Praise fo

A *CHRISTIAN SCIENCE MO*

"Woodard traces a gradual, emerging consensus of American unity. It's a dark tale. This country purchased its sense of itself as a unified whole at a high price, he writes: that of racial equality. . . . In Woodard's hands, [history] leaps to life. He shows just how powerful a form popular nonfiction can be in the hands of a disciplined writer who won't tolerate generality or abstraction. . . . The writing is relentlessly accessible. . . . This is that rare history that tells what influential thinkers failed to think, what famous writers left unwritten. . . . Woodard demonstrates that something more complicated than reason is always afoot, some swirl of politics, events, and wordless popular sentiment that sweeps the hapless thinker in its wake."
—Jill Leovy, *The American Scholar*

"Compelling . . . George Bancroft's portrait is only one of many utterly gripping depictions scattered throughout *Union*. . . . The stakes are nothing short of determining how a nation thinks about itself, how it teaches posterity about itself. In *Union*, that battle sprawls out of the narrow confines of academia and embroils the entire country—and the fight is ongoing."
—*The Christian Science Monitor*

"Woodard succeeds in demonstrating the high stakes of master narratives, versions of the past that people choose as identities and stories in which they wish to live. . . . This book will help readers grasp the staying power and the consequences of the idea—ingrained in generations—that American history is essentially a chronicle of progress, a saga of liberty unfolding under some illusive pattern of exceptionalism and divine design. . . . Woodard does make visions of history into a kind of human drama. He writes with a storyteller's pace and vividness."
—David Blight, *The Washington Post*

"A fascinating journey through history . . . *Union* is timely and thought-provoking."   —*BookPage*

"Overall, Woodard effectively shows how the country struggled to create a national myth, and an international image of unity. . . . Woodard is a gifted historiographer, and this excellent work will be appreciated by anyone interested in American history and how it came to be written."

—*Library Journal* (starred review)

"Ambitious and accessible . . . This enlightening and character-driven account will resonate with progressive history buffs."   —*Publishers Weekly*

"Sturdy American history."   —*Kirkus Reviews*

"*Union* is detailed and unflashy, and it contains many valuable historical lessons modern readers will find useful."   —*Booklist*

PENGUIN BOOKS

UNION

Colin Woodard, a *New York Times* bestselling author and historian, is the state and national affairs writer at the *Portland Press Herald*, where he received a 2012 George Polk Award and was a finalist for the 2016 Pulitzer Prize for explanatory reporting. A longtime foreign correspondent for *The Christian Science Monitor* and the *San Francisco Chronicle*, he has reported from more than fifty foreign countries and six continents. His work has appeared in *The New York Times, The Washington Post, The Economist, Smithsonian, Politico,* and dozens of other publications. A graduate of Tufts University and the University of Chicago, he is the author of *American Nations, American Character, The Lobster Coast, The Republic of Pirates,* and *Ocean's End.* He lives in Maine.

ALSO BY COLIN WOODARD

Ocean's End
The Lobster Coast
The Republic of Pirates
American Nations
American Character

UNION

THE STRUGGLE *to*

FORGE *the* STORY *of*

UNITED STATES

NATIONHOOD

COLIN WOODARD

PENGUIN BOOKS

PENGUIN BOOKS

An imprint of Penguin Random House LLC

penguinrandomhouse.com

First published in the United States of America by Viking,
an imprint of Penguin Random House LLC, 2020
Published in Penguin Books 2021

ISBN 9780525560173 (paperback)

THE LIBRARY OF CONGRESS HAS CATALOGED THE HARDCOVER EDITION AS FOLLOWS:
Names: Woodard, Colin, 1968– author.
Title: Union : the struggle to forge the story of United
States nationhood / Colin Woodard.
Description: New York : Viking, 2020. | Includes bibliographical
references and index.
Identifiers: LCCN 2019057963 (print) | LCCN 2019057964 (ebook) |
ISBN 9780525560159 (hardcover) | ISBN 9780525560166 (ebook)
Subjects: LCSH: Nationalism—United States—History. | Regionalism—United
States—History. | United States—Politics and government—Philosophy. |
National characteristics, American—History.
Classification: LCC E169.1.W6885 2020 (print) | LCC E169.1 (ebook) |
DDC 320.540973—dc23
LC record available at https://lccn.loc.gov/2019057963
LC ebook record available at https://lccn.loc.gov/2019057964

Printed in the United States of America

DESIGNED BY MEIGHAN CAVANAUGH

For my daughter, Sadie Adelaide Woodard,
who hopefully will inherit a liberal democracy
and ample royalties from this book

CONTENTS

A NOTE FROM THE AUTHOR

I have long wondered how and by whom the story of United States nationhood was created. Nearly a decade ago I wrote a book, *American Nations: A History of the Eleven Rival Regional Cultures of North America*, that argued there was never one America but several, with distinctions dating back to the differences between the various North American colonial projects and the swaths of the continent each settled in the decades and centuries that followed. I knew that these regional cultures—Greater New England, Greater Appalachia, the Tidewater, the Deep South, and so on—had their own ethnographic, religious, political, and philosophical characteristics and that most had rallied together in response to an external threat: Britain's attempt to systemize, homogenize, and consolidate its empire. At its birth, nobody seemed quite sure what the United States was. A treaty organization? A federation of sovereign nations? A nation-state in waiting? I was also aware that these questions persisted as late as the 1830s, and that the lack of answers threatened the survival of this new entity, whatever it was.

In *Union* I set out to write a book that would reveal how the story of a shared nationhood was devised, disseminated, and ultimately upheld. What I discovered in the course of my research was an intellectual battle of the highest possible stakes that spanned a century and ultimately helped explain a great deal about the age in which we now live. I have told this story through the lives of five people who made themselves standard-bearers as well as lightning rods in this struggle for the hearts and minds of millions.

The battle was initially fought between two vainglorious men who had been professional acquaintances and partisan allies—one a Harvard-educated New England preacher's son, the other a mostly self-educated South Carolinian torn in his loyalties between aristocratic Charleston and the crude and dangerous Deep Southern frontier. One believed we were a nation founded upon shared, God-given ideals, the other that we were an alliance of sovereign nations defined by blood and built on inequity. They were both unexpectedly challenged by a fugitive slave from the Maryland Tidewater, who denounced their arguments from the greatest stages in the land and from the pages of his immensely popular books. The conflict would not be settled until the 1910s, after terrorist campaigns and a war that killed hundreds of thousands, when a Deep Southern president vanquished his ideological opponents and united the federation under an ethnonationalist vision of the American identity. Even then, one of his closest friends, perhaps the most famous American scholar of his age, was laying the groundwork for a later revolution. This book tells their story.

At this writing our Republic faces existential dangers not unlike those of the 1820s, when the federation was sharply divided along regional lines and its members uncertain of what, if anything, held it together. The paths *Union*'s principal characters fought over remain before us, and the survival of the United States is at stake in the choices we make about which one to follow.

Freeport, Maine
December 2019

UNION

ONE

The enemy's forces were surrounded, artillery raining down on them from three sides, their backs to the river, huddled in fortifications from which there was no escape. All through the night and into the morning, French and rebel cannonballs blasted the town's hewn-log defenses, propelling wooden shrapnel through flesh and bone. Shells tore through buildings, buried men in their trenches, and scattered severed limbs across muddy streets. Within the collapsing walls, food was scarce, even though the commander had already expelled all the fugitive slaves who had sought shelter beneath his flag, the Union Jack.[1]

Then a red-coated drummer appeared at the top of the parapet. His arms began moving rapidly as he beat on his instrument. The soldiers of the besieging armies couldn't hear the drumroll over the din of artillery, but when a British officer appeared beside him, holding a white handkerchief above his head, the meaning was clear enough. The cannon stopped firing, the last clouds of smoke slowly rose into the sky, and the beat of the drum could be heard, signaling a desire to parley. The British officer and the drummer—the latter still broadcasting the request for a truce—stepped down from the defenses and walked slowly toward the American lines. A Continental officer ran up to greet his British counterpart and fastened a handkerchief over his eyes. He sent the drummer back over the parapet to Yorktown and led the blindfolded officer to meet General George Washington.[2]

After a solemn night beneath a clear sky "decorated with ten thousand stars," Lord Cornwallis negotiated his surrender. The day after that, October 19, 1781, his seven-thousand-man army marched out of the shattered Virginia port between rows of French and Continental troops, their regimental flags furled, the drummers playing "Welcome Brother Debtor," a tune associated with imprisonment. They laid their rifles in heaps at the rebels' feet.

The war for American independence was at an end. But what now?

THIRTEEN OF BRITAIN'S seventeen mainland North American colonies had won independence, having banded together to face a common threat to their respective political institutions, traditions, and liberties. They had created a joint military command, the Continental Army, and a sort-of treaty organization, "The United States of America," under the Articles of Confederation. Each of these American states was sovereign and independent, having agreed only to delegate defense, foreign trade, and foreign policy duties to their shared body, the Congress, which had fled from place to place during the conflict. Nobody really knew what this United States was or what it should become or even if it should continue to exist at all.

These new states' citizens didn't think of themselves as "Americans," except in the sense that French, German, and Spanish people might have considered themselves "Europeans." If asked what country they were from, the soldiers who now occupied Yorktown would have said "Massachusetts" or "Virginia," "Pennsylvania" or "South Carolina." For years to come, newspaper editors across the former colonies would refer to the new collective not as a nation but as a "league" or as the "American states" or "Confederated America," unsure of what it was or how long it might last.[3]

The ethno-cultural landscape—with all its implications for nationhood—was even more complex. The descendants of English Puritans dominated most of New England and upstate New York; those of Southern English gentry and their indentured servants and slaves populated the Chesapeake country; those of the English slave planters of Barbados controlled life in the Deep Southern lowlands. The legacy of the Dutch colony of New Netherland had shaped the development of the area around New York City, while that of William Penn's Quakers had begat an ethnic and religious mosaic (with a German plurality) up and down the Delaware Valley. The backcountry was overwhelmingly Scots-Irish, in constant friction with the coastal societies that usually governed it. If a nation can be described as a people with a sense of common culture, history, and belonging, there were, in effect, a half dozen of them within these "United States," and outside New England there wasn't a single state that wasn't divided between two or, in the case of Maryland and Pennsylvania, three of them.[4]

In the run-up to the war, one of the biggest arguments against leaving the Empire had been that a shared British identity was one of the few things keeping the colonies at peace with one another. In 1764 one anonymous letter to the editor of the *New York Mercury* warned that if the colonies achieved independence, "the disputes amongst ourselves would throw us into all the confusion, and bring on us all the calamities usually attendant on civil wars."[5] In Maryland Reverend Jonathan Boucher warned New Englanders would become "the Goths and Vandals of America," conquering their neighbors.[6] The Founding Father John Dickinson of Pennsylvania predicted that an independent British North America would collapse into "a multitude of Commonwealths, Crimes, and Calamities—centuries of mutual Jealousies, Hatreds, Wars and Devastations, until at last the exhausted Provinces shall sink into Slavery under the yoke of some fortunate conqueror." Leaving Britain, he added, was tantamount to "destroying a house before we have got another, in winter, with a small family."[7]

Wartime regional divisions were so profound that, in 1778, the British secret agent Paul Wentworth reported there would be not one American Republic, but three: an "eastern republic of Independents in church and state," a "middle republic of toleration in church and state," and a "southern . . . mixed government copied nearly from Great Britain." The differences between them, Wentworth argued, were greater than those between the nations of Europe. Even after the war the London papers reported that "the States consider themselves thirteen independent provinces, subject to no other control than their own assemblies. The authority of Congress, to which they submitted but from necessity during the war they have now almost generally thrown off." Edward Bancroft, a postwar British spy, predicted the American confederation would surely splinter, leaving only the "question whether we shall have thirteen separate states in alliance or whether New England, the middle, and the southern states will form three new Confederations."[8]

One thing was clear to the confederation's elites in the aftermath of the war: Unless a more formidable union could be negotiated, the United States would soon fall apart. "I . . . predict the worst consequences from a half-starved, limping government, that appears to be always moving upon crutches and tottering at every step," Washington wrote in 1784, and added in 1786: "I do not conceive we can long exist as a nation without having lodged somewhere a power which will pervade the whole union in as energetic a manner as the authority of the different state governments extends over the several states."[9] Everyone realized, Jefferson would later recall, that "these separate independencies, like the petty States of Greece, would be eternally at war with each other."[10]

The Constitutional Convention of 1787 was called in response to this growing crisis and yielded a legalistic remedy: a stronger federal government constrained by elaborate checks and balances between its monarchical, aristocratic, democratic, and priestly components—the presidency, Senate, House, and Supreme Court—and vis-à-vis the states themselves, which arguably remained sovereign little nations. The whole point was to ensure no one block of colonies—no one regional culture—would be able to force its will on the others. The word "nation" was conspicuously absent from the constitution that was drafted.

The United States of America came into being as a contractual agreement, a means to an end for the parties involved. No one thought they had created a nation-state of the sort that Holland or Prussia or post-

Revolutionary France was, and that central Europe's Romantic thinkers hoped the states of the German Confederation might one day become. Its people lacked a shared history, religion, or ethnicity. They didn't speak a unique language all their own. They hadn't occupied the continent long enough to imagine it as a mythic homeland, a place their people had dwelled in since time immemorial, and they'd killed or supplanted those people who did have the right to make such a claim. They lacked a common political heritage apart from the imperial ties against which they had just revolted, and they had no shared story of who they were and what their purpose was. In short, they had none of the practical or ideological foundations of a nation-state.[11]

The United States was a state in search of nationhood, a country in search of a story of its origins, identity, and purpose. It needed to find these things if it was to survive.

FOR A TIME the ad hoc remedy to this problem was to define American identity in terms of participation in the shared struggle of the American Revolution. Washington, commander in chief and founding president, was venerated almost as a monarch until his death in 1799, then promptly promoted to demigod: the father of the nation, the mythic lawgiver, a man of perfect virtue, wisdom, and morals whom "Americans" might strive to emulate. Parson Mason Weems, a hustler-cum-historian, invented stories to buttress this image and disseminated them at considerable profit in pamphlets and, later, his book-length *Life of George Washington*. Washington's birthday was made a public holiday. His remains were treated as sacred relics, their resting place fought over between Virginia (which held them) and the U.S. Congress, which had appropriated money to house them in a purpose-built D.C. shrine. Virginia won.[12]

But the beatification of Washington and his wartime supporting cast—Henry Knox, Nathan Hale, Ethan Allen, the Marquis de Lafayette—only worked as a placeholder for a national narrative for as long as 1776 remained in living memory. By the 1810s the Revolutionary soldiers and Founding Fathers began dying off, leaving a growing void where the country's sense of national identity should have been. Backcountry settlers in the Appalachian uplands had rebelled against the authority of the governments of Pennsylvania, Maryland, Virginia, and the United States in the early 1790s. New Englanders considered seceding from the federation during the War of 1812, and the governor of Massachusetts had conspired with British officials to frustrate the federal war effort.

The federation's leaders began panicking. Senators slapped a tariff on the British books they feared were brainwashing Americans in their own schools and libraries.[13] Noah Webster toiled away at compiling an "American" dictionary with distinctive words and spelling conventions in an effort to create a "national" language because, as he put it, "America should have her *own*, distinct from all the world."[14] The intellectuals who wrote for the leading journal of the era, *The North American Review*, lamented that the United States couldn't produce a history of its own—a story of itself and its origins—because its component states couldn't agree on what it should say. "It will be at best but a combination of distinct histories," one lamented, "which subsequent events only show the propriety of uniting in a single narrative." If new adhesives weren't developed, if someone didn't fashion a compelling story of what America was, the young Union was expected to fall apart.[15]

This is the story of the struggle to create that national story and, with it, an American nationhood. It is told through the eyes of the primary combatants themselves: three men born in very different circumstances at the dawn of the nineteenth century who would develop three competing answers to the United States' existential questions; and two who came of age in the aftermath of the Civil War and witnessed the triumph of one vision over the other in the second decade of a new century. It's the story of how the peoples of the United States answered those great existential questions of nationhood: Where did we come from? Who are we? Where are we going?

I end the story at the point when a broad consensus on how to answer these questions was finally achieved. It's a struggle that takes the better part of a century, a period in which we see the federation radically transformed—geographically, technologically, economically, and philosophically—into an industrial empire capable of dominating the world. This consensus was by no means final, but its contours make this a sobering and cautionary tale for readers today.

TWO

I n the late summer of 1813, on the outskirts of one of the federation's
largest towns, a dusty stagecoach arrived, carrying as one of its passengers a short, thin, wide-eyed boy with close-cropped hair. He looked
awkward, shy, and unsure of himself, standing amid the rumbling oxcarts
and boisterous street peddlers. He looked around to get his bearings, which
wasn't easy, as he was nearsighted. His new school turned out to be right in
front of him, just over a low, unpainted wooden fence abutting the west side
of the square.

Harvard College looked bigger than his old boarding school, which had
just a single building. This school contained six brick and granite structures
clustered together on the far side of the messy college yard, where great
piles of firewood surrounded a large hole in the ground where workmen
were digging the foundations for a new building. Beyond, to the north and
east, was what one student would describe as "an indefinite extent of wild
pasture and whortleberry swamp, the depths of which were rarely pene-
trated by the most adventurous freshman."

Facing the Yard across Harvard Square and Peabody Street was a row of
wooden houses, and George Bancroft may have seen his future professors
and classmates coming and going from their doorsteps. An unlucky few
were lodged in the one dwelling reputedly haunted by a woman whose husband had murdered her there in the previous century. Fortunately Bancroft's lodgings were a block away. He picked up his modest baggage and

made his way to the home of sea captain Luther Dana, probably accompanied by his roommate, Stephen Salisbury, a childhood friend from his hometown of Worcester, forty miles to the west. There he was shown to the ground-floor room where he would spend his first year in Cambridge.[1]

Some twelve-year-olds would have been intimidated. Harvard was already the preeminent higher education institution in the country. The 177-year-old institution had cultivated New England's intellectual and clerical leadership for generations, drawing students from elite families over the entire length of the Eastern Seaboard.

But young George Bancroft was not easily cowed. It was not because he was part of the Massachusetts upper class, the so-called Boston Brahmins. His parents, who lived in a farmhouse on the edge of Worcester, struggled to support thirteen children and George's sickly grandmother who would live to be ninety-seven. His mother, Lucretia, whose wealthy Tory parents had lost everything in the Revolution, dutifully followed the advice of Count Rumford, the author of thrifty New England self-help booklets like "On the Management of Fire and the Economy of Fuel" and "Of Food, and Particularly of Feeding the Poor," with its advice on the preparation of "Indian corn," macaroni, potatoes, and "the cheapest soup that can be made." "I learn'd many cheap dishes and made them satisfactory to my family," she would later recall. "I always did it with my own hands, they as cheerful and satisfied as if it was a dainty." George, the Bancrofts' eighth child, had attended Phillips Exeter Academy on a full scholarship. Harvard was awarding him one, too, both because he had graduated first in his class and also because everyone there knew his father.[2]

Aaron Bancroft was deeply immersed in the intellectual life of post-Puritan New England. The son and grandson of orthodox Calvinist deacons, he had attended Harvard during the Revolution, with excused absences to fight as a volunteer at the Battles of Lexington and Bunker Hill. He had become a prominent preacher despite holding unorthodox theological views, ideas he would pass on to his cerebral fourth son.[3]

From the beginnings of the Puritan migration in the 1630s, New

Englanders had believed they were a chosen people, tasked by God to create a more perfect society on Earth, a "city upon a hill" to guide humanity. If they all did what God demanded, they would be rewarded; if any member failed in that task, they might all be punished, so individual behavior and the shaping of children's morals were everyone's business, and public institutions—meetinghouses, public schools, boards of selectmen, Harvard itself—were tasked with creating, maintaining, and protecting their utopian society. They believed God had charged them to propagate his will and to spread it across the Earth. Much was expected of individuals, but their interests were secondary to the success of the Yankees' collective mission. Hereditary nobility, landed aristocrats, bishops, kings—the pillars of established authority in the English and, later, British empires to which they belonged—were threats to this mission.[4]

Aaron Bancroft accepted all of these beliefs, but he rejected the orthodox Calvinist view that humans were inherently depraved and that their fates were predestined: that God had already decided if individuals were damned, and there was nothing they could do in their lifetimes to alter this fact. Instead, Reverend Bancroft believed that God had given humans the ability to discern right from wrong and that they could improve their moral selves through reason and conscience to achieve salvation. "He considered reason as a primary and universal revelation of God to men of all nations and all ages," George would later say of him. "He was sure of the necessary harmony between reason and true religion, and he did not scruple to reject whatever seemed to him plainly in contradiction with it."[5]

Like most other New England intellectuals with such views, Aaron Bancroft became a Unitarian and later would be the founding president of the American Unitarian Association. During George's childhood, Unitarianism spread like wildfire through New England's political, intellectual, and business elite. Unitarians governed the publishing houses, the literary journals, the Athenæum in Boston, and Harvard itself. Through this network, Aaron published and distributed his sermons widely—John Adams praised them as "a chain of diamonds set in links of gold"—as well as his magnum opus, *The Life of George Washington*, a widely read biography released when George was seven.

This legacy—reason bound to religiosity, a passion for shaping the mind through words and letters, a faith in humankind—was passed down to young George, who would hold it close for the rest of his very long life.

It also opened the doors of Exeter and Harvard to the boy, who intended to follow his father's path and become a minister.

.FOR ALL OF ITS PRESTIGE, George did not find Harvard so different from Exeter. Indeed, by later standards, the college was little more than a glorified boarding school.

Most parents sent their teenage boys there not to train them for a particular profession but to keep them out of trouble. The college offered a solution to adolescent temptation, sin, and wickedness in the form of an unrelenting schedule of compulsory classes, lectures, meals, and homework, all overseen by stern, morally upstanding tutors and professors, many of them trained ministers. There were no academic departments, just a single curriculum consisting of thirty-three scheduled subjects that every student took in the same order during their four years of study. Most of these "subjects" were actually an intensive study of one or two texts, with instruction given during four-hour-long recitation sessions. Church services were mandatory, with stiff fines for anyone who was tardy, absent, or, most worryingly, engaged in "indecent or irreverent behaviour." Students were forbidden to travel to Boston—accessible via an eleven-seat stagecoach that made the six-mile round trip from Harvard Square only twice a day—except for Saturday afternoons, and they had to be back by eight that evening so as to pass the Puritan Sabbath eve in the required way: quietly in one's dimly lit dorm room. Tutors patrolled the grounds at night, looking for transgressors.[6]

Many of George's 301 fellow undergraduates found ways to rebel.

Some spent their Saturday afternoons in Boston taverns or whorehouses.

Others sought admittance into one of the undergraduates' covert clubs—the Hasty Pudding, Porcellian, or Pierian—where they cooked, drank, played sports or musical instruments, discussed books and newspapers and indulged in all sorts of other unsupervised and, therefore, illicit activities. They organized elaborate pranks, and shared famous past exploits with one another, like how the breakfast water in the dining hall had been tampered with one morning in 1791, causing the disruption of the annual commencement ceremonies when more than a hundred undergraduates simultaneously vomited on their parents, teachers, and peers. They lit bonfires and barrels of pitch in Harvard Yard, or wrote insulting messages to teachers, affixed them to cannonballs, and dropped them from the rooftops as their intended recipients approached. Occasionally they simply rioted, throwing bread, crockery, or buckets of ink and water at one another.[7]

George did not participate in these high jinks. While his roommate and other boys took dance lessons, skated on ponds, frolicked in Boston or at the tiny tavern on Fresh Pond, George focused on his studies and obeyed the rules. He befriended his teachers and President John Kirkland, who occasionally invited him to his house for dinner. Reverend Andrews Norton, who oversaw the library, taught biblical criticism, and was known as the "Unitarian pope," became a confidant and mentor. George's freshman-year Latin instructor, nineteen-year-old Edward Everett, would become a lifelong friend and role model, plowing a path that would lead George to see places and do things his father would never have dreamed of. Fellow students considered George a dull teacher's pet and mockingly referred to him as "Doctor Bancroft."

He excelled at what was then Harvard's most important subject, the now-forgotten discipline of "moral philosophy." This encompassed what we would today call psychology, sociology, economics, political science, and metaphysics—a comprehensive examination of human nature and how it could be perfected by rationally aligning itself with God's discernible plan. In such studies George discovered the intellectual foundations of his father's worldview: that faith and reason were compatible, that scientific investigation could reveal God's plan, and that ethical self-improvement and discipline would enable men to hasten it along. Harvard's Unitarian clergymen "tried to teach the means of leading a virtuous, useful, unselfish life, which they held to be sufficient for salvation," the historian Henry Adams would later write. "For them, difficulties might be ignored; doubts were waste of thought. . . . Boston had solved the Universe."[8]

GEORGE GRADUATED at the top of the class in 1817, was elected to Phi Beta Kappa, and was given the honor of delivering the English-language oration at the commencement ceremonies. His address was entitled "On the Dignity and Utility of the Philosophy of the Human Mind" and concluded with fulsome praise for those who chose the life of the intellectual, as he intended to do himself. "The man who has been introduced to the wonders and glories and pleasures of intellect feels himself elevated above the common sphere of mankind," the sixteen-year-old said. "He lives in an upper world and contemplates with calm indifference the labours of ordinary men, as of inferior beings, like the majestick eagle, who, heedless of the croakings of the ravens below, rises on his ample wing, 'Sailing with supreme dominion through the Azure deep of air.'"

President Kirkland didn't offer him supreme dominion, but he did help the earnest teen secure a scholarship to continue his studies for another six months so that he could earn a master's degree in theology, the next step toward becoming a minister. Some of Bancroft's classmates were going on to earn degrees at Harvard's new law and medical schools—the latter was buying cadavers from questionable suppliers in New York as local authorities had recently clamped down on grave robbers—or were entering business. Even if he'd wanted to follow such professional paths, he lacked the money and connections to do so. The ministry was what Kirkland, Professor Norton, and his parents all expected of him, and at a time when sermons were one of the main ways of shaping public opinion, the profession suited Bancroft's intellectual aspirations. He watched as Edward Everett took the pulpit of Brattle Street Church, New England's most prestigious perch, and electrified Boston's elite with daring feats of oratory. ("All his speech was music, and with such variety and invention that the ear was never tired," reported an area schoolboy named Ralph Waldo Emerson.) Bancroft had reason to hope he might one day do the same, maybe even at Brattle Street. "The plan of life, which I have adopted, indicates very clearly that I must become, either an instructor at the University, or a clergyman, or set up a high school," he told Kirkland. "There may be no need of me at Cambridge; it may be either disagreeable or impracticable to found an honourable school; I may expect, therefore, that I am to become a preacher."[9]

But as Bancroft practiced preaching and made his way through texts for aspiring divines in the shortening days of December 1817, Kirkland surprised him with a request to help him save Harvard.

Throughout his seven years as president, Kirkland had been trying to pull his tradition-bound college into the nineteenth century. The school's teaching methods were outdated and discouraged the very sort of intellectual inquiry its Unitarian trustees championed. Faculty morale was low. Professors were poorly paid, had no opportunities to do research or scholarship, and were expected to spend every waking hour surveilling and disciplining the students, dodging the occasional cannonball along the way. Kirkland—a charming, gentlemanly Harvard-trained Unitarian minister—was painfully aware that the universities of Europe put all of America's tiny colleges to shame, and he longed to adopt their reason-based, scientific approach to research and inquiry, their seminar-like teaching methods, their panoply of subject-specific academic departments offering advanced courses of study that led to a proper doctoral degree. He knew that if Harvard was to achieve this goal, it would need faculty who had been immersed in the German intellectual milieu and who could replicate the aspects of it that could serve the college's mission and bring higher learning to North America. With the financial backing of like-minded trustees, Kirkland sought to send an elite cadre of recent Harvard graduates to earn their doctorates in the Old World, hoping that on their return they could spark a New England renaissance at the Yard.

Everett, the golden boy of his generation, had been Kirkland's first emissary. Kirkland had lured Brattle Street's star preacher back to Cambridge with an endowed professorship and a two-year, all-expenses-paid trip to earn his doctorate at one of Germany's most prestigious universities. In April 1815 Everett and George Ticknor, Harvard's prospective languages professor, had departed for Göttingen's Georgia Augusta University. The tutor Joseph Cogswell, later to be appointed professor of geology and mineralogy, joined them the following year. All three were impressed with what they found there. ("What a mortifying distance there is between a European and an American scholar," Ticknor reported. "We do not even know the process by which a man is to be made one [and I expect] two or three generations at least must pass away before we make the discovery and succeed in the experiment.") They urged Kirkland to send more Harvard men in their footsteps as soon as possible.[10]

Kirkland, surveying the Yard, chose Bancroft. The hard part would be convincing the earnest young man to agree to the proposition. A PhD wasn't necessary to pursue a ministerial career, and Aaron Bancroft feared his son might be corrupted by Germany's notoriously liberal social and theological environment, where the authorship of the Bible itself was dissected as if it were merely another piece of literature.

A former U.S. president dissuaded Bancroft as well. As he pondered his decision in the spring of 1818, Professor Andrews Norton invited him along on a trip to Quincy to visit John Adams. The eighty-two-year-old received them cordially in his parlor, where Mrs. Adams presided over tea and a shifting cast of grandchildren. Norton introduced Adams to his seventeen-year-old companion and mentioned the young man would soon be studying at a German university. "With a frankness which did not at all clash with the welcome of my reception," Bancroft later recalled, "the venerable man broke out in somewhat abrupt and very decisive words against educating young Americans in European schools, insisting, and from a certain point of view very correctly, that a home education is the best for an American."[11]

It was, in the end, George's father's decision, and Reverend Bancroft placed his faith in a wealthy and worldly friend, George Cabot, a Revolutionary-era privateer who had nearly led New England to secede from the Union during the War of 1812. "Mr. Cabot emphatically advised that the offer should be accepted," George later recalled. "His opinion was positive and clear; he had no doubt about it."[12]

THREE

Nine hundred miles to the south, Bancroft's future intellectual rival, William Gilmore Simms, was also concluding his college studies, but under very different circumstances.

The College of Charleston, which twelve-year-old Simms had been attending for two years, was the oldest higher education institution in his native South Carolina. It was also, quite possibly, the worst in the Union.

It had been chartered by the legislature in 1785, and despite being granted a nine-acre campus in South Carolina's greatest city and showered with donations from patriotic plantation owners, only six students had received a bachelor's degree there by 1794. Most graduates were poorly read fourteen- and fifteen-year-olds who had followed a curriculum akin to that of a grammar school, only with less supervision. "The moral habits of many of the students were considerably depraved; of some of them shockingly so," one later reported. In a vote of confidence the college headmaster sent his own children to Harvard and Yale instead. By 1803 the school had squandered its endowment and sold off most of its campus to pay off debts. By 1811 it had become a public nuisance, with derelict buildings and pupils running amok and sometimes killing passersby with stones. "It was a cage of every unclean bird," an alumnus later recalled. "I look back with horror to my boyish days spent there."[1]

By the time William Gilmore Simms enrolled in 1816, the trustees had given up. Most of the institution's buildings were being rented out to tenants, reducing the college to a trio of loosely affiliated grammar schools operating without the assistance or oversight of the board. "Experience has shown that Charleston does not yet supply a sufficient number of youths who [are competent to] receive all the advantages of a collegiate education," they concluded.[2]

The state's anti-intellectual culture was largely responsible for the state of its education system, a fact Simms would bemoan for the rest of his life. South Carolina's founding settlers had been planters from the English colony of Barbados, members of a slaveholding oligarchy infamous throughout the Empire for immorality, arrogance, and the excessive display of wealth. In the early 1670s, as land on their island ran short, some had come to the subtropical lowlands of the future Palmetto State seeking to duplicate the West Indian slave society they'd left behind, with its gang-labor system and disenfranchised white laboring class propping up a sumptuous fortified capital of pastel town houses and crushed seashell streets. Until the eighteenth century the colony was simply referred to as "Carolina in the West Indies," and by the time Simms was finishing his studies, its people had spread their culture across the lowlands of Georgia and the southernmost part of North Carolina, and were pressing on into new territory in the Mississippi and Alabama country.

The oligarchy, which despite the American Revolution maintained ironclad control over Deep Southern political, legal, and business affairs, had little interest in public education. They hired private tutors for their own children, and sent their sons to English boarding schools and universities. South Carolina didn't create a statewide public school system until 1811, and outside of Charleston it existed primarily on paper. As late as 1850 only 16 percent of South Carolina's white children were attending school, compared to more than 90 percent of Maine's. The enslaved black majority wasn't allowed to read at all. Lacking demand, colonial South Carolina had only two higher education institutions, the College of Charleston and South Carolina College in Columbia, the state's capital. As a bright and bookish child without the means or connections to study elsewhere, Simms had to make do with the paltry education his native city could provide.[3]

SIMMS'S SHORT LIFE had already had its fill of tragedy and upheaval.

He was born on April 17, 1806, the namesake son of a Charleston tavern and grocery owner. His older brother, John, died seven months after William's birth, a few weeks before turning two. Ten weeks later his mother, Harriet Singleton Simms, bled to death giving birth to another baby boy, who expired two days later. The three were buried beside the children's grandfather in St. Michael's cemetery. Her family inscribed on her tombstone: "Happy the babe who privileged by fate, to shorter labor and a lighter weight; Received but yesterday the gift of breath, ordered tomorrow to return to death." It was all too much for William's father, whose hair reportedly turned white within a week. His business, which was on King Street at the heart of the city, promptly failed. Proclaiming Charleston "a place of tombs," the elder Simms left William with his grieving mother-in-law and disappeared into the wilds of Tennessee. At age two, William was effectively an orphan.[4]

The boy, bright but sickly, was raised by his grandmother, who was forty-five and twice widowed when he came to live with her. Jane Miller Singleton Gates, he would later recall, was "a stern though affectionate parent," who embraced the adage that children should hear everything and say nothing and "taught me the first great lesson without which we learn none—obedience." The two were nonetheless close, and he took great pleasure in the incredible family stories she told him. Her father-in-law, Thomas Singleton, a Virginian who came to South Carolina in the 1760s, became the Johnny Appleseed of tobacco, touring the backcountry to advise settlers how to plant and cure the valuable plant and sell them copies of his pamphlet, *A Treatise on the Culture of Tobacco*. ("To these instructions in a great measure," the Charleston *City Gazette* later declared, "is owing the flourishing state the culture of this great staple of Carolina is now in.") During the two-year British siege of Revolutionary Charleston, she told her wide-eyed grandson, Thomas had kept a live baboon in his basement, which he dressed in a military uniform and named for the British commandant

Colonel Nisbet Balfour; "Strut, Balfour, strut!" he would order the primate.
He spent the last three years of the war as a British hostage aboard a swel-
tering prison hulk in St. Augustine, Florida. Simms's grandmother had herself helped other patriots escape the besieged city by rowing them across
the Ashley River to safety. Her husband, John Singleton, had fought in the
backcountry, which descended into a messy civil war between Loyalist and
patriot neighbors, with terrible atrocities committed by both sides. Decades
later, these accounts would make their way into some of Simms's blockbuster novels.[5]

He was a lonely child. "I grew hard in consequence, hard, perhaps, of
manner; but with a heart craving love beyond all other possessions," he
later confided to a friend. "My mind was of a very uncompromising sort,
my temper exceedingly earnest and impassioned and my pride, springing,
perhaps, something from the feeling of isolation in which I found myself
at an early age—without father or mother, brother or indeed, kindred of
any kind," he told another. When other children played joyfully, he would
be filled with sadness. "Sickness, and suffering, and solitude crouched o'er
my cradle," he recalled. When healthy, he would go on long walks to brood
among the ruins of abandoned forts and batteries or would listen to the
fireside tales of the dozens of cotton and tobacco wagoners from all across
the Southern frontier who camped in the yard behind the Bull's Head Tavern at the end of journeys. Sometimes members of the Catawba tribe would
travel to Charleston from their reservation in the northernmost part of
their state to barter skins and handmade cooking pots. They, too, would
find a place in the books he would later write, books a young nation in
search of itself would eagerly read.[6]

Though his grandmother constantly fretted and economized, their material circumstances were actually quite stable. From his maternal grandfather, young Simms had inherited two houses in Charleston, one of which
they rented out, and as many as twenty-five slaves, presumably among
them Thomas Singleton's "faithful negro boy Cato," whom Thomas in his

will asked "to be kindly treated and kept in memory of me."* Jane hired out many of these slaves for income but, according to Simms, badly mismanaged his own inheritance. She "hoarded so religiously, as to withhold the appropriations necessary to my education," he complained, rendering it "wretchedly neglected."[7]

He watched the sons of the Charleston elite drill with private tutors or board the sailing vessels that would whisk them away to Exeter and Eton, Cambridge, Massachusetts, or Cambridge, England. Instead, Simms attended the public elementary school where his favorite instructor was the "old Irishman" who taught him to read and write. "He was the best, and he knew little," Simms later said. The other teachers, unsupervised and ignorant, showed up only two days out of five, and none could teach him arithmetic. "The teachers were generally worthless in morals and as ignorant as worthless," he added. "The whole system . . . was worthless and scoundrelly." Fortunately he was often too sick to attend classes and could direct his own studies at home. "I got books, devoured them—books of all kinds without order or discrimination, and probably in this way, acquired a thousand times more than I could have done under the ordinary school advantages." He often read late into the night, concealing his flickering bedroom candle behind a large dried goods box, and "soon emptied all the bookshelves of my acquaintances."[8]

IN THE SPRING OF 1816, months before he was to begin studies at the College of Charleston, his grandmother received a letter from the far side

---

* One of Simms's great-uncles had been bequeathed "my negro woman Nanney," and another inherited the fetus she was carrying, which was to be taken from her at age three, taught a trade, and freed when he or she turned twenty-five. "My reasons for the above request are as follows," Thomas explained in his will. "A gentleman whom I suppose to be the father of the child the wench now goes with is an intimate friend of mine and gave me 15 guineas at Camden as a fee for acting in the manner above mentioned."

of the vast young Mississippi Territory, which then included what is now Alabama. It was from William's father.

William Sr., his brother, John, and their respective slaves were farming frontier land near the Pearl River hamlet of Columbia, he wrote. He wanted his son to join him, and for the boy's grandmother to escort the ten-year-old—by boat, stagecoach, and horseback—from the genteel port where he'd spent his whole life to an unknown land beyond the borders of the civilized world. Jane refused.[9]

One day that summer, while William was walking down the street, a stranger seized him. William screamed and kicked as the man—a rough-looking fellow in his early fifties with a northern Irish accent and what Simms thought a very ugly appearance—tried to drag him away. The man claimed to be his uncle and said he was taking him to his father. William's shrieks drew the attention of his neighbors and grandmother, who stopped the kidnapping. In the aftermath the would-be abductor was able to prove he was indeed James Simms, younger brother of William Simms Sr., whose signature was on a document that James carried that granted him power of attorney in any effort to recover the boy. Jane stood her ground. Not long thereafter, she and her grandson were in court, defendants in William Sr.'s custody suit.[10]

The case was spectacular. Simms's uncle retained Benjamin Cudworth Yancey, former law partner of John C. Calhoun and chairman of the state legislature's judiciary committee. Simms's grandmother hired the legislator Robert Hayne, a future South Carolina House Speaker, attorney general, governor, and U.S. senator, and John S. Richardson, the sitting attorney general. The case was heard by an associate justice of the state's highest trial court, the nearly deaf sixty-two-year-old Elihu Hall Bay, who had a terrible stammer. "His respect for female character often led him into error, where a woman was a party," the state appeals court chief justice John Belton O'Neall would later say of him. "Such a mistake in favor of the weak and lovely never soiled *deeply* the ermine of justice." After hearing Jane's plea that she was the only parent William had ever known, Justice Bay made another unusual ruling: He would let the boy decide.[11]

The choice Simms faced was between all that he knew—his native city with its elegant town houses; its theaters, taverns, and slave market; a harbor of ships weighing anchor for the great cities of the Atlantic world; and shelves of books waiting to transport him to ancient Athens and Rome—and the southwestern frontier, a rough, dangerous, dynamic world of pioneers and ruffians, Indian warriors, and intra-imperial skirmishes known to him only from the tales of Bull's Head Tavern wagoners. On one hand there was the grandmother who had stood by him, on the other a father he'd never met and who had abandoned him as an infant. Simms would second-guess and agonize over this decision for the rest of his life.

"I declared my wish to remain with my Grandmother, and the rights of the father were set aside—I think now improperly, and as I now believe, to my irretrievable injury in many respects," he would recall. "Had I gone with my father, I should have shown less feeling, but more world wisdom."[12]

SHORTLY THEREAFTER Simms entered the College of Charleston. He read the classics and studied Latin, French, German, Spanish, and Italian. He was introduced to science and chemistry, which intrigued him enough to consider practicing medicine. "I grew apace in some things," he would say, "backwards in others." In his spare time he penned verses about the recently concluded War of 1812's "most spirited events . . . particularly which took place on the ocean."

In 1818, as George Bancroft sailed for Göttingen, William Gilmore Simms, future first man of letters of the American South, finished his formal schooling at the age of twelve. He would later observe, "My education was accordingly almost wholly nominal."[13] His postgraduate travels took him only a few blocks away, to a Charleston apothecary's shop, to begin an apprenticeship as a lowly pharmaceutical chemist.

FOUR

Earlier that year, six hundred miles north of Charleston and four hundred miles southwest of Cambridge, near the twisting, slow-moving brown waters of Tuckahoe Creek on the Maryland portion of the Delmarva Peninsula, a boy was born. He never knew his own birthday, but late in life he learned that it was sometime in February in the year 1818. He also never knew his birthplace, though it was likely either on the farm of tenant farmer Perry Steward or twelve miles to the south, at his grandparents' log cabin, tucked in a crook of the Tuckahoe, a two-mile walk across low, flat land from the hamlet of Hillsboro.[1]

His name was Freddy Bailey—Frederick Augustus Washington Bailey—and between the ages of one and six he lived with his grandparents, Isaac and Betsy Bailey, and an assortment of cousins and siblings. Isaac earned his wages as a plowman and sawyer on nearby farms, while Betsy minded the children and was sought after for her expertise in the making of fish nets, the planting of potatoes, and the delivery of babies. Freddy and the other kids played in the yard, the river, and the mud, imitating the sounds of farm animals. They ran wild through reeds and dirt roads to gawk at the bustling activity at the nearby Lee's Mill, where farmers came to grind their corn and children came to fish in the millpond. At night, after filling their bellies with cornmeal mush scooped from a tray with empty oyster shells, they climbed a ladder to sleep on a platform set in the rafters.[2]

It wasn't until Freddy was four or five that he learned his grandparents' cabin wasn't actually theirs. Someone the adults called the Old Master—a man they spoke of in ominous and fearful tones—owned it, as well as the land it sat on. Most surprisingly for young Freddy, he also discovered that this mysterious figure owned his grandmother, all the other children and their mothers, and even Freddy's mother—and Freddy, too. When you turn six years old, his grandparents told him, the Old Master will call for you, and you will go and live with him, and never return.[3]

There was something called slavery, Freddy Bailey was learning, with growing fear and sorrow in his heart, and he was one of the enslaved.

FIVE

On the evening of August 14, 1818, just as the light began to fade, the stagecoach lurched and swayed over the crest of a hill and into the Leine Valley, presenting George Bancroft with his first view of Göttingen, the university town that would be his home for the next two years.

It was a peaceful-looking city, its half-timbered buildings tightly packed within the circular mold of medieval walls that had been torn down half a century earlier, and a sight for a weary traveler's eyes. Bancroft and his traveling companion, Frederic Hedge, the twelve-year-old son of one of his Harvard professors, had spent twenty-two pleasant days crossing the Atlantic to Amsterdam, followed by eight uncomfortable ones riding in a seemingly interminable chain of stagecoaches. They had crawled across the Netherlands, Western Prussia, and the northern Electorate of Hesse, changing horses and carriages every few hours at village inns and frequently stopping at tollbooths and customs posts. "Travelling in the public coaches of Germany," Bancroft concluded, "would learn any one to bear a lingering disease without a shrug or a sigh." Now they had finally arrived at their destination, looking down upon ancient church spires and the buildings of Georgia Augusta University, the center of higher learning in Germany. "The dews of the night were gracefully receiving the heat of a warm summer's day and the meek twilight only increased the effect of the delightful vale which surrounded me," a rapt Bancroft wrote the next day. "It was a lovely eve."[1]

Göttingen was unusually quiet that evening. Authorities of the Kingdom of Hannover, of which Göttingen was a part, had recently dispatched 150 hussars to restore peace after violent street clashes and then ordered the expulsion of hundreds of students, including virtually all of the non-Hannoverians studying there. For days Bancroft and Hedge had overheard their fellow passengers speaking of "blood and war" in the city, and so were relieved to find its narrow streets calm and patrolled by soldiers.[2]

The riots pointed to the unsettled state of the "Germany" in which the two young Americans had just arrived. In the early nineteenth century, Germany was a region, not a nation-state. For hundreds of years the German-speaking peoples of Europe formed a majority of the population in more than three hundred independent kingdoms, principalities, duchies and grand duchies, counties, lordships and baronies, free cities, and independent abbeys spread across Central Europe, not to mention the Archduchy of Austria, which was itself the core of a vast multiethnic empire extending over much of East-Central Europe and into the Balkans. While Bancroft was at Harvard, Napoleon Bonaparte's empire had collapsed, and the map of Europe had suddenly been redrawn, with most of the German states, Prussia, and the Austrian crown lands agreeing to band together in a new German Confederation, a loose interstate alliance with a shared parliament that oversaw collective defense and diplomacy. This arrangement had obvious parallels with that of the young United States: a weak association whose component states considered themselves sovereign and commanded the primary loyalties of their citizens. Some thinkers argued that Germans were an extended family, sharing customs, values, and proclivities and should therefore become a united national state like France; others feared that such a plan would destroy liberty, diversity, and the peace of Europe. Bancroft would be undertaking his graduate studies within this giant laboratory of nationalism, where history-changing experiments in nation building were under way, many of them conducted by the very men under whom he studied.[3]

The student exodus had left open a wide choice of housing to the young American, allowing him to rent a desirable two-room apartment on Gotmarstrasse, just a block from the market square at the city center, where his landlord served breakfasts of coffee and brown bread. The city was better off without the disorderly students, Bancroft remarked in a letter to President Kirkland, adding that it had been "too full and could well spare the abundance." He deposited young Frederic Hedge with a tutor in a nearby village, introduced himself to most of his professors, and explored his new surroundings with enthusiasm.[4]

Göttingen was a medieval town of ten thousand inhabitants with clean and well-paved streets, Bancroft discovered, but it offered few distractions from study. Its prominent buildings—from the astronomical observatory at the edge of town to the hospital, churches, and university at its center— were plain and straightforward. Many of the houses were simple frame- and-plaster structures, and a number of the rest had obviously been constructed from stones scavenged from long-lost watchtowers. There was a single private literary club and a number of houses offering cheap meals to students, who ate quickly and in silence, hunkered down with caps on their heads. The ruins of the town walls were now capped with a raised public walkway lined with shade trees. Though he found this promenade beautiful, Bancroft did not like taking his evening strolls there because of the "swarms" of romancing young people. ("Decency is not much regarded by them, nay indecency is often outraged," he complained to an American friend, before quoting the ancient Roman poet Catullus: "*Quod indignum est, omnes pusilli et semitarii moechi.*" ("They don't deserve this, all these puny little *alleyway* fornicators.")[5]

He had a much more favorable impression of the university itself. In 1818 it was considered the finest university in Christendom, if not the most Christian of universities. Founded in 1737, it had emerged as a center of the German Enlightenment and exemplified the Central European academic ethos of *Wissenschaft*, a quest to discover new knowledge rather than the propagation of tradition and established truths. Compared to those of Harvard, its scholars had a remarkable degree of intellectual freedom to probe, question, challenge, teach, and debate almost everything but the actions and policies of the current leaders of the Kingdom of Hannover. Beneath the university library's vaulted, cathedral-like ceilings were shelved more than two hundred thousand volumes, a collection more than thirteen times the size of the one Bancroft had access to at Harvard. Forty full professors and thirty trained instructors provided lectures and directed largely independent study across the breadth of scholarship, from medicine to philosophy, politics to classics, Hebrew to Arabic. "I have come to the pure fountains of wisdom, that I may drink of her unpolluted waters and be refreshed," Bancroft giddily wrote Andrews Norton before matriculating.[6]

As he plunged into a demanding schedule, studying and attending classes from five in the morning to eleven at night, he was amazed by the university's obsession with punctuality. When the town clock struck the top of the hour, the city's empty streets were suddenly flooded with students rushing to the next class with portfolios under their arms. Each professor would begin and end exactly on time, often stopping his remarks mid-sentence. In the period between classes, the probing discussions of books, objects, paintings, and historical documents was like nothing Bancroft had experienced. "The darkest portions of history become almost transparent when reason and acuteness are united with German perseverance," he wrote Kirkland. "It is admirable to see with what calmness and patience every author is read, every manuscript collected, every work perused which can be useful, be it dull or interesting, the work of genius or stupidity, to see how the most trifling coins and medals, the ruins of art and even the decay of nature is made to bear upon the investigated subject." Teachers not only knew their material, they knew how to teach it effectively, engaging Bancroft and his classmates in provocative discussions and assignments.[7]

He was, however, horrified by everyone's decidedly un-Yankee behavior. People greeted one another with kisses, regardless of gender or state of hygiene. Students were wild, noisy, slovenly dressed, careless in their deportment, and reeking of body odor. Instructors used the Lord's name in vain—"*Ach, allmächtiger Gott; Gott im Himmel; ach, der Herr Jesus*" echoed through the streets and lecture halls—and most of them didn't appear to attend church. Professors were "for the most part ill bred," Bancroft reported, and didn't even try to assume the manners, bearing, and dignity of proper gentlemen. They spoke informally, used obscenities, told crude jokes, and appeared to have little interest in shaping society, upholding culture, or achieving fame. Instead most treated scholarship as a vocation, "cultivated simply because one can get a living by it," which was anathema to all the values Bancroft had learned from his Unitarian father and alma mater. "I had expected to find in the learned something venerable and great," he complained, adding that it was hard to "honour them for their erudition without despising them for their vulgarity and their meanness."[8]

His adviser, Johann Eichhorn, was a typical example. Although Eichhorn was friendly, cheerful, and extremely hardworking, Bancroft was troubled by his lack of social graces. "Of dignity in his deportment, or loftiness and elevation of manners he has not the slightest conception and this defect can be perceived in almost all his actions and words," he told Norton. "He is always in good spirits and very merry, but his mirth is often ill timed and his stature destitute of delicacy."

Bancroft had been warned about Eichhorn's blasphemous approach to biblical criticism, which held that the Bible was the work of humans, that the miracles it recounted were ancient people's renderings of misunderstood natural phenomena, and that many parts of it hadn't actually been written by their purported authors. Bancroft never forgave his adviser after he spoke "so obscenely" about the second chapter of Genesis—which describes God creating Eden, Adam, and Eve—that it forever spoiled the passages for him.[9] But Eichhorn did open Bancroft's eyes to the importance of evidence-based inquiry, and his theories about the operation of human societies resonated with the young New Englander. Eichhorn was one of the first historical theorists to view human societies as organisms that, once born, grew and developed according to their own character, an idea that would later frame Bancroft's worldview.

More influential in Bancroft's intellectual development was Professor Arnold Heeren, who taught classical studies, and whose work on ancient Greece would be the focus of Bancroft's doctoral thesis. From the beginning of civilization, Professor Heeren taught, the growth and development of human peoples had been influenced by a combination of the intrinsic qualities of their "race" and their environmental, geographic, and historical experiences. The European race was self-evidently the greatest, he noted, because it alone had developed laudatory conventions like monogamous marriage, the abolition of slavery, and the constitutional protection of individual liberties. However, it had not always been so: China and the East had once had their day, developing great inventions and elaborate states before the scepter of human leadership passed to the West. But while it might appear from present circumstances that Europeans were intrinsically superior, he cautioned, this didn't "prove an absolute want of capacity in our darker fellow men." Indeed, as Heeren had written in his *Reflections on the Politics of Ancient Greece*, "We will welcome the age, which shall contradict experience in this point, and which shall exhibit to us cultivated nations of negroes." Bancroft was so fascinated with this text, which used the Greek city-states as a foundation for understanding the organic evolution of human nations, that he would later be the first to translate and publish it in English. Unlike Heeren, however, he believed the torch of history was already passing from European to North American hands.[10]

For two years, Bancroft toiled away at his studies with only a few interruptions: dinner with his professors, fencing lessons, a hiking trip to the Harz Mountains during his second summer vacation, and a disappointing visit to the aged Goethe. (He "would rather take for his heroine a prostitute or a profligate, than give birth to that purity of thought and loftiness of soul, which it is the peculiar duty of the poet to raise," Bancroft sniffed.) From excursions to Weimar, Prussia, Saxony, and Austrian-controlled Bohemia— marked by frequent customs stops along arbitrary state boundaries—and conversations with his fellow students, he came to acknowledge the disadvantages of Germany's fractured political arrangements, but also appreciate the Germans' sense of having a common culture, which provided the underpinning for a potential German nation. On the intellectual front, he accepted that the Germans had many worthy innovations and ideas, but concluded many of them would only see fruition among Americans, who had the necessary piety and moral compass. "It is refreshing to see what man can do though labouring under the most unfavorable circumstances, and to think how ably all good literature would thrive if [one] could transplant it to America," he observed. "If we could graft it on a healthy tree, if we would unite it with a high moral feeling, if learning would only go to school with religion." When he returned home, he intended to do just that.[11]

The Germans, for their part, were intrigued with Bancroft and his fellow Americans, and opened their homes, salons, and clubs to them. Their hosts, Bancroft soon learned, imagined the American frontier to be an Edenic state of nature, an exotic place where civilization and barbarism rubbed shoulders in a "pre-Adamic" world of innocence. At social events they peppered him with questions about Native Americans, a people on whom Bancroft had probably never laid eyes. The questions could be silly—at dinner parties, one local luminary liked to try to provoke American guests by conflating indigenous practices with European-American ones—but through their eyes, Bancroft found himself also looking at his native country as a tabula rasa where God's plans could freely unfold.[12]

His own patriotism remained unabated. On July 4, 1820, a few months before receiving his doctorate, he and the handful of other Americans in Göttingen gathered to celebrate Independence Day. Bancroft delivered a rousing speech for the occasion that revealed his view of his country's strengths and weaknesses vis-à-vis those of Europe. He called for a dozen toasts, to President James Monroe, to the flag, and to George Washington, but also to America's literary prospects ("May riches bow to wisdom"), to her literary institutions ("May they ever be nurseries of enlightened patriots"), to her role as an asylum for oppressed peoples ("May her benevolence not prove her poison"), and to the speedy abolition of slavery ("May our country learn to practice at home this sublime lesson she has taught the world"). His speech contrasted the arbitrary tyranny of the German princes with the glorious safeguards of the Constitution America's Founding Fathers had created. "The book of time lay open before them. They could there read the fates of nations ... see the courses which other statesmen had steered and grow wise by the lessons time gave them," he asserted. "They could see the rocks on which other nations had split, and learn to guide the American ship gaily and triumphantly over the waves." He exalted in the westward expansion of the United States, which he judged to be a march to glory, wealth, and power. "The hum of business and the noise and bustles of cities are heard where in the days of our childhood the snake reposed undisturbed and the wild beast formed his lair in security," he continued. "Oh! My countrymen, never was a land blessed of heaven like ours. . . . My countrymen, we are Americans. The arts and sciences of Europe cannot make us forget it."[13]

UPON GRADUATION Bancroft set out on what would be one of the greatest European backpacking tours in history, albeit without an actual backpack. He departed on foot for Berlin in the company of two Greek students, arriving three weeks later in the Prussian capital, the largest city Bancroft had ever seen. A bustling metropolis of two hundred thousand, Berlin had impressive buildings, grand parks, and tree-lined boulevards. Pedestrians, wagons, and carriages coursed under the triumphal Brandenburg Gate and down the grand Unter den Linden toward the Prussian palace complex. At the University of Berlin he found a wealth of exciting people and ideas and, with letters of introduction from his Göttingen professors, was swept into a pageant of soirées, dances, and dinner parties.

He spent five months in the city, learned to dance, perfected his Italian and French, attended the opera and ballet, and saw his first Christmas tree. He took courses with some of Germany's leading thinkers: the historian August Böckh; the literary historian Friedrich Wolf; the educational expert Friedrich Schleiermacher, who taught that God assigned each nation a calling on Earth; and the philosopher Georg Hegel, who saw history as the record of humans' desire for freedom, itself the divine will of God. He befriended the university's founder, the philosopher and diplomat Wilhelm von Humboldt, during lively discussions about the American West, the culture and language of Native Americans, and the place of the United States in the annals of civilization. He missed a large part of a ball hosted by the Countess Amerika Bernstorff—daughter of General Friedrich Riedesel, who commanded German mercenaries fighting alongside the British in the American Revolution—when he conversed late into the night with the British ambassador, Sir George Rose, about the state of German religion. "I think with more affection of my five months in Berlin than of the two years I spent in Göttingen," he wrote Kirkland.[14]

He reluctantly left the city in February 1821 and hiked to France via Leipzig, Weimar, Frankfurt, and Heidelberg, where he spent a month studying with the historian Friedrich Schlosser. Arriving in Paris in early May, he called on Wilhelm von Humboldt's younger brother, Alexander, the most famous explorer of the age. Alexander had undertaken a five-year-long expedition to South and Central America from 1799 to 1805, capped by an extended visit with President Thomas Jefferson, with whom he'd shared intelligence about the newly acquired Louisiana Purchase. Alexander von Humboldt opened the doors of the City of Lights to the twenty-year-old American. He dined with the Marquis de Lafayette, hero of the American Revolution, and drank with Benjamin Constant, the Swiss philosopher of classical liberalism, and General Horace Sébastiani, who'd led Napoleon's troops into Moscow during the ill-fated invasion of Russia and had served as the emperor's ambassador to the Ottoman Empire. He walked through the French countryside with Washington Irving on a glorious summer visit to the rural retreat of U.S. ambassador Albert Gallatin, who had been Treasury secretary under both Jefferson and Monroe. He joined Humboldt to see a session of the Institut de France, where the scholars were debating the authenticity of a pile of bones sent from Sweden and purported to be those of the French philosopher René Descartes. He met Sir John Russell, future British prime minister, the Irish poet Thomas Moore, and the German poet August Schlegel, who was bound for Bonn with a collection of Sanskrit texts. "At that little table how many men who hold a conspicuous place in the political and literary world!" he proclaimed after dining with Sébastiani, Constant, Lafayette, Humboldt, and the craniologist Franz Gall, one of the founders of modern psychology. "I never was at so pleasant a dinner party."[15]

Bancroft had been admitted into the republic of letters, an informal transnational network of scholars, politicians, and learned men, doers of deeds, inventors of scientific disciplines, authors of epic poems, decoders of the words of the ancients, vanguards of the modern age. These experiences transformed his worldview, and enabled him to view his beloved homeland from a global perspective. He would remain in contact with many of these men for the rest of their lives, serving as a conduit between the U.S. and European worlds of letters, thought, and ideas.

In August 1821 he visited London and, lacking introductions, found it dreary. After receiving news that his older brother John, a sailor, had been lost at sea, he spent six weeks trekking the Swiss and Italian Alps alone, reflecting on the meaning of existence, the glory of creation, and the lessons of all he'd seen and learned in Paris and Göttingen. He climbed glaciers and Mont Blanc and danced, and serenaded mountain peaks as he walked for miles through pouring rain. "I could sit undisturbed amid the beauties of nature, and give way to the delightful flow of feelings and reflections, which came hurrying on me, as I sat on the Alpine rocks and gazed on the Alpine solitudes," he wrote Norton. "Never till now did I know how beautiful and how kind a mother Earth is." He saw the treasures of Milan, Venice, and Florence en route to Rome, where he arrived in late November, lean and tan, his clothes in tatters, and his beard long and unruly.[16]

On his first morning there he went directly to St. Peter's Basilica. "I threw myself on my knees before the grand altar, and returning thanks to God for guarding me amidst all the dangers of travelling, preserving me on the high seas and on shore, raising up friends and benefactors for me wherever I have been, and blessing me with health and external prosperity in an almost unexampled manner," he wrote in his diary. "I besought his Goodness in my humble petition to prepare blessings and happiness for those generous friends through whose kindness and munificence I have seen foreign countries and been able to prosecute my journey even to that city which I had ever most desired to see. My parents and every member of my family were remembered too in these moments of my life, which were too sweet and too solemn to be ever forgotten."[17]

His winter in Rome was a reprise of his season in Paris. With written introductions from Alexander von Humboldt, he was received by Napoleon's exiled sister, the Princess Borghese, at her sumptuous palace; by the Prussian ambassador Barthold Niebuhr, a leading historian of ancient Rome; and by the Baltimore-born socialite Elizabeth Patterson, the ex-wife of Napoleon's younger brother, Jérôme. He marveled at the masterpieces of Raphael, Bernini, and Michelangelo, as well as the fact that they were all a short walk away, as were the settings of much of the history and philosophy he had been studying for the past four years. "Were I to remain in Rome, till I grew tired of the place, or till I had seen all its wonders, I believe I never should move from it," he wrote Kirkland.

In May he started for home, journeying overland to Marseilles. At Livorno in Tuscany he found the frigate USS *Constitution*, Old Ironsides, at anchor in the bay and was invited aboard for tea by Captain Jacob Jones. They were soon joined by Lord Byron, who was wearing a black jacket, white pantaloons, and gaiters. Byron parried the advances of female guests but tossed the flower in his lapel to one of them on departure. The British poet was living with his mistress, Countess Guiccioli, in a villa outside a nearby village, and Bancroft managed to obtain an invitation to spend an entire day with the famous couple, conversing about literature and the affairs of the world. Byron said he hoped to visit America. Two years later he was dead, never having made the trip.[18]

On June 12, 1822, Bancroft boarded the ship *Belle* at the docks in Marseilles, bound for home, his mind full of ideas about his country and its destiny in the world.[19]

SIX

Meanwhile, in North America, Simms endured a stagecoach journey far worse than anything Germany could offer, jostling along a wilderness track that had been nothing more than a horse path only thirteen years earlier. The Federal Road led from Augusta, Georgia, 150 miles west of Charleston, to Mobile, the only port and one of the only towns of consequence in the new state of Alabama. Established as a postal link to New Orleans, the five-hundred-mile path cut through Creek tribal territory and became the principal route for settlers bound from the Carolinas and Georgia to the Deep Southern frontier.

The coach—probably a nine-seater pulled by four horses—averaged only three or four miles an hour through forests and scrub, swaying the entire time with a sickening motion. On the driver's command, the passengers would prevent the vehicle from toppling over by leaning together in one direction or the other. When it rained, the coach would frequently become "mired down" in mud and sometimes, as Simms put it, "the united energies of passengers and drivers, were inadequate to its extrication." The Marquis de Lafayette would take the exact same route while on a grand tour of America that winter, and was jostled so violently he began vomiting.[1] Stops were made at Indian agency outposts thronged with Creeks trading for liquor or at roadside hovels whose "half-breed" Euro-Creek proprietors charged exorbitant prices for bug-ridden beds and unpleasant food. The landscape, Simms would recall, was nothing but "dreary wastes."[2]

It was the fall of 1824, and Simms, now eighteen years old, a young man with a stern but open face, lively blue eyes, brown hair, and a broad forehead some thought "intellectual," was on his way to see his father. He had spent the first few of the past six years in Charleston as an apothecary's assistant. In the evening he'd written poetry and spent time with fellow teenagers in one or another of the juvenile literary clubs that had sprung up in the city, where members paid twenty-five cents a week for access to a book-swapping shelf and to debate ideas. He'd started writing a novel with one of his friends, though the project petered out after a few chapters, and at fourteen he wrote a tragedy entitled "The Female Assassin," which he later said was as bad as the title suggested. At fifteen he began publishing poetry in Charleston's newspapers under a variety of pseudonyms. Sometime before his departure for Alabama, he'd given up pharmacology. His father's invitation to visit him at his plantation on the Pearl River, south of Jackson, put any other career decisions on hold.[3]

Simms had finally met William Sr. in 1817, when he had come to Charleston on a short visit. His father was then about fifty-five years old, his six-foot frame topped by a halo of white hair. After his wife had died, he and his brother James had joined their siblings in the uplands of central Tennessee, where he became friends with a local slaveholder and militia commander named Andrew Jackson. In 1813 he and James, their slaves in tow, moved to the frontier settlement of Columbia in the newly acquired Mississippi country. They'd joined a local militia regiment during the War of 1812 and fought in a bloody and chaotic campaign against the Creeks, during which he'd survived by eating his own horse. His regiment had fought under Jackson at the Battle of New Orleans, where British forces were resoundingly defeated, and he then returned to the brothers' cotton plantation outside Columbia. The future, he asserted to his son, lay there on the banks of the Pearl River, far from the oppressive aristocratic culture of Charleston.[4]

Now Simms was on his way there, moving farther from civilization with every jolt and sway of the stagecoach.

In the interior of Georgia carriage wheels often sunk into the sandy road. The state capital of Milledgeville was a mere village of twenty-five hundred and yet, Simms said, "must be of some importance, if only considered in its general relationship to the rest of the state." The coach passed through friendly Creek settlements—travelers called them "white towns"—and avoided their hostile "red towns," whose inhabitants opposed the cession of tribal lands to the United States. Four days out from Augusta, it crossed the Chattahoochee River on a Creek-operated ferry, and Simms stepped ashore in the five-year-old state of Alabama. The group stopped at run-down wooden-palisade forts, still manned and ready to offer sanctuary to settlers should hostile Creeks attack. The coachman sometimes pressed on late into the night, lighting his way through Alabama's forests and pine barrens with smoking pine torches he'd fixed on arms extending from either side of the stagecoach. Simms slept in rude log cabins with foul food on the table and dead rattlesnakes hanging in the doorway. Bridges were often washed out, and his fellow travelers dreaded crossing the Persimmon Swamp on the route's mile-long log-and-brush causeway, which was collapsing into the mosquito-plagued water.[5]

Everywhere the atmosphere was unsettled, a land torn between indigenous and Deep Southern control, with everyone scarred by the recently concluded war between these rival forces.

Simms finally debarked at Montgomery, a five-year-old village on the Alabama River. He found shops, a bank, a courthouse, a newspaper, and a post office looking out on steamship landings piled high with bales of cotton grown on tiny slave-powered farms farther upriver. Here he, the cotton, and an assortment of passengers piled aboard a steamboat for the four-hundred-river-mile journey to Mobile and the sea. The trip could have been completed in two days, but as the steamboat stopped at every landing to take on more passengers and cotton and offload supplies and information from the outside world, it took nearly a week. Simms watched as cotton bales were slid down to remote docks from planters' warehouses high on the river bluffs, the planters' valuable slaves handling the upper station, and cheap Scots-Irish laborers the dangerous lower landing. "A steamboat has nothing romantic about it," Simms later wrote. "The incessant grumblings and gruntings of its engine, the foetid density of its smoke, sent forth in huge black volumes that impart to every thing around their own sootiness of aspect, with which one might find himself impregnated, gliding down the serpentine waters of the Alabama." Even the trees and wild flowers offered no solace, "coupled as they were with smoke and steam."[6]

Simms described the buildings of Mobile, a ramshackle port town of eighteen hundred, as being "of temporary erection, poor materials, and miserable workmanship." He was soon on another steamboat, heading northward up the Tombigbee River for a monotonous trip of a week or more to Tuscaloosa, a "rude, scattered hamlet" where his sleep was interrupted by the howl of a wolf "as he hungered upon the edge of the forest for the prey that lay within her tents." There he acquired a horse and prepared to ride westward into Mississippi, his mind "choked by the tangled vines of erroneous speculation, and haunted by passions, which, like so many wolves, lurked, in ready waiting, for their unsuspecting prey." He set out through the steamy forests of the Choctaw tribe, staying the night in "Indian hovels" and napping in the shade of the forest to escape the midday heat. One afternoon he awoke from such a rest, a few hundred yards off the trail, to realize the raised ground he'd used as a pillow was in fact a grave, with the remnants of a wooden cross. For years afterward Simms would ponder what could have driven a person from civilization to such a lonely end.[7] From Columbus, Mississippi, 250 miles from Mobile, he followed a new military road southwest toward Jackson, the state's three-year-old village capital, and from there rode or floated 90 miles down the Pearl River to Columbia, the sleepy river hamlet where his father and uncle had made their home.

In all the thousands of letters and the hundreds of stories, books, and orations he would later produce, Simms never described his reunion with his father, or William Sr.'s little plantation, or even the part of Mississippi where it was located. His published descriptions of his travels in the region conspicuously omitted his destination, or the fact that he was visiting family, as if it were a shameful secret Charlestonians mustn't learn of. From census records we know that the brothers had twelve slaves and a 153-acre farm near town. When Simms arrived, his father had just returned from a three-month tour on horseback of "the wildest regions of the Southwest," probably the Yazoo Valley and what is now northern Louisiana.[8]

In the months that followed Simms got to know his father and the world he inhabited. He later described him as "a man of great energy and enthusiasm of character, a lively and playful temper—full of humor and no small poet in the acceptation of those days." The elder Simms loved humorous writing and even wrote some himself. He'd fought the Creeks, the British, and, in Florida, the Seminoles, and revered General Jackson, a fellow Scots-Irishman. He was about sixty-three, large and "admirably formed," with a smooth, merry face, but slightly stooped with age. He was sharp-witted, ready with a quip and joke, but in more somber moments would address his son in original verses conveying his affections and leaving the young man "quite touched."[9]

He and Uncle James had been born in Larne, County Antrim, a harbor town in northern Ireland that had been a major gateway to America for eighteenth-century Scots-Irish emigrants and was a center of their unsuccessful 1798 rebellion against the British. Most of these Scots-Irish were descendants of immigrants from the war-torn Scottish Lowlands, where centuries of warfare with the English had given rise to a culture with a warrior ethos, extended cousinages, and a desire for autonomy and self-sufficiency. Queen Elizabeth had encouraged tens of thousands of these Protestant Scots to cross the narrow Irish Sea to help conquer and hold Ulster against Irish guerrillas in the seventeenth century, and the leaders of many of British North America's seaboard settlements had been pleased to direct families like the Simmses to the Appalachian frontier, where they might again hold land for England against indigenous inhabitants. From south-central Pennsylvania to the Southern uplands, they formed a culture as distinct as that of New England or the plantation country of South Carolina and lowland Georgia, a region where personal autonomy was prized and government institutions looked upon as an unwelcome intrusion.

The Simmses first settled among Pennsylvania Scots-Irish in the uplands of far northern South Carolina, probably just before the outbreak of
the Revolution. Among their neighbors in Lancaster County was the widow
Elizabeth Jackson, native of Carrickfergus, seven miles south of Larne, and
mother to a boy William Simms Sr.'s age named Andrew, future president
of the United States. By 1800 four of William's brothers and sisters had—
like Andrew Jackson—moved on to north-central Tennessee, a state overwhelmingly dominated by Ulster Scots and their descendants. But by the
1810s Tennessee was too crowded for William's liking, so he moved southward, eager to start his life anew.[10]

During the months of his visit Simms and his father toured the wilds of
interior Mississippi and Alabama, riding on horseback through Creek, Choctaw, and Cherokee territory, often far beyond the line of settlement. "Noble,
indeed, though wild and savage was the aspect of that green forest country, as
yet only slightly smitten by the sharp edges of the warrior's axe," Simms later
recalled. "I rode forty and fifty miles without sign of human habitation, and
found my bed and supper at night most generally in the cabin of the half-
breed." He spent several weeks deep in the Choctaw nation of northern Mississippi "without feeling the loss or the weight of time," though he described
the journey as "*travail* rather than *travel*," most of it on footpaths. "Some of
the Indian paths, as I experienced, seemed only to be made for the perplexity
of the stranger. Like Gray's passages, which 'led to nothing,' they constantly
brought me to a stand. Sometimes they were swallowed up in swamps and, in
such cases, your future route upon the earth was to be discovered only by a
deliberate and careful survey of the skies above." From his father he learned
how to bargain with tribal people, to imitate the accents of natives and frontiersmen, to swim across rivers, and to navigate the trails. He saw forlorn
farmsteads surrounded by trees that had been killed by girdling but had yet
to fall over, a scene of desolation that Simms likened to a battlefield "from
which the decaying forms of man and horse have not yet been removed."[11]

Most of the people living in these bark-thatched hovels were from South

Carolina or Georgia and appeared to Simms to have regressed in the absence of the "restraining presence" of the society they'd left behind, indifferent to appearances and deprived of church, schools, and "all the luxuries and charms of civilization." The children were dirty, ignorant, and slovenly, and the youths abused whiskey and tobacco, which Simms began to think of as the two "gross, brutal and terrible tyrannies of our nation." He ascribed this as being done "for gain! For the small increase, the miserable pittance, the little more to the cotton heap . . . And for this the man is willing to convert the wife into the wench, and the dear children, who might be made the noblest pillars of the noblest republic, into horse-boys, or ruffians, or something worse!" The presence of the money-obsessed "lower orders" of Southern society who settled on the frontier was corrupting the Choctaw, Creeks, and Cherokee, whom they cheated and onto whom they passed their vices. The Indians, he concluded, were "rude, uninformed, and unpolished, but still highly intellectual beings" who were being introduced to civilization by the worst sort of teachers.[12]

The frontier, in Simms's mind, was not a good influence on anyone. When he told his father, somewhere deep in the Yazoo country, that he intended to return to Charleston, the older man was surprised and aghast and delivered a fervent pitch in favor of the frontier:

> Return to Charleston! Why should you return to Charleston, where you can never succeed in any profession, where you need, what you have not, friends, family and fortune: and without these your whole life, unless some accident should favor you, will be a mere apprenticeship—a hopeless striving after bread. NO! Do not think of it. Stay here. Study your profession here. And pursue it, with the energy and talent which you possess, and I will guarantee you a fortune, and, in 10 years, a seat in Congress. Do not think of Charleston! Whatsoever your talents, they will there be poured out like water on the sands.[13]

But Simms had spent the previous months pondering his future as his horse thumped along Choctaw trails, and when he finally returned to Charleston in the spring of 1825, the nineteen-year-old threw himself into executing his plan.

He, like Bancroft, wanted to be a man of letters, and needed a compatible day job. Bancroft, returning from his own travels, had the ministry in mind; Simms chose law, and began studying it under Charles Rivers Carroll, a local attorney with literary aspirations. With one or more friends from his literary club days, he founded a journal, *The Album*, which he filled with a flood of his unsigned writings: at least sixty poems, four book reviews, two serial novellas, and six other works of fiction written and published in less than a year.[14]

Still, he felt the weight of the obstacles standing in his path—the aristocratic exclusiveness of Charleston's phenomenally wealthy elite, the shortage of readers and patrons, the condescension of the well-born toward a young man who was not. "I also well knew that [my intellect] would never be anywhere more jealously resisted than in a proud, wealthy and insulated community such as that in which I was born, in which the honors and rewards were few and for which there were hundreds of candidates," he later recalled. "I could never be, in my native place, what I might be elsewhere." For all that repelled him about the frontier, he could feel the allure of an environment where hard work and merit might matter more than connections and pedigree.[15]

So on January 12, 1826, he set out again to see his father. This time he took the sea route and came to regret it. His ship was battered by storms and plagued by smallpox during a brutal, monthlong trip around the seemingly endless Florida peninsula to New Orleans, the largest city Simms had ever seen, which he judged "a vile reservoir of infamy and baseness." He took a steamboat to Mobile, which was swamped with outcasts from the Choctaw nation who were "in the most miserable states of degradation and drunkenness, lying about the streets in numbers and perfectly nude, beggaring the town with an exhibition as disgusting to the sight as it was painful to the feelings of humanity." He again rode with his father through the Yazoo country, and possibly to Louisiana on the far side of the Mississippi River, but Simms may have seen enough. After just three weeks, he left his father and returned home, his final decision having been made.[16]

It was to be Charleston and civilization, for better or worse, over the rootless, ignoble frontier. South Carolina, he knew, was his true country, the Deep Southern lowlands, his culture. He intended to devote his life to their service.

SEVEN

F reddy Bailey's time came without warning, on a summer's morning in 1824 when he was six years old. His grandmother put a freshly ironed bandanna turban on her head, took him by the hand, and told him it was time to go to the Old Master. He left the clay-floored cabin for the last time and everything he had ever known.[1]

It was a twelve-mile walk through fields and footpaths to the Wye House Plantation, and in the heat of the day Grandma Betsy had to carry the exhausted boy on her shoulders. As they passed through a stretch of woods, the stumps, knots, and rotting logs looked to him like the legs, eyes, and ears of monsters that Freddy feared were coming to eat him. If they didn't get him, the Old Master would. He later said he had seen himself as having been selected as "a meat offering" to a "fearful and inexorable demi-god." His grandmother carried and tugged him onward, "with the reserve and solemnity of a priestess."[2]

The Wye House estate was incredible to behold, a powerful symbol of the region to which it belonged.

Maryland's Eastern Shore was part of an entirely different culture from that of the Deep South or the Appalachian frontier or tidy, messianic New England. The Chesapeake Tidewater region had its origins in the aftermath of the English Civil War of the 1640s, when hundreds of defeated Royalists emigrated to the creeks and shores of eastern Virginia. Many of these men were the younger sons of English gentry, who were not going to inherit their fathers' landed estates, who in previous generations would have had to make do with a career in the church or the army. The Chesapeake offered an alternative, a chance to re-create the manorial country estates they'd left behind, with their great houses, elegant gardens, immaculate fields, and peasant laborers. It was a self-sufficient world that shipped its output to London and other English cities. For two generations these "distressed Cavaliers" had struggled to establish themselves in light of the fact that, on a continent replete with "free" land, there was no one who was willing to take on the role of the serfs. They therefore imported thousands of indentured servants—white bondspeople compelled to work off their transatlantic fares. When by the end of the seventeenth century there were no longer enough of these laborers to be had, the Tidewater planters followed the example of the West Indies and the Deep South and brought in large numbers of enslaved Africans. Fueled by tobacco profits, this Tidewater civilization spread west into the Virginia Piedmont, south into eastern North Carolina, and north into southern Maryland, the Eastern Shore, and the southern counties of Delaware. The result, by Freddy Bailey's day, was a region modeled on a warped version of the English country manor, where poised and mannered lords like Thomas Jefferson, James Madison, and the late George Washington embraced the Enlightenment and its ideal that humans shape their own destiny, even as they presided over armies of chattel slaves.[3]

Wye House Plantation, where Freddy's "Old Master" was a mere supervisor and clerk, was the richest estate in Maryland. It encompassed fourteen thousand acres with thirty satellite farms and a total labor force of five hundred slaves. At its center was the Great House of Edward Lloyd V, the sixth-generation lord of this realm, a former congressman, three-term governor of Maryland, and a sitting U.S. senator. An elegant Georgian mansion with a pillared portico and grand wings, the Great House was flanked by formal brick courts, a dairy, a loom house, kitchens, and a smokehouse and approached via a grand oval carriage drive, a tenth of a mile long and paved in white beach pebbles that enclosed a carefully trimmed formal lawn dotted with ornamental trees. To each side were orchards and game parks, and behind the mansion the Lloyds could promenade down the gravel walks of the bowling green past fruit, vegetable, and flower gardens to the Orangerie, an elegant eighty-five-foot-long greenhouse equipped with an elaborate heating system that kept tropical plants flourishing in the mid-Atlantic winter.[4]

A side road led to the Long Green, a twenty-five-acre common lined with ramshackle slave quarters and an array of slave-operated workshops: the smithy, cooperage, carpenter's shop, and icehouses. There was an elaborate stable stocked with thoroughbreds, barns for hundreds of sheep and cows, chicken and pigeon coops, tobacco houses and warehouses. The produce of this and the Lloyds' satellite plantations were loaded on the estate's sloop, *Sally Lloyd*, and shipped directly to Annapolis and Baltimore on the other side of the Chesapeake.

Wye House was an empire unto itself, the center of an operation that produced more wheat and corn than anywhere else in Maryland. The Lloyds and their overseers were judge, jury, jailer, and executioner, effectively answerable to no one. (The house still stands, and the Wye family still lives there as of this writing, eleven generations on.)[5]

Freddy's grandma took him across the Long Green—mobbed with "children of many colors; black, brown, copper, colored and nearly white"—to the Old Master's house, a straightforward brick home at the center of the plantation's activity. She pointed out various cousins and an eleven-year-old boy and two girls, ten and eight, who she said were his siblings. Go play, she encouraged him, "they are kin to you." Before Freddy knew it, she was gone, and he threw himself on the ground and wailed for so long and so loud that his brother and sisters fetched him pears and peaches in an effort to console him.[6]

Freddy was too young to work in the fields, so he spent his days driving the cows to and from the barns, cleaning the front yard, keeping chickens out of the gardens, and doing errands for the Old Master's daughter. Slave children weren't provided with beds, so he slept on the floor of a kitchen closet wearing the knee-length hemp shirt that was his only article of

clothing. He and the other children waded for crabs and oysters to supplement the rough corn mash their overseers served them in a trough, a meal
they would devour "like so many pigs," scooping it up with oyster shells or
their bare hands. He was hungry much of the time and fought the dogs and
cats for scraps in the yard, or would beg the cooks to give him the water
that meat had been boiled in. In winter he was often cold, and resorted to
crawling headfirst into an old grain sack for warmth. When not working,
he played with the other slave children, but preferred the company of
twelve-year-old Daniel Lloyd, the third son of Master Lloyd himself, who
sometimes shared his cakes, protected him from bullies, and expanded
Freddy's horizons with intelligence on the comings, goings, and identity of
the Lloyds' many genteel visitors and houseguests. He loved to visit the
windmill overlooking the anchorage and to watch sloops and schooners
sailing out of the river for the mysterious towns and cities of the outside
world. In some respects, he would recall, Wye House was "Eden-like."[7]

He heard about the estate's most brutal aspects before he saw them himself. Bill Denby had run from an overseer who intended to beat him, planted
himself in the middle of a creek, and refused to come out; the overseer shot
him in the head. One elderly slave, who was harvesting oysters to stave off
hunger, was shot in the back by Lloyd's neighbor, John Beale Bordley, who
was offended the slave had paddled his makeshift canoe near "his" side of
the Wye River. Another white neighbor, Mrs. Giles Hicks, fell into a rage
when her fifteen-year-old slave girl failed to awaken when Hicks's infant
began crying in the middle of the night; she bashed the girl's face in with a
log, broke her breastbone, and watched her die in agony. A third neighbor
bragged of killing two slaves with a hatchet. None of these murderers were
held to any form of account. Another slave walking on the road was questioned by a passing stranger about how he was treated at the Lloyds'—not
so well, but he got enough food, he had replied, unaware that the stranger
was actually Senator Lloyd himself. The slave was subsequently separated
from his family, placed in chains, sold to a slave trader, and shipped away to
Savannah and the horrors of the Deep South, where every Tidewater slave

feared being sent. "This is the penalty of telling the simple truth, in answer to a series of plain questions," Freddy would later observe.[8]

He experienced the dark side directly one afternoon when his eight-year-old cousin Henny Bailey arrived at the Old Master's door with a huge gash across her face, her neck and shoulders covered in fresh wounds and her clothes matted with blood. She had been beaten by an overseer at one of the Old Master's farms and had walked twelve miles to beg her owner to protect her. Instead the Old Master, whose real name was Aaron Anthony, shouted that she "deserved every bit of it" and sent her straight back to what was almost certainly another beating. Freddy witnessed it again early one morning, peeking through the crack at the bottom of the closet he slept in, as the fifty-nine-year-old Anthony tortured Freddy's beautiful fifteen-year-old aunt, Hester Bailey, whom he lusted after, because she had a boyfriend. He stripped her to the waist, called her a "damned bitch," hung her by the wrists from a joist, and began whipping her with a thick cowhide strap, peeling the skin off her back as she screamed. "The louder she screamed, the harder he whipped, and where the blood ran fastest, there he whipped longest," Freddy remembered. "He would whip her to make her scream, and whip her to make her hush, and not until overcome by fatigue would he cease to swing the blood-clotted cowskin." By the time Anthony stopped, Hester had received thirty to forty lashes, and Freddy was filled with a terror that stayed with him for the rest of his days at Wye House.[9]

He learned that the adult field hands lived in constant fear of whipping or rape. That Senator Lloyd often broke up families so he could profit from the sale of children or a parent to the ever-hungry slave traders who supplied the plantations of the new states of Mississippi, Alabama, and Florida. That the adults worked in the fields dawn to dusk six days a week on a monthly allowance of eight pounds of pickled pork or herring, a bushel of coarsely ground corn, and a pint of salt. That they received two coarse hemp shirts, two pairs of trousers, and a single pair of socks and shoes each year and went naked if these wore out prematurely. That they slept together under horse blankets on the clay floors of the long house. That their children were taken away from them at the age of one and sent to live with elderly women like his grandmother, so as to make family ties impossible. They were, he would recall, little more than "human cattle . . . wielding their clumsy hoes; hurried on by no hope of reward, no sense of gratitude, no love of children, no prospect of bettering their condition; nothing, save the dread and terror of the slave-driver's lash."[10]

Within a year, the boy was dreaming of what it would be like to one day be a free man. At around this time the Old Master scrawled in his ledger book Freddy's market value: $110, the equivalent of about eight cows.

Then, on March 15, 1826, a year and a half after his arrival at Wye House, he received wondrous news from Lucretia Auld, the Old Master's daughter: He was going to be sent to Baltimore to serve at the household of Lucretia's brother-in-law, Hugh Auld. He would depart on the *Sally Lloyd* in three days' time.[11]

The elated Freddy spent much of his remaining time at the plantation in the creek, scrubbing the dead skin off his feet and knees, "washing off the plantation scruff, and preparing myself for departure." He boarded the sloop excitedly, gave Wye House one last look, and then stood in the bow the remainder of the trip, looking ahead as the open Chesapeake came into view.[12]

EIGHT

As the *Belle* entered New York Harbor on the third of August, 1822, George Bancroft stood on deck in a state of reverie on returning after so long an absence. "I thought I had never seen such deep and beautiful green as I then saw all along the Jersey shore; it seemed to me, that no country has such neat and pretty villages, such cheerful townships, such a transparent atmosphere and glowing sky as our own. I was inclined to find everything agreeable and beautiful," he recalled shortly thereafter.

But his elation wore off almost immediately.

The route home to Worcester, he realized, was "not formed after the higher laws of beauty," as were Switzerland, Tuscany, and the French countryside. "I look in vain for the land of romance, for the bold scenery or the luxuriant landscapes, which charmed me in other countries." Still, he reminded himself that "our country is the land of our hearts for different and more serious reasons . . . as the place of refuge for pure religion, for civil liberties, for domestic happiness, and for all the kindly affections of social life." He loved his country deeply, he confided in a friend. "My chance of being remembered rests upon my attachment to it."[1]

Over the next few weeks, however, the twenty-one-year-old's attachments were shaken. He'd spent the past year being embraced as a peer by Lafayette, Goethe and Byron, Irving and Gallatin, princesses and generals. His fellow New Englanders now looked at him with disapproval. He dressed strangely. He sprinkled his speech with French and German phrases. He held peculiar ideas, and expressed them in unacceptable ways. "I have grown quite estranged from my own country and countrymen," Bancroft confided to his friend Samuel Eliot. "Before winter is over, I expect to find all the superfluous excitability, which I gathered in Southern countries, chilled to a calmness fit for our colder latitudes."[2]

After a week's stay at the Cambridge home of Andrews Norton—a visit Bancroft thought had gone well—his host sent him a letter informing him he would never be welcome there again. At President Kirkland's house young George recommended a sweeping set of reforms to be enacted immediately to bring Harvard into the nineteenth century, and requested an appointment to a college professorship. Kirkland instead offered him a one-year stint as a lowly Greek tutor, and the college treasurer, Stephen Higginson, complained he only got that because he was Kirkland's pet. "Bancroft—an unsuccessful scholar . . . came here unfit for anything," Higginson wrote. "His manners, style of writing, Theology, etc., [were] bad, and as a Tutor only the laughing butt of all [of the] college." Students, hating his rigorous, German-inspired teaching methods, shouted insults outside his window at night, mocked his flamboyant walk by day, and took to singing a protest song with the refrain "Thus we do in Germany." They broke windows, disrupted classes, and complained so loudly that Bancroft was forced to relent. "I have found College a sickening and wearisome place," he wrote near the end of his brief tenure. "My state has been nothing but trouble, trouble, trouble."[3]

It wasn't his only failure. Like his role model, Edward Everett, he'd intended to earn his fame and contribute to shaping his country as a minister-scholar, and began substitute preaching at a different church on an almost weekly basis. He lacked Everett's gifts, however, and hadn't inherited his father's, either. Parishioners were displeased with his ornate, flowery orations, dripping with sentiment and short on theology. His sermon in Portsmouth, New Hampshire—which included praise for "our dear pelican Jesus"—was long remembered, but not fondly. "He hath sadly disappointed great expectations," his friend and former Harvard schoolmate

Ralph Waldo Emerson wrote in his diary after seeing him speak. Bancroft decided the ministry was not his path.[4]

Nor, it turned out, was poetry. He spent the fall of 1823 revising verses he'd penned in the journals he carried across Europe and, that October, published them in a thin volume dedicated to Kirkland. They were the sentimental reflections of a twenty-year-old European-study-abroad student, doggedly set in rhyme, and opened with his departure from Boston: "And fast away the tear he brushed/That down his cheeks too freely gushed/As swiftly from his native shore/The vessel hurrying breezes bore." The book was, in Bancroft's words, "not much cared for," and later in life he attempted to buy up and destroy every last copy.[5]

After this disappointment he found what he hoped was a way forward. Joseph Cogswell, who had preceded him at Göttingen and was now Harvard's librarian, shared his frustration with the college's small-minded governing board and craven students. Through the long, dark New England winter they devised a plan to force reform from below, by starting a German-style gymnasium, a rigorous boarding school of the sort Bancroft had become familiar with on the Continent. At the conclusion of the 1822–23 academic year, they both resigned their positions and moved one hundred miles west to the bucolic village of Northampton, Massachusetts, where they opened their Round Hill School in rented buildings that October. "We are going on very smoothly and very happily," Bancroft reported to Everett a few weeks later. "There is some comfort in shaping one's conduct by one's own inclinations and views, without being obliged to bend to the ignorance of others."[6]

But Bancroft quickly discovered he wasn't much of an administrator or a secondary school teacher either. "He was absent-minded, dreamy, and often in abstracted moods as well as very near-sighted," one pupil recalled. He showed up in class with a slipper on one foot and a boot on the other, and frequently forgot his glasses, allowing boys to play tricks on him, such as pelting him with an overripe muskmelon. "The wall back of the platform where he sat, poring over a book, was thickly bespattered with 'spit balls' thrown at him." Their teacher, the pupils concluded, was more interested in his own learning than he was in theirs.[7]

When not holding class, Bancroft was indeed deep at work researching and writing. He translated and published two of Heeren's most influential books, *Reflections on the Politics of Ancient Greece* and *Manual of Ancient History*, making them available in English for the first time. He introduced American readers to the German poet Friedrich Schiller in a review he wrote for the most prestigious intellectual periodical of the day, *The North American Review*, edited first by Everett and later by another Harvard alumnus, Jared Sparks. His essays for that magazine on Goethe and on Heeren's *Ancient Greece*—in which the Göttingen professor laid out his theories of history—attracted a great deal of notice, and a massive three-part series he wrote for the *Review*'s main competitor, Philadelphia's *American Quarterly Review*, presented a complete history of German thought for the American reading public. While he made little money from these freelance efforts, through them he had almost single-handedly become the conduit linking the German intellectual revolution with the intelligentsia of the young United States. Writing, he began to realize, could be a means by which he would stir the public, build American literature, and help influence how his country saw itself.[8]

By 1826 Bancroft had become disillusioned with teaching and watched as Everett quit Harvard and went into politics, winning a seat in the U.S. House of Representatives. Perhaps he could become a scholar-statesman, too, Bancroft thought, and so on the Fourth of July he delivered an address in Northampton offering a political vision for the future of the United States on the occasion of its fiftieth birthday. America, he said, was the great hope of all of mankind precisely because she granted genuine power to ordinary people, whose freedom to assert their own interests would keep an aristocracy from forming. "The dearest interests of mankind were entrusted to our country; it was for her to show that the aspirations of former ages were not visionary; that freedom is something more than a name; that the patriots and the states that have been martyrs in its defence were struggling in a sacred cause," he told the crowd. "The nations of the earth turned towards her as to their last hope. And the country has not deceived them."

Bancroft immediately published the speech in book form, and for the political observers who read it, his partisan leanings were clear and eyebrow raising. Bancroft was signaling allegiance not to the Federalists and Whigs who dominated New England and who believed an educated elite must guide the ship of state, but to the popular democracy of Andrew Jackson, who'd leveraged his fame as a war hero to nearly win the 1824 presidential election against Massachusetts's own John Quincy Adams, and who was preparing a rematch in two years' time.[9]

Only later would Bancroft learn that as he gave his speech, John Adams and Thomas Jefferson lay on their deathbeds. By nightfall both were gone, and millions of Americans realized that the Founding Fathers could no longer offer counsel on the questions facing the young federation.

As Bancroft contemplated his future, a twenty-three-year-old visitor from Springfield caught his attention. Sarah Dwight belonged to one of the city's most prosperous families, storekeepers who were investing in banks across New England, upstate New York, and the new state of Ohio. After a formal courtship, and an inspection of Round Hill by her father, Jonathan Dwight, the couple were wed on March 1, 1827.[10]

The marriage would prove an unhappy one, but it gave Bancroft the means both to extract himself from the tedium of Round Hill and to set himself on a path to fame and glory.

NINE

In Charleston, William Gilmore Simms was also making his way in the world of letters, but had lawyering as his base of financial support.

Returning from his second trip to Mississippi in the middle of 1826, he put down roots, marrying Anna Malcolm Giles, daughter of the Charleston merchant Othneil Giles, passing the bar exam, and accepting a job as a magistrate. Although he had a comfortable salary and some remaining inheritance from his mother, he and Anna moved to the suburb of Summerville, where the rent was cheaper. Simms threw his extra time and resources into *The Album* and, when the journal failed, started a second one, the *Southern Literary Gazette*. By his twenty-third birthday, he had a seventeen-month-old daughter, three published books of poetry, and a reputation as a respectable and effective attorney.

Like Bancroft, Simms increasingly sought to help define, guide, and nurture the development of his country. In Simms's case, however, the country in question wasn't the United States, but rather South Carolina or, in Simms's more expansive moods, the section it had spawned, comprising lowland Georgia, Alabama, and Mississippi, the only places he had as yet visited. His newspaper articles, published poems, and even the novels he was writing dwelled almost exclusively on this region's origins, character, and historical experience. Most of his fiction took place on the Revolutionary frontier of his grandparents' generation, or deep in the backcountry he'd explored with his father. While he was not unsympathetic to frontiersmen and Indians, his heroes were almost always cultured lowlanders who brought order and enlightenment to the frontier.

He loved the United States as well, but more as a fortuitous legal construct or international alliance that protected and strengthened its real, historical constituent nations, like New England or South Carolina. Without the Union, he recognized, the British would not have been defeated in either 1783 or 1814, South Carolina would have lost its liberties and self-government, and Mississippi, Alabama, and the vast U.S. territories of the Louisiana Purchase might never have existed. The "terrible vicissitudes to which our fathers were subjected" in creating "the proud and aweful edifice of our Union" were "sober truths of undisputed history" that must not be betrayed.[1]

By 1829, however, this was fast becoming a minority position in South Carolina. The federal government had passed a tariff that year that protected and fostered manufacturers (concentrated in the North) while harming exporters (like the Deep South's cotton, rice, and indigo growers). South Carolinians vigorously opposed the tariff, and when the new president, Andrew Jackson, failed to take action, many in the Palmetto State argued that the state legislature had to declare the tariff null and void. Thousands of copies of a treatise on this subject, anonymously penned by Vice President John C. Calhoun, South Carolina's leading politician, were distributed throughout the city, and politicians gathered into Nullifier and Unionist camps. Fights and violence began to break out as South Carolinians clashed over their loyalty to their fifty-three-year-old federation.

Simms vigorously supported the Unionist cause.

With his friend E. Smith Duryea, he bought a distressed newspaper, the Charleston *City Gazette*, and turned it into the leading voice opposing the "Nullies." The component sections of America, he editorialized, had engaged in a common struggle for liberty, and it would be foolish to dissolve the alliance they had forged. "A nation—a great nation has sprung into existence," he exalted, "the pride and luxury of our people and the liberty they enjoy." Nullifiers promptly canceled their advertisements in the paper, wiping out half its profits and forcing Simms and Duryea into crushing debt.[2]

On the afternoon of September 7, 1830, Simms was standing "erect as a poplar" at the entrance of the *Gazette* as a torch-lit parade of hundreds of Nullifiers came down Broad Street, celebrating their victory in the state legislative election. As they passed close by, several recognized him and hissed. Simms loudly muttered, "Cowards!" The crowd turned on him and rushed the office, wielding clubs, intending to destroy him and the printing presses within. He was seized by three assailants brandishing clubs.

There are differing accounts as to what happened next. Some said Simms dissuaded them with a pistol. (As tensions in the city increased, he had purchased two pairs to supplement the long-barreled gun he kept "always conveniently at hand.") Others claimed he was rescued by Duryea's diplomatic intervention or by the brandishing of "a weapon of some little potency." He had come within a hairbreadth of a beating that might have proved fatal.[3]

Soon afterward Simms received word from Uncle James that his father had died in Mississippi on March 29, 1830. His grandmother passed away at around the same time. His wife, who had never recovered from her pregnancy, drew her last breath on February 19, 1832, and Duryea followed a month later. As well as suffering these losses, Simms had exhausted his inheritance and was deeply in debt, with no foreseeable means to pay it.

Meanwhile, the Nullifiers had taken over the state government and were barreling headlong toward an armed showdown with their federal counterparts. "We shall have to emigrate en masse to a territory which I doubt not the [federal] government will assign us for a new state, and leave this once high, but now damnably defiled scene of brutal prosecution and tyranny to be over run by the U. States, her name and star place blotted out and her territory divided among the contiguous and more loyal states," he lamented.[4]

He would later acknowledge that his mental sufferings from deaths, debts, privations, and political tensions in this time period "nearly drove me mad."[5]

In desperation, he sold the *Gazette*, left his four-year-old daughter with his mother-in-law, packed his manuscripts and unpublished poems into trunks, and "sick, sad, and desolate" departed for New York City, uncertain if he would ever return.[6]

TEN

As the *Sally Lloyd* tied up to Smith's Wharf, Freddy Bailey gawked at the three-masted ships in Baltimore's harbor, oceangoing vessels that dwarfed the bay sloops and schooners he'd seen in the Wye River; at huge clipper ships under construction at the Fell's Point shipyard, thronged with workmen, white and black; at the crowds of pedestrians on the paved brick streets; at the seemingly endless procession of tall brick and stone buildings looming over the traffic; at the spires and cupolas of cathedrals, churches, and civic buildings, each taller than any structure he'd ever seen.

Baltimore was a fast-growing city of eighty thousand people and part of an entirely different cultural region from that in which he had been raised. While southern Maryland and the Eastern Shore were part of the aristocratic Tidewater country, central and northern Maryland had more in common with southeastern Pennsylvania, northern Delaware, and southern New Jersey, a pluralistic, multicultural milieu with origins in William Penn's xenophilic Quaker settlements on the shores of Delaware Bay. As he walked Baltimore's streets to meet his new masters, Freddy avoided bellicose gangs of Irish and German immigrant children, beheld free black shopkeepers and workmen, and witnessed white people interacting with slaves in an attitude of polite aloofness rather than the brutishness to which he had become accustomed. Baltimore had a population of four thousand slaves but was also home to the largest free black community in the Union, fourteen thousand strong, with churches, stores, and even schools of their own. The city would open the eight-year-old's mind to freedom's possibilities and torment him with the prospect of lifelong bondage.[1]

To his surprise, when he arrived at the Aulds' home, the little family was standing at the door, welcoming him with smiles, as if he were a person, not a thing.

Sophia Auld, his new mistress, greeted him in a tender, kind, even motherly fashion, and warmly introduced him to her two-year-old, Thomas, saying, "There is your Freddy" and assuring him that "Freddy will take care of you." "I was told 'to be kind to young Tommy'—an injunction I scarcely needed, for I had already fallen in love with the dear boy," Freddy would recall. "I wish I could describe the rapture that flashed through my soul . . . brightening up my pathway with the light of happiness."[2]

The astonished boy was given clean clothes, a straw bed with real covers, and full meals with good bread. Sophia Auld, raised in a pious household of antislavery Methodists, regarded him not as property, but as an older stepbrother to little Tommy. She caressed him, read him the Bible, and treated him with a kindness that left him happy but confused. "I scarcely knew how to behave towards her. She was entirely unlike any other white woman I had ever seen," he would recall. "The crouching servility of a slave, usually so acceptable a quality to the haughty slaveholder, was not understood nor desired by this gentle woman." When he'd avert his eyes, as he'd been taught to do when addressed by white people, she implored him not to. "Look up, child; don't be afraid," she encouraged him.[3]

Freddy settled into his duties: playing and looking after Tommy; running odd errands in the vast, exciting city; and watching over the house when Hugh Auld, an ambitious ship's carpenter, and the rest of the family were absent. Sophia, noticing his interest in her Bible reading, began teaching him the alphabet, and soon he was spelling three- and four-letter words. She was as proud of his progress as he was and innocently shared it with her husband.

"If you give a nigger an inch, he will take an ell," he told her angrily. "A nigger should know nothing but to obey his master—to do as he is told to do. Learning would spoil the best nigger in the world. Now, if you teach that nigger how to read there would be no keeping him. It would forever unfit him to be a slave." He claimed, incorrectly, that teaching slaves to read was illegal in Maryland, and forbade his wife to instruct the child further. "If you learn him how to read, he'll want to know how to write, and this accomplished, he'll be running away with himself." For Freddy, rooted to the parlor floor in shock, this was "a new and special revelation, dispelling a painful mystery, against which my youthful understanding had struggled, and struggled in vain, to wit: the *white* man's power to perpetuate the enslavement of the *black* man," as he later wrote. "'Very well,' thought I, 'knowledge unfits a child to be a slave.'" With that Freddy resolved that obtaining knowledge would be his goal.[4]

From then on he learned any way he could. He traded the warm bread Sophia gave him for reading lessons from the hungry Irish boys he'd befriended on the streets of Fell's Point. He gathered the loose pages from a Bible and discarded newspapers he found scattered on the street. When he went to the shipyard where Hugh Auld worked, he'd quiz workmen about the meaning of letters written on the parts of the vessels they were building, then copied them in the dirt with sticks. As Tommy grew older and started learning to write himself, Freddy would sneak off with his copybooks and repeat the lessons. He saved pocket money to buy a used copy of *The Columbian Orator*, a three-hundred-page middle school reader recommended to him by his street friends that contained eye-opening readings: an abolitionist-inspired dialogue between a master and a slave; a dialogue between an Englishman and a Mohawk Indian, in which the latter appears the more virtuous; David Everett's two-act drama *Slaves in Barbary*, in which a captured white sea captain is placed under the supervision of the black man who had heretofore been his slave; and a detailed essay on public speaking and the art of oration. "The reading of these documents enabled me to utter my thoughts, and to meet the arguments brought forward to sustain slavery," he recalled. "The more I read, the more I was led to abhor and detest my enslavers."[5]

He confided his anguish to the Irish boys he'd befriended, and they shared his sense of injustice. They told him repeatedly that they believed Freddy had as much a right to be free as they did, and that they didn't believe God had ever created anyone to be a slave. "I was no longer the light-hearted, gleesome boy, full of mirth and play, as when I had landed first at Baltimore," he later wrote. "Knowledge opened my eyes to the horrible pit and revealed the teeth of the frightful dragon that was ready to pounce on me."[6]

His relationship with the Aulds began to deteriorate as he grew into a teenager filled with rage and hopelessness. Sophia became furious when she caught him reading a purloined newspaper, and seemed conflicted herself by the moral gymnastics she had to perform to justify oppressing him. "I was human, and she, dear lady, knew and felt me to be so," he realized. "How could she then treat me as a brute, without a mighty struggle with all the noble powers of her own soul?" As Tommy entered his teens, he began treating Freddy with the haughty contempt of his class. Slavery, Freddy would come to believe, destroyed the souls of masters as well as slaves.[7]

He struggled to deal with the capriciousness of life as a human chattel. Once, at age nine, he was suddenly sent back to Tuckahoe because the Old Master and his daughter Lucretia had died and their human property needed to be divided into lots and sold or given to others. To Freddy's relief, he was returned to Baltimore after about a month, but some of his siblings were sold for profit and sent to work in the wilds of Mississippi and Alabama, where plantations had sprung up like mushrooms.

In March 1832 Hugh got into a spat with his brother Thomas, the man who still legally owned Freddy, over who would have custody of Freddy's sixteen-year-old cousin Henny Bailey, who'd been terribly disfigured when she'd fallen into a fire as a child, leaving her fingers "drawn almost into the palms of her hands." When Thomas didn't get his way, he petulantly demanded that Freddy be returned to him. With almost no advance warning, the fourteen-year-old found himself on the Lloyds' new sloop *Amanda*, bound back to the grim world of the Eastern Shore.[8]

As he was carried away down the Chesapeake, he watched steamboats passing by, en route to Philadelphia. "I watched the course of those steamers," he recalled of the moment, "and, while going to St. Michael's, I formed a plan to escape from slavery."[9]

ELEVEN

Not long after his marriage to Sarah Dwight, Bancroft sold his stake in the Round Hill School and began working for his in-laws' growing business empire. That involved a move that would take him to the frontier, but a very different frontier from the one Simms had been exploring.

In the 1810s Sarah's uncle Henry had followed the New England settlement stream out of Massachusetts, over the Hudson, and onto a six-million-acre swath of western New York that in colonial times had been claimed by Massachusetts. Virtually all of the settlers who'd colonized this region were from New England, and they established Yankee-style townships in what had been the forests of the Iroquois, with Congregational churches and public schoolhouses fronting town greens. Henry Dwight had founded the Bank of Geneva in 1817 in the lakeside village of the same name. He then convinced his brothers to join him in buying the Bank of Michigan, the largest financial institution in the young Michigan Territory, most of whose thirty-two thousand settlers were from New England or the Yankee upstate of New York.

A few years later Henry had watched as Irish workers dug a canal stretching the 363 miles from the Hudson to Lake Erie. With its opening in 1825, the Erie Canal enabled thousands of New York and Ohio farmers to ship their produce to East Coast markets twenty times faster than before, creating a staggering explosion in commerce that turned Buffalo into a city and New York City into the nation's largest port. The relative ease and comfort of barge travel attracted forty thousand passengers to the canal in its first year, an entirely unexpected phenomenon that made investors rich. The Dwight family, Henry urged, should invest in the newly accessible Western Reserve of Ohio, a portion of that nineteen-year-old state abutting Lake Erie that had been claimed by Connecticut and, as a result, was settled almost entirely by New Englanders.[1]

The Dwights decided to send Bancroft on a mission to investigate the defunct Commercial Bank of Lake Erie in Cleveland. Before the opening of the Erie Canal the bank had been overwhelmed by bad loans and suspended operations, and still owed the federal government $9,000. But its charter was still active, and the Dwights thought it might be worth buying the bank and assuming its debt in order to gain access to its difficult-to-obtain federal banking charter. In July 1831 Bancroft traveled west of the Hudson for the first time, probably on one of the horse-pulled passenger packets that departed from the Albany locks twice daily, bound for Buffalo, four days away. From there he likely took a steamboat to Cleveland, then a village of fifteen hundred that he was certain "must grow into a large city." There he discovered that no banks were operating, but its business community was bullish about a second canal already under construction that would connect the hamlet with the Ohio River and redirect the commerce of Kentucky and southern Ohio to Lake Erie and New York instead of the Mississippi and New Orleans. Bancroft needed little convincing that Cleveland and the Commercial Bank were worth the investment—so much so that he even decided to borrow $16,000 to buy shares in the bank himself.[2]

Closing the deal would require eight months of almost nonstop travel, and while in Cleveland he received word that Sarah had given birth to a daughter. He was unable to get nearer to home than Geneva, though, where he and Henry worked out the $50,000 purchase arrangement. In November he went to Washington, D.C., to lobby Congress and the Treasury Department to forgive a part of the bank's debt. In January, Sarah wrote to inform him that their infant had died; the Dwights instructed him to remain in

Washington to conclude his work. It took him until the middle of February to do so, by which point Sarah was overwhelmed with grief.[3]

Despite this tragedy, Bancroft enjoyed his time in Washington, a city that reminded him of his time in Europe. He lodged with his sister's husband, Massachusetts congressman John Davis, a rising star in the national Republican Party. Davis was being groomed for a gubernatorial run and had entrée to the capital's most exclusive social circles. Over Christmas dinner Bancroft debated the role of the free press with John Quincy Adams; the erstwhile president compared it to "the implements of war," while Bancroft likened it to grains "ordinarily the nutriment of life, but which are sometimes perverted by distillation into poisonous liquors." He was introduced to Charles X, the exiled king of France. He socialized with the man who'd defeated Adams, Andrew Jackson, and was surprised to find him of good personal character, though the White House reception Bancroft attended was marred by a throng of his vulgar followers, "the vilest promiscuous medley, that ever was congregated in a decent house . . . pouncing with avidity upon the wine and refreshments, tearing the cake with the ravenous keenness of intense hunger," and jostling the ladies. He watched Henry Clay deliver a rousing speech in support of the very tariffs that were infuriating Simms's neighbors. On another occasion he heard Everett lecture his House colleagues on the evils of slavery and the merits of helping blacks emigrate to special colonial outposts in Liberia. (Bancroft wrote his wife that he preferred to see the slaves emancipated, because "slavery corrupts the masters" by harming competition and "the sinews of industry.")[4]

During the months he spent in the capital, George filled the quiet hours with books. He read the inventor Sir Humphry Davy's treatise on human passions alongside the eminent Scottish historian George Chalmers's *Political Annals of the Present United Colonies*, a British perspective on American history that George found impressive in scholarship but scandalous in interpretation, being "full of spleen against our ancestors." This fueled an epiphany: He could do better than Chalmers. His passions, he had come to realize, were not with teaching or business. The proper stage for his life wasn't the wilds of western Massachusetts or the Western Reserve, but the world at large. "The tastes, which have lain dormant, have revived, and my mind has been aroused to greater activity," he wrote to his grieving wife. "It was an unwise thing in me to have made myself a school-master: that was a kind of occupation, to which I was not peculiarly adapted, and in which many of inferior abilities and attainments could have succeeded as well. I have felt rejoiced at being entirely emancipated from this condition."[5]

It was during that sojourn in the capital that Bancroft made the decision to write a history of his country that would help guide its people to their destiny.

Congress finally passed the Dwights' banking measures on February 10, 1832. Bancroft returned home to soothe his wife, who, over his objections, continued to wear mourning clothes. The investments he'd made would pay off, as Cleveland and the Commercial Bank did indeed boom. For the first time in his thirty-two years, he had the financial cushion that enabled him to focus on his intellectual pursuits full-time. Without telling his friends exactly what he was doing, he began visiting libraries, borrowing books, seeking advice on the location of document collections. He spent long hours at the Harvard library, the Massachusetts Historical Society, and the Athenæum in Boston.

For much of 1833 and early 1834 he did little else but write. He was at work twelve to fourteen hours a day, scrawling out words in his compact script, four lines to a page, then revising them in the ample spaces in between. Some of the pages became so clotted with ink from his alterations that it would be difficult for a printer to decode his intentions. But the pages stacked higher, and within them was a story of America and its purpose.[6]

He had settled on his theme even before he started his research.[7]

History, he was convinced, was the unfolding of God's plan for the world, and that plan was the progressive development of liberty, equality, and freedom. This Providential view of humanity's past, present, and future had been passed on to him by what he had learned from his father, his

boarding school, his college, and his faith. His professors in Göttingen and
Berlin had reinforced this paradigm, even if most of them expressed this
discernible direction of history in secular terms.

Hegel, Heeren, and Eichhorn had taught him to focus on nations—*Volk*,
or peoples—as the primary actors in history's progress. Each group had its
own intrinsic characteristics and each grew like an organism from the instructions encoded in its seed, its spirit, its *Volksgeist*. World history was
led, these professors had demonstrated, by a series of nations each taking
its turn to carry the baton of freedom and liberty as far as it was capable
before handing it off to another. Greece was succeeded by Rome; a corrupted Rome was conquered by the Teutons, the ancient Germanic peoples
who the first-century Roman historian Tacitus said were morally upstanding and democratically organized; the Teutons in turn invaded the British
Isles, passing the torch to the resulting Anglo-Saxons. It had then, Bancroft
was already certain, been taken up by British-settled North America.[8]

America *had* to be a chosen nation. Bancroft's Puritan ancestors believed themselves to be such an elect people, tasked by God to erect a city
upon a hill, to conduct an errand in the wilderness to create a more perfect
and godly society. Bancroft assumed his Greater New England region was
exemplary of the country as a whole, that its deep cultural values and ideals
were broadly shared. Those values, he believed, were unfolding from their
Anglo-Saxon germ, spreading by means of roads, canals, and steamboats to
fulfill the divine plan.

A golden age was coming for humanity, and America would lead the
way, ever forward, ever noble, ever good.

Bancroft portrayed the pre-contact Americas as having been devoid of
civilization—"a few scattered tribes of feeble barbarians, destitute of commerce, of political connexion, and of morals"—a second Eden provided by
God to enable the staging of the final act of history, away from the corruption
and despotic heritage of the Old World. Through the events of the past two
centuries, God had revealed that Spain, Portugal, and France were not the
nations that would bring his design to fruition, and that even England itself

was too weighed down by the past to lead humanity to this bright future. The continent had been made for the Americans and had waited for their arrival, providing the setting for them to build their Providential nation.[9]

Bancroft was convinced that by studying the past one could plot out the future course of God's plan for humankind and that this was the true purpose and calling of the historian. He had come to believe that it was his task to reveal not only to Americans but to the men of letters around the world the United States' character, identity, and world-historical purpose.

In the study of his hillside Northampton home he gathered books, notes, and documents from a dozen libraries and culled the parts he needed to build this story. In June 1834 the assembly was completed. He paid for the creation of the printing plates—and thus owned them—and traveled to Boston to carefully supervise the printing and binding of his book at the premises of the publisher Charles Bowen.[10]

By September volume 1 of *A History of the United States: From the Discovery of the American Continent to the Present Time* was ready for publication. It ran more than five hundred pages and covered the period to 1660, 116 years before the United States was founded. "The work which I have undertaken will necessarily extend to four or perhaps five volumes," he informed readers in the preface. "Its completion will require further years of exertion." Instead, he would end up writing twelve volumes, and even his very long life was sufficient only to take him up to 1789, almost a century short of the ever-advancing present.[11]

Inspired by all he'd seen in his recent travels, he opened the *History* with a triumphant portrait of the Union in 1834, where popular sovereignty, equal justice, and a free economy had created a utopia, peaceful and secure, prosperous and ever growing. "New states are forming in the wilderness; canals, intersecting our plains and crossing our highlands, open numerous channels to internal commerce; manufactures prosper along our waterways; the use of steam on our rivers and railroads annihilates distance by the acceleration of speed," he wrote. "There is no national debt; the community is opulent; the government economical; and the public treasury full."

A vigorous press educated the people. The immigrants who were arriving on the nation's shores were blending into a "harmonious union" with those already here. Americans had built all this on the "unproductive waste" of pre-contact North America. Explaining how they had done so, he pledged, was the object of his history, which would trace the steps by which Providence created the United States and "conducted the country to its present happiness and glory."[12]

Bancroft insisted that the country's disparate colonies—be they in the oligarchic Deep South or Puritan-founded New England—had been planted with the same seed and, despite differences in soil and climate, were all growing the same American organism. "I have dwelt at considerable length on this first period, because it contains the germ of our Institutions," he wrote. "The maturity of the nation is but a continuation of its youth. The spirit of the colonies demanded freedom from the beginning."[13]

The founders of Massachusetts had been at the vanguard of this effort, he argued. The Pilgrims' Mayflower Compact—signed to prevent a mutiny when the colonists had arrived in the wrong location—had in his telling recovered the rights of humanity and secured what he would later term the "birth of constitutional liberty." The Puritans' intolerant, collective-minded project had, in Bancroft's view, "planted . . . undying principles of democratic liberty," creating a colony that was, throughout the seventeenth and eighteenth centuries, "unconsciously becom[ing] a representative democracy." Scarcely had the first settlements been created at Massachusetts Bay, he informed readers, than their streets were "filled with the hum of village politicians . . . inquiring into their liberties and privileges. . . . The voice of the majority was the voice of God and the [essential] issue of Puritanism was therefore popular sovereignty." The Commonwealth's citizens were industrious, frugal, healthy, long-lived, and staunchly moral, protecting even animals from cruelty. Their descendants accounted for a third of the white population of the United States. "To New York and Ohio, where they constitute half the population, they have carried the Puritan system of free schools; and their example is spreading it through the civilized world."[14]

The other colonies followed suit, Bancroft maintained. In Virginia he saw not a society created by and for slaveholding aristocrats, but rather a "nearly independent democracy" and "a nursery of freemen"; if Virginia had departed from the principles of popular supremacy, universal suffrage, and freedom of religion, "it was from the influence of foreign authority" in London. He characterized Lord Baltimore, feudal master of Maryland, as among the "most wise and benevolent law-givers of all ages," securing for his people the freedom of religion, and that he was the first leader in the world to give his subjects liberty of conscience by adopting "religious free-dom as the basis of the state." He claimed that innovations had echoed back and forth between all of these colonies "like the solitary mountain, replying to the thunder, or like deep, calling unto deep."[15]

Reaction to the book was swift and laudatory. Everett read it in twenty-four hours, stopping only for sleep and church, and declared it "a work which will last while America lasts, and which will instantly take its place among the classics of our language." The historian William Prescott said Bancroft had "given us a pledge of an enduring, impartial, readable history—such as we greatly need." Everett's review in *The North American Review* went even further: "He is the instrument of Providence, to award to good men, who in times past have served or admired his native land, the just need of praise." Heeren wrote from Göttingen: "It is written with the warmth and enthusiasm the writer feels in his subject, so natural in writing the his-tory of one's own country." He called it "a life work, for it will occupy you a great part of it, and altogether it is the most agreeable, the most grateful, and the worthiest labour you could enter upon."[16]

Not everyone had such high praise. John Quincy Adams thought the book's morality "ostentatious, but very defective" and its account of early Virginia "a florid panegyric." Actual Virginians liked it even less, precisely because Bancroft mischaracterized the political positions of their aristo-cratic mid-sixteenth-century leaders, who had been loyal to the Crown in the English Civil War and not the Parliament, as Bancroft had rather pre-posterously claimed. "If we know anything (and we think we do) of the character of the early settlers of Virginia, they were a chivalrous and generous race . . . and when driven from their native country, they had bent their steps toward Virginia, as that part of the foreign dominions of England where the spirit of loyalty was the strongest," College of William & Mary law professor Nathaniel Beverley Tucker fumed in a review. "What is the meaning of this strange attempt to pervert the truth of history. . . . Is it intended to dispose us to acquiesce in the new notion 'that the people of the colonies, all together, formed one body politic before the revolution?' Against this proposition we feel bound to protest." Professor Tucker also recommended Southern readers not buy the book, and that Southern writers undertake the task of writing their own history, otherwise the New Englanders would "become our masters."[17]

Even in the face of such criticism booksellers couldn't keep Bancroft's *History* on the shelves. Within a year a third of New England's families owned a copy, and over the next decade it would go through ten editions. The images of America that Bancroft conjured up in its pages filtered into the public consciousness, where they would remain for more than a century after the book itself had been forgotten. Nathaniel Hawthorne would respond to his friend's glowing depictions of the Puritans in the pages of *The Scarlet Letter* and "Endicott and the Red Cross." One of Bancroft's chapters provided the inspiration for the artist John Gadsby Chapman's *Baptism of Pocahontas*, while another influenced William Powell's depiction of the *Discovery of the Mississippi by De Soto*, two grand paintings that were commissioned to hang in the U.S. Capitol's Rotunda, where they are still displayed today, serving as official renderings of key moments in the American national myth.[18]

TWELVE

When Simms arrived in New York City for the first time in the summer of 1832, the city had reached only as far north on the island as Fourteenth Street and was recovering from a cholera outbreak that had killed more than thirty-five hundred of its inhabitants. But for the South Carolinian, it was still a remarkable place to behold.

Founded by the Dutch in the 1640s, it had always been a place apart, a city-state modeled on Golden Age Amsterdam, a place of commerce and trade, publishing and finance, tolerant of most anything from moral and intellectual deviancy to slaveholding, and populated from the beginning by a diverse ethnic, racial, and religious mix with no one group in charge. The Erie Canal had suddenly made it the largest city in the country, with a quarter of a million people living in a dense grid of low brick and wooden houses. Church spires poked up above the fray, along with the tops of the Masonic Hall and the Apollo dance hall. A forest of masts lined the South Street wharfs as barges and steamers unloaded cargo and passengers from Ohio, Michigan, and beyond. Just to the north, overflowing outhouses, animal feces, mud, slaughterhouse gore, and household garbage mixed into a vile concoction residents called "Corporation pudding." Simms arrived a few blocks to the southwest, in the thriving commercial district at the tip of the island, at the comfortable Wall Street town house of his host, James Lawson.[1]

Lawson, a thirty-three-year-old Scotsman, had emigrated to Gotham in 1817 to work as an accountant for his uncle, a position he'd parlayed into

becoming a leading figure in the city's publishing scene. Charming and so-
ciable, a brilliant storyteller and part-time poet and playwright, he'd established friendships with authors and actors, and lent money to and performed
other small favors for publishers and editors, making himself the connec-
tive tissue between the groups. He had become, in effect, the literary agent
for the city's leading writers, including Edgar Allan Poe, William Cullen
Bryant, and John Greenleaf Whittier, and his home the hub of the literary
world, where the city's men of letters mingled with visiting celebrities. Simms
had published Lawson's work in the Charleston *City Gazette*, and the two
had become dedicated correspondents, though they had yet to meet. Simms
wound up spending most of the next three months as Lawson's guest, and
they would remain friends for the rest of their lives.[2]

Lawson opened New York's doors to his South Carolinian friend. There
were long walks with Bryant and the poet Robert Charles Sands and discussions with the actor Edwin Forrest. He spent time with the bookseller
and literary editor Evert Duyckinck, who introduced him to the publishers
James and John Harper, future founders of *Harper's Magazine*, who expressed interest in Simms's unpublished poems. Lawson, a bachelor, also
introduced him to the pleasures and practices of high-society courting, and
the two spent many hours in the charming company of the city's most eli-
gible young women and their well-connected fathers and brothers. In the
late summer, Simms retreated to Hingham, Massachusetts, outside of Boston, to finish revising the poems that the Harper brothers would publish as
Atalantis, and work on his unfinished novels. The gates to the literary world,
Simms realized, were in New York, not Charleston, and Lawson urged the
twenty-six-year-old widower to move there.[3]

When Simms returned to South Carolina, the Nullification Crisis was
still tearing the state apart, and he spent the fall and winter hiding out and
writing in Summerville, a revolver "always conveniently at hand." He wrote
Lawson that he was "already determined on expatriation and, in fact, consider myself now rather a visitor in the state than a citizen." If he could sell
his property, he would "leave tomorrow." Before year's end Simms sent the

finished manuscript of one of his novels to the Harpers and waited anxiously for a response. In the early months of 1833 they responded with enthusiasm and encouraged him to submit his other book when it was completed.[4]

THE HARPERS' PUBLICATION of Simms's first two works of fiction transformed him from a local literary figure to a rising national star. The leading journals and newspapers of the day raved about the books, and no less than Poe declared there was not another author "who surpasses him in aggregate of the higher excellences of fiction." The novella *Martin Faber* sold out four days after its September 1833 release. *Guy Rivers: A Tale of Georgia*, his first full-length novel, was published the following summer and prompted *The American Monthly Magazine* to declare Simms to be the peer of James Fenimore Cooper and Sir Walter Scott, while *The Charleston Mercury* deemed the book "decidedly the best American novel that has appeared in recent years."[5]

The stories that so riveted the reading public took seriously the sorts of people and places they rarely encountered. Martin Faber was a twisted, immoral psychopath who narrated his own tale of murder and cruelty; readers saw the world through the villain's eyes, learned how he thought, and discovered the origins of his depravity: a childhood in which morality, education, and discipline were never enforced. Some were shocked by the character's violent acts, and a few were scandalized that such a monster would be presented in the first person, allowed to speak for himself without explicit editorial condemnation.

Guy Rivers focused on the clash between the civilized culture of the lowland South and the wild, unrestrained conditions on the Southern frontier, between the respective worlds Simms and his father had chosen. Set on the contemporary frontier of north Georgia, then in the midst of a gold rush, it told the story of a young, capable, and well-bred lowland gentleman who is captured, deep in the forests surrounding the mining camps, by a criminal gang called the Pony Club, so named because they stole horses from the

Cherokee. An action-packed adventure, it, too, excited many readers but upset the Puritanical-minded with its vivid and frequent depictions of the violence, depravity, and barbarism of its subjects and their milieu. Defying convention, Guy Rivers, the leader of the gang, was an educated man, a lawyer who had chosen to abandon civilization. Characters spoke in rich dialects, from the ornamental speech of lowland drawing rooms to the colorful backwoods banter of the rough-and-tumble Appalachian frontier, to the Gullah-inflected speech of the slaves.

Simms didn't slow down. He was finishing *Guy Rivers* while *Martin Faber* was going to print, and was outlining *The Yemassee* while in New York in the summer of 1834 to help the Harper brothers prepare *Guy Rivers* for the presses. In January 1835 *The Yemassee* was on the way north on the Charleston mail packet, and Simms was already far along in the manuscript of his fourth novel, *The Partisan*, which he finished in New York that summer, even as the first chapters were going to print.

The Yemassee: A Romance of Carolina was his first full-length work of historical fiction, and proved to be an even bigger hit than *Guy Rivers*. The book was set on the South Carolina frontier during the Yemassee War of 1715–17, when a coalition of Native American groups and their Spanish allies in Florida nearly succeeded in destroying the English colony. The protagonist, the jocular, self-identified "Cavalier" Gabriel Harrison, ultimately rescues the situation with the help of his ever-loyal slave, Hector, and then reveals himself to actually be Charles Craven, the colony's royal governor. He faces a worthy adversary in the Yemassee chief Sauntee, who is depicted sympathetically and with more complexity than any of the novel's white characters. "Why comes the English to the lodge of our people?" he asks at one point. "Why makes he long speeches, full of smooth words— why does he call us brother? He wants our lands."[6]

With *The Yemassee* readers who were familiar with Bancroft's *History* were now confronted with the moral question of westward expansion, and the fact that America's growth had not been innocent or without victims.

But Simms provided them with a justification for their conquests, one he would repeat in his writings for decades to come: When two races meet, if neither will submit to bondage, the superior one is destined to conquer. One of the novel's characters, an idealistic Yankee preacher, asks, "When shall there be but one flock of all classes and colours, all tribes and nations, . . . and thy blessed Son, our Saviour?" Governor Craven responds: "Until they shall adopt our pursuits, or we theirs, we can never form the one community," united in Christian prayer, "and so long as the hunting lands are abundant, the seductions of that mode of life will always baffle the approach of civilization among the Indians."[7]

In Simms's novels, Africans, to their everlasting benefit, have happily submitted to lives of bondage. While Bancroft had decreed that, in America, "every man enjoys the fruits of his industry; every mind is free to publish its convictions," at the end of *The Yemassee*, Craven's loyal slave Hector declines his master's offer to be freed. Hector's explanation for his decision reflected Simms's conception of what African Americans thought, or ideally should have thought, about being property:

> "I d—n to h-ll, mossa, ef I guine to be free!" roared the adhesive black, in a tone of unrestrainable determination. "I can't loss you company, and who de debble [Craven's dog] Dugdale guine let feed him like Hector? 'Tis onpossible, maussa, and dere's no use for talk 'bout it. De ting aint right; and enty I know wha' kind of ting freedom is wid black man? Ha! you make Hector free, he turn wuss more nor poor buckrah—he tief out of de shop—he git drunk and lie in de ditch—den, if sick come, he roll, he toss in de wet grass of de stable. You come in de morning, Hector dead—and, who know— he no take physic, he no hab parson—who know, I say, maussa, but de debble fine em 'fore anybody else? No, maussa—you and Dugdale berry good company for Hector. I tank God he so good—I no want any better."[8]

Some version of that speech would be repeated by other slaves who appeared in his novels.

The mid-Atlantic literary scene again praised Simms's latest work. *The Knickerbocker*, New York City's leading journal, declared it "should at once take a high rank among our native fictions." The *Baltimore American* wrote that it established Simms "among the first class of modern novelists," while New York's *Advocate* noted there was "talent in every page of it." *The American Monthly* judged that Simms showed more understanding about human motives than Cooper had displayed in his entire canon. The first printing sold out in thirty-six hours, and German and U.K. editions quickly followed. Simms had joined his peers at the highest levels of American literature.[9]

The Partisan, a novel about the American Revolution in South Carolina featuring Simms's maternal Singleton ancestors as heroes, was released in November 1835, but by then the author had something other than work to focus on. Despite his intention of forsaking South Carolina, he'd returned to Charleston each winter, gratified that he was finally receiving the local respect he had long sought. With fame and at least the appearance of fortune at the age of thirty, he had won the affections of a seventeen-year-old girl from one of the highborn planter families from whom he'd always sought acceptance. "I have been wooing—I have been wooed and—have won!" he wrote excitedly to Lawson in April 1836. "The Lady has smiled . . . and said 'Yes.'"[10]

THIRTEEN

F red Bailey was one of four slaves at Thomas and Rowena Auld's home and store on Cherry Street in St. Michaels, Maryland, the others being his older sister, Eliza; his disfigured cousin, Henny; and his aunt Priscilla. Although the Aulds had plenty of food, the four slaves now had to beg and steal it to survive. Thomas had taken to assaulting sixteen-year-old Henny. He tied her by her wrists to a ring in a floor joist, whipped her naked shoulders and back with a heavy cowskin "in a manner both brutal and shocking," and left her tied down and lying there bleeding for four or five hours while he tended the store, later returning to lash her wounds open again. All the while he quoted Luke 12:47, a biblical passage favored by Southern preachers because it condoned the whipping of servants.

Over the next nine months, Fred, now fifteen, grew increasingly despondent and surly. There was little for him to read, and he missed his friends, bed, food, and relative freedom back in Baltimore.[1] He upset Auld by calling him "Captain" rather than "Master." He repeatedly let Auld's horse run away to a neighboring farm, where it knew it would find better forage, and when sent to fetch it back, Fred could count on a kindly cook offering him an ample meal. Although he was whipped each time for this infraction, it did not deter him. Fred attempted to organize a Sabbath school to teach a few of the town's black children how to read, but Auld and two other slaveholders burst in, armed with sticks, to break it up. By year's end Auld had grown so angry and frustrated that he contracted Fred out to a notorious slave breaker for the entirety of 1834.[2]

Edward Covey was a poor twenty-eight-year-old farmer who lived seven miles west of St. Michaels and had acquired a reputation for crushing the spirits of rebellious slaves. In his service Fred Bailey became a field hand for the first time, working in every kind of weather from dawn to dusk, and as late as midnight when hay needed to be cut and tied into bundles. There was more food, but little time to eat it. Fred proved to be an awkward farmer, and Covey whipped him severely on an almost weekly basis, tearing off his clothes and lashing him, "causing the blood to run, and raising ridges on my flesh as large as my little finger." Covey had rented another enslaved field hand, Bill Smith, and would lock him in a cabin each night with his enslaved cook, Caroline, in the hopes he would impregnate her. "He boasted that he bought her simply 'as *a breeder*,'" Fred later recalled. The farmer rejoiced when his chattel gave birth to twins at the end of the year.[3]

"I was broken in body, soul, and spirit," Fred recalled of his first months with Covey. "My natural elasticity was crushed; my intellect languished; the disposition to read departed; the cheerful spark that lingered about my eye died; the dark light of slavery closed in upon me."[4]

On a blazing-hot August afternoon, Fred suffered a heat stroke and collapsed in the field, unable to get up. Covey kicked him repeatedly and, when he was still unable to rise, bashed him over the head with a hickory slat, making a deep wound that soon soaked the slave's threadbare Baltimore clothes with blood. When he was finally able to stand, he feebly stumbled, barefoot, through forest, bogs, and briars back to Auld's store, looking "like a man who had escaped a den of wild beasts." He begged Auld to intervene, telling him that Covey would kill him. Auld treated his wounds with salts and sent him back the next morning, threatening to use the whip himself.[5]

To his amazement, Covey greeted him in a friendly manner. But the next morning, while Fred was getting hay from the loft, the farmer ambushed him and tried to tie him up for a beating. "But at this moment—from whence the spirit came I don't know—I resolved to fight." He seized Covey by the neck, rising as he did so. The two men grappled with each other, Covey shaking with surprise, and Fred drove his fingernails into the man's throat. When Covey's cousin tried to pull him away, Fred kicked him in the stomach. As the fight continued, the other slaves refused to help Covey and, after two breathless hours, the slave breaker finally gave up. "Now you scoundrel, go to your work," he said breathlessly. He never again challenged Fred for the duration of his yearlong indenture.[6]

Covey declined to rent Fred again, and in 1835 and 1836 Auld contracted him to a more benign farmer, William Freeland, for whom Fred worked with four other slaves. Over the course of the year—better fed and more reasonably treated—the five slaves became close. Fred secretly taught them to read, and they planned an escape for Easter weekend, 1836, intending to steal a canoe, travel to the head of the Chesapeake, and walk to freedom in Pennsylvania. Someone betrayed the plan, and the conspirators were hauled off to the Talbot County Jail in Easton.[7]

On their first day there, flocks of slave traders surrounded the jail, shouting taunts and inspecting the prisoners for possible purchase. At the end of the holiday weekend, Freeland retrieved his slaves, but left Fred behind in the jail, where he fell into the depths of despair. "My hopes and expectations were now withered and blasted," he would later write. "The ever dreaded slave life in Georgia, Louisiana and Alabama—from which escape was next to impossible—now, in my loneliness, stared me in the face . . . a life of living death, beset with the innumerable horrors of the cotton field and the sugar plantation, seemed to be my doom."[8]

After a week Thomas Auld claimed him and told him he was to be sold to a friend in Alabama. But in fact Auld had spent the previous week pacing his rooms, unsure what to do with the quarrelsome eighteen-year-old. A few days after Fred's release, he did something remarkable: He told Fred that he was being returned to his brother Hugh in Baltimore to learn a trade. When Fred turned twenty-five, Auld told him, he would set him free.[9]

Why Auld did so would remain a mystery to Fred for the rest of his life, but it set the young man on a path on which he would never have to face a whipping again.

FOURTEEN

Everyone expected that Bancroft would be at work from dawn to dusk to complete the next volume of the *History*, which was eagerly anticipated by the reading public. For two and a half years he indeed did rise early to read, write, or send inquiries to scholars, librarians, and statesmen across the United States and western Europe. Throughout 1835 and 1836, he traveled to state historical societies, to the homes of the descendants of key historical figures, to the scenes of colonial events, and to Revolutionary battlefields.

Emboldened by the reception for the *History*'s argument that America was on a divinely ordained mission to redeem humanity, Bancroft also decided it was his job not just to identify the path but to help lead his people along it, and to avoid the obstacles placed in their way. To everyone's surprise, just months after the release of volume 1, he decided to enter politics, once again following the path of his mentor, Everett. In November 1834 his independent candidacy for Northampton's seat in the state legislature ended in an overwhelming electoral defeat. In Boston *The Atlas*, aligned with the Whigs, mocked him for having been educated in "the halls of infidelity and atheism, from the dram shops and the dram cellars" of Germany. The *Boston Courier* advised him to "return from the wilderness of politics . . . to the more attractive garden of literature." The whole country cherished him as a writer, the *Newburyport Herald* proclaimed, yet rebuked him for insisting on risking his reputation on the "rocks, shoals, and quick sands of party."[1]

Bancroft, undaunted, declared his allegiance to Jackson's Democrats, reasoning that he needed a party affiliation to succeed, and the Democrats' platform as champions of ordinary men accorded with the *History*'s view that God's will was best reflected in the aggregate spirit of the American people. "The Tory regards liberty as a boon; the Whig as a fortunate privilege," he explained to the people of Springfield on July 4, 1836, while Jackson's "democracy claims freedom as an inalienable right." He stumped for Democrats across New England, debated Daniel Webster onstage, conferred with James Monroe at his Virginia estate, and earned the respect of Vice President Martin Van Buren, who declared Bancroft his "first man" in Massachusetts.

Bancroft's Whig friends—including Everett and his brother-in-law, John Davis, now governor of the state—were appalled, and many in the Beacon Hill aristocracy closed their doors to him. "*Entre nous,* don't you wish you had stuck to your trade of making books and been content with the lasting glory thus gained?" his sister Lucretia asked. "Would not your chance for immortality have been greater as the author of the *History of the United States* than as a speech-maker in Congress?"[2]

His fame indeed grew with the June 1837 publication of the second volume of the *History*, which covered three decades in the late 1600s and focused on the allegedly democratic foundations of Virginia, Maryland, Dutch New Netherland, and Pennsylvania. Slaveholding Virginia "was always 'A LAND OF LIBERTY,'" he proclaimed. The Netherlands gave Americans "the principle of federal union" and therefore shared in the liberty-guided "spirit of the age," despite New Netherland's being a corporate colony with no provisions for self-government. Across the nation Germanic peoples—English, Scots, Dutch, the German majority in Pennsylvania—had become "Anglo-Saxons in the woods again," a people with "the active instinct for personal freedom" finally freed from the impediments of Europe's feudal history. Reviewers praised the new book; scholars celebrated it; citizens purchased it in quantity.[3]

As the praise flowed in, Bancroft also experienced political success and personal tragedy. In June 1837 Sarah died, never having recovered from the birth of their third child, George. In November, Van Buren won the presidency and asked Bancroft, who had campaigned hard for him, to accept one of the most influential federal appointments in New England, the collector of customs for the port of Boston. With his wife dead and his children living with relatives, Bancroft was free to move to Boston. There he devoted his spare time into building the Custom House into a Democratic political machine via the distribution of patronage appointments and lucrative printing contracts. He founded a newspaper, the *Bay State Democrat*, to proselytize for the party and serve as a headquarters for events and visitors. Most important, within months he became betrothed to the woman who would become his second wife, Elizabeth Davis Bliss, sister of Bancroft's brother-in-law, U.S. senator and former Massachusetts governor John Davis. By the fall of 1838 he and his children had moved into her opulent home at Winthrop Place, which quickly became a literary hub of Boston.

Financially solvent, intellectually revered, and politically savvy, George Bancroft had by 1840 become the de facto Democratic boss of Massachusetts. He shaped public opinion and made speeches casting the Democratic Party as the vehicle for the Providential American destiny outlined in his history. But the Democrats were resoundingly defeated in the 1840 election, losing the presidency, the Massachusetts governorship, and both houses of Congress. The Whigs took back the Custom House, and Bancroft was coming around to agreeing with his sister that perhaps his energy could be better spent elsewhere.

By then volume 3 of *History* had appeared, and its narrative of the events of the 1690s had been greeted by further praise. Although his politicking had made him a divisive figure, he remained widely feted for his scholarship. For the next two years he dug into further research, buying the letters of Sam Adams and other historical figures, building a vast library collection at his Boston home, and hiring research assistants to copy archival records in London and Paris. He went on high-profile lecture tours, addressing the Maryland legislature and the Mercantile Library in Philadelphia, and speaking at the commemoration of the Bunker Hill Monument in Boston and a New York dinner honoring a visiting Charles Dickens. He was a houseguest of Charles Carroll, the inheritor of the greatest pre-Revolutionary fortune in America, at his twelve-square-mile slave plantation outside Baltimore. ("The housekeeping was excellent.") He visited with Van Buren, dined with senators, shared the stage with the great Transcendentalists, and hosted European dignitaries at his home.

By 1843 even the Massachusetts establishment had forgiven him his political transgressions. Harvard awarded him an honorary degree and a position on its board of governors. His *History* was fast becoming the national narrative. And to the west, Bancroft was convinced he could see America's sun rising high above the Earth.

FIFTEEN

Simms's new bride, eighteen-year-old Chevillette Eliza Roach, was the petite, dark-eyed surviving child of Nash Roach, who owned a Charleston town house and two adjacent slave plantations in the western part of the state, and styled himself an English country gentleman. Chevillette was the apple of her father's eye, particularly after her brother's untimely death in a duel fought with a college classmate to settle a dispute about a dish of trout. Roach made it clear that he was willing to do almost anything for his daughter and her husband, but that she was not to be taken away from him.[1]

Thus Simms found himself the effective lord of Woodlands, a four-thousand-acre plantation of oak and longleaf pine forests, bridle paths and ponds, ornamental lawns and sprawling cotton fields, its mansion flanked by barracks for seventy slaves. Situated near the hamlet of Midway, halfway from Charleston to Augusta, Georgia, and across the Edisto River from his father-in-law's Oak Grove estate, Woodlands made Simms the Deep Southern gentleman he'd always longed to be, elevating him into a higher echelon of society. He was, at least initially, enormously happy there, working away in the study or on the grounds, surrounded by a family he loved and house slaves he believed loved him.[2]

Woodlands was worth a small fortune but, at least in Simms's hands, generated losses as often as it did earnings. He now had more dependents than ever: his nine-year-old daughter, Augusta; his wife; and eventually nine more children, not to mention the slaves. His old debts from the Charleston

City Gazette were still unpaid, while his growing family of small children, his wife's seasickness, and Nash Roach's griping made traveling to give lectures, research history, or maintain business connections far more difficult to arrange. Simms soon found himself forced to write reviews, essays, and short fiction for magazines and journals just to keep his family solvent.[3]

He also continued to write books, a whole shelf full in the first six years of his marriage. There were more historical novels set in Revolutionary South Carolina and more short stories and novels set on the Deep Southern frontiers of Alabama and Mississippi of the 1820s and 1830s, all of them populated by crude, colorful, often violent characters—including blacks and Native Americans—that continued to scandalize gentler readers. ("If England had denounced and destroyed every writer . . . who had offended against morals in some respects," Simms noted, "Shakespeare would have been the first to burn.") He researched an entire textbook, *The History of South Carolina*, which was adopted by the state's nascent public school system.[4]

To his distress, as the 1840s began, he noticed that his books were becoming less profitable. The lack of an international copyright law meant that British publishers could steal his works, and ensured that U.S. publishers had no incentive to pay American authors, as they could simply pirate the works of English ones. Magazines had soared in popularity, cutting into the book market, and because they paid relatively well, Simms and many other authors found themselves compelled to write for them. "The mind is frittered away wretchedly by that compulsion which requires you to write to order and to measure," he lamented.[5]

It was in this environment that, in June 1842, Simms accepted an offer to become the editor of *The Magnolia*, a two-year-old literary journal that had moved to Charleston from Savannah. For a year and a half he wrote, edited, and curated the attractive monthly, shaping it into the standard-bearer of Deep Southern literature and thought. Although it had a stellar reputation and a healthy subscription base, *The Magnolia* failed in late 1843 because many of its subscribers weren't paying their fees and collecting from them in a region short on roads and courthouses proved impossible for Simms.[6]

The Simmses fell into the seasonal pattern of the slave lord: fall, winter, and spring at the plantation and a retreat to their Charleston town house in summer, when the swampy interior became "fatal to European and Atlantick life." Simms spent part of every summer in New York, nurturing his friendships and business contacts, or in Great Barrington, where he (and sometimes his family) spent weeks at a time as guests of William Cullen Bryant. Augusta Simms and Bryant's daughter Fanny became such close friends that, in 1840, they began attending boarding school together. Bryant, a progressive champion of unions, racial equality, and the common man, brought his family to Woodlands for three weeks in March 1843 and called it "one of the most pleasurable periods of my life." If his friend's reliance on slavery bothered Bryant, he did not mention it in the dispatches he wrote from the plantation, which focused on the amusing antics of the slaves. They were, he informed his *New York Evening Post* readers, "a cheerful, careless, dirty race, not hard worked, and in many respects indulgently treated."[7]

Simms also became ever closer friends with his new neighbor, the plantation lord and former U.S. congressman James Henry Hammond, a tall, handsome, and excessively arrogant man famous for his insightful conversational ability, compelling oratories, and shameless flirtation. Simms widened Hammond's literary knowledge, and Hammond in turn opened his friend's eyes to the world of politics, encouraging him to model himself after gentlemen statesmen-scholars like Jefferson and Madison. Simms was tempted by the idea and became even more intrigued in December 1842, when Hammond was elected governor of South Carolina, which put him in a position to lower the gates of the state's political citadel for his friends.[8]

His future plans weighed heavily on Simms's mind the following summer while en route on a steamship to the Bryants' Ninth Street town house. He had fought to define the American identity by bolstering that of its Deep Southern region. Now he, like Bancroft, was considering trying to lead his state toward its proper future. Was it wise? Perhaps, Simms thought, he might ask Bancroft himself.

SIXTEEN

Despite the promise of being freed in eight years, from the moment Frederick Bailey returned to Baltimore he began planning his escape.

The Aulds appeared to be keeping their promises. Hugh found Frederick a position as an apprentice shipyard caulker, where he learned how to make wooden vessels watertight by inserting tar-soaked fibers into the myriad seams between their planks. When a group of Irish laborers severely beat him, unwilling to have him competing with them for work, Hugh tried to bring the assailants to justice, only to be reminded by the magistrate that a black man's testimony was useless under Maryland law. (The white witnesses—who had been screaming "Kill the damn nigger!" during the assault—declined to testify.) Failing to obtain legal protection for his eighteen-year-old charge, Hugh moved Frederick to the shipyard where he was working, and by the middle of 1836, Frederick had become a full-fledged caulker, earning nine dollars a week. (Ironically, once completed, the clipper ships Frederick helped build were used by slave smugglers running the British blockade of the West African trade, who delivered their illicit cargo into U.S. ports in defiance of an 1808 ban on the importation of slaves.)[1]

But Frederick chafed at turning all his wages over to Hugh, and in the spring of 1838 demanded he be allowed to live, in effect, as an indentured servant, free to hire himself out as he wished so long as, each Saturday, he turned over three dollars to his master. Hugh, surprisingly enough, agreed to this, and also allowed Frederick to rent his own quarters in the city. Frederick worked hard for the next few months, saving up money for his intended escape. He discovered many of his free black workmates could read and write, and that "some of them had high notions about mental improvement." They even invited Frederick to join a debating society they'd organized—"a secret night school," he would later call it—where he began to discover a gift for public speaking. He grew enormously attached to these kindred spirits, black men whose ambition and hunger for knowledge contradicted prevailing racist theories about the African character. Samuel Dougherty, he later recalled, "would have been one of the most successful men Baltimore ever knew" had he been "a white man or had he been given anything like fair play." They stole time to read at work, "under ship's bottoms and behind logs of ship timber," making the shipyard their college. "Its timber and boards were our first copy-books, and the white carpenters writing 'larboard' and 'starboard' with chalk were our unconscious teachers." At one of their evening meetings, Frederick proclaimed he wouldn't stop until he became a U.S. senator.[2]

He also met Anna Murray, a free black housekeeper who had grown up on the other side of Tuckahoe Creek from his grandparents' cabin. They shared a grimly ironic sense of humor, a distaste for hypocrisy, and a willingness to forthrightly express indignation. Unlike Frederick, however, Anna was stoic and reserved, even among those she knew well; she couldn't read or write and had no strong inclination to learn to do so. They became secretly engaged and she was an essential coconspirator in his escape plans, saving money and even selling some of her possessions to finance his flight northward.[3]

Events came to a head in early August 1838, when Frederick decided to spend the weekend at a Methodist revival camp outside Baltimore and failed to check in with the Aulds to turn over their portion of his wages. Hugh Auld, furious, canceled their entire arrangement. Frederick was forced to return his tools and move back into the Aulds' house, but once there he defiantly refused to go to work. That week, as Hugh threatened him, Frederick realized it was foolish to further test his master's wrath. He returned to work for the next three weeks, diligently and punctually return- ing home with his entire weekly wages. But on the morning of Monday, September 3, he left the house early and never returned.[4]

FREDERICK INTENDED TO ESCAPE via a futuristic and carefully guarded technological miracle: the passenger steam train. The very first railroad in the country had gotten its start eight years earlier in Baltimore, just a few blocks from the shipyards, in the days when Frederick was taking care of little Tommy Auld. Since then, tracks had been extended in stages all the way to a ferry landing on the Susquehanna River at the head of the Chesa- peake, then onward across the rest of Maryland and northern Delaware to Wilmington. From there, Frederick knew, one could catch a steamboat up the Delaware to Philadelphia in the free state of Pennsylvania. The route, however, was under close surveillance. Blacks were allowed to ride only during daylight hours and then only if they could produce documentation proving their free status. Slave catchers patrolled the depots, ferry landings, and steamship decks; the streets; and the post road.[5]

Frederick arrived at the station in a disguise: a red shirt, a tarpaulin hat, and a black cravat tied in the careless fashion of the sailors he'd worked around on the city's docks. In his pocket was the seaman's protection cer- tificate of one of his free black sailor friends, a document U.S. sailors car- ried to prove their citizenship to prevent kidnapping by British Royal Navy press gangs. The certificate described a man with darker skin, and knowing that this document would not satisfy the ticket agent, Frederick had en- listed another free black friend to buy his ticket for him. Just as the train prepared to pull out of the station, Frederick leaped aboard, rucksack slung over his shoulders, and into the jostling, crowded Negro car. He'd practiced a sailor's vocabulary and knew ship parts from having assembled them. He hoped that patriotic sentiment would help as well, as many Americans were still angry that the Royal Navy had pressed their sailors into service during the War of 1812. As the train headed eastward across the Maryland countryside, Frederick recognized several free black acquaintances in the car, and hoped that his disguise would prevent them from recognizing him.[6]

The conductor entered the car just before the train reached the terminus at the Havre de Grace ferry landing, punching tickets and inspecting the black passengers' papers. "My whole future depended upon the decision of this conductor," Frederick realized, trying to hide his anxiety beneath a veil of calm self-possession. The conductor had been interrogating passengers in a harsh, peremptory tone, but when he reached Frederick his demeanor softened. "I suppose you have your free papers?" he asked.

"No, sir," Frederick replied. "I never carry my free papers to sea with me."

"But you have something to show you are a free man, have you not?"

"Yes, sir. I have this paper with the American eagle on it, and that will carry me round the world." And with that Frederick pulled out his seaman's protection.

The conductor merely glanced at it, punched Frederick's ticket, and moved on to the next passenger. Frederick, knowing he did not match the description on the document, later called this moment "one of the most anxious I had ever experienced."[7]

The train came to a halt and the passengers climbed off and onto the Susquehanna River ferry. As they made their way across, one of the ferry's hands approached Frederick. It was a free black he knew and he started pestering Frederick with questions: Where are you going? When are you coming back? Why are you dressed like a sailor? Frederick feared the man would draw attention to him or, worse, betray his slave status to the crew, resulting in his prompt arrest. He managed to get away to another part of the vessel and anxiously awaited arrival at Perryville, where the Wilmington train awaited. Once aboard, he realized a German blacksmith he knew well was in the same car and was staring at him very intently. Fortunately the man didn't turn him in. "He saw me escaping, and held his peace." At a whistle-stop, Frederick looked across the platform at the southbound train and, to his horror, saw seated in the opposite window one Captain McGowan, master of the revenue cutter Frederick had been caulking the week before. McGowan didn't look up until sometime after the train pulled away.[8]

Alighting at Wilmington, a slave city in a slave state, Frederick feared he would be challenged by officials or slave catchers, but no one stopped him as he walked to the docks and boarded the Philadelphia steamer. He was unchallenged all the way to that Quaker-founded city and on arrival went straight to the Willow Street depot to catch an overnight train to New York City. A short ferry ride later, not long after dawn, on September 4, 1838, he arrived at his destination, hungry, sleep deprived, and elated.[9]

WALKING THE CROWDED STREETS of Gotham that day, "dazzled with the wonders which met me on every hand," he lost himself in "the mighty throng, which like confused waves of the troubled sea, surged to and fro between the lofty walls of Broadway." He was overwhelmed with emotions: joy, anguish, and grief, but most of all relief, "like one who had escaped a den of angry lions." He was free, but he was still in danger.[10]

New York was a free state, but Dutch-settled New York City and its environs were no sanctuary for African Americans. White New Yorkers often excluded blacks from boardinghouses, hotels, restaurants, streetcars, and labor unions. Black children attended segregated schools, while adults had to demonstrate they owned at least $250 in property before they could vote. The city's merchant, banking, and insurance elites were deeply entwined with the Southern slave economy, and retailers enjoyed a lucrative trade with Southern visitors on business and shopping trips to the great city-state on the Hudson. Many planters brought their slaves with them, which state law allowed them to do for up to nine months at a time. Four years earlier, white mobs had broken up an interracial gathering at the Chatham Street Chapel and rioted for three days, driving five hundred African Americans from their homes. Informants, black and white, lurked everywhere, hoping to make a profit from the city's many slave catchers. Even free blacks were sometimes carried away by unscrupulous slavers.[11]

A few hours after his arrival Frederick encountered a man he knew, Jacob Ellis, who was one of the slaves owned by Walter Allender, son of the Aulds' landlord on Philpot Street in the 1820s. Unbeknownst to Frederick, Ellis had fled to freedom in late 1831 by somehow signing on as a member of a ship's crew. He revealed that he was now known as William Dixon, and that he had wound up at the center of a sensational and ongoing legal battle following his seizure by the city's most notorious slave catcher, Daniel Nash. He was suspicious that Frederick might reveal his true identity—in court, Ellis had claimed to be a Philadelphia-born free black—but warned him not to go to the dockyards or any of the boardinghouses that admitted blacks, as they were closely watched, and "the colored people of New York were not to be trusted." Before disappearing into the crowd, Ellis warned him to trust his secret to no one, as Southerners were everywhere in the city.[12]

Frederick, nearly penniless, slept the first night or two among stacked barrels on a wharf, uncertain where to turn and whom to trust. Without money, friends, credit, work, food, or shelter, he was becoming desperate. As he stood on Centre Street, staring at The Tombs, a massive new granite prison complex modeled on an ancient Egyptian temple, a neighbor took notice of the forlorn man in sailor's clothing. By a stroke of luck, he was a free black sailor named Stuart who was associated with the New York Committee of Vigilance, a group of African American activists who had sprung hundreds of slaves from bondage, sometimes by force. Stuart took him into his home for the night and, the next day, delivered him to the committee's leader, David Ruggles, first officer of the Underground Railroad.[13]

Ruggles, twenty-eight, operated out of an abolitionist bookstore at 36 Lispenard Street in what is now Tribeca, and was a legendary figure in the city. He had supported Jacob Ellis at his trial, faced kidnapping by slavers, boarded a Brazilian slave ship and freed its cargo, and was at that moment in the midst of an extended trial for helping a slave escape his Virginian master. With his help Frederick was able to send a letter to Anna, telling her to come and meet him. Ruggles kept the fugitive safe in his home for several days until Anna arrived, then introduced them to a black Presbyterian priest who married the couple on September 15.[14]

New York, Ruggles advised them, was not a safe place for a runaway slave. However, a skilled caulker could find work and safety in the whaling port of New Bedford, Massachusetts, deep in the protective bosom of abolitionist New England.

On the very day of their wedding, Frederick and Anna took their luggage to the docks, boarded the fast steamer *John W. Richmond*, and sailed into Long Island Sound and freedom.[15]

SEVENTEEN

It was William Cullen Bryant who first suggested Simms meet Bancroft. The poet and newspaper editor was friends with both men and knew they had many things in common. They were both failed poets, successful historians, bestselling authors, and widely recognized as leading men of letters. They had each been newspaper editors and publishers. They were both Jacksonian Democrats and believers in westward expansion. Simms was contemplating a political career; Bancroft was just concluding his. Both hoped to be appointed to diplomatic posts in Europe.

In the summer of 1843 Simms was a houseguest at Bryant's New York residence, and before he departed for a side trip to Boston in August, Bryant gave him a letter of introduction to Bancroft. "You must be already familiar with his merits as an author," Bryant wrote the famed historian. "Those of us who know him personally think there is even more occasion to esteem the man."[1]

A few weeks later Simms arrived at the Bancrofts' three-story stone town house, which stood on Winthrop Place, a tree-lined avenue in the most exclusive part of Boston. The Bancrofts' home had all the social cachet of a Charleston planter's. It had been built for the Cabots, who sold it to Elizabeth's family, members of the leading merchant, banking, and political dynasty in Plymouth. Across the street were the homes of the Lodges and Rufus Choate. Edward Everett, Daniel Webster, Robert Winthrop, and a host of other New England luminaries lived nearby.[2]

Bancroft, still thin and nearsighted but sporting grand sideburns, greeted Simms warmly. They sat down to tea and talked at great length, discussing the writing and importance of history; the internal machinations of the Democratic Party; and the increasing tensions over whether the United States should agree to absorb the breakaway Mexican province of Texas. The two shared a belief that their party's leader, former president Martin Van Buren of New York, was making a fatal political mistake by not backing annexation. They may have admitted to each other, in whispered tones, that they each preferred a little-known insurgent, former Tennessee governor James Polk, to be the one to challenge the incumbent president, the Whig John Tyler, in the next year's election.[3]

Their meeting was so companionable that Bancroft invited Simms to join him on an excursion to his in-laws' hometown of Plymouth, where the Pilgrims had, in Bancroft's telling, founded the primordial United States. Simms regretfully declined, having business to attend to back in New York, but he urged Bancroft to visit the Deep South, and to call on him in Charleston when he did so.

They parted as friends. It would not last.

EIGHTEEN

rederick and Anna arrived in New Bedford on the Newport stage-coach without enough money to pay their fare. To their relief, they were met at the terminus by Nathan and Mary Johnson, a free black couple who served as the local agents of the Underground Railroad. The Johnsons paid the coachman, collected the couple's luggage, and led them to a three-story wooden house where they could stay free of charge until they got on their feet. The Johnsons were experts on fugitive slave reentry, having helped many of the three hundred runaways then living in New Bedford. They would be safe in town, they told the Marylanders, as abolitionist sentiment ran high among its residents, who could be counted on to expel any slave hunters. They advised the couple to change their names, for safety's sake, and to conceal the specifics of where they'd come from and how they'd gotten away.[1]

Frederick was at a loss as to what name he should assume, so Johnson helped with that, too. He was then reading Sir Walter Scott's *Lady of the Lake*, the epic 1810 poem about the clash of Lowland and Highland Scots clans in the sixteenth century, whose hero was the exiled former adviser to the king, James Douglas, now a rebellious Highland chief. Frederick liked the name but added an extra *s* for distinction. Frederick Augustus Washington Bailey was now Frederick Douglass.[2]

Douglass was amazed by the level of wealth and order he saw in New Bedford, a thriving town of twelve thousand citizens, a twelfth of whom were black. "I had been taught that slavery was the bottom-fact of all wealth [and] . . . came naturally to the conclusion that poverty must be the general condition of the people of the free States," he would write. Instead, he found himself amid the riches of the whaling trade, which in this final pre-petroleum decade, provided the oil that lubricated the moving parts in locomotives, aboard steamships, and within the machinery powering the rapidly expanding factories of New England and beyond. "Nowhere in all America will you find more patrician-like houses; parks and gardens more opulent," Herman Melville, who was in town at the same time as Douglass, wrote in *Moby-Dick*. It took thousands of men to crew the ships, harpoon the whales, boil their fat into oil, load and unload the barrels from the holds, repair the hulls, sew the sails, and stock the supplies, and they all took a cut of the wealth. These laborers, Douglass found, lived in homes better furnished and supplied with conveniences—"sinks, drains, self-shutting gates, pounding-barrels, washing-machines, wringing-machines"—than those of slaveholders back in the Tidewater. On the docks, where he found his first work, he saw ships loaded far more briskly and efficiently than they would have been in Baltimore: In New England, five men and a sixty-dollar ox did the work of twenty-five slaves—an $11,000 investment—in a Southern port.[3]

The town's black families fared far better, too. Their children attended the same schools as whites, their men registered and voted on equal terms with whites, and they lived in better conditions than the free blacks Douglass had known in Maryland. Racism was by no means absent, however. When Douglass was hired on to caulk a whaling ship, the white caulkers stopped work until he was forced to sign on as a day laborer for one dollar a day, half what he would have otherwise earned. The New Bedford Lyceum refused to allow blacks to attend the lectures held there. Douglass stormed out of the very first service he attended at the Elm Street Methodist Church after witnessing the contemptuous attitude of the minister toward black congregants seeking to receive Holy Communion. Still, he found the conditions in New Bedford, where he would spend the next three years of his life, "the nearest approach to freedom and equality that I had ever seen."[4]

Through 1839 and 1840 Douglass did whatever work would pay the bills. He manned the bellows at a brass foundry and moved massive casks at a whale oil refinery. He loaded ships, dug cellars, shoveled coal, and hauled trash. The financial pressures increased as his family grew—daughter Rosetta was born nine months after their arrival, and son Lewis sixteen months after that. But Reverend Thomas James of the black African Methodist Episcopal Zion Church, himself a former slave, noticed and encouraged Douglass's speaking skills. James soon licensed him to preach and invited him to occupy the pulpit with increasing frequency. What he said in these sermons has been lost to history, but by 1841 preaching had become his primary occupation, and word of his skills had reached abolitionists in Boston and Toronto.[5]

He had by then already had contact with the abolitionists. A few months after his arrival, an agent for the Boston-based abolitionist weekly newspaper, *The Liberator*, called at his home, and gave Douglass a free subscription. The paper, he said, was like "a gospel," and its founder, William Lloyd Garrison, akin to "Moses, raised up by God to deliver his modern Israel from bondage." In its pages Douglass learned of the spread of abolitionism in Greater New England and of campaigns to abolish human bondage in the District of Columbia and the federally administered Wisconsin, Iowa, and Oregon Territories. He learned that Southern members of Congress had passed a "gag rule" three years earlier prohibiting discussion of slavery in the U.S. House, and read of Garrison's opposition to schemes to "solve" the Union's race problem by sending blacks to colonies in Africa or the Caribbean. As he read *The Liberator* week after week, he embraced its editor's principles and felt a surge of optimism about the "hopes for the ultimate freedom of my race."[6]

The Garrisonians argued that slavery degraded the entire society, and needed to be ended immediately, preferably by the secession of all free states. They denounced not only slaveholders but also the U.S. Constitution (for its sanctioning of slavery), the political system (for tolerating it), and even churches that allowed slaveholders to attend. At the same time they opposed armed resistance (they were pacifists), political organization (they thought the system impure), and voting (even for antislavery candidates). They were outspoken, idealistic, and, from a practical point of view, completely ineffective. Douglass would later split from the movement but, as a newly free slave encountering the world of advocacy for the first time, he became a devoted follower, attending and even speaking at local antislavery meetings.[7]

After one such gathering in August 1841, Frederick and Anna were invited to attend a convention of the Massachusetts Anti-Slavery Society being held on Nantucket Island, New Bedford's whaling rival, thirty miles out to sea. After boarding the steamer *Telegraph*, the couple was ordered to sit in the rain in the uncovered Negro section on the upper deck. The white conventioneers on the ship joined them there, where they passed resolutions condemning the steamship company's policies. There were more resolutions on the convention floor that day and the next. Then Douglass— six foot one, brown skinned, and strikingly handsome—stood up to speak.[8]

There's no record of exactly what he said that day, but the audience was spellbound. "I think I never hated slavery so intensely as at that moment," Garrison said of the speech. "There stood one, in physical proportion and stature commanding and exact—in intellect richly endowed—in natural eloquence a prodigy—in soul manifestly 'created but a little lower than the angels'—yet a slave, ay, a fugitive slave—trembling for his safety, hardly daring to believe that on the American soil, a single white person could be found who would befriend him at all hazards." When Douglass concluded, the audience burst into applause, and Garrison stood up and declared that Patrick Henry had never made a speech "more eloquent to the cause of liberty." John Collins, who oversaw the society's advocacy work, approached Douglass afterward, asking him to become a full-time speaker for the group.

Though Douglass feared the attention he would attract might help the Aulds apprehend him, he agreed. Before the week was out, he was on the road with Collins on a three-month trial circuit.[9]

The pair traveled by rail and stagecoach across eastern Massachusetts, southern New Hampshire, and Rhode Island and appeared in town halls, churches, and courthouses. Douglass told the story of his enslavement, his aborted reading lessons with Sophia Auld, and, with growing intensity, his struggles after his forced return to the Eastern Shore. "It was the volcanic outbreak of human nature, long pent up in slavery and at last bursting its imprisonment," one listener said. "It was the storm of insurrection—and I could not help but think, as he stalked to and fro on the platform, roused up like the Numidian Lion—how that terrible voice of his would ring through the pine glades of the South, in the day of her visitation, calling the insurgents to battle and striking terror to the hearts of the dismayed and despairing mastery." He was a forceful, living rebuke of white supremacist ideology—eloquent, razor sharp, and furious at the treatment of his people. He spoke in at least twenty towns during this trial circuit, leaving thousands of admirers in his wake. The society immediately knew they had a star, and soon all of New England would know this, too.[10]

There were also challenges. Twice that September he was thrown off rail trains after refusing conductors' orders to move to the Negro car. In the second incident, at the depot in Lynn, Massachusetts, he and Collins were beaten by six railway employees when they refused to leave their seats in the whites-only car; the railwaymen ultimately ripped their seat from the floor, dragged it to the door, and ejected it from the train with the two men still seated in it. This thuggish behavior upset the other passengers, and within days Lynn was in an uproar against the Eastern Railroad, with meetings and newspaper editorials calling for a boycott of the company. Thereafter, Garrison hired Douglass full-time, acquired a house for him steps from the Lynn depot where, surrounded by friends, he could more easily get to and from his speaking events.

The next three years were a blur. Anna, who bore a third child during that time, barely saw him. He spoke across New England and in New York City for Garrison's new American Anti-Slavery Society. He rode barges along the Erie Canal, speaking in tiny towns across the Yankee upstate of New York to Buffalo. He went to Ohio and Pennsylvania, spoke alongside the feminist icon Abby Kelley Foster, and was heard by luminaries across the Northeast. He was also pelted by mobs, forced out of speaking halls, called names, and threatened with death by drunken gangs. In September 1843 he and his colleagues foolishly tried to make a speaking tour of central Indiana, which, perhaps unbeknownst to the organizers, had been settled via the Scots-Irish settlement stream and was part of a Greater Appalachia, not abolitionist-minded Greater New England. In each town they met mobs, and in Pendleton, sixty thugs led by a man in a coonskin cap surrounded their stage and attacked the speakers, knocking out one man's teeth, and beating Douglass with clubs, breaking his right hand. One witness said Douglass would have been killed had members of the audience not rescued him. Douglass's bones were never set right, and his hand never recovered its full strength and dexterity. The incident made Douglass reconsider Garrisonian pacifism; at one point during the melee he had picked up a club himself to save a colleague from being stoned.[11]

In October 1844 Anna gave birth to their fourth child, Charles, and a road-weary father finally stopped traveling. That winter he wrote a book, the story of his twenty-seven-year-long life, from the cabin on the Tuckahoe Creek to his embarkation on the speaking tour. Seven months later, in May 1845, *Narrative of the Life of Frederick Douglass, an American Slave* was published by the Anti-Slavery Society in Boston, a brief but riveting account of the horrors and injustices of slavery.

It was a sensation. The first five-thousand-copy run sold out in just four months. By September, despite Maryland's ban on abolitionist books, the citizens of Baltimore were reading it avidly, and a correspondent reported "five hundred copies are still wanted here." The *New-York Tribune* carried a front-page review; its reviewer had "never read (a narrative) more simple, true, coherent and warm." *Littell's Living Age* estimated in March 1846 that "not less than one million persons in Great Britain and Ireland have been excited by the book and its commentators." In its first two years, it went through nine editions in the United States, five in the United Kingdom, and was translated into German and French. It made Douglass the most famous black person in the Western world.[12]

He feared, though, that it had also made him one of the most wanted as well. In the *Narrative* he had named names and humiliated some of Maryland's most powerful individuals. At any moment, he thought, their agents might seize him "and return me to a doom worse than death." His white abolitionist friends shared his concerns and, in August, organized to send Douglass into protective exile.

On August 16, 1845, Douglass and his Lynn neighbor James N. Buffum boarded the Cunard line's *Cambria*, the fastest ship on the seas, and sailed off to the east, bound for a land where his liberty might be ensured: Great Britain.[13]

NINETEEN

When James Polk was elected president in November 1844, Bancroft was elated.

He'd been a vocal supporter of the Tennessean, and at the Democratic National Convention that year, he'd helped secure him the nomination by convincing many delegates to defect from Van Buren. In the general election he'd stumped for Polk across New England and New York, even neglecting his own hopeless gubernatorial campaign in Massachusetts. His primary motivation for backing Polk was the territorial expansion of the United States, starting with the annexation of the Mexican provinces of Alta California and Texas and the assertion of full sovereignty over the Pacific Northwest, which was also claimed by Britain. It is "the manifest purpose of providence that the light of democratic freedom should be borne from our fires to the domain beyond the Rocky Mountains," Bancroft declared from the stump. Democrats "had never turned pale at the thought of extending the area of freedom."[1]

President Polk appointed him secretary of the navy, positioning him to make history, not just write about it. Bancroft did not shrink from the role, and in the eighteen months he served in the eleventh president's cabinet, the administration set into motion the greatest territorial expansion in U.S. history by fighting a war with one of its neighbors and threatening one with the other. By the time Polk left office in March 1849, the United States had annexed the Republic of Texas and the provinces of Nuevo Mexico and Alta

California and negotiated control over the Oregon Country, a combined area larger than the Louisiana Purchase and comprising most or all of the future states of Texas, New Mexico, Arizona, California, Nevada, Utah, Oregon, Washington, and Idaho.

The Mexican acquisitions were extremely controversial, both because of their imperialistic (and, thus, un-republican) character and because of the issue of slavery, which put into question whether the United States was really "extending the area of freedom." Mexico had abolished slavery in 1826. Ten years later Deep Southern slave lords helped lead a successful revolt in Texas and reinstituted slavery in their self-proclaimed republic. They wanted the United States to annex this Republic of Texas precisely in order to defend slavery, because their only alternative—an alliance with Britain to deter a Mexican attack—would have had abolitionist strings attached. "Without the advantages of slavery, Texas can never be a nation of any great importance or prosperity," the former Texas president Mirabeau Lamar declared. "Her Union with the United States will give permanency to that institution in both countries." Annexation would not only add another slave state to the Union, but it would encompass a huge territory that the enabling legislation envisioned dividing into as many as five states, completely altering the balance of power in Congress. Lamar, a native of Georgia, said Texas and the South were like Siamese twins, "bound together by a strong, natural ligament, which if severed, must bring death to both."[2]

Bancroft's *History* inspired the most spirited advocates of annexation and war. John O'Sullivan, editor of *The United States Magazine and Democratic Review* was a huge fan of the work, and had already pronounced Bancroft one of the Republic's "writers of the first class" who were helping build U.S. nationhood. In a July 1845 essay that borrowed heavily from the *History*, O'Sullivan famously declared America's "manifest destiny to overspread the continent allotted by Providence for the free development of our yearly multiplying millions." Texas's annexation that year was preordained, "the inevitable fulfillment of the general law which is rolling our population Westward." California would be next because of "the irresistible army of Anglo-Saxon emigration that has begun to pour down upon it." British Canada would follow, severing its ties with "the little island three thousand miles across the Atlantic" and "destined to swell the still accumulating momentum of our progress."[3]

Bancroft faced considerable pressure from his Massachusetts friends not to participate in the inevitable war with Mexico on moral grounds. "Now I ask if you, George Bancroft, the historian of freedom, are willing to aid in bringing into this republic that province which has restored slavery after poor Mexico had abolished it," Theodore Parker, the great Unitarian intellectual, wrote in November 1845. "If you can do that—why, what is your lecture on Roman slavery, what your whole history of freedom but a piece of brilliant declamation? I love noble words as well as you; but I love deeds worthy of noble words—love them far better."[4]

Instead Bancroft found himself appointed acting secretary of war at the height of the crisis, and on June 15, 1845, he personally wrote the orders that sent General Zachary Taylor's men across Texas to take up positions on the new southern border—the very act that precipitated the war. Mexico had never recognized Texas's independence and viewed Taylor's maneuver as an invasion of their territory, meaning military confrontation was certain. Twelve days later Bancroft gave the official eulogy for Andrew Jackson, who had died earlier that month, in a speech celebrating American expansion. "A pupil of the wilderness, his heart was with the pioneers of American life towards the setting sun," he told Congress. "His spirit rests upon our whole territory; it hovers over the vales of Oregon, and guards in advance the frontier of the Del Norte."[5]

Months later, as secretary of the navy, he gave the orders to the Pacific Squadron to seize California's ports, which effectively ended Mexican control of the province. While he had naively thought the two countries could avoid war, he publicly supported the conflict, which resulted in the occupation of Mexico City by U.S. troops and Deep Southern demands for the annexation of the entire country.[6]

William Gilmore Simms led these calls to seize Mexico, lobbying Senator

Calhoun, Governor Hammond, and others to take an aggressive stand. "Slavery will be the medium and great agent for rescuing and recovering to freedom and civilization all the vast tracts of Texas, Mexico, etc., and our sons ought to be fitted out as fast as they are ready to take the field, with an adequate provision in slaves," he wrote. "The acquisition of Texas and Mexico secures the perpetuation of slavery for the next thousand years." Opposing him was much of the Yankee intelligentsia. Horace Greeley, the New England–born newspaperman, called on Americans to "awake and arrest the work of butchery ere it shall be too late to preserve your souls from the guilt of wholesale slaughter." The Massachusetts legislature declared such an effort "a war against freedom, against humanity, against justice" with "the triple object of extending slavery, of strengthening the slave power, and of obtaining the control of the Free States."[7]

The virulence of public reaction, pro and con, to the slavery ramifications of the war surprised Bancroft and wore down his enthusiasm for serving in the cabinet. He found solace, ironically, in organizing and opening a school, the U.S. Naval Academy in Annapolis, using existing funds and instructors and a surplus military installation, and in attending diplomatic functions in the capital. But by the summer of 1846 he longed to return to researching his *History*, preferably in Europe, where many of the relevant archives were located. Polk, appreciative of his service, nominated him to be the U.S. ambassador to the United Kingdom.[8]

On October 9, 1846, Bancroft and Elizabeth boarded the *Great Western*, a luxurious transatlantic paddle-wheel steamer that had once been the world's largest passenger vessel, and set off across the Atlantic, back to a continent he hadn't seen in nearly a quarter century.[9]

He would never live in New England again.

TWENTY

S imms had also supported Polk in the 1844 election contest, but his real political loyalties were with his intimate friend and neighbor, James Henry Hammond. Their friendship, the closest and most important in each other's lives, helped shape the Deep South's view of itself, of the United States, and of the future Confederacy.

The two had a great deal in common. They were almost exactly the same age. They had each had middle-class upbringings and abortive law careers before marrying into South Carolina's planter class, which never fully accepted them. Each had edited newspapers and was interested in politics and literature. Both men presented themselves as jovial, arrogant, and uninhibited in public, but nursed private feelings of social alienation and cosmic persecution. Their primary national loyalties were to South Carolina, not to the United States. They were deeply committed to defending slavery and opposing notions of human equality, before the law and elsewhere.

Jefferson's claim that "all men are born equal," Hammond wrote in his widely discussed 1845 booklet, *Letters on Southern Slavery*, was "ridiculously absurd." On the contrary, he argued, "slavery is truly the 'cornerstone' and foundation of every well-designed and durable 'Republican edifice,'" ordained by the Bible, humane for the enslaved, and beneficent for society. He had defended the institution ably as a congressman in 1836, introducing a motion that ultimately led to the infamous "gag rule" preventing the House of Representatives from so much as discussing slavery.

Slavery, he told the House, is "the greatest of all the great blessings which a kind Providence has bestowed upon our glorious region." On his own plantation Hammond had introduced gang labor and revoked permission for his slaves to hold church services, visit the local store, or sell produce grown in their garden. The annual death rate among his slaves—sixty-five per one thousand—was twice the U.S. slave plantation average, and the child mortality rate a shocking 72 percent.[1]

Hammond's Achilles' heel was his exuberant and unrestrained sexual appetite. While attending law school in the state capital, Columbia, in 1826, he attacked his sleeping roommate, the future court of appeals justice Thomas Jefferson Withers, with what the latter described as "furious lunges" and the "crushing force of the Battering Ram." Fortunately Withers enjoyed the attention and, when apart from Hammond, wrote him explicit letters on the "extravagant delight of poking and punching a writhing Bedfellow with your long fleshen pole," letters that were successfully hidden by the state's archivists until 1980. "Your elongated protuberance . . . has captured complete mastery over you," he cautioned his friend. "I really believe that you are charging over the pine barrens of your locality, braying, like an ass, at every she-male you can discover . . . alarming the country with your vociferations."

After his 1831 marriage to the plain, shy, seventeen-year-old heiress Catherine Fitzsimmons, Hammond no longer had any need to charge over pine barrens. His wife's plantation on the Savannah River, Silver Bluff, consisted of 10,800 acres of land and 147 slaves, including seventy-four females, with a median age of twenty-five. In 1838 he purchased an eighteen-year-old girl and her two-year-old child and commenced sexual relationships first with the mother and later with the daughter, and shared both of them with his son. His wife—who Hammond said could not satisfy his "appetites"—eventually learned of these affairs and left the household for many years. Simultaneously, while in Columbia, he groomed his four nieces, aged twelve to seventeen, as sexual playthings, molesting them at least once a week. "For two years I gave way to the most wanton indulgences," he confided to both Simms and his diary. "They extended to every thing short of direct sexual intercourse ... not with one, but indiscriminately with all of them."[2]

This was the man with whom Simms, on his return from visiting Bancroft in 1843, decided to align his political fortunes.

Hammond had by then been governor for almost a year, a primarily ceremonial office that, in aristocratic style, was chosen not by voters, but by the legislature, which retained most powers under the state's constitution. Wanting to do more than strut about in the uniform he'd purchased—replete with gold epaulettes, silver embroidered stars, and a white plumed hat—he needed legislative allies, and so enlisted Simms to run from his district in the 1844 midterms. Simms agreed, and without really campaigning, won the seat.[3]

At the State House he worked closely with Hammond, improving his speeches, sharing information, and delivering rousing orations in support of the governor's initiatives. His primary task, though, was to help Hammond, who represented lowland plantation interests, against Senator Calhoun's faction, concentrated in the interior uplands, where small farmers were in the majority. In his spare time Simms was busily trying to secure an appointment to a European diplomatic post from newly elected President Polk—"one of those pleasant berths in Italy or elsewhere, where the salary is decent and the duties nominal." He might accept being the secretary of the legation in London or ambassador in Mexico, or even chargé d'affaires in Naples, but was "yet unwilling to sink into [a position] which is merely subordinate." To his disappointment he was offered nothing, even as Northern intellectuals like Bancroft and Washington Irving were granted ambassadorships. "Now could I drink black blood," Simms lamented.[4]

Meanwhile Hammond's ship crashed on the shoals of his indiscretions after his nieces' father, Wade Hampton, learned what he had been doing to them. Hampton, a kingmaker in state politics, sought his revenge in 1844 and 1845 in the form of a vigorous whispering campaign throughout the salons of Columbia and the Low Country. "Their desire was to black ball me and to mortify me and mine by keeping us out of Society and all respectable persons from coming to our house," the governor complained to his diary. Hampton's scheme worked, and Hammond was forced to withdraw to his plantation whenever the legislature was in recess. At the inauguration of the new governor at the end of 1846, he feared the Hamptons would gun him down in the streets of the capital before he could escape to the relative safety of Silver Bluff. He would subsequently be exiled from politics and polite society for more than a decade.[5]

Simms's association with Hammond did him no favors. To his shock he lost reelection to the legislature that October and, the following month, a bid to be chosen lieutenant governor by his erstwhile legislative colleagues. "I am pretty well tired of a game in which it is so easy to be beaten," he wrote Hammond. "I should regard my recent defeats as a sufficient proof that I am not the person that I suppose myself and possess but few of the endowments upon which I had but too easily been satisfied to count." Hammond, feeling defeated himself, advised that Simms devote all his energies to crafting a single literary magnum opus.[6]

Simms was by now too depressed to undertake such a project, and not only on account of his political defeats. His wife nearly died giving birth to their sixth child, Mary, on September 1, and just twenty days later fourteen-month-old Valerie died of an illness, becoming the fourth child the couple had buried in the Woodlands' cemetery. The plantation was continuing to lose money, and while Simms kept producing novels, they weren't covering his losses. In November a crack-shot attorney challenged him to a duel over an unfavorable review Simms had written in *The Southern Literary Messenger*, and he prepared for an almost certain death. "I am in a state of mental depression," he wrote Hammond shortly after a colleague convinced the aggrieved lawyer to call off the duel. "But for the condition of my wife I should be tempted, repudiated as I am here, to clear out, and try my fortune wholly in literature either in the North or Europe."[7]

Of one thing Simms was certain as he surveyed the reaction to events in Texas and Mexico in the months that followed: "A dissolution of the Union is inevitable," he wrote Lawson in the summer of 1847. Preparations for that event needed to be put in order.[8]

TWENTY-ONE

Douglass's ascent to international fame began on his 1845 Atlantic crossing.

The new side-wheel steamship *Cambria*, the pride of the Cunard line, was a wooden vessel with three sailing masts for backup power that had begun its voyages on the Boston-to-Liverpool run a few months earlier and had already set a new eleven-day transatlantic record. She carried ninety-four passengers on the trip, a mix of races and nationalities, including slaveholders from Louisiana, Georgia, and Cuba, some in comfortable first-class cabins, while others were in cramped steerage belowdecks. Douglass's chaperone, James Buffum, had tried to buy them first-class tickets, but the captain refused, sending the pair instead down into the forecastle, the least comfortable part of the ship in bad weather.[1]

On the final evening of the trip, however, the captain invited Douglass to deliver an oration on the main deck. The passengers had been passing around copies of both his *Narrative* and James Henry Hammond's *Letters on Southern Slavery*, debating their relative merits for days. In the middle of Douglass's speech, an inebriated New Orleans planter walked directly up to him, stared at him steadily for a minute, and said: "I guess you're a liar." Douglass, a witness recounted, responded with a similar insult, and the two started loudly arguing. Soon the whole crowd broke up into "a dozen stormy groups" shouting at one another. "I wish I had you in Cuba," one slaveholder called to Douglass. "We would use him up," a Georgian agreed.

Then a group of Southerners rushed the speaker, intending to toss him overboard. The captain intervened, and the parties returned belowdecks, but when the *Cambria* arrived in Liverpool, newspapers began to spread news of the incident across the English-speaking world, boosting interest in Douglass before he gave a single speech.[2]

After a short layover Douglass and Buffum took a ferry across the Irish Sea to Dublin to begin a monthlong book tour. Douglass's immediate and lasting impression of Ireland and its people was favorable. He encountered no problems when checking in at the finest hotels or sitting down next to white people in carriages, church pews, and restaurants. He was not the target of any insults, and no one challenged his humanity. "The entire absence of everything that looks like prejudice against me, on account of the color of my skin, contrasts so strongly with my long and bitter experience in the United States, that I look with wonder and amazement on the transition," he wrote Garrison in a public letter. "I breathe, and lo! the chattel becomes a man!" Hundreds came to hear his orations, and thousands purchased copies of the new Irish edition of his book, the proceeds of which supported his travels. He appeared onstage with Daniel O'Connell, the Irish nationalist who was fighting for Irish independence from the United Kingdom. Comparing the black experience in the United States with that in the United Kingdom, Douglass would later reflect on an irony Bancroft would not: "The republic meant slavery and the monarchy freedom."[3]

Douglass was shocked at the poverty of the Irish masses, whose circumstances presented a sharp contrast with those of his middle- and upperclass, English-speaking audiences. In Dublin "the streets were almost literally alive with beggars," he wrote, as well as desperate children, mothers with emaciated infants, "stumps of men, without legs, without hands, without arms." The desperate conditions within tiny country cottages shocked him: cold, suffering families living in what he judged "much the same degradation as the American slaves." Their situation was about to become even worse. That summer and fall, as Douglass journeyed between Dublin, Cork, and Limerick, potatoes were rotting in the fields, victims of a blight that some claimed had arrived with a "blue fog" that had descended on the land. The crop, on which at least a third of the island's eight million people survived, failed the following year, precipitating the deaths of a million people from starvation and disease as the island's landlords continued to export other foodstuffs to England. The experience led Douglass to empathize with and fight on behalf of other oppressed peoples. "I am for fair play for the Irishman, the negro, the Chinaman, and for all men of whatever country or clime," he would conclude from his time there, "and for allowing them to work out their own destiny without outside interference."[4]

He spent most of 1846 crisscrossing Scotland and England, his fame and reputation growing with every stop. He delivered more than a hundred speeches that year alone to audiences as large as four thousand. He met the great English abolitionist Thomas Clarkson, who'd helped end slavery in the Empire, and prominent members of Parliament. He had equal billing with William Lloyd Garrison on a joint speaking tour of England later in the year. As he saw the effect he had on audiences, and how some of Britain's most influential people approached him with interest and respect, he felt a growing sense of accomplishment and power.

As the tour progressed, however, he became increasingly irritated with his Garrisonian chaperone. Buffum accompanied him everywhere, and Douglass learned he was reporting his utterances, social interactions, and book earnings to Garrison's chief of staff back in Boston, Maria Weston Chapman. She, in turn, directed Buffum and Douglass's Dublin-based host and printer to chastise the young orator if he strayed from their pacifist, antipolitical ideological script, or if he appeared before rival abolitionist organizations. "Set someone to watch over me," he warned Chapman, "and the last blow is struck." But even as he was tempted to break with the American Anti-Slavery Society, he realized he had little choice but to remain with the organization, as he depended on them to take care of his family in his absence.[5]

He was also lonely, homesick, and worried for his family's safety. At one point in the summer of 1846 he pondered moving Anna and the children to England, to abandon his birth country and its racism entirely, but even after newspapers reported that the Aulds had vowed to apprehend him, he still believed he needed to return home. He wrote William White, one of the people who'd saved him from the murderous mob in Indiana, asking if he thought it was safe to do so. Then some of his new English friends and admirers intervened.[6]

While on a seaside break at the Newcastle home of the Quaker abolitionist Ellen Richardson and her brother, Douglass made such an impression on his hosts that they decided to try to buy his freedom from his owners. Throughout the fall the Richardsons raised funds from English abolitionists. They located Hugh Auld, who had purchased the ownership of Frederick from his brother, and, via intermediary attorneys, negotiated a purchase price of £150, a little more than $700. (The Aulds appear to have had pangs of conscience after Frederick's escape: they had already freed Henny, sold Eliza to her free black husband, and on the same day they agreed to terms for Frederick, freed one of his cousins.) On December 12, 1846, Frederick Bailey, alias Douglass, became a free man in the eyes of Maryland. Rather than celebrate, many in the Garrison camp criticized Douglass for agreeing to the purchase of his freedom papers, arguing the payment tacitly endorsed property rights in humans. "Those papers," Douglass responded, "shall be the brand of infamy, stamping that nation as a nation of plunderers and hypocrites," unwilling to confer the inalienable rights set forth in the Declaration of Independence unless they were first paid.[7]

On April 5, 1847, having given 184 speeches across Britain, Douglass reboarded the *Cambria* a changed man. Because U.S. newspapers reprinted stories from English ones, he was now far more famous in America than when he'd left. Many nationalists were angered that a black American was criticizing their country before the world. Abolitionists esteemed him. Poets were composing verses about him, including Lorenzo Sabine, an attorney in Eastport, Maine, who wrote: "Thy tongue is loosened—loosened be the ties/Which held thy brethren in the Western shores/Proclaim their wrongs, denounce the nation's lies." Douglass had realized the true extent of his gifts and no longer felt the need for mentoring from Garrison and his friends. And now he had money: the impressive sum of $2,175 given to him by British abolitionists to ensure his powerful voice would not be quieted when he reached the New World.[8]

He intended to open a newspaper.

TWENTY-TWO

It's not often that a book review helps incite a cataclysmic war, but in 1848 Simms wrote one that did just that. The main subject of his two-part essay, published in the July and August issues of *The Southern Quarterly Review*, was *The American Loyalists*, a history by a New Englander, Lorenzo Sabine.

Sabine, the self-educated son of an impoverished New Hampshire parson, had lived for twenty-seven years at the far eastern fringe of the United States, in the island town of Eastport, Maine, a place immersed in the Loyalist experience. Sabine could gaze out his windows at the Loyalist-founded settlements of British New Brunswick on the islands studding Passama-quoddy Bay. Eastport itself had been invaded, occupied, and formally reabsorbed into the British Empire during the War of 1812, an experience many locals had not opposed. Sabine had interviewed Loyalists and the children of Loyalists, read family papers they brought down from their attics, and interacted regularly with His Majesty's subjects, the fishermen, farmers, and shopkeepers of Deer Island, Campobello, and St. Andrews, New Brunswick, who came regularly to shop, trade, and visit kin on the U.S. side of the bay. The previous Revolutionary-era generation of propagandists and historians, desperately trying to emphasize the strength and unity of their weakly bound and quarrelsome new federation, had demonized the Loyalists as greedy, unpatriotic, and traitorous "others." Sabine knew the situation was more complex, and that most Loyalists had been patriotic but for king and kingdom, that leading patriots like the Cabots had made fortunes from the war, and that what constituted loyalty to one's country in 1776 was in the eye of the beholder. In the mid-1840s he set out to correct the record.[1]

The result was an 1847 book that sketched the lives of hundreds of Loyalists, opening with a lengthy historical essay that demonstrated just how widespread American Loyalism was, and how in many ways the American Revolution was actually a civil war, particularly in the Southern colonies, where Loyalism was widespread. To prove his point, he included a data table of all regular enlistees to the Continental Army by state, one that revealed that Massachusetts alone provided nearly a third of the total—67,907—which was considerably more than all six states south of the Mason-Dixon Line combined (59,943). Worst of all, on a per capita basis, was South Carolina, which provided only 6,660. "The public men of South Carolina . . . claim that her patriotic devotion in the revolution was inferior to none," Sabine continued. "As I examine the evidence, it was not so." While New Englanders had turned out in force to liberate Boston, Charleston's citizens did not rally to save their city because, in Sabine's assessment, "the inhabitants, as a body, preferred to return to their allegiance to the British crown." South Carolina "could not defend herself against her own Tories," he continued, "and it is hardly an exaggeration to add that more Whigs of New England were sent to her aid, and lie buried in her soil, than she sent to every scene of strife from Lexington to Yorktown."[2]

Simms was incensed, even though his many Revolutionary novels pulled few punches depicting the colony's bloody internecine war. This Mainer, he wrote, was "diseased by prejudice . . . the common misfortune with New England writers" who "regard her children as the saints, to whom the possession of the Earth has been finally decreed." It wasn't that Sabine's numbers were wrong—South Carolina, like Georgia, had been ambivalent about the Revolutionary cause—but rather that it was being used to question his state's patriotism. The sentiments of the majority, Simms continued, were an irrelevant test; what mattered was that a patriot minority had persevered despite the resistance of Quakers and immigrants. "We deny that you have any right to inquire into their numbers," he decreed. "They are the only true representatives of the State." New Englanders, he lamented, were distorting U.S. history and, thus, the American experiment itself. To another friend he wrote "that Yankee Histories of the United States are generally fraudulent from Peter Parley to George Bancroft."[3]

Simms's review was widely read and celebrated in Southern political and literary circles, just as Sabine's book was championed throughout Greater New England, with *The North American Review* declaring it "a better sketch than can be found elsewhere of the actual state of things during the struggle with Great Britain." Their lances would soon be taken up by others in a verbal joust that erupted into violence.

THE AMERICAN LOYALISTS further convinced Simms and his circle that secession was inevitable, imminent, and necessary to protect their society. He and Hammond formed an affectionate alliance with three other Southern intellectuals: William & Mary's Nathaniel Beverley Tucker, who had challenged Bancroft's depiction of early Virginia; the Virginia planter Edmund Ruffin, who had argued that the Declaration of Independence's promise of universal equality was "both false and foolish"; and the University of Mississippi chancellor George Frederick Holmes, who called the natural rights of liberty and equality "vain twaddle." This "sacred circle," as they called themselves, corresponded, organized political actions and publications, and developed the intellectual foundations of something new: a Southern nationhood.

They pinned their hopes for actualizing their ideas on a June 1850 convention of Southern states that was to be held in Nashville to develop a united Southern response if the U.S. government banned slavery in the vast western territories that had recently been annexed from Mexico. Simms counseled that there should be no compromises. "We want few words, and stern acts only," he wrote Tucker who, along with Hammond and Senator Jefferson Davis of Mississippi, was a delegate to the convention. "The formation of the new republic would bring us wonderfully nearer to one another." But the convention was a failure, with few attending who were not from South Carolina or the host state, Tennessee. Despite Tucker's agitation, the delegates declined to endorse secession and instead promoted a compromise that would split the new territories between slave and free areas and revoke the power of Northern state courts to provide due process rights for alleged fugitives who had been apprehended by slave catchers. Simms was appalled by the proposal but knew that South Carolina couldn't survive on its own against a hostile federal government, which would likely blockade its ports and thus ruin its economy. "The scum is uppermost and will remain uppermost until we have the storm," he fumed. "We are all anxious to relieve ourselves from the international incubus, and the question is one purely of time."[4]

There was more disappointment close to home. After Senator John C. Calhoun's death on March 31, 1850, Simms expected the governor would appoint Hammond to replace him, and he advised his friend on how to position himself on key issues coming before the U.S. Senate. To both men's shock the position was offered to a different man and, when he declined, to another, who also declined; a third man accepted, and died in office six weeks later, only to be replaced by yet another rival. Hammond, whose wife had by now left him over his fathering of slave children, fell into a deep depression. "My caste is now fixed—I am a Pariah," he wrote Simms that December. "Let all avoid me who will." Simms, too, was despondent, as more of his children died, his plantation continued to lose money, and his own political career appeared ended.[5]

But as a novelist and the editor of *The Southern Quarterly Review*, he remained one of the most prominent defenders of the South. He attacked Harriet Beecher Stowe's new blockbuster novel *Uncle Tom's Cabin*, declaring her depictions of the cruelties of slavery to be "unqualifiedly false." Slaves were, he argued, valuable property cherished and protected by their masters. Contrary to Stowe's assertions, he proclaimed that laws forbade the willful killing of a slave or the separation of children under ten from their mothers. Uncle Tom, Stowe's protagonist, was an implausibly virtuous slave, while she had depicted all the white characters in a sinister light.

Stowe, he warned, was "the mouthpiece of a large and dangerous faction which if we do not put down with the pen, we may be compelled one day (God grant that day may never come!) to repel with the bayonet."[6]

He also set himself to write a counternarrative, working feverishly in his Woodlands study when his duties overseeing the plantation and the *Review* allowed. The result, *Woodcraft*, was published in 1854 and is widely considered one of his best novels. The story, set in war-torn South Carolina at the end of the Revolution, followed the virtuous deeds of an upstanding planter who returns from the fighting to restore order and prosperity, cheered on by his loyal slaves, who had been hiding in the woods to avoid being kidnapped by Tory bandits. The planter, Porgy; his brave but vulgar lower-class lieutenant, Millhouse; and his enslaved cook, Tom, have complementary skills, accept their places in the hierarchy, and watch out and care for one another. Porgy testifies that his love for Tom is so great that he would shoot him rather than let him fall into the hands of another owner. Tom, at the end of the book, declines his master's offer to be freed. "I no guine to be free no way you kin fix it; so maussa, don't you bodder me wid dis nonsense t'ing 'bout free paper any more," Tom says. "I's well off whar' I is I tell you; and I much rudder [rather] b'long to good maussa, wha' I lub, dan be my own maussa and quarrel wid mese'f ebbry day."[7]

IN 1853, Lippincott, Grambo & Company published *The Pro-Slavery Argument*, an anthology largely consisting of Hammond's *Letters on Southern Slavery*—one of the works debated on the *Cambria* during Douglass's Atlantic crossing eight years earlier—and Simms's revised essay on "The Morals of Slavery." In this new book, a store of ammunition for Southern secessionists, Simms argued that slavery was an essential civilizing instrument through which superior peoples uplifted inferior ones by teaching them to work and eventually by incorporating them into society. In this way Norman conquerors had "raised Britain's Saxons," resulting in "the most perfect specimens of physical organization and moral susceptibilities, which the world has ever known." It was a pity that North American Indians resisted servitude, as they could have been saved and elevated to greatness via "an Egyptian bondage of four hundred years." He lamented that "the lousy and lounging *lazzaroni* of Italy, cannot be made to labor in the fields, under the whip of a severe task-master" as it would make them "a much freer—certainly a much nobler animal—than we can possibly esteem them now." Africans were happier and freer in slavery than in their natural savage condition, and Simms believed they were probably incapable of advancing to a state of full freedom, having been "designed as an implement in the hands of civilization always."[8]

Simms, spurred on by Southern pride and financial necessity, released a collection of short stories that aimed to win the South allies in New York City and Philadelphia, cities he'd long realized belonged to a different nation (or different nations) from New England. *Southward Ho!*, published in 1854, was a Chaucerian collection of tales shared among a geographically diverse set of steamship passengers bound from New York to Charleston, Simms's own seasonal commute. South Carolina, an Alabamian pontificates, was the only state that protected its cultural legacy from the masses, working "in a thousand ways" to protect the state from the people; foolish purveyors of un-checked democracy were failing to do so, leaving their people "without God or country." "One of the most dangerous of the errors which prevail among the people of the North, is their obstinate faith in the integrity of the Union," another Southerner in Simms's novel warned. "There can not be peace, so long as the south is in the minority, and so long as the spirit and temper of the north are so universally hostile to our most vital and most cherished institu-tions. Until you reconcile this inequality, and exorcise this evil spirit, that now rages rampant through the Northern States—allied with all sorts of fanatical passions and principles—Agrarianism, Communism, Fourierism, Wrightism, Millerism, Mormonism, etc.,—you may cry peace and union till you split your lungs, but you will neither make peace nor secure union."[9]

The storm was coming, Simms warned one and all. It was time to pre-pare the Southern people for a nationhood celebrating inequality, hierar-chy, and the supremacy of the Anglo-Saxon race.

TWENTY-THREE

On his return to the United States, Frederick Douglass initially created controversy with his angry denunciations of the nation and its failures to uphold its own ideals. "I have no love for America as such," he said of the country that then enslaved three million. "I have no patriotism. I have no country." The Bill of Rights, he observed, was for African Americans "a bill of wrongs." The nation was in "discord with the Almighty." The pro-slavery press savaged him.[1]

Within weeks Douglass was on the road again, traversing the mid-Atlantic and lower Great Lakes states, accompanied by Garrison. They spoke to rapt audiences, faced down racist mobs, and were Jim Crowed by steamship captains. The breakneck schedule wore both men down, with Garrison becoming so sick that he had to remain behind in Cleveland. Douglass worked his way eastward, stopping in Rochester, New York, to lay the ground for the new, more independent life he had been longing for since Ireland.

In November 1847, just seven months after returning to America, he shocked the Garrisonians by opening a newspaper office of his own in Rochester, at a far remove from the Boston-based organization.[2]

Rochester, a boomtown of thirty-five thousand on the Erie Canal, was a center of abolitionist sentiment and the nascent women's rights movement. A stop on the Underground Railroad, the town had seen the founding of a black women's abolitionist group in 1834, a white-led Female Anti-Slavery

Society in 1835, and the Western New York Anti-Slavery Society thereafter. Douglass was welcomed by the prominent Quaker abolitionist Daniel Anthony, who invited him to the enormous Sunday dinners for liberal reformers at his farm outside of town, where Douglass would meet and become close friends with his daughter, Susan B. Anthony. Located across Lake Ontario from British Canada, where hundreds of fugitive slaves made their home, Rochester was an ideal base for Douglass.[3]

His newspaper, *The North Star*, financed largely by gifts from his British abolitionist friends, was to be an African American voice against slavery, and one that was soon at variance with the pacifist, antipolitical tenets of Garrison and his followers. For the next two years Douglass and his allies marched into electoral politics, criticizing the major parties—Whig and Democrat—for their betrayal of the national purpose. "The blood of the slave is on your garments," he told Northerners after they helped elect the slaveholder Zachary Taylor to the presidency. "You have said that slavery is better than freedom—that war is better than peace." "Slavery will be attacked in its stronghold," he warned Southerners. "The compromises of the Constitution and the cry of disunion shall be more fearlessly proclaimed, till slavery be abolished, the Union Dissolved, or the sun of this guilty nation must go down in blood."[4]

Within months, however, *The North Star* was in trouble. African American subscribers failed to appear in large enough numbers, and Douglass was soon begging for money from every quarter he could. He mortgaged the Rochester home he'd just purchased for Anna and the children. While trying to write, edit, typeset, publish, and distribute a weekly newspaper, he had to rush off to deliver lectures just to keep the family fed. On the verge of a nervous, physical, and financial breakdown, he survived only through the help of one of his white English friends, Julia Griffiths, who crossed the Atlantic, moved into their house, and worked alongside Douglass at *The North Star*'s offices. She bought the mortgage on his house, loaned the newspaper money, and fund-raised from other philanthropists. From May 1849 to the summer of 1855, Griffiths helped keep Douglass intact, although she would sometimes write friends of her fears that Douglass was losing his mind under the stress. Anna was unhappy with the situation—after three years she forced Griffiths to move to a boardinghouse—and the people of Rochester were scandalized by what was, at the least, the appearance of impropriety.[5]

Sometimes Douglass sheltered fugitive slaves in his house, which itself became a stop on the Underground Railroad, receiving "passengers" David Ruggles sent on from New York City. In December 1851 a group of eleven arrived with their conductor, an intense, pistol-packing, five-foot-tall, thirty-one-year-old escaped slave named Harriet Tubman, who had personally retrieved them from the Eastern Shore of Maryland and guided them through Delaware and on to Rochester. Though she suffered from epilepsy, as the result of an injury she had received from an overseer, she made repeated trips into Maryland, rescuing siblings, cousins, and hundreds of strangers, and earning the nickname Moses. They became allies, and Douglass protected her and her passengers as they began the final leg of their journey to St. Catharines in present-day Ontario, where Tubman made her home.[6]

While on the stump Douglass condoned the use of deadly force to stop slave catchers—bloodhounds who had "no right to live"—and slaveholders themselves. He visited Harriet Beecher Stowe at her Massachusetts home, and likened her to Burns and Shakespeare, pronouncing *Uncle Tom's Cabin* to be "the *master book* of the nineteenth century." He wrote a blistering open letter to Thomas Auld, whom he told he felt thankful that his four children were "in comfortable beds, sound asleep, perfectly secure under my own roof" in Rochester, where there were no slaveholders "to rend my heart by snatching them from my arms." On the invitation of the feminist activists Elizabeth Cady Stanton and Lucretia Mott, he spoke at the 1848 Seneca Falls Convention, where he helped secure narrow passage for a measure to demand that women have the right to vote; the convention's official proceedings were printed at *The North Star*'s offices. On tour in Springfield he lodged at the home of a local wool trader who, after hours of conversation, unfolded a map, pointed to the Allegheny Mountains, and said God had placed them there "for the emancipation of the Negro race"; the man's name was John Brown. Douglass wrote an autobiographical masterpiece, *My Bondage and My Freedom*, the publication of which in 1855 would finally lift his financial worries. From the pages of his newspaper, he blasted George Bancroft for both his "hypocritical hallelujahs" on American liberty and his silence as it was being trampled to death.[7]

On July 5, 1852, Douglass delivered one of the greatest speeches in American history. In a hall just a few blocks from his home, he asked what the Fourth of July meant to a slave, a question that led him to consider what the signers of the Declaration of Independence had pledged to seventy-six years earlier: the promise of universal human equality. The Declaration, he told the mostly white audience, "is the ringbolt to the chain of your nation's destiny," its principles the soul-saving instruments to which Americans "must be true to . . . on all occasions, in all places, against all foes, and at whatever the cost." He warned, "From the round top of your ship of state, dark and threatening clouds may be seen."

> Heavy billows, like mountains in the distance, disclose to the leeward
> huge forms of flinty rocks! That *bolt* drawn, that *chain* broken, and
> all is lost. *Cling to this day—cling to it*, and to its principles, with the
> grasp of a storm-tossed mariner to a spar at midnight.

Slavery violated all those principles, he told his Rochester neighbors, and thus "brands your republicanism as a sham, your humanity as a base pretense, and your Christianity as a lie." Your hands, he told them, "are full of blood," and "a horrible reptile is coiled up in your nation's bosom . . . nursing at the tender breast of your youthful republic. For the love of God," he implored, "fling from you the hideous monster and let the weight of twenty millions crush and destroy it forever."[8]

When he took his seat, the six hundred onlookers stood and cheered, and his words quickly echoed across the nation.

TWENTY-FOUR

B ancroft returned to America, apparently unaware of the gathering storm, a crisis he had helped to create by issuing the orders that precipitated the Mexican conflict and led U.S. troops to occupy California. Everything would turn out fine, he was convinced, because he and Polk had acted in accordance with God's clear plan for their country.

Oblivious to the political and moral stakes, he stuck firmly to the *History*'s guidance. From London he had advised President Polk to annex as much of Mexico as possible. He had urged Secretary of State James Buchanan to conclude a quick, severe settlement that would ensure that "America will be the happiest, most prosperous, most envied country on earth." As U.S. troops occupied Mexico City, he was pleased to inform Polk that the British foreign minister, Lord Palmerston, considered the swift victory evidence "of the immense superiority of the Anglo-Saxon race." He wrote that Northern calls for "No More Territory" were "absurd," as he remained unconcerned about the massive expansion of slavery such subtropical annexations would certainly bring. Providence clearly wanted the United States to expand liberty, both in quality and in territory, so abolition would come about naturally and in its own time, like a flower opening in spring.[1]

Meanwhile he misjudged almost every political event of the time, from the prospects of the 1848 democratic uprisings on the European continent (he was convinced Providence would sweep the monarchies away) to the seriousness of the Irish famine, which he feared would create welfare dependency. ("Millions of the Irish fasten themselves on the public treasury of England; and exist in inert apathetic dependence as idle pensioners, pleading misery as their title to bounty, and seeking to make that bounty perpetual by their own listless indifference to their welfare," he wrote as a million people starved to death across the Irish Sea.) The tribune of liberty also had no interest in the fact that a fugitive American slave was filling lecture halls and newspaper columns from one end of the United Kingdom to another. He was also oblivious to the anger at home over the Manifest Destiny policies he'd helped to enact, and so was completely taken aback when Polk's successor, Lewis Cass, lost the 1848 presidential election to General Zachary Taylor, a development that put a premature end to Bancroft's ambassadorship.[2]

Perplexed and disgusted with politics and governance, he announced his retirement from both and in September 1849 moved his family to New York City, where he bought a town house, filled its third floor with the thousands of manuscripts he'd collected from across two continents, and set to work. As the federation careened toward dissolution, he spent every morning composing proof that it was instead destined for continued greatness. As Simms and Hammond crafted arguments for the moral goodness and desirability of slavery, Bancroft inked paeans to American liberty. As Douglass warned that America would drown in blood, Bancroft prepared volumes that confidently declared all was and would be well. In the afternoons he rode horses and in the evenings he attended dinner parties with the Astors. In the summers he and Elizabeth spent weeks at a time at Rosecliff, their seaside estate in Newport, Rhode Island, where Bancroft created and cultivated a new variety of ornamental flower, the American Beauty rose.[3]

Volumes 4 and 5 of the *History* appeared in 1852 as the federation began to run aground on the rocks of slavery and its leaders fought over the morality of the Fugitive Slave Act, the future of the Missouri Compromise, and the status of human freedom and equality in the new federal territories. Bancroft's most recent historical volumes covered the tumultuous period of the mid-eighteenth century, when British North America had expanded westward, helping place the colonies on their own path to war. In them, he again took a complacent view. God had intended that France be defeated because he did not wish the Mississippi Valley to fall into "the decaying framework of feudal tyranny." Britain had been but a "transient trustee" of the northern swath of these lands, as God had "commissioned" her to "transfer it from the France of the Middle Ages to the free people, who were making for humanity a new existence in America." The Native Americans who lived there were of no consequence, being "inferior in reason and moral qualities" and thus unable to carry forth the Providential mission. Rather, that mission had grown organically "from the intelligence that had been slowly ripening in the mind of cultivated humanity" and would ensure "the advancement of the principles of ever-lasting peace and universal brotherhood." The British colonies "resembled living plants, whose inward energies obey the Divine idea, without effort or consciousness of will."[4]

Volumes 6 and 7 appeared in 1854 and 1858 respectively and carried much the same message. At the Battle of Lexington the minutemen had acted not as individuals, but as "the slowly ripened fruit of Providence," led and nurtured by a light "combined of the rays from the whole history of the race." The events of the Revolution weren't human acts, but rather followed "laws that are much older than Andes or Ararat." The implications for his readers were clear: keep calm and let the Providential plan guide the nation forward to its glorious destiny.[5]

IN THE MID-1850S Bancroft also finally set out to begin exploring the federation he'd spent so many years praising. Until then he'd never been south of Virginia or west of Ohio, his travels almost entirely confined to the East Coast and the Yankee-settled areas of the eastern Midwest. What he saw reassured him that his thesis was correct: The United States would continue its unbroken progress toward freedom and greatness.

In the late winter of 1855 Bancroft traveled to the Deep South, where he was the guest of genteel planters who introduced him to local luminaries and took him on carriage excursions in the countryside. In St. Augustine, Florida, he was spellbound by date trees, orchards of orange trees in blossom, bananas growing wild "like raspberries," and mockingbirds as "thick as robins." In Savannah he got a glimpse of a massive slave auction—"I saw a woman with two [children] put up, and another with her infant in her arms; she wiped a tear from her eye, but stood bravely as possible"—but he was quickly whisked away by his hosts. He was shown an African American church and introduced to the ninety-nine-year-old slave who served as its minister. He heard his hosts tell affectionate stories about their own slaves, living and dead, as other slaves prepared and served his meals. In Columbia, South Carolina, he visited with Wade Hampton's twenty-five-year-old son, Frank, and former mayor, U.S. senator, and South Carolina College president William Preston, who, like Bancroft, was a close friend of Washington Irving's. At the college they called on Francis Lieber, the German-born intellectual, and President James Henley Thornwell, a Presbyterian minister and leading voice for the idea that slavery was endorsed by God. Everywhere he went he was surrounded by polite, educated, and generous men who hardly seemed the sort intent on destroying the Republic.[6]

THE PREVIOUS SUMMER, Bancroft and his stepson joined former president Millard Fillmore and a host of luminaries and journalists on a Midwestern junket sponsored by the Chicago & Rock Island Railroad and the Minnesota Packet Company for what was billed as the "Grand Excursion," the first rail-and-ship journey linking the Atlantic with the Mississippi. They traveled from Chicago to the Mississippi on special trains festooned with flags and flowers, stopping regularly to give speeches and witness military parades. At the river port of Rock Island, Illinois, they boarded five steamships for a weeklong trip upriver to Minneapolis and then down to St. Louis that left Bancroft enthralled. The river, he wrote Elizabeth, was "more beautiful than was expected or can be told." The forests, flowers, fertility, and seemingly endless extent of the surrounding prairie converted

Bancroft into "one of their most enthusiastic admirers." In St. Louis he wrote Elizabeth that the excursion had been "the pleasantest and most instructive of my life."[7]

He and Fillmore traveled back to Chicago by train and, on June 14, stopped in Springfield, Illinois, where a throng of locals waited to glimpse the former president. A local railroad attorney and onetime congressman introduced them to what a newspaper reporter called "a large concourse of citizens." Fillmore expressed his "highest admiration" for Illinois, confessing he "had no adequate idea of its immense resources until he had traversed its magnificent prairie." After a multi-gun salute and some conversation, the attorney wished them well. Bancroft didn't think much of the middle-aged Whig, an uninteresting man of little consequence who had shown he lacked the rhetorical skill and emotion to ever make a decent orator. He and Fillmore likely boarded the train without giving him another thought.[8]

Abraham Lincoln waved good-bye.

TWENTY-FIVE

Lincoln had a lot on his mind in the summer of 1854. He had retired from politics in 1849, after spending a single term in Congress fighting against the Polk administration's war with Mexico and for the abolition of slavery in D.C. and the new federal territories. Tired and frustrated, he had thrown his energies into his Springfield law practice, where he represented everyone from slandered women and murder suspects to a steamship company and the Illinois Central Railroad.

But all that had changed on May 30, 1854, shortly before Bancroft's visit, when another Springfield resident had turned the country upside down. Senator Stephen Douglas, who'd been on the opposite side of nearly every vote they cast when they'd served together in Congress, had introduced and won passage of a law that facilitated the expansion of slavery. It repealed the territorial quarantine imposed by the Missouri Compromise thirty-four years earlier, which had banned slavery everywhere in the Louisiana Purchase north of today's Arkansas and Oklahoma, with the exception of the then-new state of Missouri, where cotton planters had established a foothold along the floodplains of the river of the same name. From that moment forward, the residents of the various territories—the future states of Kansas, Nebraska, North and South Dakota, Wyoming, and Montana—would be allowed to decide on their own if they would permit slavery, a provision that guaranteed Kansas would cease to be free as slaveholders poured into it from across the border in Missouri.

. This shocked moderates like Lincoln, who had convinced themselves that the Founders had been ashamed of slavery and committed to human equality, and so had designed the Constitution in such a way that it would ensure its slow, natural extinction. It had provided for the end of the importation of slaves after 1808. Its preamble tasked the Union to "secure the blessings of liberty" for all its people. Recognizing regional differences the Founders had been forced to make concessions to the slave states—allowing three-fifths of the enslaved population to count toward the Southern states' congressional representation—but these were temporary measures, which is why the word "slavery" never appeared in the document. They had hidden it away, Lincoln would say, "just as an afflicted man hides away a wen or a cancer, which he dares not cut out at once, lest he bleed to death." As a matter of law, he held, slavery had to be respected where it existed, but the American ideals set down in the Declaration compelled the federal government to prevent its expansion, awaiting the day it died a natural death in the face of economic, demographic, and moral realities. Senator Douglas's Kansas-Nebraska Act of 1854 flouted the Founders' intent, Lincoln believed, and betrayed the Union's most fundamental values.[1]

Lincoln had started plotting to unseat Douglas that winter, shortly after the senator had first introduced the act. Lincoln's law partner, William Herndon, had set up back-channel communications with Theodore Parker, Bancroft's Transcendentalist associate, who sent them copies of his antislavery sermons. Lincoln himself started covert communications with Illinois's leading antislavery crusader, Owen Lovejoy, a man who, like Parker, he could not openly embrace if he wished to have the support of the people of central Illinois. With their speeches and papers in hand he sequestered himself in the Illinois State Library—and immersed himself in history in preparation for the fight.[2]

Lincoln must have read at least some volumes of Bancroft's *History of the United States*, as its themes are reflected in many of his subsequent speeches. His friend Henry C. Whitney read him one of Bancroft's own speeches as they traveled to court in Danville, an oration on the inevitability of human progress in which the historian asserted the unity of humankind. "Every man is in substance equal to his fellow man. His nature is changed neither by time nor by country," Bancroft said. "No science has been reached, no thought generated, no truth discovered, which has not from all time existed potentially in every human mind." All were proceeding toward a "commonwealth of mankind" whose component peoples had been "prepared, like so many springs and wheels, one day to be put together."

Bancroft's speech intrigued Lincoln, inspiring him to write one of his least successful lectures, "Discoveries and Inventions," in which he addressed how ideas and innovations built upon one another, driving progress, a process at which Americans were especially successful because the "dust of ages" wasn't present to "smother the intellects and energies of man." While Lincoln didn't share Bancroft's faith in progress or the inevitability of American destiny, he did embrace the concept that the United States had the potential to further human freedom and that the Federalists' defining cause had been universal equality. America hadn't yet achieved its promise, but it might one day do so if the slave lords' advance could be halted.[3]

When Lincoln emerged from the library late that summer he began crisscrossing the state, denouncing Douglas and the Kansas-Nebraska Act, both in solo appearances and in oratorical contests with the senator himself. His speech in Peoria in October 1854 was representative of his argument at the time, inflected by Bancroft and Parker: The United States was founded to promote freedom and equality, and slavery violated this sacred purpose. Of slaveholders he said: "That *perfect* liberty they sigh for—the liberty of making slaves of other people—Jefferson never thought of; their own father never thought of; they never thought of themselves, a year ago." Of slavery: "I hate it because it deprives our republican example of its just influence in the world—enables the enemies of free institutions, with plausibility, to taunt us as hypocrites—causes the real friends of freedom to doubt our sincerity, and especially because it forces so many really good men amongst ourselves into an open war with the very fundamental principles of civil liberty—criticizing the Declaration of Independence, and insisting that there is no right principle of action but *self-interest*." Of equality: "If the negro is a *man*, why then my ancient faith teaches me that 'all men are created equal;' and that there can be no moral right in connection with one man's making a slave of another."[4]

His solution, however, was not to elevate African Americans to equal status, but to rid the country of them. Given godlike powers, he told the people of Peoria, he would free them and send them all to Liberia, "their own native land," but he knew such a proposal was logistically impossible, there being an insufficient amount of ships and federal funds to ship millions of people across the Atlantic and supply them until they got established. "What next? Free them, and make them politically and socially, our equals?" he asked. "My own feelings will not admit of this; and if mine would, we well know that those of the great mass of white people will not." The only solution, he concluded, was gradual emancipation and expulsion, much the same plan George Bancroft had in mind. It wouldn't be until after he met Frederick Douglass that Lincoln would fully embrace the more expansive idea that many peoples could partake simultaneously in America's promise of universal equality and freedom.[5]

For now, he sought to save a white man's republic from an existential threat. "Our republican robe is soiled, and trailed in the dust," he told his audience, as Senator Douglas looked on.

> Let us repurify it. Let us turn and wash it white, in the spirit, if not the blood, of the Revolution. Let us turn slavery from its claims of "moral right," back upon its existing legal rights, and its arguments of "necessity." Let us return it to the position our fathers gave it; and there let it rest in peace. Let us re-adopt the Declaration of Independence, and with it, the practices, and policy, which harmonize with it. Let north and south—let all Americans—let all lovers of liberty everywhere—join in the great and good work. If we do this, we shall not only have saved the Union; but we shall have so saved

it, as to make, and to keep it, forever worthy of the saving. We shall
have so saved it, that the succeeding millions of free happy people,
the world over, shall rise up, and call us blessed, to the latest generations.[6]

He then climbed down from the stage to begin the mighty struggle.

TWENTY-SIX

June 26, 1854, began routinely enough, with no hint of the violence to come.

Senator Charles Sumner, a stalwart abolitionist from Massachusetts, stood up on the Senate floor during a debate on whether to repeal the Fugitive Slave Act and defended his state from a Southern colleague's charges of fanaticism. "The fanaticism which the Senator condemns is not new in Boston," he said, but was the same that at the dawn of the Revolution had opposed the Stamp Act, the Tea Tax, and the British at Bunker Hill, and that had been possessed by John Adams and John Hancock. South Carolina's Andrew Butler then rose to declare that Revolutionary Massachusetts was a slaveholding state, and that American independence "was won by the arms and treasure, by the patriotism and good faith of slaveholding communities." The United States, he continued, was the product of a slaveholders' compact, and if New Englanders continued to agitate for African American liberty, it would collapse, "and we should be better off without it."[1]

Butler then asked if Sumner would personally assist in capturing a fugitive slave. Sumner responded that he would not, adding a biblical quote that had also appeared in an important scene in *Uncle Tom's Cabin*: "Is thy servant a dog, that he should do this thing?" Butler mocked this response at length to hoots of laughter, and then he and colleagues from Virginia and Indiana criticized Sumner for his stance, which they declared tantamount to violating the Constitution and the oath each of them had taken to uphold it. They attacked the preamble of the Declaration of Independence, contending that Jefferson's argument that all men were created equal was a "self-evident lie," and what it really meant was that each state was created equal and so, ipso facto, the words actually directed Americans to respect slavery. Sumner stood his ground, and the three senators called for him to be expelled amid a barrage of insults, with Indiana's John Pettit arguing that Sumner's defense of equality meant the senator thought that "he who walks in the gutter with the vilest and most worthless is your equal."[2]

Sumner would not forget the personal insults, and would later respond in kind, but he did not wait to defend his state's honor. He consulted Lorenzo Sabine's book and promptly delivered a searing scholarly counterattack on Butler's historical assertions. Far from spearheading the Revolution, the South had supplied far fewer troops than New England, he noted, citing Sabine's detailed tables, facts, and figures, and South Carolina had been the least patriotic of all. He cited passages in Bancroft's *History of the United States* attesting to how slavery had weakened South Carolina's ability to assist in the patriot cause. "Not by slavery, but in spite of slavery was independence achieved," Sumner concluded. "It was the inspiration of Liberty Universal that conducted us through the Red Sea of the Revolution, as it had already given to the Declaration of Independence its mighty tone, resounding through the ages."[3]

In the highest deliberative chamber in the land, representatives of the four largest regional cultures were fighting a rhetorical war over the purpose and identity of the American Republic. Simms, Sabine, Bancroft, and Douglass had provided much of their ammunition.

The Fugitive Slave Law was not repealed, of course, and the Senate moved on to other matters that session. The tensions, both between Sumner and his pro-slavery colleagues and between New England–settled states and lowland Southern ones, continued to fester.

In the spring of 1856 the inevitable ramification of the Kansas-Nebraska Act was finally coming to pass: The Kansas Territory, racked with violence between pro- and antislavery settlers, asked Congress to admit it to the Union as a slave state. On May 19, after weeks of preparation, Sumner rose to deliver a speech entitled "Crime against Kansas" that would take five hours over two separate days to complete. His primary aim was to establish the illegality of almost everything that had led to Kansas having a pro-slavery government, and to demonstrate how a conspiracy of slave masters was destroying democratic institutions across the Union. He also attacked the men and states he felt were especially responsible for this state of affairs. Senators Butler and Douglas, authors of the Kansas-Nebraska Act, had sallied forth on this criminal venture like "Don Quixote and Sancho Panza," Sumner said. Butler "has read many books of chivalry and believes himself a chivalrous knight" but "has chosen a mistress to whom he has made his vows and who though ugly to others is always lovely to him; though polluted in the sight of the world, is chaste in his sight—I mean the harlot, Slavery." For her, Sumner continued, Butler surpassed "the frenzy of Don Quixote in behalf of his wench, Dulcinea." Douglas served as the "squire of slavery, its very Sancho Panza, ready to do all its humiliating offices." Together they were part of a "pirate crew" assailing the ship of state "for the sake of its doubloons and dollars" backed by a sympathetic president.[4]

When Sumner resumed his speech the following day he soon put South Carolina itself in his sights. "Were the whole history of South Carolina blotted out of existence, from its very beginning down to the day of the last election of the Senator to his present seat on this floor, civilization might lose—I do not say how little; but surely less than it has already gained by the example of Kansas, in its valiant struggle against oppression." The state, he added, suffered from the "shameful imbecility" of slavery during the Revolution and "its more shameful assumptions for slavery since."[5]

After he finished, Stephen Douglas responded: "Is it his object to provoke some of us to kick him as we would a dog in the street, that he may get sympathy upon the just chastisement?"[6]

Butler himself was unwell and at home in South Carolina, but his nephew, Preston Brooks, represented the north-central part of the state in the U.S. House and was incensed at Sumner's words against his kin and country. As a friend later explained, a Southern gentleman would never have addressed such an insult through the courts, but rather via a duel, if the perpetrator was indeed a gentleman, or a beating if he was not. Representative Brooks decided on the latter course, but waited two days for the printed version of the speech to appear. He then tried to find Sumner on the streets outside the Capitol, and failing to do so, waited the following day outside the Senate chamber for Sumner to leave his desk, where he sat franking copies of his speech that were to be mailed across the country. Brooks finally entered the chamber with his South Carolina colleague, Representative Laurence Keitt.[7]

Brooks was thirty-six but walked with a limp as the result of being shot by future Texas senator Louis Wigfall in a duel. He carried a thick, gold-headed walking stick with him at all times, so no one gave it a second thought when he approached Sumner's desk with stick in hand.

When he reached Sumner, Brooks denounced "a libel on South Carolina" and began beating the seated man. Again and again he battered the senator, who thrust himself backward in an attempt to escape the blows, ripping his desk from its anchors, and collapsing on the floor as he began to pass out. "Don't kill him," Senator John Crittenden of Kentucky shouted and rushed toward Brooks, only to be blocked by Representative Keitt, who threatened him with his own cane. "Let them alone, damn you," Keitt warned as Brooks propped up Sumner's unconscious body and broke the cane over his head.[8]

Keitt and Brooks then strode from the chamber, triumphant in their assertion of Southern honor.

As a result of his injuries, it would be more than two years before Sumner was able to return to the Senate chamber. Most prominent Southerners applauded the beating.

Butler, who rushed back to Washington on hearing of the incident, delivered a multi-hour speech on June 12 and 13 in which he justified Brooks's actions and defended South Carolina's honor at length using arguments cribbed from Simms's defense of the state's performance in the Revolution. "He approached that man with no other purpose than to disgrace him as far as he could," Butler said of Brooks, "but the stick broke." Brooks, who resigned after being censured by the House, told that chamber that he had "speculated somewhat as to whether I should employ a horsewhip or a cowhide" but was afraid Sumner would take it from his hands.

Keitt, also censured, gave his resignation speech two days later, going on for hours to defend his state's conduct in the Revolution, likewise citing Simms and repeatedly taking Lorenzo Sabine to task by name. He then counterattacked, quoting eleven Revolutionary letters from George Washington and others complaining about the Massachusetts militia, and a dozen more extracts from newspapers and the Massachusetts legislature attesting to that state's disloyalty in the War of 1812. "My colleague redressed a wrong to his blood and his State, and he did it in a fair and manly way," Butler said of Brooks. "In the feudal code of chivalry . . . the churl was never touched with the knightly sword; his person was muleted by the quarter-staff."[9]

In special elections shortly thereafter, their former constituents returned both Brooks and Keitt to their House seats, a move many Northerners interpreted as a confirmation that South Carolina did not belong together with them in the same Republic. "I do not see how a barbarous community and a civilized community can constitute one state," Ralph Waldo Emerson told the citizens of Concord shortly after the assault. "I think we must get rid of slavery, or we must get rid of freedom."[10]

MONTHS LATER Simms and Sabine exchanged letters. "I must not forget to say that Sumner properly owes his cudgeling to you!" Simms wrote the New Englander. "He followed in your tracks and relied upon your introductory essay." Sabine, already shocked by the attack on his work by Butler and Keitt, had reexamined all his sources but came to the same conclusions as before. He invited Simms to discuss the matter in person when he was next in New England, and Simms accepted.[11]

Simms had decided that this would be the appropriate time to carry the fight to the North, to convince audiences there of South Carolina's virtues and of the heresies of men like Sumner. Butler himself had been urging him "to take up the cudgels and fight his battles."[12]

It would prove to be an extremely poor decision.

TWENTY-SEVEN

Simms had been contemplating a Northern lecture tour before the caning incident, as he desperately needed the money. His plantation was still operating at a loss—Hammond claimed it was because Simms coddled his slaves—his latest books weren't selling well, and *The Southern Quarterly Review* was about to fail. Exhausted by long months spent at his writing desk and in need of a break, he had looked to his Northern friends for advice on how to organize the most profitable and efficient speaking tour of "Northern capitals and states."[1]

His plan was to cure Northern audiences of their ignorance about South Carolina's culture and history, particularly as to its patriotism in the Revolution. He intended to avoid a direct defense of slavery, but when he read Sumner's Kansas speech he pledged to "disabuse our neighbors of the notion that the south was imbecile." Simms knew New York City—and judged that his ideas would get a fair hearing there, given its legacy as a slave-trading port. What he didn't take into account was the fact that most of the rest of the state had been first settled by New Englanders and had become perhaps an even greater abolitionist stronghold than Massachusetts itself. It was the home base of Frederick Douglass and antislavery philanthropist Gerrit Smith, a sanctuary for Harriet Tubman and John Brown, and contained the most important terminus of the Underground Railroad, at the gates of British Ontario. Unwisely Simms planned to start delivering his "South Carolina in the Revolution" speech in western New York and work

his way east before entering the lion's den in Boston and triumphantly ending his tour with a grand engagement in New York.

To arrange this he turned to New York's greatest resident historian,
George Bancroft, for assistance. Bancroft lent his weight to a committee of
Gotham luminaries, which included William Cullen Bryant, who organized
a series of lectures in the city and publicized Simms's willingness to appear
elsewhere in the state. Invitations poured in from Yonkers to Buffalo, as well
as Boston and New Haven. Simms left home in late October 1856, optimistic
that his tour would be financially profitable and intellectually triumphant.[2]

It was a disaster.

He gave his first speech in Buffalo on November 11 to a standing-room-
only audience of more than twelve hundred. Despite having a hoarse voice,
Simms thought the talk had gone well, as there had been frequent applause,
though the next morning he learned that "some of the Yankees took offense
at a showing of the history which they had never seen in Yankee books."
More likely, much of their offense was a response to Simms's having framed
the entire lecture as a reply to the remarks that Sumner had made before
Brooks had beaten him senseless, thus implying that he had deserved to be
violently assaulted.[3]

Sumner's attacks on South Carolina's Revolutionary zeal, Simms told his
Yankee audience, had "poured forth with a malignant satisfaction" to "goad
and mortify the natural pride and sensibility of a hated party." These
words—not Brooks's behavior—constituted an "assault" that was "gratu-
itously wanton, hostile to all the ends of council, and grossly subversive of
all the parliamentary & social proprieties." Furthermore, Simms promised
to show these charges were false, and in doing so reveal Sumner's assault
"so wholly gratuitous" as to have "darkened [his] moral vision" and led him
to "bear false witness." This, he proclaimed, was "an outrage upon sacred
histories," a "blow" aimed "at the Dead and the Living, the past, present and
future." He concluded with a warning that "our respective countries" might
fall into civil war with each other, lest the North meet his "demand for the
justice of my country."[4]

The Buffalo audience was, according to newspaper accounts, "coldly polite," but unimpressed with the visitor's aspersions of a man who was still recovering from an actual assault. The *Evening Post* called the speech "ill-digested, bitter and to at least nine-tenths of the audience, [an] offensive defense of South Carolina politicians of the Brooks school." The *Morning Express* was even harsher: "With an impudence unsurpassed, he comes into our midst and makes an harangue abusive of a Northern State and running over with fulsome and false praise of the least deserving State in the Union."[5]

By the time Simms reached Rochester on the thirteenth, his local hosts were fretting over these newspaper accounts and considered asking him to give a lecture on another topic. In the end he gave the talk again, this time in the Corinthian Hall, the very venue where local resident Frederick Douglass had delivered his famous "What Is the Fourth of July to a Slave?" speech. The audience of a thousand was not impressed, and the reviews were brutal. "As a literary production, it is destitute of merit and reflects no credit upon the writer of a series of passable novels," the *Rochester Democrat and Chronicle* opined. "As a lecture before a literary association, it is an imposition." While he was warmly entertained at a post-speech reception, Simms was deeply stung. Northerners, he decided, had "a lack of veneration" that led them to trample all authority and to refuse to "recognize anything as sacred." When he showed up in Syracuse, his hosts insisted he change the topic of his lecture.[6]

He hoped to receive better treatment in New York City on the eighteenth; when he arrived at the venue, the Church of the Divine Unity, George Bancroft was in the audience but only one hundred other people sat scattered within the building's cavernous interior. The next morning's *New-York Tribune* delivered a harsh verdict, and compared Simms's standing in South Carolina with that of Preston Brooks. "While Bully Brooks is feasted and loaded with presents and caresses on the strength of this single gutta-percha exploit"—a reference to the caning—"Mr. Simms . . . is turned over, in his declining age, to the cold charity and empty seats of Northern lecture rooms." By opening his speech with an attack on Sumner, the *Tribune* continued, it was "too much like a covert apology for the brutality of Bully Brooks."[7]

Two days later, when Simms was to give a second lecture, this time on the charms of the southern Appalachian Mountains, only six people turned up at the Divine Unity to hear him. The host committee had been unable to sell or even give away tickets. "The church was well lighted and warmed, but none of the committee having appeared, the sexton only admitted the people to the vestibule of the church," *The New York Herald* reported. After half an hour, "the lecturer still not appearing, the gas was turned off, the doors locked, and the assembly adjourned *sine die*, looking at their tickets." Simms canceled the remainder of his tour and, as he put it, "hastened home to my forest cover, with the feeling of the wounded hart flying to the thicket."[8]

The experience shook Simms to the core. Never again would he be quite as confident in himself, nor as healthy. "You have gone North at a somewhat critical time for *you* and martyred yourself for South Carolina, who will not even buy your books, and for Brooks, whose course could at best be only *excused*," a worried Hammond counseled as soon as he read the devastating reviews. "What Demon possessed you, *mon ami*, to do this?" Simms thereafter described the tour as "my defeat."[9]

From then on, he would make no further attempt to win over the people of the mid-Atlantic states. It was time to throw himself into the forging of a new federation, one where the specter of human equality would never again disturb the white man's hall.

TWENTY-EIGHT

Not three weeks after Simms's humiliation at Rochester's Corinthian Hall, a tall, slim man with a chiseled, weather-beaten face and deep gray eyes, "ready to spring at the least rustling," appeared on the streets of the town. He had fled Kansas with his sons and the other men in his gang after perpetrating murders there, and was now headed to Frederick Douglass's house.[1]

When he reached the door, John Brown was warmly welcomed. Douglass, aware that he was in town, had sent him a dinner invitation. Brown stepped into the safety of the Douglasses' hillside farmhouse, a brick home nestled in among the trees where the orator regularly hid escaped slaves en route to nearby Canada, as they were no longer safe outdoors even this far north after the passage of the Fugitive Slave Act.[2]

Brown and Douglass had stayed in touch since their first meeting in Springfield eight years earlier. Douglass undoubtedly knew that Brown had been commanding a guerrilla band in the Kansas Territory, where pro- and antislavery settlers had been fighting a civil war over the future status of the region. He knew of the sack and burning of Lawrence, the New Englander–settled capital of a self-fashioned free-soil government. Whether Douglass was yet aware of the murders Brown had committed in reaction to the attack on Lawrence—or the near-simultaneous beating of Sumner on the Senate floor—is unknown. In the middle of the night, Brown and his men had pulled pro-slavery (but non-slaveholding) settlers out of their beds, hacked them to death with broadswords, and chopped off their hands and limbs to terrorize the neighbors, wives, and children who would inevitably find the disfigured bodies. When Douglass did learn of what Brown had done in Kansas, he condoned his acts. "The horrors wrought by his iron hand cannot be contemplated without a shudder, but it is the shudder which one feels at the execution of a murderer," he would write. "The amputation of a limb is a severe trial to feeling, but necessity is a full justification of it to reason. To call out a murderer at midnight, and without note or warning, judge or jury, run him through with a sword, was a terrible remedy for a terrible malady."[3]

In the struggle against slavery, Douglass had long since abandoned pacifism in the face of desperate times. Some of his closest friends in the free black community had fled western New York, fearing kidnapping under the due-process-deficient Fugitive Slave Act. Douglass himself feared he could be seized, his manumission papers challenged on some technicality, and then transported back to Maryland, where he would likely be killed. Any optimism he had that white Americans would find and follow their moral compass had been shaken by the passage of the Kansas-Nebraska Act and by the newly aggressive behavior of slaveholders, as demonstrated by Representative Brooks's assault on Senator Sumner, an event he said "plainly foreshadowed a conflict on a wider scale." An epic struggle between freedom and autocracy, between the natural rights in the Declaration of Independence and the hierarchical world of white supremacists, was now upon the country, and he believed it had to be fought with deadly, righteous force. John Brown, whom an early biographer would call "a modern Hebrew prophet," was willing to do whatever needed to be done, however bloody, and Douglass admired him for it.[4]

What the two men discussed that night is unknown, but they kept in very close contact thereafter, visiting each other whenever the occasion arose. Over the next two years Douglass raised money to supply Brown's gang. He acted as the older man's banker, receiving and holding funds until Brown passed through Rochester and was able to pick them up. They met

on the road, sharing a stage in Worcester and, in Detroit, seeing off a group
of Kansas slaves Brown had escorted one thousand miles so that they could
make their way across the river to freedom in Upper Canada. There Harriet
Tubman had set up her headquarters in "Black Town," a neighborhood of St.
Catharines, Ontario, populated by fugitives from Maryland's Eastern Shore.[5]

In January 1858 Brown hid out for three weeks in Douglass's home
under an assumed name, writing letters to allies and making plans to build
a fortified guerrilla base in the mountains of western Virginia where escaped slaves could find sanctuary before being shuttled to the north via a
militarized Underground Railroad. He drew elaborate diagrams of the fort
on a pair of wide boards, intriguing Douglass's children, who would listen
to Brown's stories while seated on his knee. He spoke of wanting to capture
the contents of the federal government's greatest arsenal, located just across
the Potomac from the mountains of western Maryland in a place called
Harper's Ferry. He dreamed of sparking a slave rebellion that would overthrow the slave power of Virginia, and spent hours in an upstairs bedroom,
drafting a provisional constitution for his imagined free state. He was likely
corresponding with Tubman, who had been a guest at Douglass's home just
before Brown's arrival, and whom Brown would soon visit in St. Catharines,
where he had his constitution printed.[6]

Douglass approved of Brown's plans to deploy freedom fighters in the
Southern uplands to help liberate slaves. But of Brown's occasional mutter-
ings about capturing Harper's Ferry, he later wrote, "I paid but little attention." The plan was foolish, not least because it involved attacking a federal
installation, an act that would make allies into enemies and bring the full
force of Union arms against him, not just Virginia's militia. Douglass had
warned Brown of these likely consequences, and hoped he'd listened.[7]

He hadn't.

In mid-August 1859 Douglass received a letter from Brown asking him
to rendezvous with him at his hideout, a stone quarry outside Chambers-
burg, Pennsylvania. Douglass arrived, funds for Brown in hand, on August
19, and with the help of a local accomplice, found his friend dressed as a

fisherman and calling himself John Smith. Brown embraced him, brought him into his camp, and laid out his plan to seize the Harper's Ferry arsenal and thus provoke a mass slave uprising that would liberate Virginia. "I told him, and these were my words, that all his arguments and all his descriptions of the place convinced me that he was going into a perfect steel trap and that once in he would never get out alive," Douglass later recalled. "He was not to be shaken by anything I could say." Brown asked Douglass to join him in the raid, saying his presence would help rally slaves to join them, but Douglass refused, and they parted ways.[8]

Two months later Douglass was speaking to a large audience in Philadelphia's National Hall when news broke of Brown's raid, falling on everyone "with the startling effect of an earthquake." The next day came the reports Douglass had feared but expected: Brown had been surrounded by U.S. troops led by a colonel named Robert E. Lee. Hours later the telegraph wires reported that Lee's men had breached the fort, capturing a severely wounded Brown, whom they hanged shortly thereafter. In Brown's baggage were documents and letters incriminating several abolitionists, including Douglass himself, and a warrant was issued for Douglass's arrest. "All who were supposed to have been [in] any way connected with John Brown were to be hunted down and surrendered to the tender mercies of slaveholding and panic-stricken Virginia," Douglass recalled, "there to be tried after the fashion of John Brown's trial and of course to be summarily executed."[9]

With the help of friends, Douglass fled northward, retracing parts of the route he'd followed as a fugitive slave twenty-one years earlier. After an anxious steamship ride to New York, he feared the trains to Rochester would be watched, so he took a ferry across the Hudson River to New Jersey to access a less obvious rail route home. In Rochester his allies warned that New York's governor would be compelled to comply with any rendition request from his counterpart in Virginia, so Douglass continued on to Canada. With a presidential order seeking his arrest, he feared even this was not a safe refuge and turned to the United Kingdom for sanctuary, where he arrived in early December.[10]

Six months later the unexpected death of his teenage daughter drew him home, regardless of the risk. A congressional investigative committee on the Harper's Ferry raid had disbanded, unable to find the will to gather the evidence needed to prosecute alleged coconspirators. The indictment against him had been abandoned, and the only man jailed for refusing to testify had been released. "Great changes had now taken place in the public mind touching on the John Brown raid," he discovered on returning to Rochester in that summer of 1860. "Emerson's prediction that Brown's gallows would become like the cross was already being fulfilled."[11]

With the presidential contest already under way, it seemed the hour of national reckoning was finally at hand. "The road to the presidency does not lead through the swamps of compromise and concession any longer," Douglass declared in June, after the former Illinois congressman Abraham Lincoln won the new Republican Party's nomination. "It will be a great work accomplished, when this Government is divorced from the active support of the inhuman slave system. . . . To save a prospective empire, yet to be planted in the Great West, from the desecrating footprints of inhuman oppression . . . is a consummation devoutly to be wished."[12]

TWENTY-NINE

The voices of discontent among us are but the evanescent vapors of men's breath . . . our little domestic strifes are no more than momentary disturbances on the surface, easily settled among ourselves," George Bancroft told a Cleveland audience in September 1860, less than two months before Election Day. "The love of union has wound its cords indissolubly round the whole American people [and] . . . it will keep alive for mankind the beacon lights of popular liberty and power."[1]

Bancroft had not strayed from this message for the past six years, even as the federation stumbled into one crisis after another without being able to resolve any of them. He was opposed to the Fugitive Slave Act, to the Kansas-Nebraska Act, to the beating of Senator Sumner, and, indeed, to slavery itself, but in his private letters seemed more concerned that the "radicals" of the young Republican Party would gain control than that the divine Union might shatter.[2]

Strangely he had no interest in the voices of those who were most committed to his vision of the United States—a place that championed universal freedom and equality, a Republic by and for the people that would be a beacon to the world. He opposed the candidacy of Abraham Lincoln, a man he considered stupid, inarticulate, and unworthy of the White House. Instead he became a close confidant and supporter of Lincoln's rival, Stephen Douglas, the man who wrote the Kansas-Nebraska Act and who had made crude race baiting an integral part of his campaign.

As for Frederick Douglass, Bancroft never once mentioned his name in his letters, speeches, and journal articles, despite the activist's commitment to the very ideals championed in the *History*. His failure to do so may have been a product of his casual racism, which held that African Americans were in no condition to be free, though unlike Lincoln, he seemed to believe they would one day be worthy of it, with proper tutelage. "The beginning, the middle and the end of our troubles, the origin of the disturbances, and the difficulty of their adjustment, lies in the fact that we have four millions of semi-barbarous, semi-civilised men among us, who are unfit for the political franchises of citizens," he explained to an English friend the following year. "Their masters have not virtue enough to set about training them for freedom."[3]

Douglass, for his part, was disgusted with Bancroft's hypocrisy. When the historian proclaimed things like "Our country is bound to allure the world to Liberty by the beauty of its example," the pages of *Frederick Douglass' Paper*—successor to *The North Star*—responded with contempt. As one editorial stated:

> Mr. Bancroft says we are alluring the world to Liberty. How? By legislating in favor of Slavery? By pulling down the old barns of Slavery, and building greater. Where has Mr. Bancroft been living, that with all his wisdom and erudition, he has not found out, that the great object of this Government, as developed in its policy, is the extension, the consolidation, and the perpetuity of a system of robbery, and plunder, and oppression, aptly characterized the vilest that ever saw the sun? . . . We may preach about Freedom forever; but until the three and a half millions of men, women and children, now writhing in the dust, are emancipated from their thralldom, all our nonsensical rodomontade about free thought, and free discussion, and free institutions—all the unmeaning twaddle of Fourth of July orators concerning the "beauty of our example"—will be regarded by the "world," to which Mr. Bancroft alludes, as a sounding brass, and a tinkling cymbal.[4]

Perhaps it's no wonder Bancroft ignored him: every fiber of Douglass's being stood as a rebuke to the idea that America had truly embraced its stated ideals, and his words repeatedly drew attention to the powerful counter-ideology of white, preferably Anglo-Saxon, supremacy.

In the final years before the Union's collapse, Bancroft continued friendly correspondence with Senator James Mason (an apologist for the beating of Sumner), President James Buchanan (champion of the Supreme Court's *Dred Scott* decision, which declared blacks ineligible for citizenship), and William Gilmore Simms, even as the South Carolinian was calling for the creation of a slaveholder's Union—aristocratic, hierarchical, and devoted to the belief in human inequality and bondage—that would be the antithesis of everything Bancroft espoused. But he spent most of the time working on his books.[5]

In May 1858, while Douglass was plotting with John Brown, Bancroft returned to Charleston. He went sightseeing and among the places he visited were the Calhoun statue ("which I do not exactly like"), the promenade on the Battery (full of "jumping children"), and the Sugar House, a walled torture complex where slaveholders could pay fees to have their slaves punished and incarcerated in tiny cells. Punishment, he observed to his wife, "is regulated with science; from [the] kinds of leathern paddles [approved] for flogging—twenty two cents the price of a single flogging; the blows are not one time to exceed twenty, and the instrument [is] so contrived, that it may inflict pain but not hurt the future [value] of the negro." It was during this trip that he concluded that slaves were content with their condition, a notion that Simms had been promoting in his novels for decades. "The slave loves the air, the Soil, the Sun, the water, of Georgia," he wrote after a tour of the Savannah River Valley, "and will rather spend his earnings in pleasure than buy his freedom at the cost of [separation from] his sweet native Soil."[6]

Later he enjoyed tea at Simms's Charleston town house while the master's daughter Mary played the piano. Simms and his wife took Bancroft on a delightful five-mile carriage ride "through flowering trees, pines and live oak." He enjoyed gracious evenings discussing ideas, history, and morals with the social and intellectual elite of the city, the whole party walking him back to the hotel on at least one memorable evening. "No one of that party thought then of dissolving the Union," Bancroft recalled, "as under the bright moon, after the still hour of midnight, we still lingered between the gardens brilliant with the bloom of the pink and the white oleander, or walked along the streets that resounded to no voices but our own."[7]

Thirteen months later, those same blossom-strewn walkways echoed with the thunderous sound of South Carolinian artillery shells falling on the Federal troops stationed in the harbor.

THIRTY

Simms may well have been distracted during Bancroft's visit. He had returned from New York a humiliated man, but remained a hero to South Carolinians. While Northern newspapers continued to mock him—*The Boston Daily Atlas* called his lectures "stupid" and Simms "a martyr to his own dullness"—*The Charleston Mercury* lauded him as a regional treasure. "To no one born and bred in our midst is the meed of praise more justly due," the editors wrote. "Our children have learned from his Revolutionary stories and tales of border warfare, their earliest and most impressive lessons of patriotic devotion, and our Southern statesmen have gathered from his historic ages their most full and conclusive arguments for the defense of a people basely and slanderously assailed." Lecture invitations poured in from across the South, and Simms spent much of the first three months of 1857 on the road, speaking at the Smithsonian and in most major cities between Charleston and Baltimore, receiving rave reviews at every appearance.[1]

The paid speaking events were welcome, as Simms had lost nearly $3,000 on the Northern tour. He had been forced to take loans from James Henry Hammond just to keep afloat and maintain the plantation. *The Southern Quarterly Review* folded in 1857, still owing him back wages. Reliant on his writing for working capital, he published eighteen books in the 1850s, and the quality and sales of most suffered from having been rushed into print.[2]

Between 1856 and 1859 Chevillette gave birth to their eleventh, twelfth, and thirteenth children and she was often sick and frail. Her father, Nash Roach, died in February 1858, leaving her the estate, but with binding strictures preventing Simms from liquidating assets to pay their debts. Far more devastating was the death from yellow fever of two of their sons—Sydney Roach (age seven) and Beverley Hammond Simms (four years old)—on the same day in September 1858. The Simmses had now lost seven of their children. "Oh! dear Hammond, weep for me! I am crushed to earth," Simms wrote to his friend. "I feel heart broken, hope crushed and altogether wretched." Over the coming year he fell into a deep depression, becoming an invalid "uneasy of brain and anxious of thought and sad at heart and wearied with troubles and full of cares." He had bleeding ulcers, rashes on his face, and sometimes had trouble walking. He was only fifty-three but felt himself an old man.[3]

Unlike Bancroft, Simms knew that the Union was collapsing. South Carolina, he told his friends, could not long remain within it in the aftermath of the Sumner caning, John Brown's raid, and what he regarded as Northern hysteria over the Fugitive Slave Act and the *Dred Scott* decision. He considered it his life's mission to persuade South Carolina's fellow states to leave with her and to help them forge a new, common identity as a Southern people and nation. Acutely aware of the regional geography of the South, Simms knew that the culture he championed didn't extend to the upland states of Tennessee and Kentucky dominated by the Scots-Irish, or even to Virginia, North Carolina, Maryland, and Delaware, where demographics and soil depletion had disrupted lowland slaveholders' control over state capitals. "Who are our Sister States? Not the South, but the Cotton States," he told Hammond. The goal should be to get out of the Union with at least two or three other cotton states and as many concessions as possible from the North. Liberated from federal tariffs and Yankee interference in their "peculiar institution," the prosperity of this Deep Southern confederation would draw the other slaveholding states into her orbit—first, any stragglers on the Gulf of Mexico, and then North Carolina,

Virginia, Tennessee, and Kentucky, if not others. "You may rest assured that all of this is going to happen, just as I tell you," he advised his friend Congressman William Porcher Miles.[4]

This new confederation would be "bound together by the cohesive bond of African slavery," which he judged to be a far more stable foundation on which to rest than that of the United States. Pennsylvania, New York, and New England had little to hold them together, leaving them "deadly rivals." Slavery, he argued publicly, would give this entity "all the essential elements for establishing the greatest and most prosperous, and longest lived of all the republics of the earth." It had allowed Deep Southern society to "reconcile the great problem now threatening all Europe and all the North—the struggle between capital and labor. Our labor is our capital." Whereas the United States had been little more than a political union, a Southern confederation could be a true nation, a community based on common feeling, customs, and values, not just logic and reason. "We will assume all the moral responsibilities of our institutions," he told Northerners in an open letter printed by newspapers across the Union, "and the adjustment of the account will then rest entirely betwixt God and ourselves."[5]

For Simms and his many allies in the planter class, there was considerable frustration with the cautious stance of the state's political leaders. The people, Simms complained, were far ahead of them on the road to nationhood. "We want thunderbolts, not gossamer, for the combat," he advised Representative Miles.[6]

But in November 1857 they had an incredible stroke of fortune.

With his nemesis Wade Hampton living out of state, Hammond was elected by the South Carolina legislature to occupy the U.S. Senate seat left vacant by Butler's death earlier that year, even though the disgraced governor hadn't been seeking the office. "All this is most extraordinary and to me astounding," Hammond wrote in his diary. "This is a signal triumph over all my enemies and, speaking as a mere mortal, a full compensation and more for all I have endured." Hammond, in poor health and having not kept abreast of national affairs, turned to Simms for advice, which his friend offered in copious detail. The primary goal, he advised, was to extract the South from the Union. Hammond agreed.[7]

On March 4, 1858, Hammond was catapulted to celebrity when he gave a speech in the Senate glorifying inequality, slavery, and authoritarian republicanism. Dressed in black and speaking slowly, he compared labor and political relations in the North and the South: "In all social systems there must be a class to do the menial duties, to perform the drudgery of life . . . a class requiring but a low order of intellect and but little skill," he began.

> Such a class you must have, or you would not have that other class which leads progress, civilization, and refinement. It constitutes the very mud-sill of society and of political government; and you might as well attempt to build a house in the air, as to build either the one or the other, except on this mud-sill. Fortunately for the South, she found a race adapted to that purpose to her hand—a race inferior to her own, but eminently qualified in temper, in vigor, in docility, in capacity to stand the climate, to answer all her purposes. We use them for our purpose, and call them slaves. . . . They are happy, content, unaspiring, and utterly incapable, from intellectual weakness, ever to give us any trouble by their aspirations.
>
> Yours are white, of your own race; you are brothers of one blood. They are your equals in natural endowment of intellect, and they feel galled by their degradation. Our slaves do not vote. We give them no political power. Yours do vote; and, being the majority, they are the depositaries of all your political power. If they knew the tremendous secret, that the ballot-box is stronger than "an army with banners," and could combine, where would you be? Your society would be reconstructed, your government overthrown, your property divided, not as they have mistakenly attempted to initiate such proceedings by meeting in parks, with arms in their hands, but by the quiet process of the ballot-box.[8]

This "mud-sill speech" was condemned across the North for its repudiation of the values embedded in the Declaration, fought for by Douglass, and celebrated in Bancroft's *History*: freedom, universal equality, and self-government. It was praised in the Southern lowlands for precisely the same reason. Simms declared it "eminently able and true" and wished only that Hammond had gone further. "He grapples the bull by the horns; but I hold it to be only the entering wedge."[9]

Hammond and Simms were not isolated voices. George Fitzhugh, scion of one of Virginia's most prominent planter families, argued in *The Southern Literary Messenger* that the slave states were effectively engaged in a counterrevolution, "a rolling back of the excesses of the Reformation—of Reformation run mad—a solemn protest against the doctrines of natural liberty, human equality and the social contract, as taught by Locke and the American sages of 1776, and an equally solemn protest against the doctrines of Adam Smith, Franklin, Say, Tom Paine, and the rest of the infidel political economists who maintain that the world is too much governed." Southerners would end the Founders' "profane attempt to pull down what God and nature had built up, and to erect ephemeral Utopias in its place."[10]

To further differentiate themselves from Northerners, many Southern intellectuals began arguing that the ruling class of the slave South was descended from the aristocratic Normans, who in 1066 had conquered England's crude, disorderly Saxons, from whom New England's people descended. The latter, the Alabama planter William Falconer argued in the *Messenger*, were "inherently destitute of capacity for control" and unable to "command obedience," while the former "come of that race to whom law and order, obedience and command, are convertible terms, and who *do* command, the world over, whether the subject be African or Caucasian, Celt or Saxon." In *De Bow's Review*, the Deep South's leading journal, the Mississippi attorney John Quitman Moore argued natural rights theory had been "the poisoned chalice which bacchanal statesmen pressed to the lips of the youthful nation" and in a Confederate constitution should be snuffed out in favor of an aristocratic autocracy led by a hereditary senate and presidency drawn exclusively from the landed elite. Such a system was "best suited to the genius, and most expressive of the ideas of Southern civilization" and "the exigencies of a vast empire, stretching from the Potomac to the Amazon, from the Atlantic to the Rocky mountains and the Andes, comprising Mexico, Central America, and the Indies, and resting upon the principle of the subordination of races."[11]

Shortly after he arrived in the Senate, Hammond began scheming to get Simms appointed to occupy South Carolina's other seat, whose occupant had just died. "If I could name a colleague," he wrote Simms in early April, "I mean to name you." Simms feebly protested that he had given up such hopes, and became excited when he heard a false rumor that he had been chosen, but in the end Arthur Hayne, brother of a former governor and senator, received the post. Hammond and others kept pushing for legislators to elect Simms to take over when Hayne's term ended later in the year, but nothing came of it.

The two men also held out hope that Hammond might receive the Democratic nomination for president in 1860, believing he could rally the South and supervise the dissolution of the failed Union. When Illinois senator Stephen Douglas won the nomination instead, they knew that Abraham Lincoln would win the general election and that South Carolina would secede.

Days after the vote Simms was elated. The North would split apart. California and other West Coast possessions would become independent republics. Shut out of the riches of the Southern cotton trade, Pennsylvania, Maryland, and even New York might seek to join the slaveholders' republic on Southern terms. Militia units were forming in every precinct—"squads of minute men," Simms called them—but he believed there would be no need to use them, as the Yankees would quickly see they had no choice but to accept the end of the Union.

"A war would destroy the whole confederacy of the North and make that of the South supreme," he assured Lawson in New York. "There will be no war."[12]

THIRTY-ONE

Sixty-five miles to the west, a three-year-old boy named Tommy Wilson was standing outside the gate of his brick home on Seventh Street in the center of Augusta, Georgia, looking across at the First Presbyterian Church, where his father was pastor.

A man walked by, speaking with intense excitement about the news that had just broken: Mr. Lincoln had been elected, that there was to be war.

Perplexed, the boy ran up the steps into the manse to find his father and ask him what it meant. The import of this moment stayed with the boy, given all that was to come. It would be his earliest memory.[1]

As an adult Tommy Wilson would go by his middle name, Woodrow.

THIRTY-TWO

When war finally broke out, Simms was caught flatfooted. He had been so confident of peace that he had convinced James Lawson to send his seventeen-year-old son, Jimmy, to Woodlands for an extended stay at the end of the year. As late as December 19, 1860, he was bragging to Lawson about how much food he had stowed away. "If you should get to starving times in N.Y., you have only to ship your women and children to me, prepared to eat hog and hominy, and live in dry walls away from the chariots and the horsemen," he joked with his friend.[1]

A fortnight later, after arranging weeks of charming dinner parties, serene horseback rides, and late-night coon-hunting expeditions for the boy with his son William Gilmore Simms III, Simms was at a loss as to how to get young Lawson back north to his family. Federal troops and the state militia were in an armed showdown over control of the forts in Charleston Harbor, and Simms realized an attack on Fort Sumter could take place at any moment. Steamship service had been suspended out of Charleston, so Simms had to send the boy to Savannah, even though he wasn't sure how long the steamers would be running from there, either. If fighting broke out on the seaboard, he instructed the boy, "You come back to me."[2]

Young Lawson managed to get away safely, but Simms was alarmed by the complacency of his fellow South Carolinians, who seemed unaware of and unprepared for the potential military dangers confronting them. To former congressman Miles, now an aide-de-camp to General P. G. T. Beauregard, he wrote detailed advice on how to improve Charleston's defenses, and in *The Charleston Mercury* he decried the lack of preparations to repel a potential Union landing on the nearby seacoast. His counsel was sound, but largely ignored, and by November 1861—seven months after the assault on Fort Sumter—Port Royal, Hilton Head, and much of the south coast of the state were under Federal occupation and would remain so for the rest of the war. "I was fated like Cassandra to speak the truth with nobody to listen," Simms fumed to Hammond.[3]

By now Simms was out of molasses, wool, and shoes and could find none to buy, leaving his slaves inadequately clothed and without the sugary treats Simms included in their rations to "keep them in sweet temper." His overseer had gone off to war, and his eldest son was enrolled as a cadet at the Citadel. With the ports blockaded, he and other planters couldn't export their cotton. New York and Pennsylvania had not seceded from the Union, as he had expected, and he suddenly lost access to his publishers, agent, copyrights, and royalty income. While he had faith in President Jefferson Davis and the new government of the Confederate States of America, he was unimpressed with South Carolina's leadership. "God send us relief and rescue," he told Hammond eight months into the war. "It is hardly to be found in our own men."[4]

Personal tragedies afflicted him as well. A son, not yet two, died that summer, and his three-year-old daughter, Harriet, perished on Christmas Day. Shortly after her burial, four-year-old Govan was ill with the same disease. "I have no longer any sense of security. My days and nights teem with apprehension," he confided to Miles. "I am under these successive shocks, growing feebler, rapidly aging, and shudder with a continued sense of winter at my hearth."

Three months later, on March 28, 1862, Simms was awoken at 3:00 a.m. by a bright light and discovered the attic of his house was on fire. His slaves were called in to save as many possessions as possible from destruction, and with a ladder they rescued Simms himself from an upper window moments before the cornice crashed down. The library wing of the house was saved, but the main building and its contents were destroyed, a loss he estimated at $10,000, nearly half the value of the entire Woodlands property. The only silver lining Simms could find in this catastrophe was the evidence, literally tested under fire, that his slaves had "no lack of love for their master."[5]

His uninsured Charleston town house having burned down two years earlier, Simms and his family moved into the Woodlands library and a pair of outbuildings. As he sat in a corner of his carriage house and looked out on the remains of his cherished home, Simms believed himself cursed by an angry Fate, tenaciously striking at him, each blow worse than the last. "Now that my homestead is in ruins, it would seem that the next shaft would properly be aimed at the Master," he scrawled on parchment.[6]

THIRTY-THREE

On December 10, 1861, on the eve of the first cold snap of winter, George Bancroft arrived in Washington, a city fortified against a siege, to try to roust the president of the United States into action.[1]

On the train he'd seen the evidence of the precarious state of the Union. As he crossed Maryland—a state divided by slavery—he saw soldiers posted at every bridge and station, while other detachments patrolled the fields between, ready to repel saboteurs. From Baltimore onward pickets were stationed every quarter mile along the tracks, with large encampments appearing frequently at the sidings. The train passed through the cordon of fortifications surrounding the capital, and the unfinished dome of the U.S. Capitol came into view, covered in scaffolds and surrounded by work sheds and building materials. Months earlier pro-Confederate mobs had torn up the rails and cut the telegraph wires, halting Washington's communications with the outside world for a week and leaving its inhabitants fearing that Confederate troops would overwhelm the city, capture the president, and drive Congress into exile. Now the capital was an island in a slaveholders' sea, linked to the free states by this one tenuous railway conduit.[2]

Bancroft, now sixty-one with whitening hair and muttonchops, was filled with trepidation. Secession and war had struck him like a pair of thunderbolts. Contrary to God's plan, the Union had shattered, his call to freedom and equality having been abandoned by half the country. In this time of crisis Providence had passed the nation's leadership into the most incapable hands imaginable, those of the ungainly country lawyer he'd met in Springfield six years before, a man without education, refinement, vision, or intelligence. "We have a president without brains," he'd recently written to his wife, adding that his hope lay in the fact that "God takes care of the daft." Lincoln's administration, he complained to a friend after Union forces had been routed at Manassas, an important Virginia rail junction just outside Washington, "was not for the moment equal to the national emergency" and "hardly more than suited for summer wear." "A bark canoe in a tempest on mid-ocean," he would later write, "seemed hardly less safe."[3]

Over the course of the war's first eight months, Bancroft had reconciled recent events with his Providential vision for the country. Slavery, he now more fully appreciated, was an affront to the natural rights of man and thus America's purpose and destiny. "It was a slow poison, daily contaminating the minds and morals of [Southern] people," he concluded. "By reducing a part of their own species to abject inferiority, they lost the idea of the dignity of man, which the hand of Nature had implanted within them for great and useful purposes." He excused his own role in the crisis by convincing himself that, had Texas not been annexed, it would have somehow conquered California for slavery, and that Northern Democrats' compromise with slavery had not taken place until after the 1848 election, which was coincidentally exactly when he had retired from politics. He also convinced himself that it was only the Southern oligarchs, a vestigial feudal contagion bequeathed from Europe, who backed slavery and rebellion, and that the common people of the South had been duped into joining a revolt against human liberty. "Slavery was an anomaly in a democratic country," he had concluded. "The doctrine of liberty is proved true, by the fact it will not be reconciled with slavery."[4]

Four weeks earlier he'd written to Lincoln to alert him to his findings. "Your administration has fallen on hard times, which will be remembered as long as human events find a record," he told the president. "Civil war is the instrument of Divine Providence to root out social slavery; posterity will not be satisfied with the result, unless the consequences of the war shall effect an increase of Free states." Lincoln wrote back immediately that it was "a high honor" to have received a note from the esteemed historian, and assured him he was well aware of the gravity of the situation, "with which I must deal in all due caution, and with the best judgment I can bring to it." Not satisfied with Lincoln's response, Bancroft had decided to deliver his advice in person.[5]

While in Washington, Bancroft toured the U.S. Army camps perched on the wooded heights of Arlington on the Virginia side of the Potomac. This required crossing the mile-long span of Long Bridge, showing a pass to the guards, and ascending the hills to the mansion of General Robert E. Lee, now inhabited by Union officers and surrounded by tents and artillery emplacements. From the heights he could see the campfires of the Confederate army, camped outside Falls Church, Langley, and Alexandria, and across the river behind him, the stub of the Washington Monument, whose upward ascent had been suspended by the conflict. He chatted with soldiers and met with classmates of his son, John Chandler Bancroft, who was serving with the Army Corps of Engineers. Nobody had much complimentary to say about their superiors. Visiting the lines a few months earlier, a veteran war correspondent for the London *Times* had found substandard artillery; unseasoned, poorly disciplined troops, and a lack of cavalry; such forces "may be good for Indians," he would write, but they "would go over like ninepins" in the face of an experienced foe. Bancroft, a former acting war secretary, was likewise concerned. "Keeping down my sorrow at heart for the woes of our poor country," he wrote to his wife, "which under incompetent hands is going fast to ruin."[6]

His audience with Lincoln took place on December 15 at 3:00 p.m.

Lincoln was lank and tall, with long limbs and large feet, and was clad in an ill-tailored suit. He typically approached visitors with what the London *Times*'s William Russell had called "a shambling, loose, irregular, almost unsteady gait." He was not, Russell reported, someone who would be mistaken for a gentleman. "He spoke with ease and clearness but not with eloquence," Bancroft would later say of him. "He had no accurate knowledge of the public defences of the country, no exact conception of its foreign relations, no comprehensive perception of his duties." This, he despaired, was the man who "must now venture a struggle for the life or death of the nation."[7]

Lincoln surely recognized Bancroft's pomposity and condescension but appreciated the lifelong Democrat's righteous condemnation of slavery and the corrosive effects it had on the Republic. Lincoln had almost certainly read portions of the eight volumes of the *History* that had been published to date, for their vision of America's spiritual mission was one he had already begun to make his own. (When the two later met at a White House reception in February 1864, Lincoln's face lit up. He swung a hand over his head and said: "Hold on—I know you, you are—*History of the United States*—Mr., Mr. Bancroft, Mr. George Bancroft!")

Bancroft's mission had been to convince Lincoln that the conflict was fundamentally about promoting the nation's destiny by defeating the slave-holders' uprising, and he worried that he had not gotten through to the seemingly dull-witted president. Lincoln told him he believed "slavery had received a mortal wound, that the harpoon has struck the whale to the heart," as Bancroft wrote to Elizabeth. "This I am far from being able to see." However, his conference with Lincoln did change the historian's perspective. Before the meeting, he'd predicted the war would roll back the expansion of slavery, ensuring it would slowly die of attrition in the South itself; afterward he became convinced that the war must vanquish it entirely everywhere.[8]

At the meeting's end, Lincoln asked if his guest would like to meet the new commanding general of the U.S. Army, George McClellan, whose headquarters was in a mansion several blocks away. When Bancroft said yes, the president pulled on his boots and walked him there himself.[9]

THIRTY-FOUR

T wenty months later, on August 10, 1863, Frederick Douglass also found himself in a Baltimore & Ohio passenger car, trundling southward across Maryland.

He was alone and back in his native state, where his former master still lived and many of his siblings were still enslaved, riding the very rails on which he had fled to freedom. In the twenty-four years since, whenever he arrived in Philadelphia he had felt he "was rubbing against my prison wall and could not go any further" for fear of being kidnapped and dragged back across the Mason-Dixon Line. He knew that if secessionist mobs could attack and kill Union soldiers on the streets of Baltimore they would be even more eager to do away with the nation's most famous and recognizable black activist, one who wanted slaves to murder their masters and who had given succor to John Brown.[1]

He, too, was in Washington to have an audience with the president.

Lincoln, to Douglass's elated surprise, had issued the Emancipation Proclamation on New Year's Day, a document that for all its qualifications and limited scope had, he knew, been "the turning-point in the conflict between freedom and slavery. A death-blow was then given to the slave-holding rebellion." Though it only abolished slavery where it did not already exist and theoretically would expire with the conflict, Douglass was aware that it implied more than it directly stated. It had a "spirit, a life and power beyond its letter," a federal commitment that tacitly acknowledged what he had always believed: that securing the Union required the extinction of slavery, both tactically—slavery being the keystone of the Confederate economy—and practically, as the events of the 1850s and the rhetoric of the Hammonds and Fitzhughs of the world had shown that black slavery and white liberty were incompatible.[2]

The Proclamation also made possible the recruitment of black soldiers into the Union army, and Douglass threw himself into enlisting as many as possible. "Let the black man get upon his person the brass letters, U.S.," he said, "and there is no power on the earth or under the earth which can deny that he has earned the right of citizenship." His own sons, Lewis and Charles, joined the Fifty-fourth Massachusetts Regiment, the black unit led by white abolitionist Robert Gould Shaw. But Douglass's efforts were stymied by two obstacles. The first was a Confederate decree promising to execute all black prisoners of war and any white officers found leading them. The other was the U.S. War Department's discriminatory policies, by which black recruits were paid less than white ones, denied enlistment bonuses, and barred from becoming commissioned officers. "When I plead for recruits, I want to do it with my heart," he lamented, "without qualification."[3]

Now, though he had no appointment, he was seeking to tell Lincoln in person.

Douglass's overnight train rolled into the B&O Depot on New Jersey Avenue in the early morning, and he stepped onto the unpaved street a block north of the U.S. Capitol. He was dressed in an overcoat and tie, had no luggage, and, unsure of his safety this far south, intended to return northward that evening. As he walked up C Street and Pennsylvania Avenue toward the White House he likely saw runaway slaves everywhere. There were approximately twelve thousand in the District of Columbia, where Congress had banned slavery ten months earlier. Some were shoeless and in rags, and others were dying of typhoid, smallpox, and the measles, all of which had broken out in the city. Union soldiers were also evident throughout the city, some hungover, some missing limbs, others rushing from one post to another. The Union's failed offensive in Virginia the previous summer had flooded the city with injured soldiers and the battles since, in western Maryland and the Virginia outskirts of Washington, had pressed hotels, churches, schools, and government buildings into service as hospitals. Instead of ending quickly, the war had turned into a steam-, rifle-, and artillery-powered bloodbath.[4]

In a stroke of luck Douglass ran into an ally on the street. The former Massachusetts legislator Samuel Pomeroy, a "Radical" Republican who now represented Kansas in the Senate, immediately offered to escort his friend to the War Department. On arriving, Douglass was granted a half-hour meeting with Secretary of War Edwin Stanton, who said he agreed that black soldiers should be treated equally, but then fabricated an account claiming that the Senate had defeated the necessary legislation. Douglass left the meeting encouraged, and with a pass granting the former slave freedom of movement; he headed straight for the White House.[5]

At that time members of the public could still freely enter into the executive mansion, and Douglass found a huge crowd on the stairway, all seeking to see the chief executive. "They were white; and as I was the only dark spot among them, I expected to have to wait at least half a day," Douglass told an audience not long thereafter. "I had heard of men waiting a week." He presented one of his business cards to the clerk and, in the stifling August heat, steeled himself for the ordeal.[6]

To his shock, the clerk returned two minutes later and took him straight to Lincoln's office. As he elbowed his way through the throng he could hear one man say in a despairing voice: "Yes, damn it, I knew they would let the nigger through." Douglass would later joke the man must have been a Peace Democrat, a member of the Northern faction that opposed war with the Confederacy. The president was sprawled on a chair that was too small for his six-foot-four frame, "his feet in different parts of the room, taking it easy," Douglass recalled. "As I came in and approached him, the President began to rise and he continued rising until he stood over me."[7]

Lincoln reached out his hand and shook his guest's warmly. "Mr. Douglass, I know you," he said in a tone that completely disarmed the fiery activist. "I have read about you and Mr. Seward"—the secretary of state—"has told me about you." The president, who had also been born in a dirt-floored log cabin, treated his guest as an equal and a gentleman. "I never met with a man who, on the first blush, impressed me more entirely with his sincerity," Douglass recalled months later.[8]

Douglass reiterated his message, hoping to prompt "a discourse" from the president. Lincoln readily complied, explaining that while he shared Douglass's goals, success depended on strategic patience and a carefully calculated sequence of incremental measures. Douglass complained that while Lincoln had recently issued orders to execute one Confederate for each black prisoner of war killed by the rebels, he had waited to make that decision until after the slaughter of hundreds of black Union captives. Lincoln explained that the latter had to happen before whites would support retaliation. "He knew that the colored man throughout this country was a despised man, a hated man, and that if he at first came out with such a proclamation, all the hatred which is poured onto the head of the negro race would be visited on his administration," Douglass recalled. Lincoln promised that black soldiers would eventually get equal pay, but the initial pay disparity had been necessary to secure the acceptance of their ever being armed and inducted into the army. Lincoln also took issue with an accusation Douglass had made in a recent speech that the president was a vacillator. "I have been charged with being tardy and the like," Lincoln said, and agreed that may have been true, but as for vacillating, he explained, "Mr. Douglass, I do not think that charge can be sustained; I think it cannot be shown that when I have once taken a position, I have ever retreated from it."[9]

Douglass left the meeting with an entirely changed opinion of the president. He realized that, though their tactics were different, they shared a vision of what America should be. "Abraham Lincoln will not go down to posterity as Abraham the Great or as Abraham the Wise or as Abraham the Eloquent, although he is all three," he told a Philadelphia crowd a few months later. "He will go down to posterity, if the country is saved, as Honest

Abraham," and his name would be etched side by side with that of Washington. The interview had, he wrote a friend on the way home, done "much to assure me that slavery would not survive the War and that the Country would survive both Slavery and the War."[10]

For his part, Lincoln did not record a reaction to this meeting, but he clearly saw Douglass as an ally in his quest to save the Union, a living affirmation of the path the president was preparing to point the nation toward.

THIRTY-FIVE

At nearly midnight on November 18, 1863, the president of the United States was still bent over his papers in an upstairs room of a modest home in the little crossroads village of Gettysburg, Pennsylvania, composing a speech he was to deliver the next morning.

Surrounding the town, in the fields and along the ridges, in makeshift graves and hastily covered trenches, were the bodies of at least seven thousand soldiers who had died in three days of fighting there that summer. General Lee's advance into the North had been driven back, leaving the dead and wounded scattered under a blistering July sun.

Soldiers and Confederate prisoners had haphazardly buried the bodies, with the arms and even heads of the deceased sometimes protruding from the soil, and marked the graves with boards on which they had penciled the names and units of the Union dead. Thousands of family members had descended on the wasteland, digging up corpses in search of their loved ones, sometimes leaving hair and body parts strewn about on the fields. By August the stench was unbearable, and pigs had begun rooting in the trenches. A local banker, David Wills, Lincoln's host, had alerted Pennsylvania governor Andrew Curtin to the situation, and soon found himself placed in charge of preparing a new national cemetery for the Union dead. In late October his contractors had begun the process of exhuming, identifying, and reburying 3,512 soldiers, a task they were still carrying out when Lincoln arrived there. They wouldn't finish until March, but the cemetery was scheduled to be dedicated in the morning, with the president to speak after the main oration.[1]

He'd been too busy at the White House to prepare the speech, and some claimed they had seen him working on a draft on the train, using his top hat as a makeshift writing table, but the cars were filled with dignitaries—cabinet secretaries, foreign ambassadors, members of Congress, generals—who would have wanted to converse with him. He'd had no free time since his evening arrival at the Gettysburg station, where stacks of empty coffins were piled. Wills and the main orator of the day, Bancroft's old friend and mentor Edward Everett, had walked the president to Wills's home on the main square, where both men and Governor Curtin were staying and where dinner awaited. Every home and building was filled with visitors who'd come to witness the cemetery's dedication, and hundreds crowded into the main square eager to hear the president. Lincoln stepped out, thanked them for their warm welcome, and declined their invitation to speak, as he had nothing prepared and "in my position it is somewhat important that I should not say any foolish things." A voice in the crowd called out, "If you can help it!" and Lincoln rejoined: "It very often happens that the only way to help it is to say nothing at all," causing the crowd to break into laughter. Only late in the night, after he had finished his dinner, did he find the time to write.[2]

The following morning Lincoln rode a horse in the formal procession to Cemetery Hill and sat in the front row to listen to Everett deliver his speech. It was a tour de force of erudition and scholarship, a two-hour-long oratory steeped in and referencing the tradition of ancient Greek funeral speeches, tracing the origins and progress of the war and the Battle of Gettysburg's place in it before concluding with a quotation from Pericles's funeral oration for the Athenian dead in the Peloponnesian War: "The whole earth is the sepulcher of illustrious men." As the crowd applauded Lincoln stood, grasped Everett's hand, and said, "I am grateful to you."[3]

Then Lincoln climbed onto the stage, clutching a sheet of paper, and, looking out on the crowd of nine thousand, delivered a two-minute, 271-word speech that distilled the vision of national purpose Bancroft had laid out in a million words of historical text and the appeals to achieve those ideals expressed by Douglass in hundreds of speeches, and joined them in a call for a national rebirth. "Four score and seven years ago," he began, referencing 1776, not 1789,

> our fathers brought forth on this continent, a new nation, conceived in Liberty, and dedicated to the proposition that all men are created equal.
>
> Now we are engaged in a great civil war, testing whether that nation, or any nation so conceived and so dedicated, can long endure. We are met on a great battle-field of that war. We have come to dedicate a portion of that field, as a final resting place for those who here gave their lives that that nation might live. It is altogether fitting and proper that we should do this.
>
> But, in a larger sense, we can not dedicate—we can not consecrate—we can not hallow—this ground. The brave men, living and dead, who struggled here, have consecrated it, far above our poor power to add or detract. The world will little note, nor long remember what we say here, but it can never forget what they did here. It is for us the living, rather, to be dedicated here to the unfinished work which they who fought here have thus far so nobly advanced. It is rather for us to be here dedicated to the great task remaining before us—that from these honored dead we take increased devotion to that cause for which they gave the last full measure of devotion—that we here highly resolve that these dead shall not have died in vain—that this nation, under God, shall have a new birth of freedom—and that government of the people, by the people, for the people, shall not perish from the earth.[4]

As he stepped away from the podium, the crowd was at first silent, not realizing that the president had ended, and then finally burst into applause.

Lincoln had consecrated not just the cemetery, but the war itself, defining it as a test of humanity's ability to live in a state of freedom, equality, and self-governance. He had reaffirmed America's as-yet-unmet national purpose as articulated in the Declaration of Independence, and called on its people to persevere in the existential struggle for its survival. For those who believed in this conception of the American purpose, these were words that would never be forgotten.

Across the North the dominant reaction to Lincoln's speech was ecstatic. *The Press* of Philadelphia deemed it "immortal," while *The Providence Journal* said "the most elaborate, splendid oration" could not be "more beautiful, more touching, more inspiring, than those thrilling words of the President." It had captured "the very spirit of the day," the *Detroit Advertiser & Tribune* declared.[5]

Bancroft was so taken with the speech that he asked the president to write out a copy. The resulting document, in Lincoln's hand, remained with the Bancroft family until 1949, when it was sold at auction. A few years later it was bequeathed to the American people; today it is displayed in the Lincoln Bedroom and is considered the definitive version of the Gettysburg Address. On Election Day in 1864, the lifelong Democrat would cast his ballot for the man whose intelligence he had so often derided.[6]

An ecstatic Douglass memorized the president's words and over the next seventeen months would remind him of them whenever Lincoln had, in Douglass's opinion, failed to uphold them. When Lincoln asked Congress to make emancipation permanent, Douglass attacked him for not extending full voting and citizenship rights to blacks as well. However little patience he had for Lincoln's nuanced political calculations, Douglass knew the president shared his vision. He would come to describe Lincoln as a "great and good man, one of the noblest men [to] trod God's earth."[7]

Those who did not share this vision, who continued to believe that the American nation was intended to be the homeland of an Anglo-Norman or Anglo-Saxon or simply a "white" people, did not hold the address in such high regard. The pro-slavery *Chicago Times* called it "a perversion of history so flagrant" that it could only have been willful, and charged Lincoln with linking the national purpose to the Declaration of Independence rather than the Constitution, with its tacit endorsement of slavery. "It was to uphold this constitution, and the Union created by it, that our officers and soldiers gave their lives at Gettysburg," it declared. "How dared he, then, standing on their graves, misstate the cause for which they died, and libel the statesmen who founded the government? They were men possessing too much self-respect to declare that negroes were their equals, or were entitled to equal privileges."[8]

Southerners received almost no news of Lincoln's speech. The Richmond papers, from which the rest of the Confederate press freely borrowed, carried extensive coverage of the parade and Everett's speech, but led their readers to believe Lincoln's impromptu remarks at the town square the night before had in fact been his sole address. The president had "declined to speak for fear he should perpetrate a folly," the *Examiner* reported, despite having access to the full text of the actual speech. "On the present occasion Lincoln acted the clown." Even leading men like Simms and George Fitzhugh probably didn't learn of the address until after the war, when their cause had already appeared to have been rendered moot.[9]

THIRTY-SIX

By late November 1864 the view from seven-year-old Woodrow
Wilson's gate had changed a great deal.

His father's church still stood but it was now part of a new denomination, the Presbyterian Church in the Confederate States of America,
which had broken from the national church in support of both slavery and
the Deep Southern cause. Reverend Joseph Ruggles Wilson had played a
central role in that process, inviting his counterparts across the Confederacy to hold their first convention at his church. At that meeting in December 1861, they had elected him secretary of the new organization, making
him its day-to-day leader. Charismatic, attractive, ambitious, and six feet
tall, he was the ideal front man, adored by the ladies and idolized by children. "If I had my father's face and figure," his son would later say, "it
wouldn't make any difference what I said." But Reverend Wilson said what
his parishioners wanted to hear. In January 1861 he delivered a sermon that
was a full-throated defense of slavery, praising it as a "great, beneficial, civilizing institution" that was "one of the colored man's foremost sources of
blessing" and "directly sanctioned by both the utterance and silence of
Scripture." His colleagues admired the speech and had copies of it printed
and distributed across the Confederacy. His father, the future president
would later say, was the most important and influential teacher he had ever
had, and Joseph Wilson was a Confederate nationalist of the first order.[1]

Life inside the Wilsons' comfortable home was little changed by the war.

The cooking, laundry, cleaning, and serving were still done by the slaves his father leased from the parish. Wilson's mother, the demure daughter of a prominent Presbyterian clan, tended quietly to domestic affairs. Reverend Wilson wrote sermons in his book-lined library. He was a prominent person and their town remained relatively prosperous, so Woodrow and his siblings never wanted for food, clothing, or provisions during the war. They had spent several anxious weeks in the summer of 1863 waiting for their father after his tour of war-torn Virginia as a Confederate army chaplain, but he returned safely.[2] All was not normal outside the manse, however.

The First Presbyterian had by then become an emergency hospital, its floors covered with hundreds of men who'd been wounded at the Battle of Chickamauga in north Georgia, the second most deadly battle of the war, and in the defense of Atlanta, which had fallen days earlier. The shaded churchyard was now a stockade filled with Union prisoners. A neighbor would often see young Woodrow standing on the sidewalk, "his thin pale face turned anxiously toward the groups in the grove," though she was unable to tell "which touched him the most, the stern, defiant men in their blue uniforms—prisoners in a hostile land, closely guarded night and day and marching around the enclosure while no friendly faces cheered them, or the wounded boys in gray, borne groaning into the deep recesses of the great church."[3]

What touched everyone in Augusta the most was word of the rapid advance of a Union army. Commanded by General William T. Sherman, it had just burned Atlanta to the ground, and it appeared to be coming their way.

THIRTY-SEVEN

At Woodlands the Simms family was hurriedly preparing to evacuate. As Sherman's army charged toward the sea—cleverly bypassing the Confederate troops massed to defend Augusta—Simms prepared to send his children farther inland to the relative safety of Columbia, where they would lodge in tight quarters with his son-in-law's kin. The Union army was said to be pillaging and burning everything in its thirty-mile-wide path through Georgia, and Simms knew South Carolina, seat of the rebellion, would be its next target. By December 21, when Savannah surrendered, Simms was alone, packing a railroad car with furniture and family belongings, while his slaves butchered hogs, bagged potatoes, and packed barrels with peas, rice, crushed nuts, and shelled corn—a year's provisions for his family to stave off famine. In early January, as Sherman's troops rested, a flood swept away a trestle bridge on the northbound railway, and Simms's slaves were forced to take arduous weeklong trips across the muddy roads to Columbia in wagons filled with foodstuffs, squawking chickens and ducks, and crates of priceless Revolutionary-era manuscripts, with cows trailing behind, bound for sale at the city's markets. Knowing that the Union army would emancipate any slaves who fell into its hands, Simms sent four of his own to Columbia, leased six more to a contractor repairing the railroad, gave one to his son, and hired another out to a cobbler in the town of Bamberg. "For those who remain," he wrote his son, "there will be ample provision and they have their instructions how to proceed in case of the appearance of the enemy."[1]

In the midst of the packing, Simms received word he might be conscripted into the Confederate army, despite being four months short of his fifty-ninth birthday. He wrote out a long plea to the newly elected governor, Andrew Magrath, documenting a host of chronic ailments: thirty years of hemorrhoids, "copious discharges of blood" that left him exhausted, an enlarged left testicle "which if I walk or ride becomes increased in size and subjects me to great pain," and occasional outbreaks of chills. He told the governor he would be pleased to serve in a bureaucratic capacity, but would rather die in the field than, as "a man of honour and delicacy," expose his diseased body to "the examination of a board of strangers." Governor Magrath granted him an exemption, but Simms found himself envious of his old friend James Henry Hammond, who, having died on November 13, had "escaped this crisis."[2]

At the end of January, just as Sherman's sixty thousand men crossed into South Carolina, Simms reached Columbia. With the railroad out of commission, his books remained in the Woodlands library, with most of his family's possessions stranded in a railcar on the sidings of Midway. A neighbor's wife and children had moved into the main house to try to look after it and the slaves, but they would be unable to deter a determined attack by Sherman's soldiers or by the notorious stragglers who were following in the army's wake, scavenging whatever it left behind.[3]

Sherman, to Simms's horror, had pivoted his armies away from heavily fortified Charleston and marched them due north at a lightning pace directly for Columbia, with little to halt their advance. Each day more refugees arrived in the city, choking the roads and bridges, reporting that their homes, towns, and villages had been burned, "one sending up its signal flames to the other, presaging for it the same fate," as Simms described it, "light[ing] the winter and midnight sky with crimson horrors." The city, swollen to twice its normal population of eight thousand, was now the repository of much of the wealth of South Carolina, the Charleston aristocracy having evacuated their jewelry, artworks, and books there for safekeeping in expectation that Sherman would march up the coast.[4]

On February 16, Federal shells began to fall on the Capitol, and the Confederate troops withdrew. The next morning a long column of well-fed and disciplined Union troops marched into the city center and accepted the mayor's surrender. Not long thereafter, as Simms later attested, teams of them proceeded from house to house bearing pots of phosphors and turpentine, which they spread over floors and walls and set aflame. Firemen who responded to the blazes were threatened by U.S. soldiers, who cut their hoses and drove them away. Soon a conflagration had spread over most of the city, fueled by the Confederate commander's decision to leave large piles of flammable cotton bales in the streets when he withdrew. "Very grand, and terrible, beyond description, was the awful spectacle," Simms recalled, "the blending of a range of burning mountains stretched in a continuous series for more than a mile." Winds fanned the flames, sweeping them across three-fifths of the city. At one in the morning, the Town Hall clock struck for the final time, its tower already bathed in fire. "Great spouts of flame spread aloft in canopies of sulphurous cloud—wreaths of sable, edged with sheeted lightnings, wrapped the skies, and, at short intervals, the falling tower and the tottering wall, avalanche-like, went down with thunderous sound, sending up at every crash great billowy showers of glowing fiery embers."[5]

Meanwhile some Federal soldiers looted homes and held up pedestrians at gunpoint, even as other units tried to maintain order and put out the fires. At least two young black women were raped and murdered by Union soldiers, who drowned one of them by holding her face in a mud puddle. "Regiments, in successive relays, subjected scores of these poor women to the torture of their embraces," Simms would report. By the time the sun rose, "peering dimly through the dense vapors," Simms saw desolate groups of women and children gazing vacantly at the "smoking masses of blackened walls and towers of grim, ghastly chimneys" that had once been their homes. Although General Sherman had issued orders to fight the fires, the incident would later be regarded as one of the great atrocities of the war, and Simms's eyewitness account, "The Sack and Destruction of Columbia, South Carolina," would become definitive.[6]

Simms's own refuge had been spared destruction, but a large portion of his food stores were consumed in the fire. Writing from a crowded attic apartment, he sought to discover what had happened to Woodlands. Weeks later he would learn the bitter truth: The rebuilt main house—and the 10,700 books in the library wing—had been burned by Union stragglers, along with the stables, barns, and machine, threshing, and carriage houses. Nearly half of the slaves who'd remained had been "taken off or beguiled away" by Sherman's army, along with every wagon, mule, horse, and plow. "My books! My books!" Simms lamented when he heard the news. "My heart is ready to break when I think of them." Most of his savings had been deposited in the Union Bank, which had relocated to "Heaven knows where—probably to Charlotte." With the railroad destroyed and his own draft animals lost during the Union occupation of the city, Simms had no means to get to Woodlands and no money to keep his family afloat.[7]

All he had was his pen. Fortunately, in the ruins of the local newspaper office, the publisher Julian Selby had cobbled together a rudimentary press and asked Simms to edit the newspaper he intended to produce. Though the pay would be just a few dollars a week, with no other options and a story to tell, Simms agreed. The first issue appeared on March 21, called, appropriately enough, the *Columbia Phoenix*.[8]

Simms chronicled, in multiple parts, the terrible tale of the city's destruction. He rallied his readers to resist, to turn to guerrilla warfare. "However adverse our people have been to a reunion with the Northern race," he wrote on April 6, as the Union forces were cutting off General Lee's retreating Northern Army of Virginia, "the feeling has become intensified by the brutal conduct of their armies, and the plain design of their Government to blot out the present proprietors of the South and repeople their land."[9]

His country was collapsing around him. By the end of the month, it would cease to exist at all.

THIRTY-EIGHT

L incoln, having won reelection, was sworn into office for his second term on March 4. At the ceremony Vice President Andrew Johnson, a Tennessee slaveholder who had remained loyal to the Union, delivered a drunken harangue that left cabinet members wondering about his sanity. Lincoln gave his Second Inaugural Address, which cast the war as the will of God, punishing a nation that had allowed slavery to persist. Americans hoped the conflict would soon end, he said, but warned that the Lord might prolong it "until all the wealth piled by the bond-man's two hundred and fifty years of unrequited toil shall be sunk, and until every drop of blood drawn with the lash, shall be paid by another drawn with the sword." With malice toward none, he concluded, they must "bind up the nation's wounds" and "achieve and cherish a just, and a lasting peace, among ourselves, and with all nations."[1]

Frederick Douglass tried to attend the White House reception that evening, but was blocked by two policemen who informed him that no black person could enter. As they led him away Douglass asked a passing friend to notify the president. Minutes later the guards received new orders and escorted Douglass into the gathering in the East Room, where Lincoln, standing "like a mountain pine high above all the others," recognized him immediately. "Here comes my friend Douglass," he said, taking the orator's hand. "I am glad to see you. I saw you in the crowd to-day, listening to my inaugural address; how did you like it? . . . There is no man in the country whose opinion I value more than yours." Douglass, flattered and gratified, told him: "Mr. Lincoln, that was a sacred effort."[2] On April 2 the Confederate president, Jefferson Davis, and his cabinet fled Richmond on the last open railway line. Two days later Lincoln toured their fallen capital in an open carriage, his aides fearing for his life.[3]

On April 9 Union forces cut off General Lee's retreat at Appomattox Court House, ninety miles west of Richmond. He surrendered his Army of Northern Virginia to General Ulysses Grant. Sporadic fighting would continue into the summer, but everyone knew the Union had won the war.

Five days later Lincoln attended a production of *Our American Cousin* at Ford's Theatre, six blocks from the White House. John Wilkes Booth, a Maryland-born actor who had championed the Confederate cause throughout the war, stepped into the president's box and shot him in the back of the head with a .44 caliber derringer. Booth jumped out of the box and onto the stage fifteen feet below and, dagger in hand, cried out the words of the Virginia state motto, *Sic semper tyrannis*: "Thus always to tyrants." The president died the following morning.[4]

Bancroft, once again, saw the hand of God at work. He regarded Johnson as a fellow Democrat of the old Jacksonian variety, devoted to the Union and popular democracy, and a pro-Union Southerner, the only U.S. senator from the Confederacy who refused to join the rebellion. Bancroft predicted that if slavery was forever vanquished via a constitutional amendment, Virginia would be richer and more populous than ever before, Texas would "become our Italy," and the Democrats would "be borne into power on the wings of their sound principles of finance." He secretly ghostwrote Johnson's first congressional address, wherein the new president outlined a lenient approach toward the vanquished Confederate states; promised emancipation, but not voting rights, for blacks; and reasserted the Providential destiny of the United States, which was to uphold "the sacred fire of liberty" for all mankind.[5]

Johnson rewarded Bancroft by naming him ambassador to Prussia, a position he would take up as soon as he finished work on volume 9 of the *History*. At age sixty-six, he would be returning to his intellectual homeland.[6]

Congress also honored the historian, a Democrat who had supported a Republican president in a crisis, and whose incremental approach to fostering racial equality was broadly shared under the newly completed Capitol dome. It was he they asked to deliver the official eulogy for Lincoln, he whose vision of America's ideals and national purpose had influenced so many of the slain president's most important pronouncements.

On February 12, 1866, Bancroft addressed a joint session of Congress and pronounced that their president had been the tool of God's Providence, a "child of nature, a child of the West, a child of America" who, innocently bearing the Declaration of Independence as "his compendium of political wisdom" had "lived the life of the American people, walked in its light, reasoned with its reason . . . [and] felt the beatings of its mighty heart." An ordinary man catapulted to the height of power, "he never would have succeeded, except for the aid of Divine Providence, upon which he at all times relied," Bancroft continued. "The President was led along by the greatness of their self-sacrificing example; and as a child, in a dark night, on a rugged way, catches hold of the hand of its father for guidance and support, he clung fast to the hand of the people, and moved calmly through the gloom."[7]

Through his chosen vessel, God had led America to complete "a work which all time cannot overthrow," the expulsion of slavery—"this domestic anomaly" forced on an innocent continent by Britain and Spain—and the creation of a "renovated nation" of moral unity and freedom reborn.[8]

In his speech Bancroft had assured white Americans of what most of them wanted to hear: The nation's fundamental problem had been solved, the Republic was restored, and the future promised only progress, just as he'd always predicted.

THIRTY-NINE

Jefferson Davis's desperate flight ended on May 10, 1865, in a creek bed outside Irwinville, Georgia, where his men, wife, and children had made camp. They'd been on the run for over a month, traveling across the collapsing Confederacy with Union troops at their heels, hoping to escape to Europe from a Gulf Coast port. That morning a detachment of the Fourth Michigan Cavalry surrounded the camp and apprehended the former Confederate president as he fled his tent, dressed in his wife's overcoat. He was placed under arrest, detained in Macon, and marched onto a train bound for the nearest steamship landing.[1]

On May 14, eight-year-old Woodrow Wilson again saw Augusta's townspeople scurrying about in a state of excitement. A large crowd was forming near the train station and soon spread up and down Reynolds Street. Jefferson Davis had arrived, they told one another. Wilson and his family hurriedly walked three blocks to join the waiting throng.[2]

The prisoner, fifty-six years old with graying hair and goatee, was marched up the street under heavy guard, bound for a ferry that would take him to the South Carolina side of the river. White women were weeping, while white men doffed their hats in salute to their former chief executive. The city's black residents had gathered in large numbers, as well, but in celebration. "I should have liked to have seen a volley of musketry sent among the Negroes who were holding such a jubilee," a planter's daughter commented.[3]

What young Woodrow thought of it all, he never did say.

FORTY

Spring had brought the slaves of Woodlands the prospect of both freedom and starvation.

Forty-seven of them had remained on the estate after Union stragglers had finished burning and looting, and nearly half were either small children or elderly. They had no tools, plows, or livestock; few provisions; and limited shelter. After their master had fled in early February, they hadn't heard from Simms or anyone else in the family for months. Realizing famine might strike their ravaged region, the newly liberated slaves organized themselves under the ad hoc leadership of one of their number, William Curry, and fanned out to salvage what they could to survive. They scavenged for corn, rice, and potatoes that they could use to seed the fields, made hoes from bits of iron found on the ruins of the nearby railroad line, and fashioned scythes from some old saw blades. Union soldiers gave them some of the mules they had confiscated. By early June, when the first occupation official, Colonel James Chaplin Beecher, toured the ruined plantation, they had seventy-five acres planted with food crops.[1]

Beecher was the white commander of the Thirty-fifth United States Colored Troops, and sub–assistant commissioner of the Freedmen's Bureau, a two-month-old military agency tasked with assisting and protecting newly emancipated slaves in the occupied South. A Congregational minister who'd served as a missionary in China before the war, Beecher was, by a bizarre twist of history, the youngest brother of Harriet Beecher Stowe, whose *Uncle Tom's Cabin* had so irritated Simms.

During an early June inspection, Beecher was impressed with what the newly freed slaves had accomplished at Woodlands. He pronounced the plantation to have been abandoned by its previous owners, named Curry as its new foreman, and decreed the present crop to be "the sole property of the hands of the place," with one-quarter of it belonging to Curry and the other three-quarters divided among the rest. The former slaves were not to be "molested in occupation of the houses now held by them" until at least through the harvest that fall. The provisional circuit court judge in nearby Bamberg—a town that had also been burned to the ground—confirmed the order.[2]

For the first time in their lives, the blacks of Woodlands would possess the fruit of their labor.

BACK IN HIS COLUMBIA GARRET, Simms remained unaware of these developments.

While Colonel Beecher was inspecting his plantation, Simms received a telegraph that his twenty-two-year-old son, Confederate cavalryman William Gilmore Simms Jr., had been stricken with typhoid in Chester, sixty-five miles to the north. Simms borrowed enough money to hire a wagon and traveled for days across rutted roads to reach Gilmore's bedside. "I found him delirious, raving and without sleep for five days," he recalled. Simms nursed his son back to a stable condition, but had to leave him to convalesce alone while Simms returned to town to publish the *Phoenix* and ensure his other children were fed.[3]

His situation had become desperate. With summer approaching, his borrowed attic chamber—half-filled with trunks, boxes, and piles of old lumber—was growing stiflingly hot, day and night, forcing him to sleep in an open courtyard, where he was tormented by mosquitoes. He and his family were now dressed in lowly homespun and owned not a knife or fork, chair or table. Whenever he ran into a soldier about to return to the North, he'd jot down a desperate letter for them to mail to James Lawson in New York, as the local postal service had collapsed and he couldn't afford to send a telegraph. "Can you help me any?" he asked in one, pleading for a $500 loan and directing Lawson to ask the Harper brothers for an advance on future articles for their monthly magazine. "Telegraph me as soon after the receipt of this as you can, as to what I may expect or hope." Lawson sent him some money via the American Express office, and Simms started planning a reconnaissance trip to Woodlands.[4]

Then he was arrested. Simms had continued to criticize the United States and its armies in the pages of the *Phoenix*. In late April he was still urging Southerners to engage in guerrilla warfare and to send their sons "born on horseback and with a rifle in grasp" against Union forces. By May he'd accepted the Confederacy's defeat and redirected his ire toward the Federal occupation forces in Columbia, blaming them for continued looting and a state of lawlessness in the devastated city. His publisher, Julian Selby, urged him to tone the attacks down but to no avail.

On June 24 a squad of soldiers appeared at Simms's door with orders for him to accompany them at once to appear before General Alfred S. Hartwell, head of the Union occupation force. At Hartwell's headquarters, however, Simms was able to charm the general into not only dropping charges, but also inviting him to "an elegant luncheon in an adjoining room." He was returned home, Selby later recalled, in the general's carriage with a large basket filled with champagne and canned delicacies. "He out-talked me, out-drank me, and very clearly and politely showed me that I lacked proper respect for the aged," Hartwell later explained. Thereafter members of Hartwell's staff would drop by the newspaper every day to chat with the entertaining South Carolinian. Simms had talked his way out of a jail term that he probably wouldn't have survived.[5]

While he waited for Gilmore to be healthy enough to travel, Simms instructed his son-in-law, Edward Roach, who lived in Barnwell, to go to Woodlands and order the former slaves to turn over anything that had survived the fire. "Say to [them] that if they do not obey, I shall have them tried by the Yankee officers for disobedience and misconduct," he instructed Roach, enclosing a labor contract he demanded they sign or face expulsion.[6]

Gilmore made the trip to Woodlands in August. There he trampled on Colonel Beecher's orders by displacing a family from their quarters, seizing 105 bushels of their corn, demanding ownership of a quarter of the upcoming harvest crop, and forcing former slaves to work under his direction. He denied them rations and forbade them to eat any of the corn they had grown until after the harvest. All of these decrees were endorsed by the new commander of the local occupation forces, Colonel Eugene Kozlay of the all-white Fifty-fourth New York Infantry Regiment, whose lieutenant was rumored to resolve all appeals from freed slaves by torturing them. William Curry managed to get word to Colonel Beecher, and though the Barnwell District was no longer under his authority, Beecher had his superiors restore his earlier ruling on the crops and issue him orders to return to the plantation to investigate and intervene.[7]

By the time Beecher reached Woodlands at the end of September, a vigilante group of local planters had begun terrorizing freed slaves across the district. Led by an off-duty sergeant from the Fifty-fourth New York Regiment and made up of eighteen local men, many of them friends of Simms, these "Regulators" showed up at Woodlands on October 1 armed with shotguns and revolvers. They searched former slaves' homes, threatened them, and "perpetuated sundry violences." At Henry Love's plantation they stripped four black women and severely whipped them. At the Mews's they murdered an elderly freedman. A few days later they shot another man in the arm while he worked in the Huttail plantation's fields. At the Matthews property the gang flogged two black boys—one of them belonging to Simms—"until the blood ran from their bodies" and then "dipped their handkerchiefs into the blood and said they would show the ladies how a free nigger's blood looked." The children's transgression had been to visit their friends without their former master's permission. The gang members, Beecher learned, had eagerly awaited the end of his command over the district, frequently saying they would "have it out with the niggers" as soon as he left.[8]

Beecher collected intelligence, interviewed victims, and even stayed up all night in a forest stakeout, hoping to catch the Regulators in the act. In the end, beyond restoring Woodlands' harvest to Simms's slaves, he lacked the authority and manpower to protect the district's freed people. He felt especially frustrated in regard to Woodlands, as he found William Curry to be so honorable. The former slave had even offered Simms half of his share of the harvest. "Cos Ise willing to help Masa Gilmore throo de hard times," Curry explained to Beecher.[9]

"I would gladly give one month's pay for ten days command in that District," the frustrated colonel wrote his superior at the end of the mission.[10]

The elder Simms, preparing to return to Woodlands at around the same time, was furious about his former slaves, who he claimed were stealing and refusing to work. "We have literally nothing left us but our lands," he told his New York friends. "How to dispossess the negroes is the problem."[11]

FORTY-ONE

Slavery had been defeated and the Union restored, but by the onset of the first postwar winter it appeared that Lincoln's dream to found a liberal democratic republic might have died with him.

Across the occupied Confederacy, commanders like James Chaplin Beecher were being replaced by men like Eugene Kozlay. Black soldiers who had been posted in Simms's Barnwell District and many other parts of the South to protect freed slaves were ordered back to the North to avoid offending defeated Confederates. President Andrew Johnson, in his role as commander in chief, worked to quickly restore the region's oligarchy to power, issuing a broad amnesty for soldiers and lower officials and thousands of individual pardons to higher-ranking ones. He stopped the Freedmen's Bureau's plan to redistribute some land to the slaves who had worked it, clearing the way for families like the Simmses and Hammonds to reclaim control.[1]

Then, over the second half of 1865, President Johnson let the defeated states set about re-enslaving the freed people in everything but name.

The Black Codes were a set of laws passed by slave-state governments from Louisiana to Maryland designed to force black people back into servitude and keep them there. Blacks—but not whites—were required to enter into labor contracts and, if they did not, could be arrested, fined, and forced to work on a plantation. The same punishments awaited anyone who was declared a "vagrant" under the laws, a definition that in Mississippi included those who were disorderly or deemed to "misspend what they earn." Judges were empowered to turn over any "orphaned" black child to an employer to spend the rest of its childhood in an unpaid "apprenticeship," with its former owners usually getting the first chance to claim them. In Mississippi blacks lost the right to hunt or fish and could be arrested for "insulting" words or gestures, "malicious mischief," or preaching without a license. In Virginia they could be declared vagrants if they declined to work for "the usual wages" offered, and in Florida they could be whipped or sold into a year's labor if they broke a work contract. South Carolina's codes were, not surprisingly, among the worst, imposing a severe fine on any black person who earned his living as anything other than a farmer or a servant. The Black Codes' purpose, the Louisiana Republican legislator Benjamin Flanders acknowledged, was "getting things back as near to slavery as possible."[2]

Proponents of the liberal democratic vision fought back against Johnson's intention to restore the Union as a white man's nation.

In December the Republican-controlled Congress reconvened and moved to take control of the "reconstruction" of the South from the president. "The republic cannot be lost," Senator Sumner pronounced. "Therefore the policy of the president must fail." The "Radical" Republicans sought to remake the South and the Union on the basis of equality before the law. They refused to seat representatives elected from the occupied states and renewed the Freedmen's Bureau's charter over Johnson's veto. They also overrode his veto of the Civil Rights Act of 1866, the federation's first, which guaranteed equal, race-blind treatment both before the law and in regard to citizenship. To ensure its permanence they enshrined these principles in the Fourteenth Amendment to the Constitution, passed in June 1866 and sent out for ratification by the states.

Some wanted to go even further. Representative Thaddeus Stevens of Pennsylvania called for the seizure of the lands of the richest 10 percent of Southerners—four hundred million acres in all—with forty acres given to every freedman and the remainder sold to compensate Unionists, finance veterans' pensions, and retire the national debt. "How can republican institutions, free schools, free churches, free social intercourse exist in a mingled community of nabobs and serfs?" he asked. "If the South is ever to be made a safe republic, let her lands be cultivated by the toil of the owners or the free labor of intelligent citizens." For most Republicans, however, any intervention to secure the economic equality of black people was a step too far, and Stevens's initiative went nowhere.[3]

Through it all a campaign of terror continued against former slaves. In the environs of Jackson, Mississippi, Regulator gangs murdered five blacks in as many days in the summer of 1865: one for being a preacher, two more for having witnessed the killing, another for having attended a dance, and a child whose hands and ears were cut off and throat slit for pleasure. "Negroes are often shot, as it appears, just out of wanton cruelty, for no reason at all that any one can imagine," the local Union officer told Major General Carl Schurz, who was compiling a report on the social conditions in the occupied South for President Johnson. In southern Alabama blacks were forced to continue as slave laborers until the crops were harvested, then "driven off to reach Mobile or starve." Others were hanged, beaten to death, tied to trees and burned alive, or, in the case of one woman, drowned in a river. In New Orleans and Memphis in early 1866, dozens of blacks were killed by white mobs, and entire neighborhoods laid to waste, with local police participating in, rather than stopping, the mayhem. "These people are industrious," Captain W. A. Poillon, the assistant superintendent of the Freedmen's Bureau in Mobile, protested on behalf of the former slaves. "They do not refuse to work; on the contrary, they labor for the smallest pittance and plainest food."[4]

This lawlessness led Congress to pass laws sanctioning the continued military occupation of the South and the rights of blacks to both vote and hold office. Even moderate Republicans began to consider the merits of guaranteeing universal male suffrage in a Fifteenth Amendment to the Constitution.

Unfortunately this latter effort alienated the leaders of a growing women's suffrage movement from the cause. Tensions had been building between Douglass and his feminist allies since the introduction of the

Fourteenth Amendment, the text of which the suffragists opposed because it repeatedly referenced "male" voting rights and, thus, became the first part of the Constitution to explicitly exclude women. Elizabeth Cady Stanton and Susan B. Anthony contested the Fifteenth Amendment due to its failure to guarantee women the franchise, and when Douglass and other African American allies continued to support the measure, they reacted with a surge of racist arguments. "Think of Patrick and Sambo and Hans and Yung Tung," Stanton complained, "who do not know the difference between a monarchy and a Republic, who never read the Declaration of Independence . . . making laws for [white intellectuals] Lydia Maria Child, Lucretia Mott, or Fanny Kemble." She and Anthony quit the American Equal Rights Association and from the pages of their newspaper, *The Revolution*, referred to black voters as "Sambo" and suggested that by not also giving voting rights to "Saxon women," Negroes would become their "rulers" and perpetuate the "grand rape of womanhood" that male-dominated society represented. More divisive was the fact that their newspaper was underwritten by a notorious huckster and racist named George Francis Train, a man Garrison warned them was a "crack-brained harlequin and semi-lunatic."[5]

For his part Frederick Douglass continued to support women's suffrage and called for a Sixteenth Amendment to enfranchise women, and would later use his newspaper to agitate for suffrage on liberal democratic principles. Likewise, when California representatives expressed their disdain for a measure that would allow Chinese people to vote, Douglass gave speeches across the Northeast arguing that everyone should be welcomed in the renewed Republic.[6]

While Congress debated the Fourteenth and Fifteenth Amendments, it also impeached President Johnson (for firing his abolitionist secretary of state, Edwin Stanton), but acquitted him at trial. The redefinition of America's national identity now stood in the balance. Events in the occupied territories would soon truncate this conversation, with profound effects on the health and stability of a battered Republic.

FORTY-TWO

By the first anniversary of the war's end, Simms's situation had not much improved.

He now lived in a small dwelling near Charleston's waterfront with his four- and nine-year-old sons; his adult daughter, Augusta; and her husband. Their home was surrounded by abandoned buildings with roofs covered in turkey buzzards and empty window frames facing overgrown gardens. Grass sprouted everywhere in the damaged streets. Throughout the war the neighborhood had been heavily shelled because it had been in range of artillery batteries set up on the Union-occupied barrier islands in the outer harbor. Simms's own bedchamber, he reported, was "shattered by shells, with orifices in the walls through which the winds stream and the rains beat." He was sleeping on a pallet on the floor, without a single article of furniture, surrounded by his trunks.[1]

Simms, now sixty, with short iron gray hair and a foot-long white beard, was fortunate that the owner of a Charleston newspaper had hired him as an associate editor, a job that often required that he write three columns of text a day. Unlike Woodlands, Charleston had schools for nine-year-old Govan, as well as better communications routes with the outside world, so it made sense to stay in the shattered city, especially as there was nowhere for him to stay at the plantation.[2]

At Woodlands, Gilmore, twenty-year-old daughter Mary Lawson, and eighteen-year-old Chevillette and her new husband, Donald Rowe, were sharing a two-room former slave quarters and subsisting on squirrels, cat-fish, and corn given to them by William Curry. Simms was able to buy them tools and mules, but the family could get only three or four of their slaves at a time to agree to sign on as contract field laborers. Across the South freed people generally sought economic independence, a piece of land of their own to stake out the Jeffersonian dream of yeoman farming.[3]

Simms, however, regarded their reluctance to become wage laborers as a sign of racial degeneracy. "If we arrest and put them in prison, they wish nothing better," he complained during that first postwar winter. "They re-main idle and we support them in prison." While his vigilante neighbors were terrorizing and murdering blacks, Simms reported to his New York friends that they were "perishing by thousands of exposure, drunkenness, starvation and all brutal practices." While hundreds of thousands of former slaves were on the move, trying to find family members who'd been taken from them, Simms claimed "sons abandon their fathers, mothers their in-fants, all to crowd to the cities where they quarter themselves for rations on the Government." Unwilling to work under contract, "they are most effec-tually ruined as laborers forever."[4]

Northern preachers had begun traveling the South, preaching libera-tion. One of them arrived in the Woodlands area in the middle of May 1866, and told some three thousand freed people "that, in a short time all the lands in the neighbourhood would be divided among them, in tracts of 50 acres each, that they should not work as hirelings any longer, but should become the masters and proprietors of the soil, and that the white nabobs should ride behind their carriages, and be only too happy to lift their bea-vers [i.e., hats] when they met." Gilmore and brother-in-law Donald Rowe confronted the preacher, threatening to horsewhip him for these "seditious preachings," and were promptly arrested by Union soldiers. Simms rushed up from Charleston and convinced the officer in charge to release them. "These young fellows, by their rashness, frequently get me into hot water," he complained afterward.[5]

The previous fall Simms had journeyed to New York, hoping to solicit sufficient book, magazine, and reprinting contracts to begin rebuilding a wing of the Woodlands main house. Little had come of it. In Charleston the city's respectable classes were selling their family silver, paintings, books, and furniture in order to buy food. The less fortunate tramped from house to house, begging for employment. "The terrors of famine threaten a vast multitude," Simms reported in early 1867. By winter's end he realized he would have to abandon the city, withdraw the boys from school, retreat to the plantation, and try to live off the land. But he still needed money to build a place to live, his only shelter there being a twelve-by-sixteen-foot brick outbuilding. The only thing he had left to sell was his treasured Revolutionary War manuscript collection, now kept at his friend Evert Duyckinck's New York home for safekeeping.[6]

Of all his possessions, the collection was the one valuable he had personally ferried to Columbia ahead of Sherman's advance. He had hoped to find the time and financial support to edit and publish the Laurens family letters himself, and had instructed Duyckinck to let no one else see that part of the collection. Earlier that winter he'd been irritated to learn that his rival George Bancroft, at work on the last volume of his *History*, had asked to inspect the manuscripts. ("I should be unwilling that Mr. Bancroft should have free range among the papers," he responded, strictly limiting the historian's access to a portion dealing with a single battle.) After publishing a slim volume of select letters, he authorized the sale of all twelve hundred manuscripts to the Long Island Historical Society for $1,500. Money in hand Simms headed to Woodlands to oversee construction of a modest four-room house on the site of the burned mansion.[7]

The situation was by then desperate throughout South Carolina. The 1866 and 1867 harvests had been poor, and famine stalked the land. Malnourished mules and horses dropped dead in their harnesses, dooming the next crop, as well. "There is not more than one planter in fifty who has corn enough to last him a single month, not more than one in two hundred who has enough for two months, none that have any that can last three months," Simms reported in early May. "A great many will almost or quite starve." At

Woodlands the twelve-member family of freedman Jim Rumph was already starving, including an infant and septuagenarian grandparents. "We have done for them all that we could and now can do no more," Simms wrote *The Charleston Courier* in an anonymous plea for emergency food aid. "Our own resources are exhausted." Mass starvation was avoided only via the efforts of New York society circles that, organizing as the Southern Famine Relief Commission, bought and shipped and distributed 170,000 bushels of corn that spring and summer, along with donated clothing, potatoes, and pork. The next harvest was also terrible, and by spring 1868, Simms was relying on corn shipments from the federal Freedmen's Bureau itself to keep the plantation going. "A dread despair of every thing has seized upon our people," he declared. "Not only [is] everybody ruined . . . every body is sternly bracing himself up to the encounter with a worse ruin, and for such a catastrophe as shall form a fitting and grand climax to such a ruin." The South, he predicted, "is doomed to be the Ireland of the Union."[8]

Focused on survival, Simms wrote little about the wider state of affairs in what would be his final years, when his visions for America and the South were being supplanted by those of his ideological enemies. What commentary he did offer was bitter and defiant. As Congress extended the military occupation of the South and made readmission to the Union contingent on the embrace and protection of black civic and political rights, Simms denounced them as despots. "We may submit, as a conquered people to the chain, but we shall not hug it, nor embrace the knees of the Conquerors," he wrote a New York friend. "We shall only loathe them the more, and feel ourselves at all times free of all obligations."[9]

In May 1868 he confided to the Virginia novelist John Esten Cooke that there was only one solution to "the problem" of Northern "Radicalism": a white exodus to escape an inevitable black uprising. "*We* have to make the passage of the Red Sea," he began.

> The negro emerging from the control of his master becomes first
> a vagabond. His next step makes him a larcener. The progress is

rapid from petty to audacious thieving, and his next advance is to felony. He becomes a burglar; commits arson, murder and highway robbery and, soon thereafter, he bands with numbers and begins the war of race, by plundering and burning towns and villages.

Seven millions of whites will not rest long under the rule of 3 millions of negroes; or if they do, the natural question will be, as it has long been with me—"Is our race worth saving?" Brood over it, organize promptly in every precinct; get good weapons, establish places of rendezvous, provide signal and pass words, seek your places of rendezvous through the woods and not by the highways, and keep your powder dry.[10]

At that very time white gangs were committing highway robbery and murder and plundering and burning black towns and villages across the South. They'd already formed secret organizations with secret signals and passwords, riding through the night, often in disguise, to torture and kill "impudent" freedmen, Yankee schoolteachers, and, most especially, Republican Party leaders ahead of that year's presidential election. The largest of these groups called itself the Ku Klux Klan, and by Election Day it had murdered a thousand blacks in Louisiana, hundreds in Georgia, and dozens in South Carolina, including the black state senator Benjamin Randolph, one of a handful of blacks elected the year before.[11]

SIMMS'S HEALTH DECLINED through 1868 and 1869, as he wrote and published two novels serialized in newspapers. Through the summer of 1869 he suffered under "a score of Demons in the several shapes of Indigestion, Constipation, Vertigo, hemorrhoids, all complicated with old age, toils inconsistent with age [and] . . . privations to which I have been unaccustomed." He told his son-in-law he preferred "dying in the harness" to "expiring by degrees like the tail of a snake whose head has been hammered." He began suffering fits of shivering that left him bedridden for days at a time. In May 1870 he described to Lawson his ailments as "a complication of dyspepsia, Dysentery and a great disturbance of the urinary organs," and said that his kidneys and liver were both implicated. (Later scholars believe he was dying of colon cancer.) A regimen of mercury and some mysterious "blue pills" that worked his intestines "like a Gopher in his hole" may have worsened his suffering.[12]

On June 9, 1870, while staying at his daughter's Charleston home, Simms got up to walk downstairs and was suddenly, in her words, "death struck" with cold sweats and quivering. The family physician arrived and said Simms had only hours left to live. Most of the Simms children did not seem to believe the end was near, however, and remained at Woodlands as their father faded away. On June 11 he said his final words: "Where is Gilmore? It won't be long." At five o'clock that afternoon, William Gilmore Simms died at the age of sixty-four.

A family friend who prepared his body for burial could not straighten his fingers, which "refused to take any other position but the natural one, drawn up as if to write."[13]

FORTY-THREE

The wounded soldiers slowly disappeared from Woodrow's father's church, bound either to their loved ones at home or bound to their graves. The Union prisoners had been liberated, returning the grounds to the sparrows, finches, and mockingbirds. The household slaves' lives continued much as they had before, though Woodrow's father now paid them wages. Letters resumed from family members in Ohio. Uncle James Woodrow could visit again, bearing terrible eyewitness stories of the great fire in Columbia, which stopped one block short of the Theological Seminary where he still taught. The Wilsons were lucky; their prosperous town had been spared destruction, and Reverend Wilson's church and livelihood remained secure. Woodrow himself remained insulated from the worst effects of his region's postwar collapse.

The boy left no written record of these years, for the simple reason that he could not read or write. He didn't learn the alphabet until the age of nine and was twelve before he was properly literate. As an adult he would remark that he thought he might be one of the slowest readers on Earth, and his writing was so plodding he would teach himself shorthand to compensate. Scholars still debate whether he was actually dyslexic, or perhaps afflicted with some other learning or psychological disability.[1]

In the spring of 1870 Reverend Wilson accepted a posting as the professor of pastoral and evangelistic theology and sacred rhetoric at the Columbia Theological Seminary. In September the family—Woodrow's parents, two older sisters, and three-year-old brother—moved out of their comfortable Augusta manse, crossed the river, and made their way to South Carolina's ravaged capital. Woodrow was then thirteen.[2]

Columbia's ten thousand residents all seemed in the throes of rebuilding. Along its wide avenues, some still lined with orange and magnolia trees that had survived the war, houses and stores were sprouting up among the burned ruins, rubble piles, and ghostly chimney stacks. In the city center, on a slightly raised plateau, the unfinished capitol had been patched together with temporary plaster and wooden planks. The sounds of hammers and saws echoed through the town.

The Wilsons moved into a rented home on Pickens Street across from the seminary, a two-story brick Greek Revival mansion with Doric columns whose shaded grounds took up an entire city block. Woodrow was enrolled in a private school run by Charles H. Barnwell but continued to look to his father as his greatest teacher. "He was good fun," he would later recall. "And by constant association with him, I saw the world and the tasks of the world through his eyes." He helped his father with his administrative work for the Confederate Presbyterians—now renamed the Presbyterian Church in the United States*—and spent spare hours in the seminary library, his father having given him a key.[3]

Wilson had little to say about his years in the capital. He usually described himself as having grown up in South Carolina rather than Georgia and in later life referred to "my own very happy boyhood in Columbia."[4]

The city, however, was in the midst of some of the most tumultuous events in Southern history, most of them taking place at the State House, just four blocks from the Wilson home. Woodrow would later express very harsh judgments about what he and some of the country's most prominent white supremacists claimed had occurred there.

Under the protection of the U.S. Army and the directives of the

---

* Since 1983, when it merged with other factions, it has been known as the Presbyterian Church (USA).

Northern-controlled U.S. Congress, South Carolina's black majority had taken control of the January 1868 constitutional convention, rewriting the state's fundamental law along liberal democratic terms. The new constitution established universal adult male suffrage, abolished debtors' prison and the (previously stringent) property requirements to run for office, and provided for the popular election of presidential electors (who had until then been appointed by legislators). It integrated public schools and colleges, required universal education for children six to sixteen, and apportioned the state's electoral districts based on population rather than wealth. South Carolina white supremacists were outraged, expressing their condemnation in ethnonationalist terms at their own convention, headed by the leading men of the old order:

> The black man is what God and nature and circumstances have made him. That he is not fit to be invested with these important rights may be no fault of his. But the fact is patent to all that the negro is utterly unfitted to exercise the highest functions of the citizen. The government of the country should not be permitted to pass from the hands of the white man into the hands of the negro. . . . As citizens of the United States we should not consent to live under negro supremacy, nor should we acquiesce in negro equality. Not for ourselves only, but on behalf of the Anglo-Saxon race and blood in this country, do we protest against this subversion of the great social law, whereby an ignorant and depraved race is placed in power and influence above the virtuous, the educated and the refined.[5]

The November 1868 elections produced a 78–46 black majority in South Carolina's lower house, and sent 10 blacks to the 21-seat senate, where Republicans also enjoyed a majority. There, in the year before the Wilsons' arrival and for six years thereafter, former slaves and free blacks who had previously not been allowed to vote or serve on a jury, promulgated a sweeping agenda founded on the natural rights and equality of men. In their first eighty-nine-day session they lifted the death penalty from all crimes save murder; forbade common carriers of all sorts to discriminate based on race; ratified the Fifteenth Amendment, guaranteeing to all races the right to vote; established a racially integrated state orphanage; doubled teacher salaries at the University of South Carolina; and issued bonds to enable the purchase of lands to be subdivided and sold to small-scale farmers.[6]

In a state that had previously been controlled by large slaveholders, the Old Guard was reduced to a handful of lawmakers from the overwhelmingly white up-country. The others had been displaced by men like William J. Whipple, one of South Carolina's first black lawyers, who could match wits and words with the racists in the chamber, quoting historical statistics and the verses of John Greenleaf Whittier. "What we demand," he said in response to the suggestion that blacks should be grateful for what whites had recently granted them, "is equality before the law. We don't ask this as a favor because we are black men, but we demand it because we are men." Robert Smalls was a self-educated Beaufort slave who, in 1862, commandeered a Confederate gunship in Charleston and led twelve other slaves to freedom, fought in the war for the U.S. Navy, and returned after Appomattox to build a black-owned railroad serving the Charleston docks. Unlike Smalls, dozens of other recently emancipated slaves couldn't confidently read or write and spoke only the Gullah dialect, but proved quick students of parliamentary procedure. Other newcomers included Robert Brown Elliott, a black native of Liverpool, England, who was educated at High Holborn Academy and Eton, was a Royal Navy veteran, and was associate editor of the *South Carolina Leader*, one of the new African American newspapers that had sprung up across the South. Elliott was one of fifteen blacks elected to Congress in this period, taking the U.S. House seat once occupied by Preston Brooks.[7]

The Old Guard, including Wilson's father, did not like these developments. White conservative papers mocked the legislature's proceedings, with racialized descriptions of the legislators and contemptuous remarks about the low-status dialect of some of the newly emancipated slaves. "In all of the history of all the states, and the history of Europe, Asia, Africa, and Australia, there is no record of such a body of 'lawmakers' as now disgraces the capital of South Carolina," the Chattanooga journalist Horace Redfield wrote on an 1873 visit. "The mass of them are for sale like sheep in the shambles, with the exception that they sell themselves." Northern conservatives were also highly critical. "Twenty three (House members) are white men, representing the remains of the old civilization . . . good-looking, substantial citizens," the journalist James Pike wrote in *The Prostrate State*, a popular diatribe against alleged black misrule in South Carolina. "This dense negro crowd they confront do the debating, the squabbling, the lawmaking, and create all the clamor and disorder of the body. . . . It is barbarism overwhelming civilization by physical force."[8]

Outside the legislative chamber, it was the Old Guard that was using physical force. The reign of terror against the black population accelerated during the 1870 and 1872 election cycles, with the Klan assassinating elected officials and beating and terrorizing would-be Republican voters regardless of race. In Eutaw, Alabama, the Klan opened fire on a crowd of two thousand blacks attending a Republican rally in front of the county court house, killing four and injuring fifty-four. In Laurens County, South Carolina, a local Republican election victory prompted the Klan to chase 150 black residents from their homes and execute 13 of them. Congressional investigators found that in the nine months after the 1870 vote, thirty-eight South Carolina blacks were murdered by masked vigilantes, and hundreds more were beaten, shot, whipped, or disfigured by having their ears cut off. That winter thousands slept in the woods to avoid being dragged from their beds and beaten or killed by these terrorists. Outside Spartanburg, a crowd of fifty masked men pulled white schoolteacher William Champion from his bed, blindfolded him, whipped him until he nearly passed out, then brought four black captives before him. "They made me kiss the negro man's posterior, and held it open and made me kiss it, and as well as I remember a negro woman's, too, and also her private parts, and then told me to have sexual connection with her," Champion told investigators. When he refused they beat him, forced him to whip one of the black captives, and threatened to murder him if he voted Republican. "They asked how I liked that for nigger equality. I told them it was pretty tough." Such testimony filled thousands of densely packed pages in the committee's thirteen-volume report.[9]

WILSON, AGED FOURTEEN TO SEVENTEEN when these events were taking place, did not comment on them in his diary. He was focused on his dreams for the future.

At school the headmaster's son found Wilson "extremely dignified" but said he was not an impressive student. "He was not like the other boys," he later recalled. "He had a queer way of going off by himself." Indeed, by sixteen Wilson had become immersed in a fantasy world of his own creation, in which he was "Thomas W. Wilson, Lieutenant-General, sixth Duke of Eagleton, Commander-in-Chief, Royal Lance Guards," a Knight of the Garter, a Knight Commander of the Star of India, a Knight of the Bath, and a member of Parliament. He filled page after page of his diaries with his orders to imaginary subordinates populating this imperial British universe, some of whom bore the names of his classmates, whom he promoted or demoted to new ranks, positions, or hereditary titles. In time he became Vice Admiral of the Red and drafted voluminous descriptions of the capabilities and armaments of the ships under his command, including the flagship he had personally designed, HMS *Renown*, which was "the fastest vessel in the world." He was still at it by seventeen, at which time he had become Lord Wilson and presided over the Royal United Kingdom Yacht Club, which kept careful censuses of the nationalities of its members, admitting English, Irish, and Scots only. Over the desk where he wrote out these imaginary orders he hung a portrait of the late British prime minister William Gladstone, whom he called "the greatest statesman who ever lived." He told a friend that he intended to become one, too.[10]

His family worried about his scholastic performance. Uncle James Woodrow urged the teen to "learn if you will . . . for heaven's sake, boy," lest he wind up with insufficient education to be a gentleman, let alone a scholar or a statesman. Their concerns were well founded. In the fall of 1873 Reverend Wilson used his influence to enroll his son at Davidson College, a Presbyterian institution located just one hundred miles to the north, on whose board he served. While Wilson received decent grades, he was unhappy, depressed, and soon manifested a "cold" that kept him tucked away in his room for much of the time, writing out general orders to his imaginary subordinates. At the end of the school year, he dropped out and moved back in with his family.[11]

FORTY-FOUR

Douglass did everything in his power to cajole, shame, or inspire Northerners to stand up to the violence unfolding against African Americans across the former Confederacy.

Traveling thousands of miles each year by train, wagon, and horseback, he addressed hundreds of audiences and hundreds of thousands of people from Maine to Nebraska, from the Virginia shores of the Potomac to the Upper Peninsula of Michigan. He purchased a failing black newspaper in Washington, D.C., and used it to add his voice to the national media conversation. His message remained clear and uncompromising, even as he saw the prospect of victory start to vanish.[1]

His argument was American greatness was built upon its foundational principles: justice, equal rights, and self-government. The federation had come into being burdened with the heavy curse of slavery, which stood in contradiction to these values. The Union's victory in the Civil War had lifted that curse, and the country now had the opportunity to fulfill its promise by embracing all people as equally human. Despite the past strains between them, he appeared at women's suffrage conventions convened by Elizabeth Cady Stanton and Susan B. Anthony, speaking in support of the effort. When conservatives questioned the wisdom of the proposed Fourteenth and Fifteenth Amendments, Douglass went to his study and crafted a speech that outlined the case for a liberal civic nationhood as powerful as anyone had presented before or since.[2]

That speech, delivered across the country during the winter of 1869–70, described America as having a "composite nationality" that encompassed all the peoples of the world. "I want a home here not only for the negro, the mulatto and the Latin races, but I want the Asiatic to find a home here in the United States, and feel at home here, both for his sake and for ours," he said.

> Our greatness and grandeur will be found in the faithful applica-
> tion of the principle of perfect civil equality to the people of all
> races and of all creeds. We are not only bound to this position by
> our organic structure and by our revolutionary antecedents, but
> by the genius of our people. Gathered here from all quarters of the
> globe, by a common aspiration for national liberty as against caste,
> divine right government and privileged classes, it would be unwise
> to be found fighting against ourselves and among ourselves, it would
> be unadvised to attempt to set up any one race above another, or
> one religion above another, or prescribe any on account of race,
> color or creed. . . . The outspread wings of the American eagle are
> broad enough to shelter all who are likely to come. . . .
>
> We shall spread the network of our science and our civilization
> over all who seek their shelter, whether from Asia, Africa, or the
> Isles of the Sea. We shall mould them all, each after his kind, into
> Americans; Indian and Celt, negro and Saxon, Latin and Teuton,
> Mongolian and Caucasian, Jew and gentile, all shall here bow to the
> same law, speak the same language, support the same government,
> enjoy the same liberty, vibrate with the same national enthusiasm,
> and seek the same national ends.[3]

To advocate for this vision Douglass even went to the White House un-invited to confront President Johnson face-to-face about his Confederate-friendly Reconstruction policies. Johnson received Douglass on February 7, 1866, and listened as he invoked Lincoln in his calls for black suffrage. The president responded with a rambling forty-five-minute-long speech that combined obliviousness with insult. Johnson claimed he had always been a friend of blacks, arguing that though he "owned slaves and bought slaves, I have never sold one." His own life, he continued, had been encumbered by his slaves' need for food, water, clothing, and shelter. "Practically, so far as my connection with slaves has gone, I have been their slave instead of their being mine," he explained defensively. "I do not like to be arraigned by some who can get up handsomely rounded periods and deal in rhetoric, and talk about abstract ideas of liberty," he continued. The Declaration of Independence and its assertion of equality under the law was a "kind of theoretical, hollow, unpractical friendship [that] amounts to but very little."

Johnson further advised Douglass that the only way to avoid a race war in the country was for "the people" to be obeyed, and in the Southern states "the people" didn't want Negroes to vote. At this point Douglass tried to interrupt him, protesting that political equality was the best way to avoid a racial conflict, but the president cut him off. As he turned to leave, Douglass remarked to one of the black men who had accompanied him that if the president wanted them to heed the people, they would have to go and "get the people right."[4]

When Robert E. Lee died in 1870, newspapers in both the North and South extolled the Confederate general's noble heroism. From the pages of his own newspaper, the *New National Era*, Douglass argued that the "rebel chief" deserved none of these "nauseating flatteries," as his heroism had been in devotion to an evil cause. When invited to speak at the 1871 Memorial Day ceremony in Arlington National Cemetery—a Union burial ground founded on the lawns of Lee's Virginia plantation—attended by the new president, Ulysses S. Grant, Douglass questioned why Confederate soldiers were being venerated at all. "We are sometimes asked in the name of patriotism to forget the merits of this fearful struggle, and to remember with equal admiration those who struck at the nation's life, and those who struck to save it—those who fought for slavery and those who fought for liberty and justice," he told Grant and his cabinet.

I am no minister of malice. I would not strike the fallen. I would
not repel the repentant, but may my "right hand forget her cunning
and my tongue cleave to the roof of my mouth" if I forget the difference between the parties to that terrible, protracted and bloody
conflict. If we ought to forget a war which has filled our land with
widows and orphans, which has made stumps of men in the very
flower of their youth, sent them on the journey of life armless, leg-
less, maimed and mutilated; which has piled up a debt heavier than
a mountain of gold—swept uncounted thousands of men into
bloody graves—and planted agony by a million hearthstones; I say
if this war is to be forgotten, I ask in the name of all things sacred
what shall men remember? . . . We must never forget that the loyal
soldiers who rest beneath this sod flung themselves between the
nation and the nation's destroyers.[5]

As the Ku Klux Klan continued its campaign against former slaves
across the South, Douglass condemned the Southern-dominated Democratic Party as the "party of murder, robbery, treason, dishonesty and
fraud." Democrats were "the apostles of forgetfulness" because "their pathway has been strewn with the whitened bones of their countrymen." He
warned that "the slave demon still rides the southern gale and breathes out
fire and wrath," ever seeking to rekindle the "smoldering embers of the Lost
Cause." He dismissed the argument that blacks should remain silent in the
face of Klan attacks. "You, colored man, must not say that there is even a
possibility of danger to the midnight riders and murderers by whom you
are slaughtered, lest our saying so will be considered as an invitation to a
war of races," he editorialized. He questioned why some white Americans
expressed reservations about using federal power to protect blacks' liberty
(via enforcement of federal and constitutional law) when they had championed its use to protect slavery (via the Fugitive Slave Act). There could be
no peace, he warned in April 1871, while the KKK "moves over the South
like the pestilence that walketh in darkness and wasteth at noon-day."[6]

On the night of June 2, 1872, Douglass's Rochester home burned to the ground. Neighbors and family members helped rescue his books from the flames, knowing they were the most important thing to him. To his dying day, Douglass was certain the fire had been a case of arson. No one was ever arrested. Douglass scavenged what he could from the ashes and moved his family to a town house in Washington, D.C., just steps from the Capitol.

There, as the federation pondered the future of the South, Douglass hosted and befriended two of the first three African Americans elected to the U.S. Senate, former slave Blanche Bruce of Mississippi and Louisiana's Pinckney Pinchback. The latter was never allowed to take his seat due to an election controversy in the state, so he returned to his home state, where he served as governor for a month in the winter of 1872–73. Bruce would be the only African American to serve out a full term in the chamber for nearly a century, and the only one from a Southern state until 2019, when South Carolina's Tim Scott completed his term. In 1875 seven African American colleagues were elected to the U.S. House, a number that would not be seen again until 1969. The doors of democracy were about to close on nonwhite people in the region of the country where most of them lived.[7]

The political mood had begun to turn against Douglass and the cause of universal civil and political rights. The Panic of 1873, a terrible economic depression, shook the country and reordered many Northern whites' priorities. Banks, railroads, and businesses were failing at an alarming pace. Restoring economic stability became more important than black equality, and the reintegration of Dixie was likely to further that cause. President Johnson's successor, Union general Ulysses Grant, had championed the freed people's cause, but his administration was mired in corruption scandals. White families, many of whom had lost husbands or sons in the war, were losing patience with the seemingly endless occupation and democratization effort in the South. In the 1874 midterm elections the Republicans were dealt a devastating defeat, and overnight a House majority of 110 became a Democratic majority of 66. Eight governorships flipped, including that of Massachusetts, which had never before elected a Democratic chief executive. "The election is not merely a victory, but a revolution," *The New York Herald* proclaimed.[8]

In his Fourth of July address to a largely black audience in the Anacostia section of Washington, D.C., the following summer, the fifty-seven-year-old Douglass said he feared that the patriotic feelings of the white population were about to return to their traditional channels. "If war among the whites brought peace and liberty to blacks," he asked, "what will peace among the whites bring?"[9]

FORTY-FIVE

A s America's second revolution faltered, George Bancroft was paying little attention, as he was engaged in trying to reshape the course of European history.

In Berlin he quickly entrenched himself in the highest political and cultural circles. Fluent in German language, thought, and customs, he was feted by Prussia's intellectuals, flattered by its nobles, respected by its emperor and, most important, befriended by its history-making leader, Count Otto von Bismarck, chancellor of the newly created North German Confederation and soon to be chancellor of an entirely new nation, the German Empire.

Bismarck, fifteen years younger than Bancroft, was the stern-willed architect of German unification, a project he had famously told Prussian legislators "will not be resolved by speeches and majority decisions . . . but by iron and blood." In 1866, the year before Bancroft's appointment as ambassador, Bismarck had launched a lightning war (*Blitzkrieg*) against the Austrian Empire, replacing the German Confederation, which had existed in Bancroft's student days, with the larger, more formidable, more centralized North German Confederation, with an imperial parliament and federated structure. At the beginning of the war, an assassin shot Bismarck three times on Berlin's Unter den Linden; he helped subdue the assailant, walked home, and had to be convinced to seek medical treatment for the wounds caused by multiple bullets having glanced off his ribs. Bismarck, already contemplating how to cow Germany's primary rival, France, dropped in on the new ambassador at his home shortly after his arrival, engaging him in a conversation on race wherein Bismarck held Germans to be a "male" or superior race, and the Celts, Slavs, and German Swabs to be "female" ones, "unfit for the conduct of public affairs, defective in judgment and energy," observing that ethnic Russians were incapable of more than "three or four hours a day" of intellectual work. Soon the two men were horseback riding through the Tiergarten and spending time at Bismarck's country manor in eastern Pomerania, to which no other foreign diplomat ever had been invited. Bismarck hung a portrait of Bancroft on his wall. Bancroft came to believe that the budding autocrat was the reincarnation of George Washington.[1]

Soon Bancroft's diplomatic reports were extolling the Prussian position on almost every issue. Germany was the most American polity in Europe, he proclaimed, a liberty-minded people struggling to establish a more perfect union. Their federation was allegedly modeled on that of the United States, their parliament an homage to Congress, their chancellor an instrument of Providence seeking to secure individual freedom. He considered that the constitution they adopted while Bancroft was ambassador—which lacked the separation of powers and placed a monarchy front and center—had "sprung from the application of the principles which guided the framers of the constitution of the United States." Any attack on Prussia from France or Austria would be nothing less than "hostility to the human race," and the Prussians clearly sought only freedom and security. Under Bismarck, peace, he told his superiors in Washington, would continue.[2]

The Franco-Prussian War took him completely unawares. Bismarck had carefully provoked France, enabling him to rally the southern German statelets to his cause, by releasing a cynically edited telegram. The message, which made it appear the German emperor had insulted a French diplomat would, Bismarck assured his friends, "have the effect of a red rag on the Gallic [French] bull." Emperor Napoleon III, confident that he was the stronger power, took the bait. Six weeks later the more mechanized and

disciplined Prussian army was occupying Paris, and Germany was finaliz-
ing the annexation of Alsace-Lorraine.

Bancroft sent Bismarck a letter congratulating him on winning "during
a war of defence, more military glory than the wildest imagination conceived of," which would bring "the German hope of a thousand years to its
fulfillment." Bismarck leaked the letter to the press, and soon all of France
was cursing Bancroft's name. In occupied Paris Victor Hugo wrote a poem
denouncing the historian-diplomat as "a vile affront of a man," "a dwarf to
whose pettiness, with the addition of venom, remains a dwarf," a flatterer of
"sinister majesty" who should simply depart. "Let us despise you," he added.
"May you have title to hatred."[3]

Bismarck, in turn, declared Bancroft "the perfect American ambassador" and successfully lobbied the Grant administration to keep him on
when it came into office. Bancroft would remain in the post for a total of
seven years, seizing every opportunity to research German archives for anything that might contribute to the tenth and final volume of his *History*.

Of American affairs during this tumultuous period, Bancroft had relatively little to say. He applauded the Senate's decision not to impeach President Andrew Johnson—it had "agitated the public mind of Europe"—and
expressed concerns about extending voting rights to former slaves. "The
emancipation of three or four millions of slaves and the conferring upon
them all civil rights of personal and property seemed to me . . . a great
moral achievement," he wrote in early 1868, but political rights should be
rewarded more gradually. "The best policy for the South would have been
to give at once the suffrage to the most intelligent of the coloured race; and
to extend it by degrees as the rest, in this generation or the next, should
have become educated and manifestly capable of exercising their right with
discretion." (He did not advocate for this system to be applied to unedu-
cated whites.) Senator Reverdy Johnson of Maryland sent Bancroft two
pamphlets he had written arguing for noninterference in Southern affairs
on the grounds that it would subject whites to the "dominion of an ignorant
African race." Bancroft wrote back in agreement: "Instead of warring against

all existing institutions I hold that the wise statesman does not attempt impossibilities but decides every question as it presents itself on the side of freedom and in this manner assists to bring the actual state nearer and nearer to the best possible state." Providential history couldn't be rushed, he continued to argue, unless it was a matter of leading the Teutonic peoples to their destiny.[4]

In 1874, after visits to Budapest, Constantinople, and Cairo, the Bancrofts packed their books, manuscripts, and cases of wine into crates, bought tickets for themselves and their indispensable German valet, Carl Hermann Braatz, and prepared to return to America—not to Boston or New York this time, but to Washington, D.C.

The Bancrofts' new home, 1623 H Street on Lafayette Square, was a hundred yards from the White House lawn. It had a library and study on the third floor where George could write his books, and a spacious and gracious dining room provided a setting for Elizabeth to entertain diplomatic, intellectual, and presidential guests. The garden offered George a place to grow hydrangeas that would be the envy of society. In the stable were horses they could ship to their Newport mansion where they fled to escape the summer heat. The seventy-four-year-old Bancroft looked forward to a life of comfortable, intellectually challenging writing and contemplation, and to the completion of his life's work, the story of the American people and their conquest of freedom.[5]

Of the collapse of Reconstruction, Bancroft would have almost nothing to say.

FORTY-SIX

Throughout the 1876 presidential campaign, the Klan and other vigilante groups continued a campaign of murder and intimidation, overwhelming the U.S. marshals and federal troops tasked with protecting the integrity of the vote. In South Carolina the former Confederate brigadier general Martin Gary wrote and distributed a thirty-three-point plan to win the election via the deployment of armed Democratic Party paramilitary units, or "rifle clubs," tasked with suppressing Republican turnout. Each member was "honor bound to control the vote of at least one negro by intimidation, purchase, keeping him away or as each individual shall determine how he may best accomplish it." Blacks, Gary advised, should not be persuaded by argument, but rather "by their fears. . . . Treat them so as to show them you are a superior race, and that their natural position is that of subordination to the white man."[1]

Then South Carolina's killings resumed: a black legislator in Darlington County; six black men lynched in Edgefield County, two more in Marlboro. In Hamburg, across the river from Augusta, Georgia, paramilitaries surrounded the National Guard armory and opened fire on the mostly black guardsmen inside, ultimately killing two. The white vigilantes then rounded up twenty-five blacks, formed a circle around them, and proceeded to murder five of them. In Ellenton, white mobs slaughtered blacks working in the fields or walking down the street, killing as many as a hundred over several days and promising "to carry the election if they had to wade in blood up to their saddle girths."

When the votes were counted, several black-majority counties that had voted overwhelmingly Republican in the previous postwar elections flipped hard to the Democrats, with turnouts a third higher than before. With some voters bragging that they had voted eighteen or twenty times, "the election," a correspondent for *The Atlantic Monthly* reported, "was one of the grandest farces ever seen."[2]

There were similar results in Florida, Louisiana, and Mississippi, where Yazoo County, the heart of the Delta country, recorded only two votes for the Republican presidential candidate, Rutherford B. Hayes. Voting irregularities threw the South Carolina, Louisiana, and Florida results into dispute, leaving the Democratic candidate—white supremacist Samuel Tilden of New York—with 184 electoral votes, one short of an Electoral College victory. Both sides knew that if all three disputed states went for Hayes, he would win the election 185–184. The election was thrown to Congress to resolve.

For months the House of Representatives wrangled over the ballots as newspapers North and South reported rumors that underground militia units in both sections were preparing for a second civil war. In the end the parties made a deal: Hayes would become president, but white Southerners would rule at home. Federal troops withdrew from their posts protecting the state houses in Columbia and Baton Rouge. Democratic "Redeemer" governments took power, rolling back civil rights protections and public school spending while reintroducing many of the Black Codes. The Supreme Court issued an 1876 decision that effectively annulled the Fourteenth and Fifteenth Amendments by ruling their protections applied only to the actions of state governments, not individuals. "The negro will disappear from the field of national politics," *The Nation* observed. "Henceforth the nation, as a nation, will have nothing more to do with him."[3]

Woodrow Wilson, age twenty-one, applauded the result. "The only thing our country requires to regain former prestige as a nation of mental and political giants is that in one mighty occasion have it close the lesions of all parts of the country to which the late war came so near being fatal," he said in one of his first public speeches. "Let us each one do everything in his power to promote that union of hearts for which the Southern people are so eager if their Northern brethren will only meet them halfway, and the North and South will soon be seen marching hand in hand in their great progress with the world."[4]

Frederick Douglass, for his part, tried to see a ray of light in the darkness. "Though freedom of speech and of the ballot have for the present fallen before the shotguns of the South, and the party of slavery is now in the ascendant, we need bate no jot of heart or hope," he began telling audiences. "In the future, patriotic millions, with able captains to lead them, will stand as a wall of fire around the Republic, and in the end see Liberty, Equality and Justice triumphant."[5]

FORTY-SEVEN

I n the fall of 1878, in Wisconsin's modest lakeside capital, Madison, a young man arrived to begin a year of remedial studies at the state university. Five-eight, 130 pounds, with large silver-gray eyes and a friendly, approachable demeanor, he was a promising student from tiny Portage High School, a day's travel to the north, where his graduating class had just eighteen members. Admissions officers at the University of Wisconsin required he enroll for a preparatory year, as they weren't certain that his public education had sufficiently prepared him for college. They needn't have worried. In fifteen years, Frederick Jackson Turner would be one of the most famous scholars in the United States.[1]

Turner was born in Portage on November 14, 1861. During his childhood the central Wisconsin town of three thousand was only a generation old and was still very much a frontier settlement. In Turner's boyhood Winnebago and Menominee traders came to town to sell their furs and handicrafts, and citizen posses occasionally captured horse thieves and hanged them from village trees. In spring men could be seen steering massive rafts of rough lumber planks through town on the Wisconsin River from the lumber camps to the north, guiding them down waterfalls and river bends with a long oar and sleeping in shifts in shelters constructed atop the timbers. In town could be heard a cacophony of languages—Gaelic, Dutch, German, Swedish, and Welsh—as a third of the inhabitants were immigrants. Turner and his friends sometimes played in the ruins of Fort

Winnebago, a wooden military post built to secure the two-mile portage to the Fox River from the tribe of the same name. The wilderness felt close at hand. One of the only area boys to have preceded Turner to study at the state university in Madison was a Scottish immigrant child named John Muir, who had helped his family carve a farm from the "pure wilderness" a few miles outside Portage and experienced what he called a "sudden baptism in Nature's warm heart," prompting him to later become one of the world's most famous naturalists.[2]

Turner's parents were leading citizens in the town. His father, Andrew Jackson Turner, owned and operated the local newspaper, *The Wisconsin State Register*, and represented the area in the state legislature. Andrew Turner was a Republican loyalist and the emerging party boss of Columbia County. While Frederick was an infant, his father editorialized fiercely for Abraham Lincoln. When the boy was attending primary school, Andrew was stubbornly refusing to acknowledge the Grant administration's corruption, dismissing the epic Crédit Mobilier scandal—in which the Union Pacific Railroad bribed the vice president and other senior officials with millions of dollars of company stock—as no more than "a ruse of the Confederate press." He denounced racists, but also counseled against efforts "to force universal suffrage on the South." When Frederick Douglass came to speak in Portage in December 1875, Turner urged his readers to attend, telling them, "You will be denying yourselves much if you fail to go to Pettibone Hall tonight and hear Frederick Douglass," and fourteen-year-old Frederick was likely in the audience to hear the great orator describe the deleterious effects of slaveholding on the civic life of the District of Columbia. The elder Turner was sympathetic to African Americans, but he believed the future of his party was more important than racial justice. His son would grow up with a similar point of view.[3]

Frederick, the oldest of the three Turner children, was his father's constant companion. He shared the elder Jackson's love for fishing, joining him on hikes and canoe trips to lakes and streams across Wisconsin, some outings lasting for weeks. As a teenager, he learned to set type on the newspaper's press to help meet the *Register*'s deadlines and, as he grew older, he wrote a recurring feature on the clever sayings of important people. He joined his father on electioneering tours through the small towns of central Wisconsin, watching him convince Republican caucus goers of the merits of his preferred candidates. He was regaled with stories of the area's history, which Andrew Turner, unlike most journalists of the era, painstakingly fact-checked against original documents and eyewitness accounts before putting them in print.

At Frederick's high school commencement he delivered an award-winning oratory on the importance of newspapers to democracy. "The daily press is one of the greatest of civilizers and public teachers and is a necessary adjunct of every free government," he pronounced. It "joined the Past and the Present and made them one." When he left for college, he intended to become a reporter.

In Madison Turner found a nascent university not much bigger than the liberal arts colleges of the day, with a total student enrollment of four hundred. The history department consisted of just a single professor, who also taught classical languages. Fortunately for Turner, that professor was William Francis Allen, a teacher of extraordinary ability and generosity whom he would always count as the greatest academic influence on his life. Allen was in many ways a younger version of Bancroft—the Massachusetts-born son of a Unitarian minister who graduated from Harvard, studied in Göttingen under Heeren, traveled Europe, and believed America to be the inheritor of liberty's flame, passed down from the Teutons to his Puritan ancestors by way of Anglo-Saxon England.

But Allen had also served as a wartime schoolteacher for newly emancipated slaves around Port Royal, South Carolina, which Union forces had occupied from 1861 onward, and during the postwar occupation was the superintendent of Negro schools in Charleston. He'd been fascinated with the Gullah dialect and customs of the former slaves, and when he was only in his twenties had compiled and published the first scholarly text on Negro slave songs. He was fully versed in the cutting-edge social science of the day, Darwinism, which led him to believe societies evolved like organisms, adapting to their particular environments. When eight years later he published a book entitled *History Topics for the Use of High Schools and Colleges*, Bancroft's *History of the United States* was at the top of his U.S. history reading list. At a time when most professors emphasized rote learning and memorization, Allen set his students to work in the state and local archives, doing original research for classroom assignments. Turner did his on the early land claims in the Portage area and then published the results in his father's newspaper for the benefit of readers.[4]

Young Turner excelled at his studies, despite having to drop out for a year while recovering from a near fatal case of spinal meningitis. He honed his public speaking skills and helped found the university's newspaper. He loved studying and teaching history but couldn't see a way to support himself as a historian: When he graduated in 1884 there were only twenty professors of history in the entire United States, and the country's oldest college history department had existed for only three years. Instead he spent the next year in Madison working as a newspaper reporter, covering the state legislature for the *Milwaukee Sentinel*, *The Wisconsin State Journal*, and Chicago's *Inter Ocean*. His skilled reporting exposed a Democratic corruption scheme involving the Wisconsin State Fair and uncovered information that foiled a coup against University of Wisconsin president John Bascom.[5]

In the spring of 1885, William Francis Allen took a European sabbatical and asked Turner to serve as his substitute as an instructor in history. Turner agreed and immediately knew that he never wanted to do anything else. When Allen returned, Turner took a job as an assistant lecturer in elocution and, a year later, assumed responsibility for his overworked mentor's U.S. history courses. By early 1887 he was teaching fourteen hours of lectures a week and even more when Allen twice fell ill for weeks at a time, leaving the entire history department in the care of his twenty-six-year-old prodigy. Somehow Turner found the time to pursue his own master's degree, conducting research at the State Historical Society of Wisconsin for a thesis on the history of the early French fur trade. His industriousness caught the eye of the university's new president, Thomas Chamberlin, who offered Turner his dream job: to be head of a new American history department.[6]

There was, however, one caveat: Turner had to first earn his doctorate in history. In the 1880s there was only one school in the United States that offered the degree, Baltimore's Johns Hopkins University, an innovative new higher education institution modeled on the German research universities that had, in just eleven years of existence, become the most prestigious graduate school in the country. In September 1888 the young scholar packed his bags and began his travels to his generation's Göttingen.[7]

FORTY-EIGHT

On dropping out of Davidson in the spring of 1874 on account of his "cold," Woodrow Wilson spent fifteen months living with his parents, who had moved to Wilmington, North Carolina, after the elder Wilson fell out with his superiors at the Columbia Theological Seminary. Woodrow knew no one in the modest port town and spent his days alone, reading and studying, or on the waterfront, dreaming about his imaginary naval command. He was withdrawn, shy, and dignified. The Wilsons' African American butler called him "an old young man."

After this peculiar interlude, his father enrolled him at another Presbyterian institution, the College of New Jersey, soon to be known as Princeton.[1]

As Joseph Wilson was still expecting his son to become a minister, Princeton was a likely choice, given its strict rules (undergraduates were forbidden to play cards, make loud noises, or leave campus without permission), conservative trustees (who chose faculty members based on their piety rather than their scholarship), pro-Southern orientation (in the early 1850s, two-thirds of the student body had come from the future Confederacy), and blunt racism (blacks weren't allowed to apply). What he probably didn't know was that the students—much like those at Harvard in the 1810s—were often in revolt against the boarding school atmosphere. They set fire to the boardwalks, detonated homemade bombs outside unpopular teachers' doors, and rioted in the streets. Woodrow soon discovered the school cared more about extracurricular activities than academics. Princeton introduced baseball, football, and student journalism while Wilson was enrolled there, and he loved them all. He neglected his studies, but was elected president of the baseball club and appointed managing editor of the *Princetonian*. Despite his aloof demeanor, he made a dozen lifelong friends. For decades afterward he would pine after his halcyon college days.[2]

Wilson was living outside the South for the first time, an experience that bolstered his reactionary politics and Southern identity. "He was very full of the South and quite Secessionist," classmate Robert McCarter later recalled. "One night we sat up until dawn talking about it, he taking the Southern side and getting quite bitter." He almost came to blows with some Northern students during the contested 1876 election and was barely able to contain himself when Hayes assumed the presidency. On July 4, 1876, he lamented America's Centennial in his diary: "How much happier we would be now if she had England's form of government instead of the miserable delusion of a republic. A republic too founded upon the notion of abstract liberty! I venture to say this country will never celebrate another centennial as a republic. The English form of government is the only true one." He recorded his outrage at universal male suffrage in his textbooks, claiming it was inconsistent with eight hundred years of English liberty and "the healthy operation of a free government." Just before graduation in 1879, he withdrew from a prestigious debate contest rather than be forced to argue in favor of universal suffrage, a decision that garnered praise from his parents. "Universal suffrage is at the foundation of every evil in this country," he confided in his diary.[3]

Wilson knew he wanted to be a statesman—he'd sometimes inscribed his calling cards "Thomas Woodrow Wilson; Senator from Virginia"—but allowed his father to pressure him into becoming a lawyer instead. He spent a miserable year studying law at the University of Virginia, grumbling to his friends about the school's emphasis on academics rather than college life. "The Law is indeed a hard task master," he confessed to a Princeton friend. "This excellent thing, the Law, gets as monotonous as that other immortal article of food, Hash, when served with such endless frequency." He skipped so many classes that he was nearly expelled, a number of them sacrificed to carry on an unsuccessful courtship of his first cousin, who lived forty miles to the north.

In the middle of his second year, after months of complaints about a persistent cold, he suddenly abandoned his studies and returned home without packing his books or saying good-bye to his friends. Two months later he wrote a classmate, asking him to send a bundle of clothes he'd left behind, and claiming he'd left because "my doctor found my digestive organs seriously out of gear." He spent the next sixteen months back in his parents' Wilmington home, studying for the bar exam and writing articles that no one would agree to publish. "The determination of the Saxon race of the South that the negro race shall never again rule over them is, then, not unnatural and it is necessarily unalterable," one read. "They are bound . . . to maintain an [sic] united resistance to the domination of an ignorant race."[4]

In May 1882 the twenty-five-year-old Wilson moved to Atlanta to work in the law offices of a University of Virginia schoolmate, Edward Renick. He passed the Georgia bar that October and began practicing a profession he disliked, surviving on a monthly allowance from his parents. "I am unfit for practice," he wrote a Princeton classmate seven months later. "The atmosphere of the courts has proved very depressing to me. I cannot breathe freely nor smile readily in an atmosphere of broken promises, of wrecked estates, of neglected trusts, of unperformed duties, of crimes and of quarrels. . . . My natural, and therefore predominant, tastes every day allure me from my law books; I throw away law reports for histories, and my mind runs after the solution of political, rather than of legal, problems." His calling, he realized, was political science, and the means of pursuing it would be to become a university professor. He secured the help of his uncle James Woodrow and some of his Princeton classmates and quickly learned that the one truly great graduate school in the country was to be found in Baltimore.[5]

He applied to the Seminar on Historical and Political Science at Johns Hopkins and, though denied a fellowship, enrolled in September 1883.

THE SEMINAR was first introduced into the curriculum by George Bancroft's research assistant, Austin Scott, who had studied in Berlin, where he helped the then ambassador compile the last volume of his *History* and was now helping him prepare a two-volume history of the creation of the Constitution. It had recently come under the direction of thirty-three-year-old Herbert Baxter Adams, another Massachusetts-born, Harvard-trained graduate of the German university system, who had helped Scott replicate the *seminarium* education they'd received in Germany.

At the Bluntschli Library on the second floor of Hopkins Hall, Wilson and his fellow students met around a long table to present and discuss one another's original work. Adams encouraged them to approach history in a scientific fashion, collecting evidence, subjecting it to scrutiny, and comparing conflicting accounts of an event in an attempt to ascertain the truth of what had actually happened. On the tables were the latest magazines in the field, including an innovative journal published by the seminar itself, *The Johns Hopkins University Studies in Historical and Political Science*, the first real academic historical journal in the country. The tall shelves lining the walls contained the eight-thousand-volume collection of the library's namesake, the late Johann Kaspar Bluntschli, a constitutional law scholar who had been Adams's mentor at the Heidelberg University. On the wall was inscribed the seminar's mission statement: "History is past Politics and Politics is present History." It was an extraordinary intellectual environment and the primary catalyst for the development of academic history in the United States, graduating rigorously trained scholars who would staff new history departments across the country.[6]

Wilson, having committed to an academic career, appreciated the intellectual intensity, but soon became annoyed with Adams's professional obsession: Teutonism.

More even than Bancroft, Adams was taken with the idea that the germ of American liberty had originated in the Black Forest of Germany, so much so that he had convinced himself that many institutions in early New England—the town meeting, the town common, the appointment of select-men, and so on—also had their origins in ancient German forms. Consis-tent with this theory—and to foster research skills—he required each of his students to conduct an original examination of the institutional history of his home community. Wilson, who saw himself as a thinker, not a re-searcher, hated it. "I found that they wanted to set everybody under their authority to working on what they called 'institutional history,' to digging, that is, into the dusty records of old settlements and colonial cities . . . and other rummaging work of a like dry kind, which seemed very tiresome in comparison with the grand excursions amongst imperial policies which I had planned for myself," he wrote to his fiancée, Ellen Louise Axson, whom he'd met that summer.

After a month of this research, he begged Adams to let him instead focus on a critical study of the U.S. Constitution, to which Adams agreed. He spent much of his time writing what would become his first book, *Congressional Government*, a treatise on the "living reality" of U.S. government. Wilson prepared it without ever once having visited Washington, just a short train ride to the south, where he might have actually observed his subject in action. In the book he argued that the presidency and political parties were too weak, Congress and its component committee chairs too strong, and the best solution to the problem was to adopt the British parlia-mentary system, wherein the leaders of the executive branch are all drawn from the legislature, where they remain members. The book has not aged well.[7]

Wilson made several close friends at Hopkins, among them a young North Carolinian named Thomas Dixon Jr., who sat on his right in the sem-inar room. Dixon's father was a slaveholding Baptist preacher, his mother the daughter of prominent South Carolina planters, and his uncle and boy-hood hero was the leader of the local Klan, about which Dixon had already written a sympathetic play. Tall, thin, and dark-eyed, Dixon was intense, performative, and could "whirl words and ideas at an audience as few men can." The two Southerners spent hours discussing politics and the South in Wilson's drafty boardinghouse room overlooking Mount Vernon Place. "We became intimate friends," Dixon recalled. Wilson introduced him to the editor of the *Baltimore Mirror*, for which he became a freelance drama critic, and at the end of the term tried to talk him out of dropping out of school to become an actor. "Wilson thought I was allowing my enthusiasm to carry me too far," he said. "But I said Good bye to my comrade on Mt. Vernon Place and went to New York."[8]

They would keep in touch. A year later *Congressional Government* was published and received widespread, if mixed, reviews. Dixon wrote with effusive praise. "You don't know how proud it made me," he said. "I just jumped up and yelled 'Three cheers for Wilson.' . . . I would give anything to be able to shake your hand and talk it over." The following year he took it upon himself to propose to the trustees of his alma mater, North Carolina's Wake Forest College, that Wilson be awarded an honorary doctorate of law on the strength of the book. "Your name was magic when I suggested it to the Faculty for approval," he added. That honor helped Wilson a great deal in his professional ambitions.[9]

By early 1886 Wilson had become restless. He and Ellen Axson were eager to be married, the book was selling well, and he felt his "mental and physical health" would be "jeopardized by a forced march through fourteen thousand pages of dry reading" to complete his degree. His friends and teachers tried to convince him not to leave Johns Hopkins, but Wilson was adamant. On the strength of his book, he put himself out in the job market and eventually accepted an offer to teach at Bryn Mawr, a new women's college located just over the border in southeastern Pennsylvania. Ellen was displeased; as a traditional Southern woman she didn't think women should be straying from their conventional roles and pursuing higher education. Wilson agreed. "Lecturing to young women of the present generation on the history and principles of politics is about as appropriate and profitable as would be lecturing to stone-masons on the evolution of fashion in dress," he confided in his diary, adding that his students' minds were like a vacuum through which his speeches passed without generating heat. Not surprisingly he clashed with the college's highly credentialed female deans and administrators, annoyed female postdoctoral fellows with his condescension, and within a year was looking to escape to somewhere more masculine.[10]

Belatedly realizing his need of a doctorate, he convinced Adams to pull some strings at Johns Hopkins and let him submit *Congressional Government* as a dissertation and to take a set of required exams carefully geared to ensure he would pass. In June 1886, he was awarded a PhD he had not really earned.

As Wilson flailed around for a job during the following year, Adams arranged for him to deliver paid weekly guest lectures to the seminar. Each week for five weeks each term for the next decade, Wilson spent several days in Baltimore as a visiting lecturer in political science, a position that enhanced his reputation and gratified his intellect.[11]

There, as the fall term of 1888 began, Wilson met one of his new students, a promising young professor from Wisconsin named Frederick Jackson Turner.

FORTY-NINE

Wilson and Turner likely encountered each other for the first time in the seminar room on a chilly mid-February night in 1889. Lean, gregarious Turner, twenty-seven years old, would have been seated with his fellow graduate students around the long, dull red wooden seminar table under portraits of Bancroft, von Holst, Ranke, and Bismarck. Tall, austere Wilson, thirty-two years old, would have been standing under the gaslights that hung from long pipes descending from the high ceilings, his shorthand or typewritten notes in hand, delivering a lecture on one or another aspect of the administrative arrangements of governments, past, present, and future. Seated among the students or at the side tables would have been Herbert Baxter Adams and his assistant, John Franklin Jameson, who nine years earlier had been awarded the very first doctorate in history ever issued by a U.S. institution.[1]

Turner's first impression, recoded shortly thereafter in a letter to his own fiancée, was that Wilson was "homely, solemn, young, glum, but with that fire in his face and eye that means that its possessor is not of the common crowd." Wilson's lecture intrigued Turner and, discovering they were both lodging in Mary Jane Ashton's McCulloh Street boardinghouse, approached him one evening in the parlor. Soon they were engaged in the first of many long, intense, intellectually rewarding conversations that would shape the future direction of both men's work. Their dialogue lasted so long that Ms. Ashton finally had to break it up. "Well, gentlemen," she observed, "you have drank all the cider, eaten all the cake, and it is after eleven o'clock. I confess to being sleepy."[2]

The Republican newspaperman's son from Yankee Wisconsin and the Deep South–raised, Democratic-voting, Scots-Irish Presbyterian minister's boy had a number of things in common.

First, each had already spent months or years immersed in Herbert Baxter Adams's seminar room, "the temple of the Teutonist cult," as one scholar called it. Fueling Adams's ideas were the findings of Charles Darwin in the natural sciences, which by the 1870s had inspired social scientists to try to apply evolutionary ideas to humans and their institutions. The British essayist Herbert Spencer had argued that the staggering and ever-growing inequality in those industrializing times was due to natural selection, coining the phrase "survival of the fittest" and arguing that those "not sufficiently complete to live . . . should die" to "make room for the better." This bolstered the idea that societies grew like organisms from an inherited seed, but suggested that as they did so they would adapt to the conditions they encountered. This helped explain, theorists of the 1880s thought, the differences between the "races," an especially elastic term in those days that conflated ethnicity, nationality, and race. At Hopkins and elsewhere, social scientists obsessed over the characteristics and relative qualities of the "French race," the "Anglo-Saxon race," and the "Aryan race," as well as the "Negro," "Mongolian," and "Caucasian" ones. Both men were receptive to these ideas before coming to Hopkins, Turner having been introduced to them by Professor Allen, Wilson by his uncle James Woodrow, a man who became so enthusiastic about evolutionary theory it had gotten him expelled from the Columbia Theological Seminary.[3]

As children of the South and Middle West respectively, each was also keenly aware of the differences between the regions, and the blind spots that their New England–dominated faculty had about the contributions each had made to American life. Both felt compelled to represent and account for their regions. Each man had not simply a passion for history, but a desire to use it to weave a more accurate and fulfilling story of how and why their nation had formed and where it was going.

Evening after evening, as the chilly Baltimore winter gave way to spring, they talked, quizzing each other about their parts of the country: Wilson wanted to know how German immigrants in the Midwest would react if the United States and Germany ever went to war; Turner wanted to know how Southerners justified the nullification of federal laws in the 1830s or secession in the 1860s. Wilson pontificated about the power of leadership and the shortcomings of the separation of powers, and shared his ambition to enter politics; Turner shared his observations on life on the Euro-American settlement frontier. They talked about the growth of the national idea and the American nationality and agreed that the West's role in both developments was very great and thoroughly neglected by historians.[4]

"All my ideas and ambitions were broadened and enriched by Woodrow Wilson's conversations," Turner would later recall. "I dare to think that these conversations had some effect upon the later history of the country as well as upon Mr. Wilson and myself."[5]

Inspired by what they had shared with each other and what Hopkins had shared with each of them, they returned home that spring to begin researching what would be the most influential works either would ever produce.

FIFTY

The true manner of living in old age is to gather a circle of friends who are devoted to the culture of truth, think with the freedom of men gifted with reason, and patient or even fond of differences of opinion," George Bancroft explained to a friend shortly after his return to the United States. "If but half a dozen of such men would but meet weekly at dinner at my house I should find instruction and delight, and beguile the infirmities of years by the perennial, never-ending enjoyment of friendship and intelligence."

At their comfortable homes in Washington and Newport, the Bancrofts re-created the graceful, intellectually engaging cosmopolitan milieu they had enjoyed in London and Berlin. They hosted dinners for diplomats and generals, intellectuals and senators, presidents and emperors, the tables decorated with the rare roses George cultivated in the conservatory or in the garden behind their mansion in Washington. President Chester Arthur said that when it came to socializing, the president was "permitted to accept the invitations of members of his cabinet, Supreme Court judges and Mr. George Bancroft," and his peers appear to have followed the rule, regardless of political party. Ulysses Grant and his wife joined President Arthur at Bancroft's table in 1882. The following year Arthur returned to dine there with the new German ambassador, Baron Karl von Eisendecher, a close personal friend of Bismarck's. President Grover Cleveland, his wife, two cabinet secretaries, and a senator dined in May 1887, then stepped across the hall into the Bancrofts' reception room where another 250 guests awaited. One 1878 banquet featured General William Tecumseh Sherman, Supreme Court Chief Justice Morrison Waite, the former New York City mayor Fernando Wood, and what *The Washington Post* deemed "a brilliant assemblage of the wealth, the wit, and the worth of the Republic." One houseguest recalled his hosts asking him whom he would like to join them at dinner. "Why not have the Presidential aspirants?" he replied. Bancroft "threw up his hands with a gesture of applause quite common with him and said, 'Delightful, we'll have them,'" and in short order they were all there.[1]

In old age Bancroft had achieved a unique social status. In January 1879 the U.S. Senate voted to give him floor privileges, the only private citizen to have ever been granted them. At all important official ceremonies, a seat would be reserved for Bancroft behind the president, alongside the cabinet officers and Supreme Court justices. He often dined at the White House and, on his eighty-sixth birthday, John Jacob Astor hosted a banquet for him at his Newport mansion, with guests that included Jerome Napoleon Bonaparte II, the would-be heir to the imperial throne created by his infamous great-uncle.[2]

Though he had withdrawn from public life, Bancroft never stopped working. His second-floor library swelled and eventually took over much of his living quarters, colonizing the walls of his bedroom, and crowding him into a small bed. A little writing table with two candles stood near its head. "He keeps pen and paper all night," Carl Hermann Braatz, their loyal German valet, said to a visitor in 1883. "If a thought strikes him, he jots it down." He woke at 5:00 each morning and set to work on whatever project was at hand until 8:30, when he would dress and come downstairs to breakfast—"fruit, a cup of chocolate, an egg and a roll," according to Braatz—and wouldn't eat again until dinner. Moderation, he told those inquiring about his impressive octogenarian fitness, was essential, both for health and for working efficiency. He then returned to his desk until early afternoon, received visits for an hour or two, and then—so long as the temperature was above forty degrees—set out on a two- or three-hour horseback ride. Such rides took him from the H Street mansion to the leafy country lanes of Arlington or Maryland's peaceful Montgomery County. When he was eighty-five, he thrice rode the thirty-two-mile round-trip to the Great Falls of the Potomac with no sign of fatigue. When in Newport, he rode a white steed up and down the beaches. "He always said that the habit of equestrian exercise which he kept up through life, even while residing in London and in Berlin, kept him fresh for literary work, and contributed to health and long life," his frequent riding companion, Librarian of Congress Ainsworth Spofford, recalled. On the men's return trips Washington street children would gawk at Bancroft—wiry, rosy cheeked, his long white beard flapping in the wind and a twinkle in his blue eyes—and yell, "Here comes grandfather Santa Claus on his fine horse!" Dinner would follow, usually with a circle of amicable guests, and by ten he would be asleep, at least until a fresh thought summoned him to the writing table.[3]

In 1874 Bancroft set to work on a revised "Centenary Edition" of his *History*, which appeared two years later, a six-volume version incorporating new material he'd discovered in the decades since the earlier editions had first appeared. No sooner was this completed than he began composing a sequel, the two-volume *History of the Formation of the Constitution of the United States of America*, with the help of Austin Scott. This appeared in 1882 and sold well, if only because it was hard to resist reading an account of the Early Republic written by a man who had met John Adams, interviewed James Madison, and dined with the Marquis de Lafayette. On its publication he wrote his sister a note about the importance of their cheering each other "as we draw nearer and nearer to the shores of eternity which are already in full sight," and within weeks he embarked on another epic project, the "Author's Final Revision," an updated and abridged version of the *History* published, also in six volumes, between 1883 and 1885. Even his wife's death in March 1886 didn't stop him from writing and hosting banquets. A month after his wife's passing, the eighty-five-year-old took the overnight train to Nashville, where he stayed with President Polk's widow, Sarah, convinced her to let him take possession of her husband's papers, and—after a visit to Lookout Mountain—was soon back at 1623 H Street, transcribing presidential papers in preparation for a biography of his former boss.[4]

Through all of Bancroft's late work, his thesis never changed. In 1882 he affirmed that the ideas in the introduction to his first volume in 1834 were essentially correct: "The intervening years have justified their expression of confidence in the progress of our republic." The Civil War had been the nation's final struggle; henceforth the United States would float down the Providential stream to a land of milk, honey, and human freedom. The violent collapse of Reconstruction and the imposition of a racial caste system on four million fellow Americans gave him no pause. His faith was not shaken by violent clashes between workers, corporate security personnel, and National Guardsmen over wages, job security, and safe working conditions. The emergence of an industrial proletariat and the exhaustion of free federal land grants in the West did not provoke concern in him that perhaps the Jacksonian dream had failed. As the 1880s began, Bancroft's early-nineteenth-century worldview was in fact becoming less and less relevant to the problems afflicting the nation.[5]

His reputation in scholarly circles was also in retreat. The younger generations of scientific historians gathered around Herbert Baxter Adams looked askance at Bancroft's methods, his shortcomings in sourcing and accuracy, his flights of poetic rhetoric in support of conclusions unsupported by solid documentary evidence. In 1884 they created a vehicle for the professionalization of the discipline, the American Historical Association, which sought to bring order, training, and cohesion to the exploration and dissemination of the nation's story. The group met to create a curriculum for public high schools—the first held in Madison with receptions at the Turner home, where Woodrow Wilson was a houseguest—and successfully won a charter from Congress, which they hoped would lead to an alliance with the federal government to construct the national narrative, as European countries did through their ministries of culture. Although Bancroft was a symbol of all the AHA was seeking to displace, his political standing was such that the association elected him to the largely ceremonial position of president in 1865. "The movements of humanity are governed by law," he reassured them in his subsequent address to their annual meeting. "It is true that the sparrow, when the time comes for its fall to the ground, obeys a law that pervades the Kosmos; and it is equally true that every hair in the head of a human being is numbered. The growth and decay of empire, the morning lustre of a dynasty and its fall from the sky before noonday; the first turning of a sod for the foundation of a city to the footsteps of a traveller searching for its place which time has hidden, all proceed as it is ordered." If "discerning the presence" of this law was proving difficult, it was because "of the infinite variety of the movements of the human will and of the motives by which it may be swayed," making it hard for statesmen to forecast coming events. Adams and his followers may have been dubious about this assertion, but the many nonacademic attendees in the audience received the stately, reassuring speech with pleasure.[6]

As the country grew less recognizable, Bancroft retreated further into the past or the pleasant company of social gatherings. Only one public policy issue prompted him to lift his cudgel: the infernal and unrepublican decision to introduce paper currency, rather than specie, or coins made of metal that had an inherent value. "Return to specie payment," he demanded. "Until that event occurs our glorious constitution lies bleeding." The public paid little attention to the arguments he disseminated in a pamphlet—that democracy and hard money existed hand in hand—as they, like Bancroft himself, belonged to a world that no longer existed. Bancroft would not engage in contemporary policy debates again.[7]

In 1884 newspapers had begun reporting each of his birthdays as if they might be his last, a death watch for a man who had outlived nearly all his contemporaries. For years he confounded them by returning from Newport in fine condition, but now Bancroft was beginning to show signs of his advanced age.[8] He stopped riding horses or walking out of doors after dark, and his German valet was always at his side, indoors or out. He would lose his thread of thought in conversation, or become confused about the identity of the person he was speaking to. The former U.S. Speaker of the House Robert Winthrop was called to his bedside in May 1889, only to realize that Bancroft thought Winthrop was his brother, Francis Winthrop, who had been in Bancroft's Harvard class and had been dead for seventy years.

Shortly before leaving Newport in the fall of 1890, Bancroft caught a persistent cold. For weeks he lingered, bedridden, at his H Street home, as visitors came to pay their respects. Senator George Hoar saw him at the end of December and reported that he'd engaged him with "fresh and vigorous thought on new topics" with "a quickness and vigour of thought and intelligence and spoke with a beauty of diction that no man I know could have surpassed." But before the visit ended, the ninety-year-old lost the thread of the conversation, his memory clouded, and the visit came to an end. Not three weeks later, on the afternoon of January 17, 1891, George Bancroft died, two days after losing consciousness.[9]

President Benjamin Harrison ordered the flags flown at half-staff before attending the funeral at St. John's Church, located a block from both the White House and Bancroft's home. There the president was joined by his cabinet, the justices of the Supreme Court (many of whom served as pallbearers), and much of Washington's diplomatic, military, and congressional establishment. The commissioner of the civil service, a young man named Theodore Roosevelt, was in attendance. The German ambassador laid a wreath from the emperor of Germany on the silver-handled casket. Several hundred people waited outside on the street, the men with hats in their hands. After the service the casket was placed on a horse-drawn hearse, which the mourners followed through Lafayette Park and down Pennsylvania Avenue to the B&O station. There it was loaded onto a special car and at 2:00 p.m. began its journey to Worcester, where his life had begun nearly a century before, in a very different America.[10]

FIFTY-ONE

The situation in the former Confederacy was growing more dire. With the black vote suppressed, Redeemer governments representing the interests of the old planter oligarchy had taken control. They began slashing funding for public school systems, public health agencies, insane asylums, and other institutions that benefited the poor. They adopted literacy tests and poll taxes knowing that, in practice, they would rarely be applied to white voters. Surprisingly, the freed peoples' most prominent champion said very little about the situation.

The Compromise of 1877 had led Frederick Douglass to make his own compromises. He had campaigned hard for Rutherford B. Hayes and was relieved when the Republican took the oath of office (in a private ceremony, to avoid assassination). At the same time, Douglass's financial situation was desperate. He had to support his wayward sons and their children, as well as various siblings and half siblings who had reached out to him after being emancipated, in addition to his own household on Capitol Hill. Speechmaking was his only reliable form of income, but the rigors of the travel were wearing the sixty-year-old down. In the spring of 1878 Douglass reached out to President Hayes, hoping for a political appointment. The president nominated him for the position of the Marshal of the District of Columbia, a federal official who helped run the federal courts, thereby making Douglass the first African American to serve in a position requiring Senate approval. Northern newspapers prematurely celebrated an end to the color line. "An ex-slave is now marshal of that old Babylonian city," Michigan's *Muskegon Chronicle* trumpeted. "Verily Babylon has fallen!" Washington's lawyers protested, but ultimately, Douglass would later report, they were not "half as malicious and spiteful as they had been industriously represented as being."[1]

As a member of the administration, Douglass was now dependent on both his salary and the self-dealing and nepotism that had by this time become routine in the federal government. (After the next president, James Garfield, made him the District of Columbia's Recorder of Deeds in 1881, Douglass hired his children to staff the office and approved payments to various relatives for unspecified freelance work.) For several years he was uncharacteristically silent in response to his bosses' abandonment of African Americans in the South. When he did speak out, it was usually to discourage blacks from joining the growing exodus from the authoritarian region, warning if they did so, "the late rebellion will have triumphed." Most of those fleeing—people who had seen their neighbors and relatives tortured or murdered for trying to vote—knew it already had.[2]

In this period he returned three times to the Eastern Shore. In St. Michaels he met with the bedridden Thomas Auld, who confessed that he'd always disliked slavery and had always known Douglass was "too smart to be a slave." In Easton he spoke at the court house, where he'd been imprisoned nearly half a century earlier, after a gracious introduction by an elderly man who had been his jailer. A fellow ex-slave helped him walk the fields and shores of the Tuckahoe until they found the site of his grandmother's cabin, where Douglass knelt and collected handfuls of soil to bring home to Washington. At the Wye House plantation he was received as an honored guest by Senator Lloyd's great-grandchildren, and sat with them on the veranda of the Great House, looking out over the ornamental lawns and gardens. "A more tranquil and tranquilizing scene I have seldom met in this or any other country," he recalled.[3]

Much of his spare time in 1879 and 1880 was spent writing his third and final autobiography, *Life and Times of Frederick Douglass*, which appeared in 1881. In this book the descriptions of the Aulds were less venomous, his reflections on his former masters more forgiving and philosophical than they had been in his prewar narratives. "The abolition of slavery has not merely emancipated the negro, but liberated the whites," he reflected. The book, however, didn't sell as well as he'd hoped, leaving his family reliant on government paychecks.[4]

In August 1882 Anna died after a short, paralyzing illness, at age sixty-eight or sixty-nine at their new home in Washington's Anacostia neighborhood. In the coming months Douglass suffered what appears to have been a nervous breakdown. He spent a month recovering at the rustic Poland Springs hotel in southern Maine, then several weeks in New Hampshire's White Mountains. "The main pillar of my house has fallen," he lamented. "Life cannot hold much for me, now that she has gone."[5]

He emerged more fiery and determined than he had been in years. At a convention of black Republicans in Louisville he condemned the South's use of the "lynch law" and "lynch courts" to confound the results of the Civil War. Racism "hunts us at midnight, it denies us accommodation in hotels and justice in the courts, excludes our children from schools, refuses our sons the chance to learn trades and compels us to pursue only such labor as will bring the least reward." He demanded the federal government enforce African American voting rights and distribute aid to public schools. If it did not, blacks would rightly conclude "they have been abandoned by the Government and left to the laws of nature." As for the Republican Party, Douglass told the audience that if it "can not stand for a demand for justice and fair play, it ought to go down."

Days afterward the Supreme Court effectively nullified the Fourteenth Amendment, declaring that the equal protection clause did not prohibit discrimination by non-state actors and that the Civil Rights Act of 1875—which prohibited discrimination in hotels, transportation, theaters, and other public-facing businesses—was unconstitutional. White Southerners were now, in effect, allowed to set up apartheid regimes. Back in the capital Douglass spoke to a mass protest meeting of more than two thousand, stating that African Americans had just been "grievously wounded, wounded in the house of our friends," a reference to the fact that many of the concurring justices were Republican appointees. "It presents the United States before the world as a nation utterly destitute of power to protect the constitutional rights of its own citizens upon its own soil. . . . A wrong done to one man is a wrong done to all men. It may not be felt at the moment, and the evil may be long delayed, but so sure as there is a moral government of the universe, so sure as there is a God of the universe, so sure will the harvest of evil come." He later said the decision showed that "the cause of justice to the black man" had been steadily losing ground among white people since Appomattox. "The colored citizen felt as if the earth was opened beneath him."[6]

On January 24, 1884, Douglass quietly married Helen Pitts, a young Mount Holyoke–educated white woman twenty years his junior who worked as one of his clerks in the Recorder's Office, without first telling his sons, who worked alongside her. The marriage scandalized Pitts's family, many black activists (who felt he'd betrayed his race), and much of the national press (shocked by what was the first interracial marriage of a famous black man). Some well-known figures defended him——both Elizabeth Cady Stanton and former U.S. senator Blanche Bruce said Douglass should be able to marry whom he pleased—but the couple was hounded for years.[7]

Others criticized his decision not to immediately resign as the D.C. Recorder of Deeds when a Democratic president, Grover Cleveland, assumed office in 1885. Needing the money, Douglass stayed on for a year with Cleveland's blessing. This dalliance with what was still the party of white supremacy led one black editor to denounce him as living solely for himself "and not for the race." Douglass argued that his job wasn't really a federal one, but rather a District of Columbia position, and pointed out that Cleveland had shown a lack of racial animus by inviting him and Helen to receptions at the White House. Regardless, in March 1886 the Cleveland administration asked him to step down and, at sixty-eight, he was unemployed.[8]

After a short flurry of speaking engagements, he and Helen withdrew to

Europe for a year, the first semblance of a vacation the former slave had ever had. They did the grand tour: London and Paris, Genoa and Rome, Egypt and Greece. They climbed to the top of the Great Pyramid of Cheops—"I would not undertake it again for any consideration," he said— explored the Forum and the Acropolis, saw some of his old abolitionist friends in England, and visited the grave of Theodore Parker in Florence. Everywhere, he later told a U.S. newspaper, they were treated with respect. The same wasn't true for the speaking tour he undertook in March 1888, which took him to black churches in Charleston and Augusta, during which he was mocked by a local leader (who wouldn't debase himself "at the feet of a thick-lipped nigger demagogue") and denied restaurant service at a North Carolina train station.[9]

In the election that year he stumped for the Republican candidate, Indiana senator Benjamin Harrison, and after Harrison's inauguration wrote asking to be reappointed to his old position at the Recorder's Office. Instead he would receive the most prestigious appointment of his entire career, serving as U.S. ambassador and consul general to the only country on Earth that had been founded by a successful slave rebellion. In the fall of 1889 he and Helen moved to Haiti.

FIFTY-TWO

Turner returned to the University of Wisconsin in the summer of 1889, and that fall took up a full teaching load as Allen's sole assistant professor in history. He designed an advanced lecture course inspired by his discussions with Wilson and by Herbert Baxter Adams's lectures, which examined the rise of local institutions with a novel emphasis on how they contributed to Western and Southern sectionalism. In December, just three weeks after Turner and Caroline Sherwood were wed, Allen caught a severe cold, which proved fatal. His death left the young newlywed to teach his courses in addition to his own and also to attend to the final page proofs of the late scholar's final book, *A Short History of the Roman People*. While his wife was pregnant with their first child, Turner also somehow managed to prepare for his doctoral examinations, travel to Baltimore to take and pass them, and then complete his dissertation—on the development of trading posts in Wisconsin.[1]

It was not at all clear if university president Thomas Chamberlin would consider Turner to replace his mentor, who had been an Ivy- and German-educated scholar of national standing. Woodrow Wilson, despite not knowing Chamberlin or anyone else at Wisconsin, wrote to the president and the head of the board of regents in his support of his friend: "I take it for granted that there is practically no doubt about his succeeding Prof. Allen, by whom he was so admired and whose natural successor he would seem to be," Wilson told them. "I am writing, I am sure, in the interests of historical scholarship in America in thus insisting upon being allowed to speak in his praise." Herbert Baxter Adams sent a commendatory letter as well, and in the spring of 1891, Turner was, to his great surprise, made full professor and chair of the department.[2]

All the while, a new conception of how American history should be studied had preoccupied him. History, he was coming to believe, was an ever-changing undertaking because the needs of the present were themselves constantly changing. Men like George Bancroft, responding to the needs of the early nineteenth century, sought to plot the will of God from historical evidence, and did so almost entirely through the experiences of statesmen and nation-states. Bancroft had written at a time when the country's birth was still in living memory, when almost the entirety of the U.S. population lived east of the Mississippi, when the nation's interregional struggles were seen as North versus South, if they were acknowledged at all, and when New Englanders like himself dominated the discourse, ascribing their own region's characteristics and origins to the country as a whole. For Americans at the dawn of the twentieth century, however, many factors were missing from this picture: an understanding of the influence of immigration, geography, economics, and market relations and of competing settlement streams as they fanned out to colonize the North American continent over nearly three centuries, creating multiple regions or "sections" as they went. A new approach was needed, an interdisciplinary approach, one that took into account events in the Old World and the New, the West as well as the East, the institutions and aspirations of the common people and not just those of the political elite.[3]

He was imagining nothing less than a new blueprint for how to reconstruct the American past and, thus, understand its meaning.

In August 1890 Turner first put forward these ideas in a speech to a gathering of Wisconsin schoolteachers. He was, appropriately enough, trying to enlist their support for the founding of an adult education program, through which the university would send scholars like himself across the state to spread culture and knowledge among ordinary citizens. His address, refined and eventually published in essay form in the October 1891 edition of the *Wisconsin Journal of Education*, remains a landmark in American historiography, a detailed program for modern scholarship that was decades ahead of its time. History "is more than past literature, more than past politics, more than past economics," the essay, "The Significance of History," concluded. "It is the self-consciousness of humanity—humanity's effort to understand itself through the study of its past." This effort was vital to producing good citizens and statesmen alike, and America was not doing as well as it needed to in either area; Bancroft was the only historian-statesman the country could yet boast of, and the community was being denied a clear view of itself because of partiality and mythmaking.[4]

Through Turner's efforts—he even got Adams to come to Madison to lecture in support of his ideas—the university extension program was inaugurated. He was soon traveling to remote quarters of the state to deliver standing-room-only lectures to farmers, woodsmen, shopkeepers, and high school students about the colonization of the continent, the development of the Early Republic, and the rise of Jacksonian democracy. As he revised and repeated his talks—in a packed Milwaukee church, an overflowing Poynette meeting hall, a frigid Oshkosh assembly—his ideas developed and crystallized. He told the Madison Literary Club in February 1891 that American history was "the history of the application of men and ideas to the physical conditions" they encountered as they colonized the continent; that historians should focus not on Pocahontas, but on how the colonization of Wisconsin, Kansas, and California had affected the individuals who settled those states. "The story of the peopling of America has not yet been written," he explained. "We do not understand ourselves."

Another year of teaching, of expanding his family and building the history department passed. He and Caroline now had a daughter and an infant son. His department was fortified by the addition of a Johns Hopkins classmate, Charles Haskins. Turner was still so overtaxed with his workload that when the undergraduate newspaper, *The Aegis*, asked him to submit an essay on his research on early Wisconsin history, he missed his deadline month after month. In October 1892 he finally turned the piece in—not one about Wisconsin's past, but "Problems in American History," which appeared in the November 4 edition of the paper and would change the trajectory of a generation of American historians.

The essay argued, in an entertaining and accessible way, that American self-definition had been confounded by the myopia of the country's Eastern-born historians. "The whole drama of the development of the United States has been presented on the stage between the Allegheny Mountains and the Atlantic," he wrote. In reality, he continued, "the fundamental, dominating fact in United States history [is] the expansion of the United States from the Alleghenies to the Pacific."

> The true point of view in the history of this nation is not the Atlantic coast; it is the Mississippi Valley. The struggle over slavery is a most important incident in our history, but it will be seen, as the meaning of events unfolds, that the real lines of American development, the forces dominating our character, are to be studied in the history of westward expansion. . . .
>
> American history needs a connected and unified account of the progress of civilization across this continent with the attendant results. Until such a work is furnished we shall have no real national self-consciousness; when it is done, the significance of the discovery made by Columbus will begin to appear.

Historians had to enlist geologists, mineralogists, biologists, and geographers to understand this phenomenon. They had to comprehend the regional differences in settler culture, environment, and immigration to determine how the presence of free land on the frontier had encouraged democracy. "What the Mediterranean Sea was to the Greeks, breaking the bond of custom, offering new experiences, calling out new institutions and activities," he concluded, "the ever retreating Great West has been to the eastern United States directly, and to the nations of Europe more remotely."[5]

Copies of that November 4 edition of *The Aegis* were widely disseminated within the scholarly community. Not everyone appreciated the significance of its arguments. Simon Patten, an economist and the future dean
of the University of Pennsylvania's Wharton School of Business, wrote that
it would provide "a very helpful way of looking at our social problems,"
which suggested he hadn't read attentively, while Johns Hopkins classmate
Charles Andrews, a historian at Bryn Mawr, argued that historians should
instead stay focused on the colonial period. But some did grasp its importance.[6]

Woodrow Wilson was eager to speak about it when, just after Christmas, he arrived in Madison for the meeting of the Committee of Ten, a
blue-ribbon panel of historians convened by the National Education Association to make recommendations on how the country's rapidly prolif-
erating public high schools should teach history and how history teachers
themselves should be taught. Turner, whom the Ten invited to their meeting, put Wilson up at his house, and he read aloud to him a draft of a new
paper that delved deeper into one aspect of his research blueprint—the significance of the frontier. At one point Wilson interrupted to suggest a phrase
to help define this concept: "the hither side of free land," for which Turner
was most appreciative.[7]

Turner was preparing this paper at the request of Herbert Baxter Adams
himself, who had held "Problems in American History" in high regard and
wanted his thirty-one-year-old protégé to present the new paper at the next
meeting of the American Historical Association. The AHA's 1893 meeting
was to take place within and as part of one of the most audacious man-
made spectacles in history: the White City at the Chicago World's Fair and
Columbian Exposition.[8]

If ever there was an opportunity to make his mark on the profession and
the nation, Turner knew this would be it.

FIFTY-THREE

Albert Bushnell Hart, the Harvard historian, was overseeing the creation of a three-volume series of college textbooks for the Longman, Green & Company publishing house that would together cover the sweep of U.S. history from Columbus to the present. He wanted Wilson to write the final book, covering the period from 1830 to 1889.

This was an unexpected offer, given that Wilson wasn't a historian by either training or temperament, but rather a political theorist. He had no interest whatsoever in doing original research—in digging in the "dusty parchment"—and apparently never did any until the day he died. His work relied entirely on published sources and his own ideas, usually delivered in what he deemed his "literary style," heavy on rousing rhetoric and grand pronouncements, and doggedly committed to British spelling conventions. He was, however, already something of a star in his field, and he agreed to take on the assignment, promising to turn the manuscript in by the end of 1890, then twenty months hence. It would take him more than three years to deliver.[1]

Wilson was by then at Wesleyan College, having broken his contract with Bryn Mawr to take the new offer. Work on the textbook was slow, partly due to the combined teaching demands of his Wesleyan undergraduates and the graduate students at Johns Hopkins. He also procrastinated, however, traveling to New York to see his old classmate Thomas Dixon Jr. In the six years since they'd sat in seminar together, Dixon had bounced from acting to state politics and then to Baptist preaching, and Wilson saw him electrify a boisterous crowd in his church's modest brick building at Twenty-third and Lexington. ("Tom Dixon is a lovely fellow," he told his companion. "I see in him the same charm that endeared him to me at Johns Hopkins.")[2]

After a year of missed deadlines and tactful prodding from Hart, Wilson sequestered himself in the Wesleyan library for the summer of 1891, reading influential histories, biographies, and essays for the first time. He received helpful advice on Midwestern and Western sources from Turner and read von Holst's *Constitutional and Political History of the United States* and Jefferson Davis's two-volume *Rise and Fall of the Confederate Government*. He relied heavily on the infamous white supremacist Edward Pollard's *Lost Cause*, which argued that slavery was benevolent and that the Civil War had been a clash of the incompatible Puritan and Cavalier civilizations. He studied a new biography of William Gilmore Simms written by one of his Johns Hopkins seminar students, William Trent, which illuminated much of the late writer's life, work, and thought. He also pursued the writings of the South's new literary star, Thomas Nelson Page, whose blockbuster novels and widely circulated historical essays essentially created the Romantic "moonlight and magnolias" image of the antebellum slave plantations. All of these authors were included in the textbook's prominent bibliography and source lists. Frederick Douglass's work and very existence were never once mentioned.[3]

Slowly, painstakingly, through the summers of 1891 and 1892 and in scraps of time during the school year, Wilson wrote his compact volume, which would be entitled *Division and Reunion, 1829–1889*. In its introduction he promised he would present the events of this divisive era with an "impartiality of judgment," a pledge that proved very attractive to a white reading public that had tired of the rancorous debate over the meaning of the Civil War. After considerable editorial work by Hart, who succeeded in reining in some of Wilson's stylistic shortcomings and interpretive biases, the book appeared in the spring of 1893 as a 326-page textbook with five colored, fold-out maps. Contained within was an outline of the post-Confederate vision of the re-united states Wilson would further as president, a sectional reconciliation based on shared Anglo-Saxon interests.[4]

The book was novel in that it gave greater attention to the role of the Middle West and Far West in the national story. Reflecting his conversations with Turner, Wilson described the new states that appeared in the Appalachian highlands and Ohio Valley in the first decades after the Revolution as being "at a much greater remove from old tradition and settled habit, and . . . in direct contact with difficulties such as breed rough strength and a bold spirit of innovation." Their settlers brought "a sort of frontier self-assertion which quickly told upon our politics, shaking the government out of its old sobriety, and adding a spice of daring personal initiative." The backcountry settlers' influence was apparent in 1829, when the Scots-Irish Andrew Jackson won the presidency, creating "for good or for ill" a new "distinctively American order of politics" that overshadowed even the Revolution and laid the groundwork for the Civil War. Wilson saw the frontier much as Simms had, as a place of rich potential in need of the civilizing hand of the conservative, learned leaders of the seaboard; he recognized, however, that that battle had been joined and lost, sweeping away the country's closest analog to the English gentry, the gentleman planter.[5]

What attracted most comment, however, was Wilson's treatment of his native South and its slave system. "It would seem plain," now that an entire generation had come of age since the Confederacy's defeat, he wrote, "that the charges of moral guilt for the establishment and perpetuation of slavery . . . made against the slaveholders of the southern States must be very greatly abated, if they are to be rendered in any sense just." Slaves, he asserted, "were almost uniformly dealt with indulgently and even affectionately by their masters." Under those owners with "the sensibility and breeding of gentlemen," slaveholding was "apt to produce a noble and gracious type of manhood, and relationships really patriarchal." Field hands, he claimed "were comfortably quartered, and were kept from overwork both by their own laziness and by the slack discipline to which they were subjected." The brutality described in *Uncle Tom's Cabin* was "in every sense exceptional, showing what the system could produce, rather than what it did produce as its characteristic spirit and method." Conditions were worst in the border states, where Northerners were most likely to witness them, he asserted against all evidence collected before or since, because there slaves were more tempted to run away and, thus, were punished more often.[6]

As for the causes of the Civil War, Wilson had nothing to say about Brooks's caning of Sumner, but plenty of criticism of William Lloyd Garrison and his fellow abolitionists. The Garrisonians' demand for an immediate end to slavery had, Wilson claimed, "powerfully repelled the mass of people, rendered deeply conservative by the inheritance and practice of self-government, deeply imbued, like all of their race, with the spirit of political compromise, patient of anomalies, good-natured too, after the manner of large democracies, and desirous of peace." John Brown had stirred Southerners' legitimate fears of slave insurrections, which "meant massacre and arson, and for the women a fate worse than any form of death or desolation." The South, he claimed, had been entirely correct that it had a legal right to secede, but had wound up on the wrong side of history, because the other sections of the country had radically changed their interpretations of the Constitution since 1787, while Dixie had supposedly held steady to its precepts, becoming, in effect, an Early Republic in amber.[7]

Wilson outright condemned Reconstruction, arguing that black enfranchisement had created "an extraordinary carnival of public crime set in under the forms of law," marked by rampant corruption and extortionary taxes. He acknowledged, in passing, that whites had tried to prevent blacks from voting and that "sometimes this effort took the most flagrant forms of violence," but insisted that this had quickly passed, leading Congress to wisely scale back federal enforcement measures in 1872. The Supreme Court decisions that neutered the Fourteenth and Fifteenth Amendments were implicitly praised for "recalling Congress to the field of the Constitution." The mass slaughters in Hamburg, Vicksburg, Colfax, and New Orleans were not mentioned in the book at all, and the only reference to the Klan was in a subsection heading that had been added by the editors.[8]

While Wilson had no moral objections to slavery, he believed it had been bad for the South because it had stultified economic and social development, creating masses of poor whites, which he called "one of the most singular non-productive classes that any country has ever seen." Such people lived in a wretched state of subsistence because of their "pride of freedom," and lack of "energy and initiative necessary to support themselves decently" coupled with a shortage of wage-labor jobs. Since the war, however, Wilson wrote, the region had been "freed from the incubus of slavery" and had developed and industrialized at a rapid pace, all but eliminating the socioeconomic distinctions between it and the other regions of the country. Other problems may have arisen—"hot conflicts between capital and labor"—but "the new troubles bred new thinkers, and the intellectual life of the nation was but the more deeply stirred."[9]

"The century closed with a sense of preparation," he concluded, "a new seriousness, and a new hope."[10]

The book received a mixed reaction. Turner wrote to congratulate Wilson on what was "in style . . . your most attractive work"; some chapters, he said, were "destined to live with the classics of our literature and history," but his entire argument about the South having remained true to the Constitution was false. The region "did not remain preserved by the ice of slavery like a Siberian mammoth. She changed greatly." *The Nation* agreed, saying this assertion amounted to "dealing in contradictions which are self-destructive." In his review von Holst said: "Wilson does not duly appreciate the part played by the purely moral element in the irrepressible conflict." One particularly virulent Southern newspaper, the *New Orleans Daily Picayune*, criticized the book for not giving a glowing enough account of slavery. "The pictures that he draws of their miseries would be appalling if they were not ridiculous," it said. "Every one who knows anything about it understands that the slaves before '61 were far better off than the inhabitants of the slums and sweatshops of New York are today."[11]

Most critics applauded, however, embracing an account that let white Americans put the Civil War and civil rights behind them. "While in all probability he will not satisfy extremists North or South, he has come as near to the Right as any writer has done or, in our opinion, will be able to do," Kemp Plummer Brattle, president emeritus of the University of North Carolina, proclaimed in a typical review. "Dr. Wilson has earned the gratitude of seekers after truth by his masterly production." Wilson's father even snuck in praise, writing anonymously in New York's *Church Union* of his son's brilliant reputation. "In our judgment, Prof. Wilson has given the very best account which has yet been written of those causes which led to our civil war, of those other causes which brought it to an end, and of that third class of causes which served to promote the reunion of the States after such a terrible severance," wrote the elder Wilson, author of *Mutual Relations of Masters and Slaves as Taught in the Bible*.[12]

Wilson now began considering a book on the entire sweep of U.S. history. He wrote a colleague at South Carolina's Erskine College, asking how he thought such a work might be received in the South, and was assured it would be welcomed warmly. He shared his ambition with Turner, who likewise gave ample encouragement. Soon he was back in the Wesleyan library, reading areas of history he'd never before studied, and preparing what he might have hoped would be the work to replace that of George Bancroft.[13]

It would take an ambitious Hollywood director to make his dream come true.

FIFTY-FOUR

When Douglass and Helen arrived in Port-au-Prince on October 15, 1889, the Haitian Republic was just recovering from a year of chaos prompted by the mysterious shooting death of a presidential candidate. General Florvil Hyppolite, a member of a prestigious Franco-African family, was now ensconced in the National Palace, having been elected president by the parliament after months of provisional rule, supported by U.S. arms shipments. Hyppolite's rivals were hoping to topple his regime, and the United States was looking for consideration for having helped him hold on to his office: a lease to the strategic harbor of Môle-Saint-Nicolas for use as a naval base to refuel the coal-powered warships of the day, enabling America to project its influence over the northern approaches to the Caribbean.[1]

Douglass soon found himself caught between his ideals and the more cynical aims of American foreign policy in an imperial age.

He had hoped U.S. influence could be used to further democracy and freedom on the troubled island, having been inspired by its beauty, flowers, forested mountains, and glorious aquamarine bays. He'd been moved by his first official audience with President Hyppolite (who said he was "the incarnation of the idea which Haiti is following"), the salutes he received from assembled soldiers, the pomp of the National Palace, and the moment when the military band of a republic created by a slave uprising played "The Star-Spangled Banner" in honor of their guest, a former slave.

But in late January 1891 Rear Admiral Bancroft Gherardi—the Louisiana-born son of George Bancroft's sister Jane and the Corsican refugee Donato Gherardi—arrived aboard his newly commissioned flagship, the cruiser USS *Philadelphia*. As commander of the North Atlantic Squadron, Gherardi summoned the ambassador aboard and informed him—"in his peculiar emphatic manner"—that President Harrison had designated him, not Douglass, to lead the long-stalled negotiations over the lease of Môle-Saint-Nicolas. Douglass tried to warn Gherardi that the one thing all Haitians emphatically agreed upon was that no outside power should ever control so much as a speck of their territory, and that any effort to bully them for a lease to Môle was certain to fail.[2] Gherardi went with bullying.

In his first meeting with President Hyppolite, the admiral declared "it was the destiny of Môle to belong to the United States" and that no other powers would be allowed to occupy it, even if Haiti wanted only to lease it to them. He bluntly reminded Hyppolite that he'd promised to pay back the United States for helping him take power, and insisted that this was the way to do it. "No better way could have been devised to arouse the suspicion of the Haitian statesmen and lead them to reject our application for a naval station than to make such representations as these coming from the decks of the flag-ship of Rear Admiral Gherardi," Douglass observed.[3]

By spring a fleet of seven U.S. warships was anchored in Port-au-Prince, a show of force that alarmed and enraged Haitians. Douglass informed the State Department of his opposition to the admiral's strategy, which apparently favored the use of military force to seize the base. "We appeared before the Haitians, and before the world, with the pen in one hand and the sword in the other," he recalled, a debasement of what he had long argued to be the country's ideals. Hyppolite refused to be intimidated by the threat.[4]

The duties, stress, and tropical heat had all begun to wear down Douglass, who was now seventy-three, and a May 1891 insurrection in the capital was the final straw. At one point he and Helen had to barricade their villa doors with furniture and lie on the floor as bullets tore through the air and rebels and soldiers clashed on the street outside. By the time they were able to evacuate to a relatively secure hotel, Hyppolite's forces were executing fighters in the streets, and the rat-a-tat of a Gattling gun filled the air.[5]

On June 27, the Douglasses boarded the steamer *Prince Willem III*, bound for New York and retirement.[6] Hyppolite had a parting gift for Douglass, however. Six months after his return to Washington, the president appointed him First Commissioner of the Republic of Haiti to the Columbian Exposition, to be held in Chicago in 1893. Douglass, perhaps the country's most famous black man, was to oversee the construction of a pavilion to honor a turbulent black republic in the middle of the White City.[7]

FIFTY-FIVE

Chicago had edged out New York and Washington, D.C., for the right to host the 1892 World's Fair and Columbian Exposition, an event that was to both commemorate the four hundredth anniversary of the European discovery of the Americas and serve as the eleventh in a series of international exhibitions held since 1851 celebrating the world's industrial and technological progress. Chicago in the 1890s was a boomtown like no other. The rapidly expanding national railroad network had made the lakeside city a key distribution and processing center, gathering in livestock, grains, lumber, iron ore, and coal and shipping out chilled, canned, and cured meats, barrels of beer, crates of furniture and tools, iron and steel girders, rails, machine parts, ships, and railcars. In a single decade it had doubled its population to one million and created a business elite of staggering wealth. The latter bankrolled the fair, eager that it be bigger and more awe-inspiring than any before it, including those held in Paris, London, and New York. Not wanting their boisterous young city to be dismissed as provincial, they insisted the Exposition be a set-piece of U.S. power and influence, an event that would redefine America's place in the progress of the world and Chicago's place in America.[1] Building it was such an enormous undertaking that it opened a year late.

The fairgrounds spread over 690 acres on the shore of Lake Michigan, with more than two hundred neoclassical buildings set on artificial lagoons, lakes, basins, canals, and islands, connected by walkways and surrounded by landscapes created by the renowned designer Frederick Law Olmsted, planner of New York's Central Park. The largest of the colonnaded exhibition halls was so huge that it could have housed the Great Pyramid, U.S. Capitol, Madison Square Garden, and London's St. Paul's Cathedral with room to spare. At the fair's center was the Court of Honor, where gondolas floated on a long, lakelike basin amid shimmering fountains and a gilded, sixty-five-foot-tall statue of a classical figure representing the Republic, a globe in one of its outstretched hands. The entire complex was wired and lit by a new and dazzling technology, electricity, generated by huge Westinghouse dynamos housed inside the palatial Electrical Building, dazzling visitors accustomed to kerosene lamps and the dim, dangerous twilight of the era's gaslit city streets.

Fifty countries built grand pavilions to showcase their national culture and homegrown innovations. Japan built an entire Buddhist temple; the Netherlands transported three hundred of its South Seas colonial subjects to the Exposition grounds so that they could build model Javanese, Fijian, Hawaiian, and Maori settlements in a two-hundred-thousand-square-foot exhibition area and entertain visitors with dances, acrobatics, and folk medicine. Each of the forty-four U.S. states erected its own building— Wisconsin's featured a twenty-two-thousand-pound block of cheese—and railroads brought passengers directly into the fairgrounds' specially built train terminal.

The main gate was at the far end of the mile-long Midway Plaisance, a honky-tonk amusement arcade that became the model for American fairs and carnivals thereafter. At one end of the Midway, the railroad engineer George Ferris built a steel structure meant to one-up Gustave Eiffel's Tower, a 264-foot-high wheel that, with the assistance of huge steam boilers, could lift great cars full of passengers high over the city. Along the way down the strip, visitors could gawk at the lesser civilizations of the world: a village of Dahomey tribesmen (who quickly tired of being asked about cannibalism), a group of miserable Inuit (made to wear their fur clothing under the August sun), a scale replica of Donegal Castle, where Irish linen weavers could be seen at work, and an entire Cairo neighborhood, with a mosque and shops, inhabited by two hundred North Africans and a host of camels. Outside the gates on a fifteen-acre site just across Stony Island Avenue, Buffalo Bill Cody built an eighteen-thousand-seat stadium where he and his company performed their world-famous Wild West Show twice daily. The Exposition's official buildings were all painted in white lead and oil, giving them a gleaming alabaster look, dazzling at night under the artificial light. People quickly began calling the fair the White City.[2]

To acknowledge the four hundredth anniversary of Christopher Columbus's crossing, the organizers held a "Dedication Day" on October 21, 1892, six months before the park was ready to open, and when most of it was a muddy construction site. The federal government declared a new holiday for the occasion—Columbus Day—and backed a youth magazine editor's scheme to have public school pupils across the country simultaneously read a new "Pledge of Allegiance" that morning. The editor, the Baptist minister Francis Bellamy, later said that when writing the pledge—which did not include the words "under God"—he considered incorporating the terms "fraternity" and "equality," but realized the former would upset the robber barons, the latter Southern racial sensibilities. "That would be too fanciful, too many thousands of years off in realization," Bellamy recalled. "But we as a nation do stand square on the doctrine of liberty and justice for all. That's all any one nation can handle. So those words seemed the only roundup of past, present, and future."[3]

Frederick Douglass attended the dedication ceremony and stood with 140,000 other spectators inside the capacious Manufactures and Liberal Arts Building to hear a choir sing Handel's *Messiah* beneath what was then the world's largest open-span roof. The "strange and weird hum and buzz of one hundred thousand voices blended into one sound, like the road of many waters," he recalled, a phenomenon nobody in the crowd had ever experienced. He was awed by the fair's "profusion of wonders and perfections of architecture" which provided a "scene of human works more suggestive of sublime and glorious ideas" than could be beheld anywhere else. But he was already concerned about how the Exposition was handling racial issues.

President Harrison had failed to appoint a single nonwhite person to the body tasked with overseeing the fair, the 208-seat Board of National Commissioners. Nor was there a black individual among the 185 full and alternate members of the Exposition Board of Lady Managers, which appointed a white woman from Kentucky "to represent the colored people." Outreach efforts by African American and Native American groups seeking to play a role in planning exhibits representing their cultural contributions were rebuffed, and of the thousands of people employed by the Exposition, there were only two blacks performing nonmenial tasks, and both were lowly clerks. Douglass was the highest-profile black person involved in the Exposition, and he occupied that position only because he was representing a foreign country.[4]

Shortly thereafter he wrote an essay for a special issue of *Campbell's Illustrated Weekly* about the Exposition. The ceremonies, "glorious as they were," were marred by racial exclusion, "an intentional slight to that part of the American population with which I am identified." How could eight million citizens, people who had helped build the country, not be represented in the greatest display of its history and progress? "If their exclusion was an intentional humiliation of the race, the occasion was not well selected for that purpose," he wrote. "The celebration of the discovery of this continent was too great to be small. If, on the other hand, it was intended to conciliate any spirit of slavery which might still exist in one section of our country, it was an ill-advised concession; a fruitless act of obeisance to an anachronism and a mere superstition of the past." The inclusion of just one black person in a prominent position, he concluded, "would speak more for the moral civilization of the American republic than all the domes, towers and turrets of the magnificent buildings that adorn the Exposition grounds."[5]

No such changes were made.

THE EXPOSITION OPENED the following May. The Haiti Pavilion, a
dome-topped, veranda-fronted Grecian building set between the German
and Spanish complexes, had been completed months before, ahead of
schedule, and served as Douglass's base for the six months the Exposition
was open to the public. He worked out of an office in one of its wings and
received guests and well-wishers in the rotunda, where Haitian coffee was
served for ten cents a cup. At the pavilion's dedication that January, Douglass had delivered a speech to a largely black audience that assigned a
world-historical mission to Haiti and the slave rebellion that had founded
that republic. "Until Haiti struck for freedom, the conscience of the Christian world slept profoundly over slavery," he said.

> It was scarcely troubled even by a dream of this crime against
> justice and liberty. The Negro was in its estimation a sheep like
> creature, having no rights which white men were bound to respect,
> a docile animal, a kind of ass, capable of bearing burdens, and re-
> ceiving strips from a white master without resentment, and with-
> out resistance. The mission of Haiti was to dispel this degradation
> and dangerous delusion, and to give to the world a new and true
> revelation of the black man's character. This mission she has per-
> formed and performed it well. . . . Whatever may happen of peace
> or war Haiti will remain in the firmament of nations, and, like the
> star of the North, will shine on and shine on forever.[6]

On opening day President Grover Cleveland headed down the Midway
in a procession of twenty-three black carriages, passing under the nearly
completed Ferris Wheel and past the streets of Cairo before stopping at the
massive Electrical Building. Before a rapt audience he turned a golden key,
launching the power plant into operation. Fountains came to life, flags un-
furled automatically from their poles, thousands of lights flickered on. The

battleship USS *Michigan*, anchored in the lake, fired a salute. The general admission gates were flung open, and a crowd of half a million began to file in to see the triumph of the New World's industrial civilization on display.[7]

THE TURNERS ARRIVED six weeks later. Dropping their bags in the dormitory room they were staying in on the Gothic campus of the new University of Chicago, Turner's wife and friends hurried to see the nearby Exposition. Turner remained behind, struggling with what would be a lifelong affliction: procrastination.

The World's Fair sought to celebrate not just material achievements but the triumph of knowledge and ideas. So while twenty-seven million visitors strolled the fairgrounds proper in and around Jackson Park, another seven hundred thousand attended the 1,283 lectures organized by the World's Congress Auxiliary, where nearly four thousand experts from ninety-seven nations and colonies and all the states and territories of the United States shared the latest findings in every imaginable discipline, from bacteriology to literature. The speakers, carefully chosen, were to establish "mutual acquaintances and fraternal relations" with one another and help seek "practical means by which further progress might be made and the prosperity and peace of the world advanced." The congresses were held eight miles to the north, in a massive new three-story building that would afterward be turned over to the Art Institute of Chicago for use as a museum.[8]

Through the good graces of Herbert Baxter Adams, Turner was scheduled to speak at the end of the second day of a three-day congress on history, organized to operate in tandem and conjunction with the American Historical Association's annual meeting. His paper, a deeper examination of one theme of his "Problems of History" essay, was to be entitled "The Significance of the Frontier." Turner had spent most of the spring and summer researching his topic in the Wisconsin State Library but as he had failed to finish writing it, he spent the next few days completing the piece in a small, hot dorm room. He attended the welcoming reception on July 10 and the morning session on the eleventh, then returned to the dorm to resume his writing. On July 12, the day of his speech, Buffalo Bill invited all the historians to see his show during their afternoon break. Turner declined because he was still at work on his talk.[9]

The other historians took a train down to Buffalo Bill's stadium and witnessed historical memory being created and disseminated to the masses. The huge production featured Indian attacks—on a settler's cabin, on the Deadwood stagecoach, on Colonel Custer—and the vengeance sought for the white victims. The West had been won, the show emphasized, by the bullet, but it cleverly managed to reverse aggressor and victim, with aggrieved Euro-American conquerors forcefully responding to senseless, inexplicable Native American attacks. The show's enormous cast included Indians who had actually fought at the Little Bighorn, white and Latino men who had worked as cowboys or army scouts, and Cody himself, a one-time scout who had decided to bring the frontier West to life onstage because he had little doubt that the frontier had vanished. The opening programs handed out to the visiting historians that day spoke of how the "rapidly extending frontier" had been a reality just ten years earlier, but was "at present inapplicable, so fast does law and order and progress pervade the Great West." If anything could have prepared these academics for what Turner had to tell them, Buffalo Bill's show should have been it.[10]

Turner's paper was the last of four read that evening, and immediately followed an undoubtedly riveting discourse entitled "Early Lead Mining in Illinois and Wisconsin." Turner's audience, many of them tired and dusty from Buffalo Bill's show, was not particularly attentive when he finally stood up and began to present what would be one of the most influential essays in the history of U.S. historical study.

He opened with a quotation from the superintendent of the 1890 census, attesting to the fact that the frontier was now closed, as "the unsettled area has been so broken into by isolated bodies of settlement that there can hardly be said to be a frontier line." This, the young historian stated, was "the closing of a great historical movement," the nearly three-hundred-year-long westward conquest of the North American wilderness, a historical drama that had resulted in the birth of the American people and their unique character. His thesis statement, which would be cited in thousands of future textbooks and academic papers, followed almost immediately: "The existence of an area of free land, its continuous recession, and the advance of American settlement westward explain American development."[11]

What made America unique, he continued, and different from England and Europe, was its frontier, and once Americans made their way through the Cumberland Gap and into the great, continent-sized Mississippi Valley, they left the constraints of their European cultural pedigrees behind. There, in primitive conditions, the "most rapid and effective Americanization occurred," as settlers were taken "from the railroad car," stripped of "the garments of civilization," and placed in "the birch canoe" and in "the hunting shirt and the moccasin." Soon they were "planting Indian corn and plowing with a sharp stick," taking scalps "in orthodox Indian fashion" and shouting war cries. "In short, at the frontier the environment is at first too strong for the man," Turner continued. The result was something new, something truly American, and it affected all the groups who went there, be they Scots-Irish or Palatine Germans or English Yankees like himself. "The frontier promoted the formation of a composite nationality for the American people," he added. "In the crucible of the frontier, the immigrants were Americanized, liberated, and fused into a mixed race, English in neither nationality nor characteristics." Faced with the Indian threat, the residents of these federal territories looked to the U.S. government for protection, fostering loyalty to the nation, and not to their half-forgotten state of origin.[12]

The West, then, was the real place of America's birth, not New England or the Chesapeake Country or the plantations of the Deep South. Even the slavery question itself, when "right viewed" became but "an incident" in the United States' story. For on the frontier, settlers embraced self-reliance and independence, qualities Turner argued fostered democracy, democratic constitutional arrangements, and the vigorous local civics he had grown up with in Portage.[13]

His paper had a disquieting implication, however, and one Turner would wrestle with for the rest of his life. If the frontier was now closed, did that not mean that all of this American inheritance was now to be lost?

Those in the crowd, if they were paying attention at all, did not raise this point. Indeed most reacted with bored indifference. To save time the congresses were intentionally designed so as to exclude formal discussion, but there was apparently little appetite for it, even after the session was adjourned and the historians and members of the public were free to leave the hall and head out into the warm Chicago night. In their dispatches the following morning, most of the newspaper reporters covering the event didn't mention Turner's talk at all. Nor did the official account of the proceedings prepared by the program's head for *The Dial*, the famous literary journal of the Transcendentalists, even as it praised the valuable contribution made by the author of the paper on early Wisconsin and Illinois lead mining. A few days later his own father wrote a letter to relatives praising Turner's admirable post-congress services as the family's guide to the Exposition, but said nothing about his speech.[14]

TEN DAYS AFTER THE TURNERS returned to Madison, Woodrow Wilson arrived in Chicago to attend the Congress on Education. He spent an afternoon doing a rapid reconnaissance tour of the Exposition "to know where to linger during the few afternoons that remain available."[15] The next day he gave a pedantic address on whether universities should impose liberal arts course requirements on students in law, medicine, and theological schools. Yes, he argued, because specialization was a "disease" that left professionals "lamed and hampered by that partial knowledge that is the most dangerous form of ignorance. I would no more employ a physician acquainted with the general field of science than I would employ an oculist who was ignorant of the general field of medicine." As he was giving his talk in Hall 7 of the Art Institute, Frederick Douglass was in Hall 33, delivering what a newspaper reporter called a "characteristic speech" on the education of colored youth. Douglass's session began thirty minutes after Wilson's, however, so they probably never saw each other.[16]

Three days later, Wilson boarded a night train to Madison to visit Turner and try to convince him to take a job with his new employer, Princeton University.

BY AUGUST, DOUGLASS was consumed with the controversy generated by the Exposition commissioners' decision to designate August 25 "Colored People's Day." His friend Ida B. Wells, an antilynching activist and a cofounder of the NAACP who had been born into slavery thirty-one years earlier, insisted that blacks should boycott the event, especially after learning that fair organizers had ordered two thousand watermelons to be served that day. "The self-respect of the race is sold for a mess of pottage," she wrote, "and the spectacle of the class of our people who will come on that excursion roaming around the grounds munching watermelon will do more to lower the race in the estimation of the world than anything else." Douglass differed, eager to seize the stage they'd begrudgingly been given to speak out against oppression. They agreed to disagree.[17]

On August 25 Douglass made his way to the stage in Festival Hall, possibly passing the booth fitted out by the R.T. Davis Milling Company, wherein a fifty-nine-year-old former Kentucky slave named Nancy Green played a character named Aunt Jemima, flipping pancakes in a red bandanna while telling soothing stories about folk life in the Old South. He was so appalled to see that the fair organizers had indeed erected watermelon stands throughout the grounds that he nearly called off his speech. In the end he relented, addressing a crowd of one thousand mostly black fairgoers.[18]

As he began to speak, some whites at the edge of the audience began heckling him. Douglass faltered for a moment, his hand holding the typewritten text of his speech beginning to shake. Then he threw the papers on his lectern, pulled off his glasses, and, as one attendee recalled, "tossed back

his head, ran his fingers through the lion-like mane of hair," and overwhelmed the hecklers "as an organ would a penny whistle."[19]

"There is no negro problem," Douglass roared. "The problem is whether
the American people have honesty enough, loyalty enough, honor enough,
patriotism enough to live up to their own constitution." He charged whites
with tolerating the mobs that had taken the place of law, mobs who "hang,
shoot, burn men of my race without justice and without right." He denounced the United States as a tyranny and said blacks "only ask to be
treated as well as you treat the late enemies of your national life." He asked:
"Why in Heaven's name do you take to your breast the serpent that once
stung and crush[ed] down the race that grasped the saber and helped make
the nation one and [thus] the exposition possible?"[20]

The crowd was roused; Ida Wells gave Douglass his due. "I swelled with
pride over his masterly presentation of our case," she said, "which had done
more to bring our cause to the attention of the American people than anything else which had happened at or during the fair." But Douglass's speech
was clear: His vision—Lincoln's vision—for a second, postwar Republic
had been stillborn. The South was defining the whole nation now and had
thereby won the peace.[21]

FIFTY-SIX

When the Exposition closed, Douglass was in poor health. He suffered from diarrhea and a persistent cough, and his writing hand had become unsteady. He confided to his sons that he felt worn out. The seventy-five-year-old had but sixteen months left to live.[1]

He did not spend them idly. Despite his infirmities, he continued to accept speaking engagements: Detroit that October before returning home; Boston and New Bedford the following year; a huge crowd at Metropolitan AME Church in the center of Washington after that. At each appearance he delivered what would be his final speech, one that called out America for surrendering its ideals and warned Americans that by depriving blacks of the protections of law, they had placed everyone's liberties in peril. Gone was his optimism about the essential goodness of the American people, his belief that the Civil War had vanquished the liberal Republic's foes, that right would triumph over wrong.

"I have sometimes thought that the American people are too great to be small, too just and magnanimous to oppress the weak, too brave to yield up the right to the strong, and too grateful for public services ever to forget them or to reward them," he began. "I have fondly hoped that this estimate of American character would soon cease to be contradicted or put in doubt. But events have made me doubtful.

Lawless vengeance is beginning to be visited upon white men as well as black. Our newspapers are daily disfigured by its ghastly horrors. It is no longer local but national; no longer confined to the South but has invaded the North. The contagion is spreading, extending and overleaping geographical lines and state boundaries, and if permitted to go on, threatens to destroy all respect for law and order, not only in the South but in all parts of our common country, North as well as South. For certain it is, that crime allowed to go unpunished, unresisted and unarrested, will breed crime.

When the poison of anarchy is once in the air, like the pestilence that walketh in darkness, the winds of heaven will take it up and favour its diffusion. Though it may strike down the weak to-day, it will strike down the strong to-morrow.[2]

He was not optimistic about the country's prospects. "When the moral sense of a nation begins to decline, and the wheels of progress to roll backward, there is no telling how low the one will fall or where the other will stop," he continued.

The downward tendency, already manifest, has swept away some of the most important safeguards of justice and liberty. The Supreme Court, has, in a measure, surrendered. State sovereignty is essentially restored. The Civil Rights Bill is impaired. The Republican party is converted into a party of money, rather than a party of humanity and justice. We may well ask, what next? The pit of hell is said to be bottomless. Principles which we all thought to have been firmly and permanently settled by the late war have been boldly assaulted and overthrown by the defeated party. Rebel rule is now nearly complete in many states, and it is gradually capturing the nation's Congress. The cause lost in the war is the cause regained in peace, and the cause gained in war is the cause lost in peace.[3]

He concluded this speech, most frequently titled "Why Is the Negro Lynched?," with a reference back to the country's Providential, Bancroftian purpose, and the Revolution that had "announced the advent of a nation, based upon human brotherhood and the self-evident truths of liberty and equality.

"Its mission was the redemption of the world from the bondage of ages. Apply these sublime and glorious truths to the situation now before you," the orator, now portly and with hair gone completely white, intoned. "Based upon the eternal principles of truth, justice and humanity, with no class having cause for complaint or grievance, your Republic will stand and flourish for ever."[4]

ON THE MORNING of February 20, 1895, Helen and Douglass rode down to Pennsylvania Avenue to attend a conference on women's suffrage, where he sat on the stage next to his old friend Susan B. Anthony. In the late afternoon they returned to their Anacostia home for a short rest before he was to give a speech to a neighborhood black church. At 7:00 p.m., Douglass started down the hall toward his waiting carriage, then stopped, fell slowly to his knees, and collapsed on the floor, Helen at his side. His heart had stopped.[5]

On learning of Douglass's death the following morning, the U.S. Senate voted to adjourn as a gesture of respect. The measure passed 32–25, with all of the Southern senators opposed.[6]

FIFTY-SEVEN

Turner was not discouraged by his paper's reception at the World's Congress.

While teaching his university classes back in Madison, he energetically promoted the frontier thesis in every way he could think of. He incorporated it into his graduate seminars. He made it the subject of public lectures throughout the Midwest. He wrote the entry for "Frontier" in *Johnson's Universal Encyclopedia* and arranged to have the paper reprinted in both the *Proceedings of the State Historical Society of Wisconsin* and the annual report of the AHA. But his real breakthrough came with a piece in *The Atlantic Monthly*, whose editor Walter Hines Page suggested he use his framework to explain the upcoming 1896 presidential election and the outburst of "populism"—a movement essentially championing the interests of small farmers—in the Middle West. "The free lands are gone, the continent is crossed, and all this push and energy is turning into channels of agitation," Turner's article said of the West. "The forces of reorganization are turbulent and the nation seems like a witches' kettle." It was not a matter of concern, he concluded, because the White City had shown that the West was capable of serving as "an open-minded and safe arbiter of the American destiny." Midwestern newspapers fawned over the piece, and *The Boston Herald* praised it for offering "the first reasonable explanation for the wild-eyed Populists" who sought to bring "free silver and anarchy" to the White House. Turner's thesis was not to be ignored any longer.[1]

Turner formulated his theory at exactly the time that the United States—an industrializing, urbanizing, continent-spanning, immigrant-attracting goliath—needed a new origin story that could explain how it had gotten where it was and where it might be going. It didn't hurt that his view of the future was optimistic. The frontier was gone, he argued, but the people it had forged were ready to take on the challenges ahead, imbued, as they were, with the spirit of democracy. Americans, having weathered the Civil War and its untidy aftermath, were reassured that their nation's destiny was to be the torchbearer of freedom in the world, and Turner had provided a rationale that didn't rely on the fuzzy metaphysics of Protestant theology or Divine Will, but rather the latest scientific doctrines: environmental adaptation and evolution. The up-and-coming generation of scholars and intellectuals, eager to overthrow stale arguments about Teutonic "germs," eagerly embraced his work and helped push it to the front of academic and popular consciousness.[2]

By 1897 Turner's work was in demand by prominent magazine and journal editors across the country. He was asked to write high-profile reviews for *The Atlantic Monthly*, *Political Science Quarterly*, and the AHA's prestigious new journal, *The American Historical Review*. Woodrow Wilson tried to poach him to teach at Princeton. Textbook authors cribbed from him. Teachers studied his essay in special sessions at professional conventions. Imitators parroted his theme in public lectures and popular articles, while speaking requests for Turner himself poured in. He was suddenly an intellectual star on par with Wilson, only with a more solid commitment to research and far better writing skills. At the dawn of the twentieth century, everyone seemed to know who Frederick Jackson Turner was.[3]

As a researcher, however, Turner had lost interest in the frontier almost as soon as he had returned from the White City. He was focused on what he was beginning to see was an even more consequential aspect of America's westward colonization experience: sectional differences.

Turner by now had come to realize that when he had developed his

frontier thesis, he had been relying on the experiences of his own tier of
"the West," the eastern portion of the Upper Mississippi Valley. This swath
of territory included Wisconsin, Michigan, Minnesota, and parts of Ohio
and Illinois and had been colonized by a settlement stream originating in
New England, one that included all of his own English Puritan ancestors.
As he pored over new maps of soil geography compiled by the Department
of Agriculture and the color county-level maps of voting patterns, economic characteristics, and social behavior in new editions of *Scribner's Sta-
tistical Atlas of the United States* or *Appletons' Annual Cyclopædia*, he saw
that other parts of "the frontier" had been settled by entirely different peoples. The behaviors, institutions, and adaptations of the settlers William
Gilmore Simms had visited and written about on the Mississippi and Alabama frontier were distinct from those of his father's friends and neighbors
in the Michigan and Wisconsin Territories, or his grandfather's a generation earlier in the Adirondacks of northern New York. Inhabitants of the
Southern uplands and Ohio Valley, the lands of Simms's and Wilson's Scots-
Irish forebearers, had yet another experience.[4]

Ever curious, Turner began obsessively researching the subject, even as
various publishers waited in vain for manuscripts of books on the frontier
thesis they had contracted him to write.

Turner loved teaching and showered attention and support on his graduate students. Beginning in the spring of 1895 he enlisted them to undertake a deeper probe of regionalism, asking them to examine sectional
behaviors during the American Revolution and in the great congressional
debates of the Early Republic. He encouraged undergraduate seniors to do
their honor theses on such topics, generating studies on the behavior of
Wisconsin legislators in the mid-nineteenth century or presidential voting
patterns before and since. Others were tasked to probe additional influences that might account for sectional differences: possible links between
the location of iron manufacturing plants in Pennsylvania and that state's
voting patterns on the tariff or the biographical details of every congressman who served between 1819 and 1829. As the data accumulated, Turner

became convinced that U.S. history had to be completely rewritten to account for the role of competing regional sections.[5]

"We need to trace the colonization of these separate regions, the location, contributions, and influence of the various stocks that combined to produce their population," he soon advised his fellow scholars. "The whole history of American politics needs to be interpreted in the terms of a contest between these economic and social sections," some of them comparable to "the greater nations of Europe" and even the empires they'd created. The frontier, he decided, wasn't the most important component of the program he'd laid out a few years earlier in "Problems of History."[6]

In the midst of his joyful research, however, tragedy struck. The Turners had been living a bucolic life in their lakeside home two blocks from the university library. Turner took canoe trips after classes, played tennis on weekends, and went off on fishing expeditions in the northern Wisconsin woods whenever time allowed. Caroline was an avid birdwatcher and Audubon Society member. In warm weather they rode a tandem bicycle around town. In winter, they read by the fireside. When Frederick was traveling or writing on deadline, Caroline would take their three children to visit her parents in Chicago, where the eldest daughter Dorothy was, at five, able to recite on demand a phrase from one of his economist colleague Richard T. Ely's works, "Political economy is the housekeeping of the state."[7]

In February 1899 a cold snap struck the city, driving temperatures to twenty-nine below zero while Turner's youngest, five-year-old Mae, was struggling with diphtheria. She died on the eleventh.

Eight months later their middle child, seven-year-old Jackson Allen, started suffering acute stomach pain. His doctor did not realize it was appendicitis until after the organ had ruptured, and the boy died in agony on October 11.

After his son's death Turner withdrew for weeks, and when he returned to teach his classes he seemed a shadow of his former self. Friends said the spark in his eye had gone and that it never really returned. Caroline was admitted to a Chicago sanitarium where she stayed for the better part of a year. After her discharge, their grief remained so unbearable that Turner took a leave of absence from the university.[8]

The little family of three packed their bags, rented out their home, and departed for Europe, leaving America's frontier and sections to fend for themselves.

FIFTY-EIGHT

Wilson, meanwhile, was developing his own theories of history.
The first was identifying the importance of Anglo-Saxon supremacy to American life. It was an idea he had been attached to since boyhood and he'd elaborated on in *The State*, a short textbook he'd published in 1889. Certain races were "progressive," enabling them to successfully manage highly sophisticated forms of government. The Aryan "race"—which included the majority of European peoples—was the most important of these, accounting for the most advanced modern governments. Some races were "stagnated," like the Chinese, while others were savage, lacking the patriarchal, monogamous family systems Wilson believed to be the building blocks of civilized life.[1]

Such discipline—"discipline generations deep"—was the reason America stood at the forefront of democracy and civilization. By living for generations under the English monarchs, America's Anglo-Saxon people had learned self-control and self-government, Wilson instructed *The Atlantic Monthly*'s readers in 1902, which accounted for why English North Americans had created a republic and French North Americans had not. "No doubt a king did hold us together until we learned how to hold together of ourselves," he continued, building a case for why Americans should rule over lesser peoples. "No doubt our unity as a nation does come from the fact that we once obeyed a king." The Philippines, which the United States had seized in the 1898 Spanish-American War and where its Marines were then putting down an independence movement, "can have liberty no cheaper than we got it." Its people should submit to American colonial tutorship, as "they are children and we are men in these deep matters of government and justice."[2]

This was the mistake the United States had made after the Civil War, he explained in a 1901 *Atlantic Monthly* essay on Reconstruction. Blacks were "unschooled in self-control," their base instincts having never been "sobered by the discipline of self-support." They were "insolent and aggressive; sick of work, covetous of pleasure—a host of dusky children untimely put out of school. . . . They were a danger to themselves as well as to those whom they had once served." It was fortunate, he wrote, "when at last the whites who were real citizens got control again," closing the "dark chapter of history" when other races had briefly enjoyed political equality.[3]

At the 1896 meeting of the American Historical Association in New York, Wilson delivered a lighthearted tribute to Turner, praising him for the "dethronement of the Eastern historian" and for reminding them all "that we do not constitute the nation here on the Eastern Coast." But he quickly pivoted to an attack on how Northerners treated his home region. "They speak of the South as if it was not part of this country," he complained. "The historian wishes the Southerner to be regretful in regard to his past. He wishes him to be apologetic in regard to his past. . . . There is nothing to apologize for in the past of the South—absolutely nothing to apologize for."[4]

Earlier that year Wilson had traveled to Washington to join his uncle James Woodrow, Simms's biographer William Trent, and the writer Thomas Nelson Page in the founding of the Southern History Association, an organization that aimed to promote the South's historical legacy. Wilson was elected as a vice president, as was Page, whose writings championed the Klan, disparaged blacks, and praised the virtues of slavery. The articles in the association's journal regularly praised Southern society for its diligence in protecting the purity of the Anglo-Saxon race, particularly now that Northerners had stopped meddling in their affairs. "The solidarity of our race is becoming daily a more potent fact which the historian of the present and future must keep before his eyes," Trent observed. Wilson would re-main an officer and active dues-paying member for as long as the organiza-tion existed.[5]

PRINCETON HAD FINALLY HIRED Wilson as a full professor in 1890, and he, Ellen, and their three young daughters now lived in a genteel half-timbered home a short distance from campus. He was an enormously pop-ular lecturer, and the college let him take a month's leave each year to continue his graduate teaching at Johns Hopkins. Universities and colleges kept trying to tempt him with offers of a presidency, which he was able to leverage into pay raises that made him far and away the best-paid teacher at Princeton.[6]

But whenever under stress—and meeting his book deadlines was stressful—Wilson would suddenly develop gastrointestinal problems, a combination of diarrhea and constipation that sometimes caused him to cancel a week or more of classes. In February 1895 the eminent physician Francis Delafield declared his problem to be an "excess of stomach mucus" and showed Wilson how to rid himself of it each day by sticking a siphon down his own throat, filling his stomach with water, and then pumping all the contents out. He diligently did this for many years, even after other phy-sicians informed him that the procedure was dangerous and unnecessary.

In May 1896, near the end of the term, he started feeling especially run-down. He developed a facial tic. A doctor diagnosed him as having an in-testinal kink caused by his stomach tube. Wilson's father, now widowed and living with them in Princeton, feared his son was going to die. His friends convinced him to take a leave of absence and recover in Europe.

A few days before his ship was to leave, Wilson woke up unable to use his right arm—the result, although he didn't realize it at the time, of a small stroke. He sailed for Britain anyway, teaching himself to write with his left hand on the twelve-day crossing, apparently without difficulty. He went horseback riding through Scotland, searched (unsuccessfully) for a trace of his grandfather in Carlisle, visited colleagues at the University of Glasgow, and took side trips to political essayist Walter Bagehot's birthplace in Somerset and the campuses of Cambridge and Oxford (whose medieval courts, quads, and cloisters took his heart in "a mere glance"). Within a month he felt few symptoms at all, despite having to go two weeks without pumping his stomach because he'd broken his siphon. "I emptied my stomach just now," he wrote Ellen from a Winchester hotel room in July. "It was clearer than I've ever seen it. Isn't that jolly?" He returned to Princeton in August a much healthier man.[7]

With great effort and the help of another recuperative trip to Europe, Wilson completed his *History of the American People* five years later. Once again he had done no original research, had never set foot in an archive, and appears not to have read most of the scholarly papers he included in the work's bibliography. Instead he relied entirely on other people's work— hastily read and often poorly digested—and his own articles in *The Atlantic Monthly* and elsewhere, from which he cribbed entire passages. He paraphrased (and popularized) Turner's arguments regarding the American frontier and parroted the sanitized depiction of Southern plantation life in his friend Thomas Nelson Page's *Old Dominion*. As with his other books, Wilson regularly substituted rhetoric, stilted poetic images, and overdrawn metaphors for empirical evidence. He shrugged off errors and later admitted, "I wrote the history of the United States in order to learn it. That may be an expensive process for other persons who bought the book."[8]

As he awaited publication by Harper & Brothers in the spring of 1902, he received a tremendous, happy, and life-changing surprise: Princeton's trustees had fired President Francis Patton and had unanimously elected their star professor to take his place. As news broke on June 10, the Wilsons were flooded with congratulatory telegrams—from Turner and President Teddy Roosevelt, Page and Hart, Jameson, Ely, and Uncle James Woodrow. To all he wrote essentially the same response: "I shall take more heart in what I have to do because men like yourself are so generous in believing in me."[9]

The inauguration turned into a gala event that brought home to Wilson just how much influence he'd accumulated. The ceremonial procession was led by former president Cleveland, and President Roosevelt was slated to be at his side, bowing out at the last minute only because he'd injured his leg and was temporarily unable to walk. The guests who assembled to watch him take his oath included Mark Twain, New Jersey governor Franklin Murphy, financier J. Pierpont Morgan, former House Speaker Thomas Reed, and Carnegie Steel chairman Henry Frick, who had survived an assassination attempt during the Homestead Strike, a deadly confrontation between Pennsylvania steelworkers and Carnegie's hired guards. Wilson was not the only one to notice the caliber of his admirers.[10]

A HISTORY OF THE AMERICAN PEOPLE appeared shortly thereafter to popular acclaim and scholarly derision. "The reader who is unacquainted with the details of wards and presidential administrations, party problems and personal prejudices, will find the *History* a disappointment after the pleasure of examining the pictures is past," *The Dial* reported. Bryn Mawr's Charles Andrews said it was destined to become "in its way" a classic, as it was "the sort of work that will make a man sleep better" with "nothing pessimistic or chicken-hearted" or supportive of anti-imperialist causes. *The Critic* said Wilson "appealed to the emotions, to sentiment, rather than to cold reason" and was "unable to formulate a conception concisely." It predicted that the book's "very vagueness . . . and consequent absence of detail" would probably help the *History* in the marketplace.[11]

The public and the popular press made it a success. *The New York Times Saturday Review* praised its lack of footnotes and deemed it "the most important work that has fallen off the press in a long time." *The Book Buyer*, targeted at booksellers, praised its spirit of sectional reconciliation, which was "its most solid claim to eminence," and its depiction of "the consistency of our general character from almost the beginning down to the very present." Harper & Brothers did brisk sales, and over the next seven years

Wilson would earn over $40,000 in royalties at a time when a full university professor's annual income was less than a tenth of that.[12]

Champions of an ethnically defined nationhood were indebted to Wilson, as the book furthered the white supremacist arguments in *Division and Reunion*, but in a format more accessible to a mass audience. He cast newly freed slaves as "dupes . . . easily taught to hate the men who had once held them in slavery" and the effort to give them political rights as a wish "to put the white men of the South . . . under the negroes' heels." Wilson likened the infamous Black Codes to "such remedies as English legislators had been familiar with [since] time out of mind." He claimed the Ku Klux Klan had formed "for the mere pleasure of association, for private amusement" by people who went about on sheet-covered horses as "pranks" and had accidentally discovered they could create "comic fear" in the blacks they descended on. He wrote that the Klansmen discovered Negroes "were easy enough to deal with"—they supposedly took the hint and returned to servility—but Yankee teachers who'd come to give "lessons of self-assertion against the whites" proved "less intractable" and so sometimes "came mysteriously to some sudden death."[13]

Of the hundreds of lynchings and mass killings of blacks that had been voluminously documented for the U.S. Congress, Wilson's *History* made no mention.

Immigrants also became a problem after 1880, Wilson asserted. "Throughout the century, men of the sturdy stocks of the North of Europe had made up the main strain of foreign blood which was every year added to the vital working force of the community, or else men of the Latin-Gallic stocks of France and Northern Italy," he began.

> But now there came multitudes of men of the lowest class from the South of Italy and men of the meaner sort out of Hungary and Poland, men out of the ranks where there was neither skill nor energy nor any initiative of quick intelligence; and they came in numbers which increased from year to year, as if the countries of the south

of Europe were disburdening themselves of the more sordid and hapless elements of their population.

The Chinese, "with their yellow skin and strange, debasing habits of life, seemed to [whites] hardly fellow men at all, but evil spirits" provoking unfortunate but understandable mass killings on the West Coast.[14]

Looking to the new century, Wilson closed on an optimistic note. An overseas empire had fallen into America's lap when "Spain's empire had proved a house of cards; when the American power touched it it fell to pieces." This had occurred just after the Americans' own frontier had closed, "as if out of the very necessity of the new career set before them." The former Confederate states were "readjusting their elective suffrage so as to exclude the illiterate negroes and so in part undo the mischief of reconstruction," and the North had now wisely "withheld its hand from interference." Better days were finally at hand under the wise tutelage of the "sturdy stocks" of Anglo-Saxon America.[15]

FIFTY-NINE

The Turners returned from Europe in April 1901, a few months earlier than initially planned due to their lack of funds. Although they lived frugally, renting modest lodgings above a wineshop in a rural Swiss village for much of the time, on arriving in Boston they had to borrow money to pay for the train fares the rest of the way home.

Frederick was humbled by what he'd seen in the valleys, villages, and cities of Italy, France, and Switzerland, frontierless places where the power of settled tradition, cultural inheritance, and shared historical experience was impossible to ignore. Europeans had an aesthetic appreciation that Americans lacked and had achieved artistic and architectural accomplishments that he believed his traditionless countrymen would require centuries to match. Now that the U.S. frontier was closed, he wondered, might the distinctive traditions of America's various regions begin to develop deeper roots? If so, what would it mean for the country's shared future?[1]

He returned to Madison to confront the persistent demands of the various publishers for whom he'd agreed to write books. Instead of completing these outstanding obligations, however, Turner accepted a new one. Albert Bushnell Hart asked him to write a book on whatever subject he selected for a new series of "scientific" histories to be published by Harper & Brothers as the *American Nation* collection. Turner agreed and chose as his topic the sectional development of the Middle West between 1819 and 1829, the decade when much of the initial settlement of that area took place. He dug into library collections, enlisted the help of graduate students, and consulted with geographers, sociologists, and cartographers. When he missed his deadline in the summer of 1904, Turner promised Hart the completed manuscript would be coming "at once." A year later, Hart remained empty-handed, and Turner gave up his summer vacation in 1905 to toil away in his hot attic study, managing to produce the first three chapters. The rest would be delivered in October, he promised Hart, but the editor wouldn't actually receive them until December.[2]

This would be the only original book-length work Turner published in his lifetime. *Rise of the New West, 1819–1829* explored the federation's sectional divisions in that seemingly placid era of its history, cleavages that would bring the country to open warfare a few decades hence. "In the minds of some of the most enlightened statesmen of this decade, American politics were essentially a struggle for power between rival sections," Turner explained in the book, finally published in 1906. "Even those of most enlarged national sympathies and purposes accepted the fact of sectional rivalries and combinations as fundamental in their policies."[3]

Rise of the New West received glowing reviews, but its sectional thesis wasn't embraced as enthusiastically as "The Significance of the Frontier in American History" had been. When he presented his argument before the American Sociological Society's 1907 annual meeting in Madison, scholars were skeptical. He showed them slides of county-level maps revealing clear regional divides in various presidential elections and correlated them to per capita slaveholding rates or the prevalence of certain soil types. He described the differences between New England, the Scots-Irish–dominated backcountry, and the aristocratic, slaveholding lowlands. And he predicted these differences were only going to grow with time. "Divesting myself of the historical mantle, in order to venture upon the role of prophet," he began, "I make the suggestion that as the nation reaches a more stable equilibrium, a more settled state of society . . . the influence of the diverse physiographic provinces . . . will become more marked.

Statesmen in the future, as in the past, will achieve their leadership by voicing the interests and ideas of the sections, which have shaped these leaders, and they will exert their influence nationally by making combinations between sections, and by accommodating their policy to the needs of such alliances. Congressional legislation will be shaped by the compromises and combinations, which will in effect be treaties between rival sections, and the real federal aspect of our government will lie not in the relation of state and nation, but in the relation of section and nation.

Sections, many of the sociologists countered, were clearly dying away under the forces of nationalization and post-Reconstruction reconciliation. "The extension of railways, the diffusion of knowledge through universal education, the unification of religious thought, the rise of the telephone and the rural mail delivery, and the development of common interests," one responded, "make a more homogeneous nation, and cause mere sectional interests to decline."[4]

Across the nation, all of Turner's audiences wanted him to continue discussing his frontier thesis. He was invited to lecture on this topic at Harvard in 1904, where his theory deeply impressed one young student, President Roosevelt's cousin Franklin. Turner was poached by Harvard on the strength of his frontier work and moved to Cambridge as a full professor in 1910, the same year he was elected president of the American Historical Association.

His thesis about the frontier was now being incorporated into high school and college history textbooks and courses.[5] But as he had researched *Rise of the New West* and then his planned magnum opus on U.S. sectionalism, the data Turner encountered had him increasingly concerned about the validity of his most famous idea. Had the frontier really been an economic "escape valve" for the urban proletariat, as he had argued? The data showed farmers were migrating to the cities and that urban wage laborers did not seek rural life in large numbers. Was Far Western frontier life really as democratic and egalitarian as that of Portage had been? The overwhelming evidence was that it was often lawless, violent, and corrupt. Did the West really make settlers "new men," or did the traditions of the competing sectional settlement streams hold firm in the new environment, as *Rise of the New West* argued? Had he perhaps missed something in having entirely ignored the fact that the West hadn't been peopled by the peaceful settlement of "free land," but rather had been taken from its indigenous people in a violent conquest?

The year his book was published, he already had enough doubts that he declined an invitation from his friend Charles Haskins to defend the frontier thesis against a mildly critical scholar at a forthcoming joint meeting of the national economic and historical associations. Turner claimed it would take too long to gather "the necessary data for proper analysis" in defense of a thesis he'd produced thirteen years earlier, and said it had admittedly suffered from generalizations. The fact was, Turner was no longer sure he could defend it.[6]

SIXTY

It was the conservative millionaire George Harvey who first promoted Woodrow Wilson's candidacy for president of the United States. As his publisher, Harvey knew Wilson's work well. A onetime reporter for Democratic newspapers, Harvey had served as an aide to two New Jersey governors and as managing editor of the *New York World* before making his millions as a partner in a streetcar syndicate controlled by two major party donors. In 1899 he'd bought *The North American Review* and been appointed president of Harper & Brothers and editor of *Harper's Weekly* by J.P. Morgan after the firm defaulted on its debts to him. Harvey hated unions, championed big business, and felt confident that Wilson shared his view, particularly as Wilson had praised the use of force to crush strikes and had written of the "alien" agitations of immigrant union activists in his *History*. Harvey liked Wilson immediately upon meeting him at his inauguration as Princeton's president, and by 1906 was talking him up as a potential president of the United States.[1]

In 1908 Harvey, who had a great deal of influence, single-handedly managed to get Wilson, a political neophyte, seriously considered as William Jennings Bryan's presidential running mate by planting editorials in both the *New York World* and *The North American Review*. Two years later he saw a more promising stepping-stone for Wilson in the open seat for governor of New Jersey, a position that had been held by Republicans for nearly two decades. He knew the 1910 midterm election was shaping up to be a Democratic landslide, as President Taft's conservative economic and environmental policies had alienated progressive Republican followers of his predecessor, Theodore Roosevelt. Wilson had the perfect profile, Harvey believed: a conservative Democrat who could mimic the language of the progressives, but had no experience or friends in politics, and would therefore be entirely dependent on Harvey and his fellow kingmakers. That Wilson had refused to allow Bryan, an unrepentant progressive already known as the Great Commoner, to speak on Princeton's campus during the 1908 campaign only reassured Harvey as to Wilson's conservatism. "We now expect to see Woodrow Wilson elected Governor of the State of New Jersey in 1910 and nominated for President in 1912," Harvey wrote in the May 1909 issue of *Harper's Weekly*. All he needed was Wilson's consent.[2]

Wilson demurred at first, though he agreed to start putting himself in the public eye by giving political speeches, with which he began attracting newspaper attention. Harvey lined up the New Jersey political bosses—led by former U.S. senator James "Big Jim" Smith, a fabulously corrupt Irish Catholic who controlled much of the Democratic primary vote—and started laying the groundwork for Wilson's future presidential bid. By the time Wilson agreed to run for the party's nomination, Harvey was able to assure him that he would win it "by acclamation." Wilson did, and despite the hostile things people discovered he'd written about Hungarians, Poles, and labor unions, he rode the Democratic wave to the governorship that November. That night Democrats also flipped control of the House of Representatives, ten Senate seats, and three other governorships, prompting President Taft to describe it as "a tidal wave and holocaust all rolled into one general cataclysm."[3]

If Harvey and Smith were elated, their gratification was short lived, as Wilson turned on them before he was even inaugurated. Smith, who had donated $50,000 to Wilson's campaign, wanted the new, Democrat-controlled New Jersey legislature to elect him to an open U.S. Senate seat. To his shock Wilson refused to support him, backing the progressive challenger, James Martine, instead. Wilson knew he needed to tack to the left if he was to win the White House, and in the off-year election he campaigned throughout the state against the Smith machine's candidates. Smith never forgave him, though Harvey remained under the belief his protégé would return to their fold as president.[4]

Less than a year after taking office, Wilson announced his presidential run and started crisscrossing the states to campaign in what were the nation's first primary contests against three more experienced candidates: the party's popular House Speaker, Champ Clark of Missouri, Representative Oscar Underwood of Alabama, and Ohio governor Judson Harmon. After Wilson lost in Florida, Alabama, Massachusetts, Washington State, California, and Maryland, in desperation he began attacking big business directly, accusing cartels of crushing the have-nots, of ruining markets, of undermining the Republic. "If you want to oust socialism," he told the annual dinner of the Economic Club of New York, "you have got to propose something better. It is a case, if you will allow me to fall into the language of the vulgar, of 'put up or shut up.'" They applauded, confident that he was a noncontender about to be returned to the obscurity of Trenton.[5]

But something extraordinary happened at the Democratic National Convention, held in an armory in Baltimore.

As none of the seven candidates had earned anywhere near the two-thirds majority of the delegates required for victory—after all, only twelve of the states had held primaries—the contest devolved into over five days of votes, backstage intrigue, and in-party fighting. Although Wilson started far behind front-runner Champ Clark—and at one point had drafted a concession speech and was about to release his delegates to vote for someone else—he slowly gained ground with each round of balloting, especially after William Jennings Bryan threw his support behind him. On the forty-sixth ballot, Wilson narrowly emerged as the party's compromise choice.[6]

In November Republicans split their vote between the deeply unpopular Taft and the not-popular-enough former president Teddy Roosevelt, who ran as the candidate of his own Bull Moose Party. His opponents divided, Wilson won forty of the forty-eight states, and his party captured both houses of Congress. When confirmation of his victory reached him, Wilson went out on his porch to greet supporters. His twenty-three-year-old daughter, Nell, recalled she felt "a sense of awe, almost of terror—he was no longer the man with whom we had lived in warm sweet intimacy. . . . He belonged to them."[7]

SIXTY-ONE

The black carriages pulled away from the White House at 10:27 in the morning, surrounded by members of New Jersey's Essex cavalry troop, bearing drawn sabers. In the front carriage President Taft and President-elect Wilson sat side by side in top hats and broad coats. Four black horses drew them slowly onto Pennsylvania Avenue, flanked by Secret Service men in frock coats and followed by a second carriage carrying the incoming and outgoing vice presidents and, on foot, the White House press corps. Taft and Wilson looked to be enjoying themselves—both were beaming in nearly every photograph that was taken of them that day.[1]

A crowd said to be the largest in the city's history—100,000 to 250,000 strong—had gathered on the sidewalks and reviewing stands to watch them pass on their way to the East Portico of the Capitol, where Wilson would be inaugurated. They cheered as the carriages passed, a few for "Bill" but the vast majority for Wilson, and newspaper reporters said most of the latter were Southerners. Wilson was the first Democrat to win the White House since 1893, *The Washington Post* noted, "and the stalwarts from Dixie were determined to take advantage of it."[2]

Dixie was indeed elated. Wilson was the first Southerner elected to the presidency since before the Civil War, and he had done so by winning the former Confederacy by staggering margins, including taking every single county in South Carolina, Mississippi, Louisiana, Florida, and the Virginia Tidewater, and nearly every one in all the other former slaveholding states. While voters in some parts of the country disapproved of his statements about blacks and new immigrants—New York's Hungarian community had protested his having described them as "a coarse crew, bred in unwholesome squalor"—the Southern electorate loved him for it. Thomas Dixon Jr. was so ebullient at his friend's victory that he dedicated his new novel, *The Southerner*, to him. Wilson, *The Atlanta Journal* had declared, was the one person who could "restore the South to her rightful place in the councils of the Union." The South had rejoined the Union in the 1870s as "conquered provinces," the previous morning's edition of the *Nashville Banner* observed. "But now unquestionably the South is again 'in the saddle.'"[3]

For weeks Wilson had been expressing his lifelong desire to reconcile the sections of the United States on Southern terms, not through the old doctrine of states' rights, but by investing the federal government with the spirit of the lowland South. "I would fain believe that my selection as President by the people of the United States means the final obliteration of everything that may have divided the great sections of this country," he told the people of his hometown of Staunton, Virginia, adding he would be happy to be "the instrument in drawing together the hearts of all men . . . in the service of a nation that has neither region, nor section, nor North, nor South." President Taft recognized what Wilson's victory meant for sectional reconciliation, having told the annual conference of the United Daughters of the Confederacy that his successor would "give to our Southern brothers and sisters the feeling of close relationship and ownership in the government of the United States."[4]

The president from Ohio and a president-elect raised in Georgia and South Carolina smiled amiably for the crowds as the carriages picked up speed for a final, dramatic climb up Capitol Hill, the cavalrymen's horses breaking into a canter alongside them.

AT 12:30 P.M. THE OFFICIAL delegation began filtering out of the Capitol and into their reserved seats on the reviewing stand. They made for an impressive display of the extent of Southern influence and power in Washington.

First came Edward Douglass White Jr., chief justice of the Supreme Court, a rimless black cap on his head, Wilson's Bible in his hand, with the other justices trailing behind him. The namesake son of a governor of Louisiana, Chief Justice White had been raised on the family sugar plantation, had served as a lieutenant in a Confederate cavalry unit during the war, had joined the Ku Klux Klan during Reconstruction, and, as a justice, helped support the constitutionality of racial segregation. Associate Justice Joseph Lamar was a close childhood friend of Wilson's, having grown up next door to the Presbyterian manse in Augusta, while Justice Horace Lurton of Kentucky had been a Confederate cavalryman and was detained for months at the prisoner of war camp at Johnson's Island, Ohio.[5]

Next came the new congressional leadership. There were rousing cheers for Wilson's primary rival, House Speaker Champ Clark, who had been born and raised in Kentucky and represented an Appalachian-settled section of Missouri where Jim Crow laws were the norm and lynchings not unusual. The president pro tem of the Senate, Augustus Bacon, another Confederate veteran, had presided over the "redemption" in Georgia as Speaker of the lower house of the state legislature and had recently penned his will, which provided for the establishment of a "whites only" park in his native Macon. Oscar Underwood, chair of the powerful House Ways and Means Committee, was a Kentucky-born congressman from Alabama. He was just one of an army of committee chairmen from the lowland South, the result of the fact that chairmanships were based on seniority and that that part of the South was effectively a one-party state, meaning most incumbent Democrats could serve as long as they wished.[6]

The crowd cheered as Wilson and Taft appeared side by side, the former looking much thinner, the latter much stouter in their frock coats. They waved before taking their seats at the center of the stage. The new cabinet soon followed, including Wilson's suave campaign aide and future son-in-law, William McAdoo, a virulent racist from Marietta, Georgia, who had built the first railway tunnel under the Hudson and would become secretary of the Treasury; campaign press secretary Josephus Daniels, editor of Raleigh's *News & Observer* and a close friend and confidant of Thomas Dixon Jr. 's, who believed black suffrage to be "the greatest folly and crime" in U.S. history and was to become Wilson's navy secretary; and Postmaster General Albert Burleson, the son of Texas slave planters. "Half the members of his cabinet were born where negro mammies crooned the first lullabies that fell upon their baby ears," *The Washington Post* observed. "The solid South is solid with the new era in Washington. One who desires to get along here will do well to say 'you all' and 'we all.'"[7]

Ellen and the Wilson daughters stood by their seats for a time, taking in the incredible throng, from the rows of West Point cadets keeping the flag-waving crowds at bay to the great bank of mysterious "motion picture machines," ready to memorialize this symbolic commemoration of sectional reconciliation and Southern redemption.

At 1:34, Chief Justice White came forward. Wilson rose, set down his silk hat, and stepped forward to face him as the official spectators stood at attention. He raised his hand. "Then came a remarkable illustration of what American institutions really mean," the *New York Times* reporter on the scene wrote. "A man born in the South took the oath as president and it was administered by a man who fifty years ago was in arms against the government." White asked if Wilson would solemnly uphold the Constitution.[8]

"I do," Wilson said as the crowd went wild. Following tradition, he opened the Bible, bowed, and kissed a random passage.

His lips landed on the forty-third verse of Psalm 119: "And take not the word of truth utterly out of my mouth."[9]

SIXTY-TWO

The proposal to begin segregating the United States government was introduced at one of Wilson's first cabinet meetings, held on April 11, 1913.

Postmaster General Burleson informed his colleagues that it was "very unpleasant" for whites to have to work alongside blacks on the cars of the Railway Mail Service, which handled most of the nation's long-distance postal transportation, because "it is almost impossible to have different drinking vessels and different towels or places to wash." In fact, it was unpleasant to have to work near black people at all. He very much wanted the new administration to segregate immediately all departments of the federal government. This, he added, "was best for the negro."[1]

Treasury Secretary McAdoo responded that segregation might be impractical in his own department, given that black and white clerks worked side by side in many buildings, but he thought the idea had merit. Just nine days earlier his handpicked assistant secretary, John Skelton Williams, had been shocked while on a tour of the Bureau of Engraving and Printing to see black and white women working alongside one another, an arrangement he said "must go much against the grain of the white women." In another room white women labored in close proximity to black men, prompting Williams to ask one of the former loudly if she was not offended. Williams had already issued orders that such racial mixing must cease throughout the bureau's factory floors, even though his subordinates had been unable to find any instances of the workers asking for these changes. McAdoo thought such practices ought to be extended.[2]

Wilson assented to the segregation proposals, noting that he had "made no promises in particular to negroes, except to do them justice."[3]

BURLESON ACTED FIRST.

In the main Post Office building, a grand Classical Revival structure on Pennsylvania Avenue that would one day house the Trump International Hotel, black employees were suddenly informed they were no longer welcome in the cafeteria. "As no restaurants in Washington were open to colored people," supervisors explained, "the government could not be expected to furnish one." WHITES ONLY signs appeared on all the bathroom doors in the nine-story, five-hundred-thousand-square-foot building, save the ones in the basement, where many of the black employees now retreated to eat their lunch.[4]

In the cars of the Railway Mail Service that operated on Southern routes, black clerks were reassigned to night shifts and the most difficult runs and forced to use designated toilets located in the least convenient parts of the train. Local postmasters put up separate windows for white and black customers and demoted black civil servants. At headquarters most of the department's black clerks were reassigned to the Dead Letter Office, where they were seated in one corner of the room and screened off from their white workmates by a row of lockers.[5]

McAdoo followed suit in July, ordering the segregation of all the buildings, divisions, and offices of the Treasury Department in Washington and in all states south of the Mason-Dixon Line. At the department's Bureau of Engraving and Printing, factory floor workers were separated by race. Black women were told to eat their lunch in the lavatories, and any who protested were fired. Black clerks were reassigned to rooms with poor lighting and ventilation. Others were separated from their white colleagues by makeshift partitions. The FOR COLORED ONLY bathrooms were all located in the basement of the five-story, five-acre building. Register of the Treasury James C. Napier, who was an Oberlin-educated lawyer born to Tennessee slaves and who had been appointed by Taft, resigned after Assistant Secretary Williams made it clear these new orders would not be rescinded. He was among dozens of African American appointees who were replaced with whites in the coming months, including Union war hero and Reconstruction congressman Robert Smalls, who was dismissed as collector of customs in Beaufort, South Carolina.[6]

By the fall similar practices had spread to the Government Printing Office, the Marine Hospital Service building, and Josephus Daniels's Navy Department. Whites were also being appointed to positions traditionally reserved for African Americans, including ambassador to Haiti. "Not only are our employees being segregated, they are being dropped from and demoted in service," *The Cleveland Gazette*, that city's African American newspaper, warned from Washington. "Separate street cars and a stringent segregation in everything now look assured."[7]

These policies were a direct assault on Washington's black middle class, which had grown substantially over the previous thirty years under the protection of the Pendleton Civil Service Act of 1883, a law that ensured hiring was based on competitive examinations, not race. The number of African American federal workers had since climbed from 620 to 12,000, with nearly half of them employed by the Treasury and Post Office Departments. While blacks had few opportunities for professional advancement in the states that surrounded the capital, its stable, well-paying federal jobs helped support some of the country's best black public schools, the elite Howard University, and a network of black-owned hotels, restaurants, law offices, and philanthropies. For two generations the District had been an island of possibility in the South's Jim Crow sea.[8]

Many African American leaders had believed Wilson's campaign pledges, the carefully worded statements the candidate had prepared that appeared to commit him to the cause of racial fairness.

They were primed to abandon the Republican Party because, on racial issues, it had ceased to present a stark contrast to those of the Southern-dominated Democrats, having repeatedly chosen sectional reconciliation over a defense of racial equality. Theodore Roosevelt's overt racism had repelled them; as president he had infamously discharged an entire black regiment for "rioting" in Brownsville, Texas, and refused to reverse his decision when it was proved they were innocent. Reassured by Wilson's apparent progressivism and his promises to "help them" and treat them "justly," blacks had organized pro-Wilson clubs, and leaders like Alexander Walters, a prominent bishop of the African Methodist Episcopal Zion Church; Booker T. Washington of the Tuskegee Institute; and National Equal Rights League founder William Monroe Trotter campaigned for the New Jersey governor. The NAACP's newspaper, *The Crisis*, endorsed him. It is estimated that, on Election Day, as many as 30 percent of African American voters cast their votes for Wilson.[9]

As word of the Wilson administration's segregation policies spread, many black leaders and their white allies convinced themselves they were some sort of mistake. "I cannot believe that either President Wilson or [his chief of staff Joseph] Tumulty realizes what harm is being done to both races on account of the recent policy of racial discrimination," Booker T. Washington wrote. "Narrow little people in Washington are taking advantage of these orders and are overriding and persecuting the colored people in ways that the President does not know about."[10]

Oswald Garrison Villard, grandson of William Lloyd Garrison, chairman of the NAACP, and a longtime Wilson ally, wrote the president in July to alert him to the distress his subordinates' policies had triggered. "The colored men who voted and worked for you in the belief that their status as American citizens was safe in your hands are deeply cast down, and know not how to answer the criticisms they receive on every hand," he warned. "Should this policy be continued we should lose all that we gained in the last campaign in splitting the negro vote." He begged Wilson to publicly affirm "that your democracy was not limited by race or color; that the fundamental scientific political truths" he had articulated in his campaign apply "to every being whatever his situation, whatever his color."[11]

Wilson wrote back that the policies had been initiated by the department heads, but were "as much in the interest of the negroes as for any other reason. . . . I sincerely believe it to be in their interest. And what distresses me about your letter is to find that you look at it in so different a light." Villard spent months imploring Wilson to issue a public statement in support of black equality, and even drafted a proposed statement for the president to consider issuing. He pleaded his case in vain.[12]

Wilson's personal position finally became clear to all on November 16, 1914, when William Monroe Trotter and a delegation of prominent African Americans came to the White House for an audience with him. At forty-two years old, Trotter was one of the country's most prominent African American intellectuals, the Harvard-educated editor of *The Guardian*, Boston's preeminent African American newspaper. He was an uncompromising activist for racial equality and had no time for the gradualism of the white-dominated NAACP or Booker T. Washington's willingness to accept segregation, which made Washington, in Trotter's words, the "Benedict Arnold of the Negro race." The softening of Republican support for racial equality had also led him to endorse Democratic candidates for ward elections in his hometown of Boston and, in 1912, Woodrow Wilson's candidacy for president, which probably helped him be granted a meeting that day.

In both substance and temperament, however, Trotter was a person likely to draw out Wilson's carefully veiled racism: he was direct, fearless, and proud.[13] Wilson, for his part, was not on his game; First Lady Ellen Wilson had died of Bright's disease that summer, a tragedy that wore away much of the president's patrician self-restraint and didactic circumlocutions.

By this time the civil service was requiring applicants to attach photographs of themselves with their applications, and black hiring plummeted.

Trotter told the president this and other discriminatory policies were destroying the very foundations of black citizenship and asked him if he had "a 'new freedom' for white Americans and a new slavery for your Afro-American fellow citizens." Wilson retorted sharply that if blacks didn't approve of his policies, they should vote for someone else in 1916. He told Trotter he should "strip this thing of sentiment and look at the facts": Segregation prevented "friction" between the races and, thus, improved the administrative efficiency of government. Blacks were being too sensitive, and their opposition to Jim Crow would only make things worse. Trotter pushed back, arguing, "We are not here as wards. . . . We are here as full-fledged American citizens, vouchsafed equality of citizenship by the federal Constitution." He told Wilson that it was absurd to argue that segregation reduced racial tensions, given that "for fifty years white and colored clerks have been working together in peace and harmony and friendliness."[14]

At that Wilson lost his composure, accusing Trotter of blackmailing him by suggesting he would lose black political support. "If this organization is ever to have another hearing before me it must have another spokesman," the president snapped. Then he dismissed Trotter from the Oval Office.

Trotter went directly to the reporters who had been waiting outside and told them what had happened. Reports of the incident—and editorial cartoons depicting Wilson throwing Trotter down the front steps of the White House—spread quickly around the world. There was no mistake, Jim Crow's supporters and opponents now both agreed: President Wilson was championing the segregation of the government that had won the Civil War.

SIXTY-THREE

Wilson hadn't wanted to speak at Gettysburg on the fiftieth anniversary of Lincoln's address, as he had planned to join his family on their New Hampshire vacation for some "much needed rest." His aides urged him to reconsider.[1]

The festival, a celebration of sectional reconciliation planned for July 1 to 4, 1913, was an enormous undertaking, spread out over 280 acres. A great tent was erected for the official speeches, which were to be given, it turned out, in hundred-degree temperatures. Congress had appropriated nearly $2 million to pay the train tickets of any Civil War veteran who wished to attend, and the U.S. Army created an entire tent city to feed and accommodate the fifty thousand elderly men expected to show up. Laborers dug ninety latrines, while an army of twenty-seven hundred cooks prepared food. The newly formed Boy Scouts of America deployed hundreds of youngsters to help the veterans get around. A medical battalion stood by to aid the sick "with fifteen horse ambulances and two automobile ambulances," and thousands of regular troops kept order.[2]

Just before noon on the final day of the festival, the president arrived on a special train from Washington. In frock coat and top hat he stood for photos with the governors of Pennsylvania and Virginia before entering the grand tent to give his address.

Tens of thousands of men who'd fought on that very battlefield fifty years before sat in the stands, some in blue uniform, some in gray, their faces creased, their chests covered in medals and service ribbons. Nine Confederate generals had recently led their former soldiers in a rousing rebel yell in that tent, an act that would have been unthinkable at Gettysburg just three or four decades earlier. General Bennett Young, grand commander of the United Confederate Veterans, declared that what made the gathering remarkable was that his men had "come as Confederates" with "no explanations sought or expected." Judge Alfred Beers, commander in chief of the Grand Army of the Republic, saluted the Southern veterans on behalf of those of the North, happy that a "war waged by men of the same race, men of the same bravery" had ended in this "meeting of brothers."[3]

There were no black veterans in the tent, or outside it. The only African Americans involved in the event—with its 53,407 veterans, 50,000 spectators, and tens of thousands of staff—were the laborers digging the latrines, erecting the tents, and handing out blankets.[4] Nor was there any mention of slavery, of the fact that 1913 also marked the fiftieth anniversary of the Emancipation Proclamation. Speakers did not dwell on the content of Lincoln's famous address nor seek to discuss the country's failure to take its message to heart. "We are not here to discuss the Genesis of the war," Virginia governor William Hodges Mann explained, "but to talk over the events of the battle here as man to man." The causes and moral purpose of the war had been excluded from the event to facilitate the "peace among whites" of which Frederick Douglass had warned.[5]

Wilson stepped before the crowd, doffed his hat, and spoke holding his speech in his left hand and his top hat in his right. "We have found one another again as brothers and comrades in arms," he proclaimed, "enemies no longer, generous friends rather, our battles long past, the quarrel forgotten."

> How complete the union has become and how dear to all of us, how unquestioned, how benign and majestic, as state after state has been added to this our great family of free men! How handsome the vigor, the maturity, the might of the great nation we love with

undivided hearts. . . . Come, let us be comrades and soldiers, yet to
serve our fellow men in quiet counsel, where the blare of trumpets
is neither heard nor heeded and where the things are done which
make blessed the nations of the world in peace and righteousness
and love.[6]

Wilson's message was that the last, best hope on Earth was in fine shape,
secure in its achievement of freedom, and ready to improve the rest of the
world.

At the close of his fifteen-minute speech he shook hands with those on
the platform, walked between the lines of his Pennsylvania police escorts,
got into his car, and was whisked to the station, where his New Hampshire–
bound train departed shortly thereafter.

He had been in Gettysburg for a total of forty-six minutes.[7]

SIXTY-FOUR

While much of the nation celebrated the end of sectionalism, Turner was more engaged with it than ever.

He reached the conclusion that the United States wasn't really a nation like France or Italy, but rather a continent of "potential nations," each "likened to the shadowy image of the European nation, to the European state denatured of its toxic qualities." He came to believe that America was "in reality a federation of sections rather than of states," that "state sovereignty was never influential except as a constitutional shield for the section," and that "sectionalism was the dominant influence in shaping our political history upon all the important measures."[1]

He had come to appreciate that environmental factors—climate, geography, soils—might not account for all of the differences between the regional cultures, which he believed numbered at least eight, at least in the near term. "The influence of the stock from which they sprang, the inherited ideals, the spiritual factors, often triumph over material interests," he would later write. "The section does not embody the racial and national feeling of the European state, its impulse to preserve its identity by aggression conceived of as self-defense. But there is, nonetheless, a faint resemblance."[2]

Political parties and "common national feeling" acted like an "elastic band," holding these geographic provinces together, he thought, and only when they became regionally defined, as in the 1850s, did the country risk a civil war. When in proper equilibrium, these provinces could be dynamic forces, "fields of experiment in the growth of different types of society, political institutions and ideas" and "breakwaters against overwhelming surges of national emotion." Therefore, any comprehensive national vision for the United States would have to explicitly take these regional cultures into account, or it would effectively represent an effort by one region or another to impose its vision and ideals upon the federation as a whole. A genuine national vision, he came to believe, had to incorporate the sort of ideals Bancroft and Lincoln had articulated. "For, underneath all, there is a common historical inheritance, a common set of institutions, a common law, and a common language," he would eventually write.

> There is an American spirit. There are American ideals. We are members of one body, though it is a varied body. . . . However profound the economic changes, we shall not give up our American ideals and our hopes for man. . . . We shall point to the Pax Americana, and seek the path of peace on earth to men of good will.[3]

Unfortunately Turner was writing very little, even on this topic.

For a decade after moving to Harvard in 1910, he produced fewer essays and reviews than he had earlier in his career, and not a single book. Scholars would later ponder his lack of scholarly activity. The shock of the death of two of his three children likely played a role, some argued, while his colleague Edward Channing attributed it to the time he spent focused on his graduate students and their work. ("Turner is a dear fellow, but he has no idea of the value of time," the historian observed. "He has never written any big books.") Or it may simply have been due to the fact that while he loved research and teaching, he found writing a joyless and exhausting chore. *Rise of the New West*, his only original, book-length work, had made it to press only in response to Hart's constant and skillful badgering. Whatever the reason, his passion was clearly in the chase, not the kill. He was forever in search of one more bit of evidence or another box of papers, or anxious to have a graduate student probe an intriguing tangent.[4]

Whenever possible, he and Caroline spent their free time in nature. They summered in a weather-beaten seaside cottage at Hancock Point, Maine, where Frederick caught flounder and befriended local fishermen. They went tent camping in Yellowstone and in Montana's Bitterroot Mountains; took long hikes through the Cascade Range; and went trout fishing on the streams of northern Wisconsin and New England. On the porch of their Brattle Street home in Cambridge, Turner would sometimes pitch a tent where, late at night, he could almost imagine he was far away from the now-sprawling city of one hundred thousand.[5]

He tried to interest academic colleagues in the importance of sectionalism. He joined the American Geographical Society and the Association of American Geographers, and at their joint meeting in 1914 showed them some five dozen lantern slides of election returns and soil samples. He returned to the Art Institute of Chicago for the American Historical Association's meeting that December to read a paper entitled "The Significance of the Section," showing how the New England–settled sections of the lower Great Lakes states had voted Republican in every election since that party's founding, while those states' Scots-Irish–settled parts voted Democratic. He spent months preparing a series of eight lectures on sectionalism in the 1830s and 1840s for Massachusetts's influential Lowell Institute. None of that work received the kind of attention his 1893 paper on the frontier had.[6]

Indeed, the influence of the frontier thesis continued to spread. His graduate students had become tenured professors, together constituting a veritable pantheon of influential twentieth-century academic historians, including Merle Curti, Carl Becker, Edgar Eugene Robinson, and Herbert Bolton, who disseminated his ideas to yet another generation of intellectuals in classrooms across the country.

ONE HIGH SCHOOL TEXTBOOK WRITER, Columbia University's David S. Muzzey, built much of his work around Turner's frontier thesis, citing *Rise of the West* continuously and repeating many of Turner's arguments.

Published in 1911, Muzzey's *An American History* would sell millions of copies and remain in print into the 1970s. It was for half a century the required textbook for a majority of U.S. public school history students. In some periods it sold more copies than all of its competitors combined. The baby boomers, their parents, and grandparents were all raised on Turner's frontier theory, a legacy that would extend across popular culture.[7]

Muzzey also embraced Woodrow Wilson's work, citing *Division and Reunion* and, especially, *A History of the American People* numerous times. Proper Americans, the textbook suggested, were Anglo-Saxons like Wilson, Turner, and Muzzey. "Before 1880 over four fifths of all the immigrants to the United States were from Canada and the Northern countries of Europe, which were allied to us in blood, language, customs, religion, and political ideas," it explained. "They were a most welcome addition to our population, especially in the development of the great farm lands of the West" because they "assimilated rapidly with our people, cherished our free institutions," and begat children who were "the most American of Americans." But now Hungarians, Poles, Russians, and Italians were replacing them, people who allegedly hadn't come "to build up new homes in the new land" but rather to act as tools of corrupt bosses and *patrones* who "debauch the city government."[8]

Again echoing Wilson, Muzzey argued that Charles Sumner and his fellow abolitionists had foolishly "let their sympathy for the oppressed slave confuse their judgment of the negro's intellectual capacity." Reconstruction had been a terrible error because it sought "to reverse the relative position of the races in the South, to 'stand the social pyramid on its apex,' to set the ignorant, superstitious, gullible slave in power over his former master." Foolish Northerners had been "poisoning the minds of the negroes against the only people who could really help them begin their new life of freedom well—their old masters." The resultant violence by the KKK was therefore understandable but also "greatly exaggerated by the carpetbag officials, who reported to Washington."[9]

And so the stage was set for the full realization of this particular narrative of American purpose. Thomas Dixon Jr. was already waiting behind the curtain.

SIXTY-FIVE

I n the two decades since Woodrow Wilson had seen him preaching against Tammany Hall at New York's Twenty-third Street church, Dixon had turned from sermons to oratory, from oratory to novels, from novels to plays. He'd succeeded at all of them.

Six feet tall, gangling, with coal-black hair and dark, scintillating eyes, he was possessed of preaching skills that attracted huge crowds, and even the city's most prominent Baptist, John D. Rockefeller, who befriended the North Carolinian and offered a half million dollars toward the construction of a great temple in Midtown. When more established rival Baptist churches sabotaged the plan, Dixon resigned his pulpit, severed ties with the denomination, and started his own "People's Church" in a rented hall at the Academy of Music. He delivered fiery denunciations of the corruption at City Hall, was once arrested for libel, and, after a decade, retired from formal sermonizing to pursue a lucrative speaking career in which he began denouncing the "black peril."

In 1901 he turned his hand to writing, filling books with racist venom. His first novel, *The Leopard's Spots*, was a rejoinder to *Uncle Tom's Cabin*, wherein the hero restores Anglo-Saxon leadership to a town in post-Reconstruction South Carolina through his volunteer work as head of the area's Ku Klux Klan. "The Anglo-Saxon is entering the new century with the imperial crown of the ages on his brow and the scepter of the infinite in his hands," Dixon's triumphant protagonist announces. "Our old men dreamed of local supremacy. We dream of the conquest of the globe." It received terrible reviews but quickly sold more than one hundred thousand copies. White readers, North and South, were ready to embrace his message.[1]

Dixon's next novel, *The Clansman*, appeared in 1905, and was an even greater success. The novel's protagonist returns from the Civil War to find his South Carolina town under anarchical black rule. "For a thick-lipped, flat-nosed, spindle-shanked negro, exuding his nauseating animal odour, to shout in derision over the hearths and homes of white men and women is an atrocity too monstrous for belief," the hero declares. "This Republic is great . . . because of the genius of the race of pioneer white freemen who settled this continent, dared the might of kings, and made a wilderness the home of Freedom. Our future depends on the purity of this racial stock." When black men rape a neighbor, the protagonist becomes the Grand Dragon of the South Carolina Klan and rides to save his own love interest—the daughter of a barely disguised Thaddeus Stevens—from a similar fate. The Stevens character then recognizes the South's plight and blesses the Klan's disenfranchisement of black voters. "Civilisation has been saved," the novel's hero proclaims on the last page, "and the South redeemed from shame."[2]

Shortly after *The Clansman* arrived in bookstores, Dixon started work on a stage adaptation of the novel that incorporated some plot features from *The Leopard's Spots*. It opened in Norfolk in late September 1905, with Dixon watching anxiously from the wings to see if the four live horses in the production would behave as they galloped across the stage in Klan costume. When the curtain fell the audience reacted with explosive applause, as if a cache of dynamite had been set off inside the theater. "What a tame thing a book compared to this!" Dixon thought. A month later the production opened in Charleston, and a reporter for the *New York Evening Post* described the audience's emotional reaction: "Every reference to the maintenance of the power of the white race is greeted with a subdued roar," he wrote. "When the cause of the carpetbagger and the Black League seemed in the ascendant, there was hissing. But it was not such hissing as one hears directed toward the eyebrows of the villain in the ordinary melo-drama. The whole house, from pit to roof, seethed. At times the actors could not go on. . . . To those who have the future harmony of the two races at heart," the reporter concluded, "the presentation of 'The Clansman' must come as a crushing blow." Dixon esteemed this assessment and quoted it in an article he wrote for *The Theatre* magazine to promote the play's New York opening.[3]

The production was a staggering triumph, playing to packed theaters in both North and South. It was often criticized in Northern papers and was condemned by the African American press, but the controversies gener-ated free publicity and ever greater returns for its producer. For the next three years Dixon had two theater companies touring the country simulta-neously, enabling him to buy a town house on New York's Riverside Drive, where he wrote a third novel celebrating the Klan and organized the pro-duction of several more plays. He lost much of his fortune in the Panic of 1907, when the New York Stock Exchange lost half of its value, but none of his enthusiasm. Dixon's ultimate motivation, he would repeat again and again, wasn't making money—it was to influence "the minds of millions" with his arguments. And that led him to film.[4]

At the time, motion pictures were looked down upon as cheap enter-tainment for the vulgar masses. Most "flickers," as they were called, were ten or fifteen minutes long, shoddily produced, and shown to working-class audiences for five cents a ticket in storefront theaters that were there-fore called nickelodeons. "The screen was still being used as a toy to amuse morons," Dixon complained. "Why not appeal to the people hungry for real amusement, inspiration and instruction?" He intended to bring *The Clans-man* to the screen to show that it could be done.[5]

First he formed a partnership with the inventors of Kinemacolor, a color motion picture process far ahead of its time, and sent crews to accompany one of his acting troops, filming impromptu scenes in homes and fields as they toured the South in the winter of 1911–12; the project failed after burning through a great deal of money. In the years leading up to World War I, Dixon pitched his idea to all the leading motion picture companies. "I tried to show them that there were millions of people with brains who had never seen the inside of a motion picture theatre who could be reached," he later recalled of these meetings with producers. "The children couldn't see it." One group actually laughed at him, calling *The Clansman* "historical beeswax."[6]

But in the spring of 1914, an upstart studio approached him out of the blue, seeking to buy the rights to the book. It couldn't afford his initial $10,000 demand, so Dixon begrudgingly agreed to $2,500 and a quarter of the film's profits. He may have been encouraged that the man behind the offer, Mutual Film's head writer, had acted in one of his plays back in 1906. His name was David Wark Griffith, and their partnership would essentially create Hollywood and make the motion pictures filmed there the most influential force in American popular culture.[7]

D. W. GRIFFITH, another Confederate officer's son, was born in Kentucky in 1875. He'd spent much of his adult life as an itinerant actor. He'd produced a play at the age of thirty-two, and when it failed he lowered himself to accept an acting job at a small New York movie studio, Biograph. Shortly thereafter the studio's director was stricken by a serious illness and Griffith took over the position. By 1909 he was directing twelve to thirteen "flickers" a month. Unlike many of his peers he quickly realized that the new medium could be liberated from the constraints of live theater, that films could be shot in most any location, and each scene from multiple angles and vantage points. "The film-play shows the actual occurrence and is not hampered by the size of the stage nor the number of people to be used," he suggested, when this was a revelatory idea. "For a film-drama we can go afield and get anything we want. If there is a shipwreck to show, we also picture the angry sea and the restless waves."

Griffith's audiences were impressed by these innovations, and his bosses at Biograph supported the bizarre experiments he proposed, such as two-reel movies (with run times as long as twenty-four minutes) or having crews travel great distances to shoot scenes on location. In 1910 they sent Griffith and his entire production team to Los Angeles to film a movie about Mexico-era California. While scouting locations for the film, Griffith stumbled across a village set in the hills called Hollywood. *In Old California* would be the first motion picture ever filmed there. He kept returning to the hamlet to film ever more ambitious productions until 1913, when he startled Biograph's management with a $36,000, four-reel, sixty-one-minute-long feature, *Judith of Bethulia*. When they insisted that the film be hacked up and released as several movies, Griffith resigned to join Mutual Film, taking most of Biograph's studio cast with him. In five years, he promised his partners, they would all retire as millionaires after having made the greatest motion pictures in history.[8]

It was at that point that one of his writers handed him a copy of a screenplay by his onetime boss, Thomas Dixon Jr. *The Clansman* was just what he'd been looking for.

DIXON AND GRIFFITH spent more than a year in a loft in New York's Union Square working on what was then the most ambitious screenplay ever written. It would be epic, at least twice the length of *Judith of Bethulia*, and would depict the entire sweep of the Civil War, Reconstruction, and the "redemption" of the South. It would capitalize on the rising white supremacy that was already evident in school textbooks, scholarly histories, popular novels, and the opinions of the Supreme Court. It would capitalize on Northern angst about the flood of non-Protestant immigration and on the near universal concern that the United States might be pulled into the Great War, which had just broken out in Europe. It would be released as Americans marked the fiftieth anniversary of Appomattox, exploiting the growing public interest in how the Civil War should be remembered.[9]

As *The Clansman* dealt with postwar events, Griffith had to write much of the opening prewar half of the screenplay. To help Griffith better understand the Old South and the war, Dixon gave him his friend Woodrow Wilson's *A History of the American People*. "The white men were roused by a mere instinct of self-preservation," he read in Wilson's book, "until at last there had sprung into existence a great Ku Klux Klan, a veritable empire of the South, to protect the Southern country." Wilson's words impressed Griffith so much that he quoted them on one of the title cards that appeared in the finished film. In fact he would quote Wilson's *History* three times in the feature, on the intentions of Northern Republicans ("to 'put the white South under the heel of the black South'") and on black elected officials in the late 1860s ("men who knew none of the uses of authority, except its insolences"). The second half of the screenplay drew largely on Dixon's book and stage adaptation, including its lurid fantasies about black rapists, its triumphant Klan riders, and its heartwarming scenes of white reconciliation.[10]

When Griffith left for Hollywood to begin production, Dixon said he "filled his trunk with books from my library and bade him Godspeed." Shooting began on July 4, 1914, at the Reliance-Majestic Studios on Sunset Boulevard. Over the next four months Griffith oversaw a production of unprecedented scale. In the rural San Fernando and Big Bear Valleys, Confederate and Union armies clashed. Artillery pieces on loan from the California National Guard roared to life, casting smoke across the locations. Cavalry units charged over California fields. At the studio Griffith's team painstakingly re-created the interior of Ford's Theatre as it was the night Lincoln was assassinated, drawing upon descriptions in a ten-volume biography written by two of the slain president's aides. They also built a duplicate of the interior of the house chamber of the South Carolina State House at the height of Reconstruction from a photograph in a Columbia newspaper and populated it with legislators, many of them actors in blackface. They brought scenes from Wilson's *History of the American People* to life: blacks frightened into "a veritable ecstasy of panic" by ghostly Klansmen; black vagrants "looking for pleasure and gratuitous fortune"; and

Thaddeus Stevens's effort to bring "the veritable overthrow of civilization in the South" by recognizing African Americans' civil and political rights.[11]

Behind the cameras and in the editing room, Griffith brought all of his cinematic innovations to bear. There were sweeping shots of urban and battlefield landscapes, of quick-cut close-ups of characters in conversation, of body parts, and even of the hooves of galloping horses. He presented plotlines that ran in parallel and text cards describing what people were saying. He shot some scenes at night, lit by magnesium flares, and others from cameras mounted on moving platforms. Budgeted at $40,000, the film ultimately cost $110,000, but it was a spectacle like no one had ever seen before.[12]

The final product was three hours long. It opened with a scene of African slaves arriving at a Colonial-era auction, with a title card reading "The bringing of the African to America planted the first seed of disunion." It introduced two white antebellum families: the Stonemans in Pennsylvania and Washington, D.C., and the noble Camerons on their South Carolina cotton plantation, a bucolic realm of happy, well-treated slaves and genteel, dignified masters. Stoneman sons fell in love with Cameron daughters, puppies and kittens played together, and all appeared idyllic. But in Washington, viewers were introduced to House Speaker Austin Stoneman—the thinly disguised Thaddeus Stevens character and patriarch of the clan— and his lustful, sexually aggressive "mulatto" housekeeper, "the great leader's weakness that is to blight a nation," a title card explained. Stoneman, his judgment clouded by Negro sexuality, brought war on the South for having the temerity to secede; the young white couples were separated; war brought ruin on the South and infernos to Atlanta and Columbia. The Cameron and Stoneman boys came face-to-face on the battleground, where one was wounded and the other, recognizing him, gave him medical attention. The camera lingered on still shots of the battlefield dead. The South surrendered.[13]

During Reconstruction, African Americans in the South Carolina legislature were depicted with their feet on desks or addressing their colleagues with fried chicken drumsticks in their hands. Good blacks remained loyal to their masters, protecting them from Union looters; bad ones ran wild in the streets as innocent white families cowered in their houses, or pursued white girls with the intent of raping them. Then the Camerons donned their sheets, rode out as the Klan, and saved one of the young heroines from a black attacker, whom they castrated with their swords. Witnessing these events, the Stonemans finally accepted the Southern point of view on race relations and, the audience read, the "former enemies of North and South are united again in common defense of their Aryan birthright." With white supremacy restored, the penultimate scene showed America's black population being loaded onto ships in New York to be deported "back to Africa," with a title card that read "Lincoln's solution." The final allegorical scene was shot in color: the God of War dissolved into an image of Christ, and one of the white, cross-sectional couples witnessed a beautiful City of Peace appearing in the distance. "Liberty and Union," a title card declares, "one and inseparable, now and forever!"[14]

Dixon, on first seeing the film at a special New York screening, was struck speechless. "When the last flash had faded I wondered vaguely if the emotions that had strangled me were purely personal," he recalled. "I had not been alone in my emotions. Every one was as excited as I and they were expressing themselves with far more eloquence than I could command." When he finally found Griffith he was still too dazed to speak. "But you like it?" Griffith asked. "Don't make me laugh," Dixon whispered, "or I'll cry—." He made one suggestion: The film should be renamed *The Birth of a Nation*.[15]

SIXTY-SIX

The film began a preview run at the grand nine-hundred-seat Loring Opera House in Riverside, California, on New Year's Day, 1915, supported by an advertising campaign touting it to be "the greatest film ever made." Audiences were not disappointed, and the local papers deemed it a fair and powerful telling of history. An enthusiastic Griffith told reporters the film would be shown only "in the best theaters and to the most educated and refined people in the United States." It had to be. The film had cost so much to make that there was little chance it would earn a profit at five or ten cents a ticket. Griffith intended to charge as much as two dollars, a day's wages for a blue-collar worker.[1]

As Griffith prepared for its February 8 premiere at Clune's Auditorium in Los Angeles, word of the film's content quickly circulated around the city. The local chapter of the NAACP, an alliance of black and liberal white leaders, was alarmed that a film celebrating the Klan's reign of terror was to be shown to thousands of people. At the time, motion pictures, plays, and other artistic productions were not understood to be forms of constitutionally protected speech, and municipal officials regularly censored or banned public performances that they regarded dangerous to public order and morals. The NAACP asked the Los Angeles City Board of Censors to prevent the film from being projected within the city. When the board declined, the NAACP petitioned the chief of police to intervene to protect public order, which he might have done had a judge not issued an injunction against him. On opening night seventeen policemen guarded the auditorium's entrances to ensure demonstrators didn't disrupt the event.[2]

This was a very dangerous portent, for if the film were banned in major markets like New York, Boston, and Chicago, it might be impossible for Griffith to pay off its debts.

Despite—and possibly because of—the protests, the premiere was a smashing success. The three-thousand-seat theater was packed, and the applause at the final curtain was overwhelming. The *Los Angeles Times* confirmed that it was indeed "the greatest picture that was ever made," and the auditorium was sold out for days in advance. Scalpers were selling tickets at a 250 percent profit, and by mid-September over 350,000 people had seen it. (Los Angeles's population was only 400,000 at the time.) Griffith knew he had made a blockbuster. He turned to Dixon, his older, more famous, and far better connected collaborator, to help head off government intervention. "The sinister forces that had provoked me to write the story were gathering to suppress it," Dixon lamented. The Motion Picture Association, "an unorganized little mob," would be of no help. They were on their own.[3]

"In the emergency our minds turned to Woodrow Wilson," Dixon later recalled. "If we could get the backing of the President we would have a powerful weapon with which to fight the Sectional conspiracy. . . . I had reasons for believing, if I could avoid the politicians and get his ear before they found out what I was after, it might be done."[4]

Wilson and Dixon had stayed in touch. After Wilson's election Dixon successfully recommended fellow North Carolinian Josephus Daniels to serve in his cabinet. He was thrilled when Wilson's lieutenants began segregating federal agencies, but was concerned that the measures didn't go far enough. "I am heartsick," he wrote the president in July 1913 to protest the appointment of a black Democrat, Adam Patterson, to lead the Register of the Treasury. "Please let me as one of your best friends utter my passionate protest. Unless you can withdraw his name the South can never forgive this." A black man overseeing white female employees was "a serious offense against the cleanness of our social life," and Dixon urged Wilson to change course and "purge Washington of this iniquity." Wilson wrote back, "We are handling the force of colored people who are now in the departments in just the way they ought to be handled . . . a plan of concentration which will put them all together and will not in any one bureau mix the two races." But Patterson withdrew his name for consideration the following day, because Wilson had failed to stand up for him in the face of fiery, race-based opposition from key Southern senators. "He had made good all my predictions," Dixon assured his filmmaking colleagues.[5]

Dixon's gambit worked. Wilson received his old friend in the Oval Office on February 3, 1915, "with the same cordial dignity with which he used to welcome me into his room in Mount Vernon Place." They chatted about their Johns Hopkins days and then Dixon got to the point. He wanted the president to see Griffith's film, "not because it was the greatest ever produced or because his classmate had written the story and a Southern director had made the Film, but because this picture made clear for the first time that a new universal language had been invented." He told the president it represented "a new process of reasoning by which the will could be overwhelmed with conviction."

"I cannot go to a theatre, just now," Wilson told him. "As you know Mrs. Wilson's death holds the White House in mourning." A long silence followed as the president contemplated the request. *The Birth of a Nation*'s Los Angeles premiere was still five days away, but he was familiar with his friend's blockbuster book and hit play and must have at least skimmed *The Southerner*, Dixon's revisionist novel casting Lincoln as a committed white supremacist, which the novelist had dedicated to Wilson two years earlier. "You might set up your machine in the East Room," the president finally offered. "I'll invite my Cabinet and their families and we will see it here."[6]

As a grateful Dixon prepared to go, Wilson stopped him. "I want you to know, Dixon, that I am pleased to be able to do this little thing for you, because a long time ago you took a day out of your busy life to do something for me," he said, in reference to Dixon's securing him the honorary degree from Wake Forest in 1887. "It came at a crisis in my career, and greatly helped me. I've always cherished the memory of it."[7]

The White House screening was set for February 18. By then gallant hooded Klansmen confronted pedestrians from dramatic color posters on display throughout New York City, while Wilson's erstwhile supporters Oswald Garrison Villard and William Monroe Trotter were preparing what would be the first African American civil rights protests in U.S. history. Courts were deliberating the merits of censorship in Los Angeles, and the National Board of Censorship was about to review the film.

Griffith joined Dixon, one of their business partners, their projectionists, and several of their friends in the East Room of the White House to present the twelve-reel film to the president and his guests.[8]

Wilson greeted Dixon and his associates with cordial handshakes and treated them in what Dixon described as a "gracious and beautiful way." They had heard Wilson was "austere and inapproachable," but came away regarding him as, in Dixon's words, "the foremost exemplar of true American democracy."[9]

The lights dimmed, and the projector whirred to life. Griffith had hired a composer to arrange an orchestral score for the film, and forty musicians were slated to perform it in the pit of the Liberty Theatre during the New York premiere, but in the East Room, the executive branch watched in silence. One of those in attendance said Wilson appeared lost in thought during the three-hour viewing. Dixon recalled that when the credits rolled, Wilson turned to him and said: "It is like writing history with lightning. And my only regret is that it is all so terribly true."[10]

After the president left the room, his physician, Cary Grayson, picked up Wilson's copy of the program as a keepsake. Wilson had been so overcome by the film that he'd crumpled it in his hand.[11]

THE FOLLOWING MORNING, newspapers as far away as St. Louis published short dispatches on the screening, giving the film at least a tacit presidential imprimatur, but an ecstatic Dixon wanted even more. He told Griffith that the justices of the Supreme Court of the United States should see it and, if they accepted their invitation, they could ask members of the Senate and House of Representatives to come as their guests. The idea was outlandish, but Griffith approved at once.[12]

Dixon called in a favor, and Josephus Daniels telephoned Chief Justice Edward Douglass White Jr. and asked him to receive his friend that very morning. Twenty minutes later Dixon was standing on White's doorstep. Mrs. White directed him to the study, which he first thought empty until he noticed a grizzled head buried in a sheepskin wrap behind an enormous pile of books. Dixon waited in uncomfortable silence for the chief justice to acknowledge his presence. When he finally did, his eyes flashed with irritation behind bristling brows.

"Well, well, sir," White growled, "what can I do for you? Mr. Daniels telephoned me that you were coming over—"

Dixon nervously explained that President Wilson and his cabinet had witnessed a remarkable film, which he would like to show the justices that night in a private screening. White cut him off.

"Picture!" White exclaimed. "The Supreme Court of the United States see a picture! Of all the suggestions I have ever heard in my life—what sort of a picture?"

Dixon hesitated. "A great moving Picture."

"Moving Picture!" White growled angrily. "It's absurd, sir. I never saw one in my life and I haven't the slightest curiosity to see one. I'm very busy. I'll have to ask you to excuse me."

Dixon stood apprehensively, his thoughts racing. "But, Mr. Chief Justice," he blurted out, "my story is one that will interest you, because you are a Southerner who lived through the period of Reconstruction."

"Reconstruction," White muttered. "What has Reconstruction to do with it?"

"Every thing to do with it," Dixon hastened to explain. "In scenes of vivid life we have told for the first time the story of the Crucifixion of the

South by the politicians of 1867, the story of the sudden rise of the Ku Klux Klan—"

"You tell the true story of the Klan?" White interjected in a soft voice and after a pause said, "I was a member of the Klan, sir. Through many a dark night, I walked my sentinel's beat through the ugliest streets of New Orleans with a rifle on my shoulder." He looked at Dixon. "You've told the story of that uprising of outraged manhood?"

"In a way I'm sure you'll approve."

"I'll be there!" White promised.[13]

Griffith rented the banquet hall of perhaps the grandest venue in the city, the new, thirteen-story Raleigh Hotel, a Beaux Arts establishment opposite the Post Office headquarters on Pennsylvania Avenue. There, at eight o'clock that evening, Dixon and Griffith welcomed the members of the National Press Club, the diplomatic corps, thirty-eight U.S. senators, fifty House members, and the justices of the Supreme Court—five hundred people in all. As the film rolled, Dixon watched how it affected the most powerful individuals in the country. "We had not only discovered a new universal language of man," he realized, "but that an appeal to the human will through this tongue would be equally resistless to an audience of chauffeurs or a gathering of a thousand College Professors."

> They could not forget what they had learned. They saw it done. It became part of their personal experience. It ceased to be History, and became fact in conscious life.
>
> As I watched the excited crowd of Judges, Senators and Members of Congress file out of the hall and heard their tense comments I knew that we were going to surprise our foes when a fight to the finish should be called.

The next morning's *Washington Post* reported the audience had "cheered and applauded."[14]

· · ·

MEANWHILE THE NAACP had asked the New York Police Department to prevent the film from opening by using its powers to suppress public nuisances. Griffith and Dixon's attorney, the former New York congressman Martin Littleton, called on the city's magistrate of courts, and reported that the president and much of the Washington establishment had seen the film. The magistrate, William McAdoo, telephoned the White House, confirmed the story was true, and advised the police to protect the theater from demonstrators to ensure the screenings were not disrupted. Meanwhile the National Board of Censorship, also based in the city, concluded that the film could be shown provided that Griffith cut some of the rape scenes, a lynching sequence, and the deportation of blacks at the end. The publicity surrounding the controversy increased interest in *Birth of a Nation*, but Griffith was taking no chances and spent $12,000 on an advertising campaign.[15]

On March 3, patrons of the Liberty Theatre were greeted by ushers dressed as Confederate and Union soldiers or in formal dresses from the 1860s. Inside was a standing-room-only crowd, and hundreds of disappointed New Yorkers were turned away from the box office. A full symphony orchestra played the score, creating an experience a reporter for the *New York American* said had "the force of a whirlwind," leaving spectators breathless. As in Los Angeles, the audience exploded in applause at the final curtain. Despite protest marches on City Hall by blacks and their allies, *Birth of a Nation* continued to be shown twice a day, filling the enormous theater with rapt fans, including schoolchildren on field trips. In the first month nearly one hundred thousand New Yorkers saw the film. It would continue its run there for a record-breaking forty-five weeks, with 802 performances, 872,000 paid viewers, and a gross of a staggering $600,000.[16]

The NAACP and its allies turned their attention to Boston, where the film was scheduled to premiere on April 10. If it was to be stopped anywhere, it would be in that hub of antebellum abolitionism and Radical Republican sentiment, headquarters of Monroe Trotter's National Equal Rights League and his *Guardian* newspaper. The film was denounced from pulpits and newspaper pages. Its opponents met with the city's mayor, James Curley, and asked him to ban it, as he had Dixon's *The Clansman* in 1906; when the film's producers countered that President Wilson had endorsed the production, the two hundred blacks in the room hissed for more than a minute. Curley refused to suppress the film but ordered scenes of a rape, an interracial wedding, Stoneman with his "mulatto" mistress, and black legislators running amok in the South Carolina State House be cut.[17]

Griffith responded with full-page ads in the Boston papers. There would be a forty-piece orchestra in the theater and eighteen thousand extras and three thousand horses onscreen. He did not mention that thirteen Pinkerton guards would be scattered throughout the audience, or that police would be on call at the entrance alongside the ushers in their Civil War uniforms.

The opening was a smashing success. During intermission Griffith stepped onstage and was so moved by the audience's applause that he could barely speak. Within a few days, tickets were sold out for a month in advance.

On March 5, Wilson replied to a thank-you note Griffith had sent him the night before the opening, expressing his interest in any films he made in the future. "If it is possible for me to assist you with an opinion about them at any time," the president pledged, "I shall certainly try to do so."[18]

SIXTY-SEVEN

A t seven o'clock on the evening of April 17, 1915, William Monroe Trotter left his newspaper office on Boston's Scollay Square and strode purposefully down a sidewalk toward the Tremont Theatre, possibly in the company of a dozen or more colleagues. He would later claim to have made the trip alone, intending to see for himself if Griffith had actually made the cuts to the film that Mayor Curley had ordered.[1]

As he approached Number 176, Trotter could see a crowd of hundreds of protesters gathering across the street, on the edge of Boston Common. The last of the theater's patrons were starting to trickle into the broad vestibule, passing through a detail of city policemen armed with nightsticks and revolvers guarding the entrance against any attack.

In the lobby ticket booth, the Tremont's owner-manager, John Schoeffel, who'd built the grand structure with a partner in 1889, recognized Trotter as he entered the vestibule, followed close behind by a number of well-dressed men and women. Hours earlier the police had warned Schoeffel of a plot to disrupt the 8:30 showing and had shared their plan to respond. Schoeffel picked up the telephone and told the exchange operator to connect him with the Lagrange Street district police station around the corner. He then gave the ticket clerk instructions.

Moments later Trotter arrived alongside the ticket line rail and saw that the clerk was now refusing to sell tickets to black patrons but still allowing white ones to buy them. He joined the line and urged those who had come in with him to do so, too. A white man walked up to him and punched him in the face.[2]

When a police sergeant came into the lobby, Trotter urged him to arrest his assailant. "We can't arrest him," Sergeant Martin King told him. "He's a policeman."

On the street outside a hundred more policemen had arrived from the Lagrange station, where they had been waiting in reserve. They formed a cordon and began preventing blacks from entering the theater.

When Trotter finally reached the ticket window, the clerk informed him that there were no tickets for sale. Policemen began pulling blacks from the line by force. "The police have no right to put you out," Trotter told them. Sergeant King ordered him to leave. When Trotter refused, the officer told him, "I charge you with inciting a riot and I'll arrest you for disturbing the peace," taking Trotter in hand and ordering his men to take him to jail.

"Stand for your rights," many of the 125 people crowded in the lobby chanted as policemen poured in to clear them away. Reverend Aaron Puller, a Baptist pastor and protégé of Booker T. Washington's, was shoved out the door. He tried to reason with a sergeant on the sidewalk, arguing there was no need to use force, when another police officer struck him on the side of the head. When the sergeant said, "Lock him up," at least three officers leapt on him, putting him in a choke hold and dragging him to the precinct. "Kill the nigger!" someone in the crowd screamed.

The lobby cleared, and the police waited, more than a hundred strong, occasionally stomping on the feet of anyone who ignored their instructions to move along.

Inside the enormous auditorium the entire front row was occupied by plainclothes policemen assigned to protect the stage. High above another detachment guarded the projection booth, with officers assigned to protect the electrical wires powering the projectors. Sixty policemen in all sat among the spectators, some scattered in the balconies or on the main floor. Never before or since had a film required such security. Never before had African Americans taken civil disobedience to this level.

Halfway through the showing, as an actor in blackface playing an ex-slave named Gus chased a twelve-year-old white girl through a Carolina forest, a twenty-six-year-old named Charles Ray rose from his seat in the tenth row and flung a decidedly rotten egg at the center of the screen. As the theater filled with the rank odor, plainclothes policemen tackled Ray and removed him from the auditorium.

When Woodrow Wilson's quotes appeared on the title cards, many of the two hundred African Americans in the audience hissed. A little after eleven, as the film concluded with its rapturous color scene of white American unity, protesters unleashed a number of stinkpots—containers filled with ammonium sulfide—creating a rush for the exits.

Outside, Trotter and Reverend Puller, both by now released on bail, had been trying to address the crowd, only to be repeatedly directed to move on by the police. Suddenly the two thousand mostly white theatergoers appeared, rushing across the lobby for the exits. The mostly black crowd outside pressed ahead to block the doors. One woman, twenty-two-year-old Clara Forsky, was arrested, as were two young men who tried to free her from the police. Witnesses described the scene as a near riot, a hairbreadth from turning violent, that was barely quashed by the overwhelming police presence. Based on reports of his agent on the scene, Thomas Dixon gleefully claimed that "a thousand stalwart policemen" had put down "a mob of ten thousand misguided colored men" with nightsticks, driving them off like the Klansmen in the film.[3]

The Tremont remained encircled by police throughout the night.

THE EVENTS that evening in Boston sparked the beginning of something extraordinary: the first mass black civil rights demonstrations in U.S. history.

The following afternoon, an angry crowd of two thousand African Americans and two hundred whites filled Faneuil Hall to hear speaker after speaker denounce the film's depiction of blacks, antebellum slave life, the

Klan, and a whites-only American identity. The United Irish League's Michael Jordan spoke, criticizing Wilson, whose name provoked hisses every time it was mentioned. Frank Sanborn, an eighty-three-year-old abolitionist who'd been arrested for helping John Brown plan the Harper's Ferry raid, said the film was as "an assassination of history." Trotter asked why blacks should support Mayor Curley if he wouldn't protect them "from this Southern misrepresentation of our race." The meeting broke up three hours later with the understanding that the attendees would reassemble on the state house steps at nine the next morning.[4]

Governor David Walsh announced he was canceling that day's showings of *Birth of a Nation* and ordered two hundred state troopers to deploy around the Tremont. Deputy Police Commissioner George Neal forbade the Lynn Elks Lodge from screening the film that day as well, as it was "not a fitting production for Sunday entertainment."

On Monday morning a mixed-race crowd of one thousand gathered on the steps demanding action and occasionally singing "We'll Hang Jeff Davis to a Sour Apple Tree," sometimes with Dixon's name substituted. Governor Walsh consulted with his attorney general and promised to support a bill allowing the suppression of inflammatory films. Hundreds poured into the municipal courthouse that afternoon, where Judge Thomas Dowd was considering a request to ban the film.[5]

On Monday night the Tremont reopened to a sold-out screening, protected by a ring of police, while a white crowd of hundreds watched from the adjacent Boston Common to see if there would be violence. A thousand people were turned away from the box office, but seats had been reserved for Police Chief Neal and Judge Dowd. "I fear that unless this play is stopped, in a week or ten days there is grave danger of trouble in Boston," Herbert Johnson, pastor of the city's largest Baptist church, told a reporter after the show.[6]

Three hundred blacks attended the legislative hearings the following afternoon, while Trotter met with the governor to ensure his continued support for the suppression bill. Across town Judge Dowd ordered an additional cut to the film, the scene in which a black rapist pursued a twelve-year-old girl. Another 2,500 attended a rally at the Tremont Temple, where the speakers included the former Harvard president Charles W. Eliot.[7]

By the end of the month, the NAACP's national membership had grown by 50 percent, to seven thousand. At the end of May, by which time Governor Walsh had signed the law creating a new state censorship board, another 350 had joined, a pace that would continue through the year. The NAACP's membership had previously been concentrated in major urban areas, but ten new branches popped up in smaller Midwestern cities and towns like Carbondale, Cairo, and Peoria in Illinois; Columbus and Dayton, Ohio; Terre Haute and Vincennes, Indiana; and St. Paul, Minnesota. At the end of April, Boston witnessed the largest political gathering of African American women in its history when eight hundred met in Roxbury to create a protective league to protest the movie and further their civil rights. "Shall we fight for our existence or not exist because we are black?" Dr. Alice McKane, the first black woman to practice medicine in Georgia, asked her fellow attendees. "I say fight, fight to the bitter end, fight until the last drop of blood is gone."[8]

There were a number of victories elsewhere in the country. Dr. John Hopkins, a black member of Wilmington, Delaware's city council, convinced his colleagues to ban the movie and any other play or film that promoted racial tensions. Elnora Gresham, the African American president of the Women's Club of Cedar Rapids, spearheaded a similarly successful effort. Harry Smith, editor of the *Cleveland Gazette*, a black paper, did the same in Ohio's largest city, while Illinois lawmakers banned it throughout the state. "We have winged the bird at least," the NAACP journal, *The Crisis*, could claim that summer.[9]

THE BIRD FLEW NONETHELESS. Once convened, the new Massachusetts censors' board declined to suppress *Birth of a Nation*, seeing no threat to public morals or order, as did the governor of Ohio and the mayors of

Baltimore, Philadelphia, and Atlantic City. The tensions in Boston led Wilson's chief of staff to pressure him to issue a statement condemning the film. Wilson declined.[10]

The film, now shorn of a few of its most egregious scenes, was shown in prominent venues across the country, each rented by Griffith and his partners, with projection handled by a dozen production troupes who traveled the central and eastern states simultaneously. It ran for twenty-two weeks in Los Angeles, seventeen weeks in San Francisco, and was reported to be selling $125,000 worth of tickets every week. Dixon had predicted the protests would make him a millionaire, and he was right. The film would gross $18 million in the United States alone.[11]

While many Northern whites saw the film as balanced and historically accurate, even if they found that the imagery was sometimes crude, the effect on Southern audiences was profound, and nowhere more so than in Georgia.

While *Birth of a Nation* had been taking the country by storm in the summer of 1915, William Joseph Simmons was laid up in bed, having been struck by a car. A failed religious educator with a penchant for fraternal orders, Simmons was inspired by the film's publicity to organize a second Ku Klux Klan, the first one having been suppressed in 1871. He acquired a copy of the old Klan's rules and set about creating an updated version. When he learned Griffith's film would open in Atlanta on December 6, Simmons applied for a state charter, made some uniforms, and rallied fifteen of his friends. On Thanksgiving night they took a tour bus to Stone Mountain, a promontory outside the city, and erected a fiery cross to announce the Klan's rebirth. There was good reason to do so that night, Simmons later told an interviewer, as "something was going to happen in town the next week that would give the new order a tremendous boost."[12]

That something was the premiere of *Birth of a Nation* at the Atlanta Theatre. On the evening of the opening Simmons and his followers paraded down Peachtree Street, armed, hooded, and on horseback. Arriving at the theater on Exchange Place they unslung their rifles and fired off a salute.[13]

Outside the box office stood a long line of people that had formed when tickets went on sale at nine that morning. The line would be there the next day, from 9:00 a.m. to 6:00 p.m., and for every day of that week. The city's hotels were packed with theatergoers drawn from all over the state and from Alabama, Mississippi, and Florida as well. "No amusement attraction outside grand opera has ever attracted to Atlanta the number of persons from out-of-town that *Birth of a Nation* brought here last week," *The Atlanta Constitution* would report. In that morning's paper, next to an ad for the movie, Simmons had taken out an ad of his own, announcing the KKK's return and its desire for new members.[14]

"There has been nothing to equal it—nothing," a reviewer for *The Atlanta Constitution* concluded. "Not as a motion picture, nor a play, nor a book does it come at you, but *as* the soul and spirit and flesh of the heart of your country's history, ripped from the past and brought quivering with all human emotions before your eyes." As a recruiting tool for white supremacists, it was also wildly successful.[15]

Within days some of the ushers outside the theater were wearing Klan robes, while merchants did a busy trade in bas-reliefs of Klansmen and other KKK-inspired merchandise. Simmons's group grew from fifteen to several hundred, including a few old men who'd served in the original Klan, each pledged to Anglo-Protestant supremacy, or as they preferred to call it, "100 percent Americanism."

By the summer of 1921 there were more than 850,000 Klansmen, spread across every part of the country.[16]

SIXTY-EIGHT

On January 16, 1917, more than two years into the most destructive conflict in human history, the German foreign minister, Arthur Zimmermann, sent a coded telegraph message to his country's ambassador in Mexico City. Germany would begin unrestricted submarine warfare on the first of February, Zimmermann informed his subordinate, and if that provoked the United States to declare war, the ambassador was to offer a deal to the Mexican president: ally with us, and we will help you "reconquer the lost territory in Texas, New Mexico and Arizona."

Ironically Zimmermann sent the message from the U.S. embassy in Berlin, as Germany's transatlantic telegraph cables had been severed at the start of the war. As a courtesy U.S. diplomats had been transmitting messages to and from Germany's New World embassies via Copenhagen, London, and the transatlantic cable to Washington. What Zimmermann didn't know when he sent the coded cable was that British intelligence had broken the codes and was secretly listening in on all transatlantic traffic via a relay station signal on Land's End, the westernmost tip of England, a station that existed to boost the power of the signal for the 2,500-mile trip under the sea. On February 20 London shared the decoded telegram with the Wilson administration, hoping it would prompt the reluctant Americans—already angered by the sinking of the *Lusitania* and a host of American ships—to declare war. The tactic worked.[1]

"The world must be made safe for democracy," Wilson proclaimed in his war message to Congress on April 2. "Its peace must be planted upon the tested foundations of political liberty."

He then proceeded to destroy those very foundations at home.

At his insistence, Congress passed a raft of authoritarian legislation: the Sedition Act, the Espionage Act, and the Trading with the Enemy Act. Together these acts criminalized criticizing or disagreeing with either the war effort or the government. The Sedition Act forbade anyone to "utter, print, write, or publish any disloyal, profane, scurrilous, or abusive language about the form of government of the United States or the Constitution of the United States, or the military," military uniforms, or the flag; to display the enemy's flag or "promote the cause" of the enemy; or to advocate in any way to reduce the production of "any thing or things, product or products, necessary or essential to the prosecution of the war." At the Post Office Department Burleson oversaw the purging of the mails of antiwar newspapers and even personal letters. Opponents of the war, including Socialist presidential candidate Eugene Debs, were given long prison terms simply for speaking against the conflict, prompting the creation of what would become the American Civil Liberties Union.[2]

The president cast suspicion on German Americans who, at that time, often used German in their schools, churches, and newspapers, particularly in a vast stretch of the mid-Atlantic region and central Midwest that had been settled under the inherited cultural assumptions of the Delaware Valley's eighteenth-century Quaker founders: that the good life meant many peoples living side by side, each retaining their own cultures. This was anathema to Wilson and the vision of a unitary white America celebrated in his *History* and by *The Birth of a Nation.* "I can not say too often," he said, "any man who carries a hyphen about with him carries a dagger that he is ready to plunge into the vitals of this Republic whenever he gets ready."[3]

Under the Alien Enemies Act he required 250,000 citizens of German descent to register at their local post offices, to carry registration cards at all times, and to submit to the surveillance of the new Enemy Alien Registration Section of the Department of Justice, headed by an ambitious twenty-three-year-old agent named J. Edgar Hoover. Some 6,300 were arrested; 2,048 were placed in internment camps for the remainder of the war, including 29 members of the Boston Symphony Orchestra and their music director, Karl Muck, who had been falsely accused of refusing to play "The Star-Spangled Banner." A half-billion dollars' worth of property was confiscated from the suspects, ranging from a trio of horses and a carload of cedar rugs to a Chicago brewery and a pencil-making factory in New Jersey. The standard of evidence was extremely low; one man was placed in a camp for twenty-seven months because the agents who searched his house found a short satirical poem he'd written that was mildly sympathetic to the plight of the German army's conscripts.[4]

Germans stopped speaking their mother tongue, changed the spelling of their names, and sought to move out of historically German neighborhoods. German books were pulled from library shelves and burned, while high schools suspended German language classes. Individuals were careful about what they said in public, particularly after a mob in Collinsville, Illinois, lynched a coal mine laborer, Robert Prager, for being insufficiently patriotic. "The lesson of his death has had a wholesome effect on the Germanists of Collinsville and the rest of the nation," the local newspaper reported.[5]

Conditions for African Americans had grown even worse. After rumors that a black man had tried to rob a white one in East St. Louis, a white mob descended on the town on July 1, 1917, and commenced three days of slaughter. Blacks were beaten or stoned to death, beheaded with butcher knives, and hanged from trees. Homes were set on fire and the occupants shot down as they fled. Others were killed as they tried to swim or raft across the Mississippi to safety after the police closed the only bridge. By the time the National Guard secured the area days later, the black quarter of the city had been reduced to ashes, and twenty-nine whites and as many as two hundred blacks were dead. It was the first of more than three dozen "race riots" to break out over the next two years, resulting in the destruction of prosperous black districts in Tulsa, Omaha, Knoxville, and Chicago.

In Norfolk a mob attacked a homecoming celebration for black soldiers returning from the European front. The death toll from a two-day assault on the black sharecroppers of Elaine, Arkansas, was more than two hundred.[6]

The NAACP and other black organizations repeatedly called on Wilson to denounce the violence, but he refused.[7] From his point of view the nation was more unified than ever. "I am convinced that not a hundred years of peace could have knitted this nation together as this single year of war has," he told Red Cross volunteers at New York's Metropolitan Opera House in the war's final months. "Better even than that, if possible, it is knitting the world together."[8]

SIXTY-NINE

A t the eleventh hour of the eleventh day of the eleventh month of 1918, the guns finally fell silent over No Man's Land.

Eight and a half million soldiers had died, many of them killed by artillery shells or suffocated with poison gas; fifty thousand were Americans. Some thirteen million civilians had starved to death or had perished from disease or been killed outright by combatants during this "war to end all wars." The Great Powers, apart from the United States, were completely exhausted, but it was clear to everyone that Germany, outnumbered and outsupplied, would eventually lose if the fighting continued. The Germans sought an armistice, which the Allies granted on the condition the kaiser surrender his weapons, ships, planes, and trucks; withdraw from Alsace-Lorraine (which Germany had seized in the Franco-Prussian War); and submit to the Allied occupation of the Rhineland, the industrial region bordering Belgium. A peace conference would be held in Paris in January 1919 to determine the future shape of the world.[1]

Woodrow Wilson arrived in Europe in late December, making him the first sitting president to set foot on the continent. He came armed with a plan, Fourteen Points, for world peace. The parties to the conflict—which together with their colonies accounted for most of the land on Earth—should commit to open peace treaties, free trade and navigation, and de-militarization; occupied countries should be freed; and the European nations long ruled by the Ottoman, Austrian, and German Empires should be given independent states of their own. Supervising this would be a League of Nations, a sacred covenant of sovereign states.

If the sacrifices of the Civil War resulted in sectional reconciliation and U.S. unity, Wilson believed the sacrifices of the World War could achieve the same for Europe and the world. "Thousands of our gallant youth lie buried in France. Buried for what?" he would ask. "For the salvation of mankind everywhere, and not alone for the salvation of America." He said that the day would come when any man who opposed "the united service of mankind under the League of Nations will be just as ashamed of it as if he now regretted the union of the states."[2]

The parallels with America did not stop there, however, for Wilson intended to build his peaceful, more perfect world on the foundations of white supremacy.

His lofty principles of democracy and national self-determination were to be extended only to European nations and to Anglo-Saxon settler countries like the United States, Canada, Australia, New Zealand, and apartheid South Africa. Poles, Hungarians, Romanians, Czechs, and Serbs deserved their own national states. African, Arab, Indian, and Pacific Island peoples did not.

A racial hierarchy would be imposed on the former colonies of the defeated Central Powers in the form of League of Nations mandates. The relatively advanced races of the Near East would be granted Class A status, a form of provisional statehood, but under the tutelage and assistance of a paternal power "until such time as they are able to stand alone." Several former German colonial possessions in Africa were categorized as Class B peoples, requiring indefinite imperial supervision by white overseers. South-West Africa and the Micronesian people's Caroline, Marshall, and Palauan island chains were relegated to Class C, places to be treated as the outright possessions of more advanced nations. That Britain, France, the Netherlands, Belgium, and the United States would maintain control over Indians, Egyptians, Vietnamese, Algerians, Congolese, and Filipinos went without question.[3]

A new edition of *A History of the American People* had been published in 1918, without any revision of Wilson's racist perspective. He never distanced himself from *The Birth of a Nation*, or his work being quoted in it, complaining only about the fact that it was "unfortunate" the production had returned to Washington at the height of the war, as it was depressing sales of war bonds in the city's African American neighborhoods.[4] While in office he intervened in the affairs of black- and Latino-governed countries in Central America and the Caribbean more often than any other president before or since, invading Mexico in 1914 (and many times thereafter), Haiti in 1915, Cuba in 1917, and Panama in 1918. U.S. forces occupied Nicaragua throughout his presidency. The Haitian occupation, which lasted for two decades, was directed by Secretary of the Navy Josephus Daniels, who dispatched mostly Southern Marine units to impose a Jim Crow regime in the world's first black republic, replete with segregated hotels, forced labor, and summary executions. "He is carrying on a reign of terror, brow-beating and cruelty, at the hands of Southern white naval officers and marines," W. E. B. DuBois charged. Twenty-first-century historians estimate at least two thousand Haitians were killed during the occupation.[5]

In Paris Wilson discovered that many subject peoples had taken his Fourteen Points to heart and were expecting him to champion their causes. He ignored the pleas of a delegation from Korea, then a colony of Japan, for independence. He refused a meeting request from a twenty-nine-year-old Vietnamese man, Nguyen Ai Quoc, seeking his support for democratic reforms in his French-ruled country; later Nguyen would adopt the nom de guerre of Ho Chi Minh. Monroe Trotter showed up as well, having traveled to Europe incognito as a steamship kitchen servant because the Wilson administration had refused to grant him a passport. Trotter petitioned conference commissioners to grant black Americans "such equal rights as are to be given the ethnical minorities in Austria, Ireland, or the Jews in Poland." Wilson also refused to see him.[6]

African Americans' greatest ally in Paris turned out to be the Japanese delegation. Its members arrived proposing a fifteenth point that Wilson could never countenance: that the principle of racial equality would be incorporated into the Covenant of the League of Nations, including a guarantee that citizens of all member states could travel within the others without discrimination. For the Wilson administration this would have meant that the United States would have had to guarantee equal treatment to Japanese, Haitian, and Liberian citizens in hotels, restaurants, transportation, and government offices, rights nonwhites did not have in Southern and Appalachian states. Wilson had also pledged to prevent Asians from immigrating to the States. "We can not make a homogenous population out of a people who do not blend with the Caucasian race," he had bluntly stated in a 1912 campaign press release. "Oriental coolieism will give us another race problem to solve and surely we have had our lesson."[7]

When the Japanese forced a vote on their measure by the League of Nations Commission, it passed 11–5, with the United States and the British Empire among those opposed. Wilson, who chaired the meeting, arbitrarily announced that the measure had failed for lack of unanimity. The commissioners were outraged, as two previous decisions—establishing the League's headquarters in Geneva and acknowledging a U.S. sphere of influence in Latin America—had both passed with opposition. Wilson unilaterally declared that the issue was too important to allow passage with merely a more than two-to-one margin. His audacity ensured that the League's Covenant would remain silent on racial equality.[8]

TOWARD THE END OF MARCH, Wilson's aides noticed he was looking haggard and that he had developed a twitch in one eye. On April 3, shortly after lunch, he was stricken with severe diarrhea and vomiting. His head and back hurt, and he shook with coughing spasms. His temperature hit 103. White House physician Cary Grayson was concerned, especially as he'd been keeping a secret from the president for the past four years: His arteries were irreversibly hardening. Five days later Wilson remained confined to his room and was forced to hold his meetings with other heads of

state there. He remained in a weakened state for the remainder of negotiations.[9]

His personality and positions now underwent a dramatic change.
Whereas before he had been furious with France's hard-line position against
Germany, in the days afterward he inexplicably yielded to its demands. No
limits would be placed on the reparation payments imposed on Germany,
which would be officially identified as the aggressor. He dropped objections to the kaiser's being tried for "war guilt" and suddenly developed an
intense personal dislike for the German delegation. The president, previously anxious about the adoption of his Fourteen Points, unexpectedly now
regarded their acceptance as inevitable. He batted away Lloyd George's plea
that he soften his stance against Germany, telling the prime minister, "You
make me sick!"[10] Herbert Hoover, one of Wilson's aides at the conference,
noticed that the normally incisive president suddenly "groped for ideas,"
and Wilson himself complained of short-term memory problems. Lloyd
George believed that Wilson had suffered a stroke.[11]

Wilson returned to Washington that July in a triumphant mood, confident that the treaty and the League of Nations would solve the world's problems and would be easily ratified by the Senate.

Inexplicably, though, he treated the Senate's leaders with condescension.
"The stage is set, the destiny disclosed," he lectured them during a critical
hearing. The treaty was made "by the hand of God" and therefore "we cannot turn back," he proclaimed. "We can only go forward, with lifted eyes
and freshened spirit, to follow the vision." After the hearing, it was clear he
did not yet have the votes he needed for passage, as the Republican senator
Henry Cabot Lodge and others feared the implications of Article Ten,
which pledged all League members to respond to an attack on one as an
attack on all. Instead of negotiating with the skeptics, Wilson barnstormed
the country, rallying voters to his vision of the League as the Providential
instrument of peace.[12]

On September 25, 1919, Wilson stumbled while climbing the stage in Pueblo, Colorado, to speak on behalf of the treaty's ratification. At the lectern he spoke slowly and haltingly and kept losing his train of thought. Afterward, on his private, eastbound train, he complained of a headache. Edith Galt, a woman sixteen years his junior whom he'd married sixteen months after Ellen's death, noticed that evening that his left arm was in a strange position. By breakfast the following morning he was slurring his speech. Edith convinced him to cancel the scheduled speaking stops and directed the presidential train to continue directly to Washington. Wilson appeared to have recovered by the time they reached Union Station, walking unassisted to the waiting automobile.[13]

On October 2 Wilson awoke unable to feel the left side of his body. Edith helped him to the bathroom but shortly thereafter heard him collapse. She found him splayed out in front of the toilet, unconscious, his head bleeding from where it had struck the toilet paper dispenser. She got him to bed somehow before calling Dr. Grayson, who soon determined he had suffered a severe stroke and that his left side was paralyzed. Appointments were canceled and visitors—including cabinet secretaries—were sent away. Edith wondered if he should resign; Grayson told her doing so would undermine Wilson's life's work and, thus, his will to live. They decided nobody could know how serious his illness was.[14]

The president didn't leave his bedroom for months. He was unable to stand until after Christmas and didn't attend a cabinet meeting until April 10. His speech, thinking, and left arm never properly recovered. For months the First Lady was in effect the president, transmitting orders and feedback to the cabinet in written memos. She and Dr. Grayson wouldn't allow even the president's chief of staff to visit him.[15]

Senator Lodge formally submitted the treaty for a ratification vote in November 1919. Senator Gilbert Hitchcock, chair of the Democratic Senate caucus, visited the president in an effort to save the treaty by negotiating a compromise with Lodge over the commitments in Article Ten. The meeting did not go well.

"Let Lodge compromise," Wilson growled at Hitchcock.

"Well, of course he must compromise also," the senator replied, "but we might well hold out the olive branch."

"Let Lodge hold out the olive branch," Wilson persisted, as Grayson and the First Lady looked on anxiously.[16]

The president's refusal to make any concessions ultimately doomed the treaty and the League, leaving Europe without an administrative mechanism to manage the peace and setting the stage for the rise of Adolf Hitler.

FOR HIS PART Wilson refused to believe he was seriously impaired. He insisted he could continue his duties and intended to run for a third term. Dr. Grayson finally rebelled and let party leaders know his patient was physically and mentally compromised and would never recover. Wilson was by then so unpopular that the state of his health was almost a moot point. In November 1920 his would-be successor, Ohio governor James Cox, founder of the Cox newspaper chain, was spectacularly defeated by the Republicans' uninspiring, disengaged candidate, Warren Harding, who hadn't even bothered to campaign. Harding's victory remains the biggest popular vote landslide in the history of presidential elections, with more than 60 percent of voters casting their ballots for him.

The Wilsons moved to a house in Washington's Kalorama neighborhood, where the former president died in February 1924, his foreign policy legacy in tatters.

The ethnonationalism he'd cultivated, however, lived on, largely unchallenged within the federation's white majority. The Klan continued to grow, claiming four to six million members by the mid-1920s, and by then owned 150 magazines and newspapers, two colleges, and a motion picture company. Showings of *The Birth of a Nation* remained a central part of their recruiting strategy.[17]

Months after Wilson's death, Congress passed an Immigration Act imposing rigid, racially based quotas aimed at maximizing immigration from

Northern Europe and minimizing it from the rest of the continent, and prohibiting Asian, African, and Arab peoples entirely. "Thank God we have in America perhaps the largest percentage of any country in the world of the pure, unadulterated Anglo-Saxon stock; certainly the greatest of any nation in the Nordic breed," Senator Ellison Smith, Democrat of South Carolina, told his colleagues in support of the measure. "It is for the preservation of that splendid stock that has characterized us that I would make this not an asylum for the oppressed of all countries, but a country to assimilate and perfect that splendid type of manhood that has made America the foremost Nation in her progress and in her power, and yet the youngest of all the nations."[18]

Across the South monuments were erected in honor of the men and women who fought to realize that vision of America. One now stood on what had once been Robert E. Lee's lawn, presiding over the hallowed grounds of the Arlington National Cemetery, a gift of the Daughters of the Confederacy. President Wilson had spoken at its unveiling on June 4, 1914, Jefferson Davis's birthday, expressing his pride that lives would no longer be "disturbed and discolored by fraternal misunderstandings." The heroic white woman standing on its plinth was draped in Confederate and U.S. flags.[19]

SEVENTY

I n the spring of 1918 the New York publishing house of Henry Holt was expecting to receive the finished manuscript of Turner's magnum opus, which had by then been some twenty years in the making.

Originally commissioned as a sequel to *Rise of the New West*, the book had evolved into a masterwork on the role of sections in the development of the nation in the 1830s and 1840s, the calm before the intersectional storm. Turner had assured his editors many times that the manuscript would soon be delivered, but years turned to decades, decades to the passing of a generation, and still the work remained little more than an outline, an idea, and an enormous and expanding set of filing cabinets filled with research notes.

But in June 1917, Turner was asked to deliver a series of eight talks at the prestigious Lowell Institute on the very topic of his book, "The United States and Its Sections, 1830–1850." Turner and the publisher were elated: Now he would be forced to put his ideas to paper. His new editor at Henry Holt, Edward Bristol, hurried a revised contract to the historian, specifying delivery of the manuscript within one year in exchange for a generous 15 percent royalty on sales. Turner agreed and toiled away to prepare the lectures, an effort that nearly broke him.[1]

By the time he gave his first talk in February 1918, he was physically and emotionally exhausted. Though only fifty-six, he had high blood pressure and vascular problems. Veins broke in his eyes. His doctor warned that further stress of this sort could prove fatal. In April, shortly after Turner delivered his last lecture, Bristol asked for a status report, as Holt wanted to include the volume in its fall catalog. Turner replied it was not quite finished and retreated to his cottage on Hancock Point, Maine, to recuperate with his wife, daughter, and grandson. He made no progress on the book that summer, nor in the academic year that followed, nor the summer after that, nor even during the 1919–20 academic year. In his weakened state it was all Turner could do to teach his Harvard classes, and that left him so drained he needed an entire summer on the Maine coast just to recover.[2]

His colleagues intervened, alerting Harvard president Lawrence Lowell to the historian's dilemma. Lowell acted immediately: Turner was offered a year's sabbatical at full salary so as to "complete for publication one or more books on American history." But at the end of the 1920–21 sabbatical year, all Holt had in hand were eight maps showing county-level distribution of literacy, ethnicity, political registration, and staple crops. Lowell extended Turner's sabbatical by an additional six months, during which time he managed to write only a very rough draft of the book's introduction. He was excused from teaching for half of both the 1922–23 and 1923–24 academic years, but produced only three of the projected twelve chapters.

Yet again, Turner was running in circles in his research, seeking ever more information to try to solve difficulties he had encountered in the data. The central problem was that, because of his early academic training, he believed that the political and social differences between U.S. sections were ultimately determined by physical geography. He expected that as the distinct Euro-American settlement streams had spread westward, they would have evolved over time in reaction to the physiographic regions each encountered. Like Darwin's finches in the Galápagos, settlers would adapt to environmental conditions and, thus, assimilate with one another throughout a given physical region. "In the midst of more or less antagonism between 'bowie knife Southerners,' 'cow-milking Yankee Puritans,' 'beer-drinking Germans' and 'wild Irishmen,' a process of mutual education, a giving and taking was at work," he explained, resulting in "the creation of a new type, which was neither the sum of all its elements nor a complete fusion in a melting pot."[3]

The data, however, kept confounding this hypothesis. The Scots-Irish settlement stream into the lower parts of Ohio or Illinois still did not at all resemble the New England Yankee–dominated one in the north of those states, despite shared physical geography. "Why does Indiana not show the same facts in regard to glacial influences as her neighbors on either side," he scribbled in his research notes. Had he been prepared to accept that culture, not geography, was the more determinative force, the answer would have been obvious: Most of Indiana was settled via Kentucky and the up-land South by Scots-Irish, and its people had different ideas about freedom and liberty, church and state, government and individuals than the post-Puritan Yankees who dominated the early settlement of Michigan or Wisconsin. He was not prepared to see this. In his notes to himself he scribbled instead: "Are there concealed geographic influences?"[4]

Desperate to complete the book, he resigned from Harvard in September 1924 so as to be able to work on it full time. He and Caroline moved back to Madison, but instead of writing the remaining chapters, he commenced major revisions of the three he had completed. He then asked Holt to return the maps he'd submitted so he could have them updated and re-drawn. It was becoming clear to his editors, if not the historian, that the book would never be completed.

The Turners eventually moved to Pasadena, California, where Frederick's old friend, Max Farrand, hired him as a researcher at the Huntington Library. There he spent his twilight years, with summers back at Hancock Point, filling more drawers full of notes for the book. In 1930, with his heart severely weakened, he dictated very rough drafts of six more chapters. He died of heart failure on March 14, 1932, hours after resolving an obscure point regarding Calhoun and the Compromise of 1850.

His final words were: "I know this is the end. Tell Max I'm sorry that I haven't finished my book."[5]

EPILOGUE

The national consensus that America was effectively an Anglo-Saxon-led ethnostate outlasted Wilson's presidency by more than three decades. From *Dick and Jane* to *Leave It to Beaver*, from Barbie dolls to "flesh"-colored crayons, children were taught they lived in a Euro-American society. In the South a racial apartheid system was extended, to include everything from public parks to graveyards. In the North administrative discrimination frequently confined nonwhite people to certain neighborhoods based on their race by not granting them mortgages or insurance policies in any other areas. In all regions of the country Jews and Catholics were also denied access to elite colleges and social clubs. Over Wilson's objections women had won the right to vote in 1920, but remained excluded from entire professions, and most elite clubs, colleges, and universities. Homosexuality was a criminal offense.

The federal government actively resisted making diversity an official part of American life. As a result of the ethnic and racial quotas in the Immigration Act of 1924, by 1960 eight in ten immigrants were European, and the proportion of foreign-born people in the country had fallen by almost two-thirds. Once-threatening European ethnic groups—Irish, Québécois, Italians, Slavs—had been slowly, begrudgingly admitted into the camp of belongers, a category that had been rebranded from "Anglo-Saxon Protestant" to "Christian" and, in some circles, even "Judeo-Christian" white.

The two world wars vividly demonstrated the dangers of ethnonationalism, of dehumanizing "the other," from the mechanized slaughter of soldiers on the battlefield to the industrialized murder of millions of civilians
in Nazi slaughterhouses. *Herrenvolk* democracy—self-rule for a master
race—was a much more difficult principle to champion after Adolf Hitler's
example. The notion that the world was best run by Teutonic, Anglo-Saxon,
or Aryan minds was discredited on the killing fields of the Somme and
Verdun, at Auschwitz and Babi Yar. The world's nonwhite supermajority
also witnessed the allegedly superior Europeans routed by Japanese forces
first at Port Arthur and then in British Malay, Singapore, Burma, the Dutch
East Indies, French Indochina, and the U.S. Philippines.

Mass conscription during the world wars produced multiethnic units
and multiracial armies, whose members felt they'd earned the rights to full
citizenship and consecrated them with blood sacrifices. During World
War I, tens of thousands of African Americans served in France, where
they were treated as equals by French civilians and officers, enraging Southern white officers and alarming President Wilson, who feared "it has gone
to their heads." In World War II hundreds of thousands of black soldiers
were deployed to England in preparation for D-Day and to Hawaii en route
to the brutal island-hopping campaign across the Pacific. On both fronts
they encountered a desegregated environment where the local population
did not discriminate against them, while white Southern soldiers caused
trouble by harassing or even assaulting the nonwhite Allied troops of the
British colonial forces. "The more I see of the English, the more disgusted I
become with Americans," an African American army lieutenant, Joseph O.
Curtis, wrote home. "After the war, with the eager and enthusiastic support
of every negro who will have served in Europe, I shall start a movement to
send white Americans back to England and bring the English to America."
Returning African American soldiers, some of them decorated war heroes,
had little patience for racial segregation at home.[1]

Domestic white supremacy was also exposing the gap between pro-
fessed American ideals and the reality on the ground. What made America

superior to the Axis powers, as every Hollywood depiction of World War II touted, was its righteous inclusion and tolerance, its commitment to democracy, human dignity, and the rule of law. Yet Nazi Germany and Imperial Japan were able to release factually accurate propaganda citing lynchings and race riots to paint Americans as hypocrites and oppressors in the eyes of millions of Asian, African, and Middle Eastern residents of European and U.S. colonies. As the full horror of Adolf Hitler's rule became clear with the Allied liberation of German death camps and discovery of mass graves, his prior praise for the Southern caste system and other American efforts to keep their "Teutonic element" pure by "not mixing with any other racial stock" gave pause to readers of Southern papers who had praised his regime's policies before the war.[2]

The Cold War greatly increased the stakes. The United States engaged in a nuclear-armed struggle for global hegemony with the Soviet Union, with the newly independent, nonwhite nations of Asia, Africa, Latin America, and the Middle East the primary battlefield. Soviet Communism was avowedly antiracist and egalitarian, and Moscow treated its nonwhite clients with respect, inviting African students to study on full scholarships at Soviet universities. Meanwhile African diplomats and senior government officials had trouble renting suitable housing or getting seats at restaurants in Washington and New York. Mali's ambassador was driven off every beach he tried to visit in Maryland and Delaware one summer, while Haiti's agriculture secretary wasn't allowed to check in to the Biloxi hotel where the international conference to which he had been invited was taking place. In 1950 U.S. Ambassador to the United Nations Henry Cabot Lodge warned that racial discrimination had become "our Achilles' heel before the world," and by 1957 Vice President Richard Nixon was advising President Eisenhower: "We cannot talk equality to the peoples of Africa and Asia and practice inequality in the United States." W. E. B. DuBois, the African American historian and civil rights advocate, laid out the problem succinctly: "It is not Russia that threatens the United States so much as Mississippi."[3]

Over the course of a decade the world watched—and the Soviets obtained

powerful propaganda material—as Arkansas National Guardsmen and a
jeering white mob blocked silent, respectful black children from entering
Little Rock Central High School; as townspeople beat black college students trying to order food at a Greensboro, North Carolina, lunch counter;
as a white mob killed a British newspaper reporter and wounded 165 federal marshals in an effort to prevent a black man from enrolling at the University of Mississippi; and as the uniformed authorities of a U.S. state
attacked peaceful protesters in Selma, Alabama. Caught between increasingly fearless civil rights activists and the blinding scrutiny of the world's
media, presidents were forced to act, however unwillingly at times, to dis-
mantle the ethnonationalist consensus over which Woodrow Wilson had
presided. Harry Truman desegregated the military and the civil service and
told Congress that the only way to "inspire the peoples of the world whose
freedom is in jeopardy" was to "correct the remaining imperfections in our
practice of democracy." Eisenhower sent the 101st Airborne to end the
standoff at Little Rock Central High School—the first time federal troops
had been deployed to enforce civil rights since Reconstruction—while the
federal judiciary effectively declared Jim Crow unconstitutional in its 1954
Brown v. Board of Education decision. In 1963 John F. Kennedy delivered a
nationwide address to propose sweeping civil rights legislation. "We preach
freedom around the world, and we mean it, and we cherish our freedom
here at home, but are we to say to the world, and much more importantly,
to each other that this is a land of the free except for the Negroes," he said.
"That we have no second-class citizens except Negroes; that we have no
class or caste system, no ghettoes, no master race except with respect to
Negroes? Now the time has come for this Nation to fulfill its promise."[4]

His assassination left it to his successor, Lyndon Johnson, to oversee
passage of the 1964 Civil Rights Act and the 1965 Voting Rights Act, which
effectively restored the Fourteenth and Fifteenth Amendments, plus a new
immigration act that undid the race-based quota system of its 1924 predecessor. "A century has passed, more than a hundred years, since equality
was promised," he told the nation. "The time of justice has now come."[5]

Simultaneous civil rights movements had compelled a return to the lost American promise of equality and self-government, a civic nationhood, not an ethnic one. The civil rights movement had toppled Southern apartheid by organizing boycotts, sit-ins, marches, and civil disobedience. Activists challenged Northern racism using terms that would have been familiar to Lincoln and Douglass. "When the architects of our Republic wrote the magnificent words of the Constitution and the Declaration of Independence, they were signing a promissory note to which every American was to fall heir," the Reverend Martin Luther King Jr. said in his most famous speech. "This note was a promise that all men—yes, black men as well as white men—would be guaranteed the unalienable rights of life, liberty, and the pursuit of happiness." The feminist movement demanded social, professional, and sexual equality for a gender that made up the majority of the population. Gays and lesbians fought the police and discriminatory ordinances. Latinos struggled against racial discrimination across the Southwest, where a Southern-style caste system had long prevailed. Elite colleges began partially dismantling their old boys' networks, and public universities rapidly expanded to increase educational opportunities.[6]

For a generation of Americans born from the late 1960s through the early 1990s, liberal civic nationalism became the received national narrative. Racism and prejudice were believed to be on the wane; equal opportunity was on the rise. With the collapse of the Soviet Empire in 1989–91, Western intellectuals even convinced themselves that the nation-state itself was destined for extinction, the triumph of liberal democracy and global capitalism considered to have become so complete that they had rendered nationhood obsolete, here and abroad. The dark side had finally been vanquished, and tossed into the dustbin of history alongside the tenets of Soviet Communism.

It hadn't, of course. America's ethnostate project has lived on, hiding in the blind spots of the intelligentsia, fed table scraps by politicians, and nurtured in the churches of illiberalism. Then, in November 2016, it was swept back into the White House, and a newly elected president began trying to exclude people from America based on their religion, from disaster aid based on their race. He built internment camps for migrant toddlers, embraced the world's most brutal foreign dictators, and eroded U.S. alliances with other liberal democracies. He could not bring himself to convincingly condemn the neo-Nazis who'd marched on the streets of an American city carrying torches and chanting "Jews will not replace us."

The battle over America's soul hadn't ended. Perhaps it never will.

ACKNOWLEDGMENTS AND SUGGESTED READING

I delved into the creation of the United States' national narrative at a time when the federation seemed on the verge of coming apart. Donald Trump was—is—president, and the ugly language of ethnonationalism is again spoken from the White House. The U.S. Senate, its committees controlled by Southerners, has to date played along, and at this writing nobody is really sure if the Supreme Court would step in to defend a civic nationalist vision of the Fourteenth and Fifteenth Amendments. History doesn't repeat itself, but it rhymes, somebody once said—not Mark Twain apparently—and whoever it was is right once again.

My research took me to the Library of Congress in Washington, D.C., where I opened a folder holding George Bancroft's invitation to attend the 1889 memorial service of President James Garfield at the Capitol Rotunda on the very day President George H. W. Bush's body was lying in state there, just across First Street Southeast. At the National Portrait Gallery I was able to come as close as one can to standing face-to-face with all five of my primary subjects, and much of the supporting cast; this included happening upon Christian Schussele's 1864 portrait of an apocryphal gathering of the great American writers of the early nineteenth century at Washington Irving's home in New York's Hudson Valley, with Simms at the far left, Bancroft at the far right and Hawthorne, Emerson, Longfellow, Cooper, Bryant, Irving, and others in between. At the Cosmos Club archives I was able to confirm that Bancroft, who lived a few doors away, never joined and that Wilson's candidacy, to my surprise, was not sponsored by the racist novelist Thomas Nelson Page (whose Washington mansion now houses the Church of Scientology). Bancroft's H Street home is long gone, but in Anacostia, Douglass's desk stood in his library waiting for him to sit down again to write.

The bulk of Bancroft's papers were at the Massachusetts Historical Society in Boston, including the letters he sent home from Göttingen and Berlin as a young man. In Concord, New Hampshire, I found Simms's letters to Lorenzo Sabine, tucked away in the granite temple that is the New Hampshire Historical Society.

My thanks to the staffs of all of these organizations for what they do to preserve our history and for their kind assistance along the way.

Bowdoin College's Hawthorne-Longfellow Library was my research home away from home throughout this project, and I'm greatly appreciative of the college's generosity in providing access to its collections for local residents generally and this researcher in particular. Throughout two years of work, the library staff kept me supplied with texts, not least the remarkably comprehensive published volumes of the letters and papers of three of my subjects.

John W. Blassingame, John R. McKivigan, and Peter P. Hinks have given the world a great gift with their ongoing series, *The Frederick Douglass Papers*, currently consisting of ten volumes over three series covering his speeches, his correspondence, and meticulously annotated editions of Douglass's three autobiographies, from which I learned so much. For Simms, I'm indebted to Mary C. Simms Oliphant, Alfred Taylor Odell, and T. C. Duncan Eaves for assembling *The Letters of William Gilmore Simms* in five volumes. Every Wilson scholar benefits from Arthur Link's epic sixty-nine-volume *The Papers of Woodrow Wilson*, which on their own take up an entire floor-to-ceiling library shelf; it's a pity so many of these scholars also followed Link's lead in apologizing for or simply covering up Wilson's racism and the central role it played in his presidency. These collections are essential reading for anyone interested in these three men, how they thought, what they did, and whom they knew.

Nobody has ever created quite as comprehensive published editions of Bancroft's or Turner's papers, though Mark Antony DeWolfe Howe provided some highlights in his two-volume *The Life and Letters of George Bancroft*, published in 1908. Turner's life became the life's work of historian Ray Allen Billington, who wrote several biographical works about him, including the indispensable *Frederick Jackson Turner: Historian, Teacher, Scholar*, which won the 1974 Bancroft Prize, appropriately enough.

Union spans a century and, as such, owes a debt to scores of historians and biographers, essayists and orators, newspapermen and diarists, congressional investigators and writers of doctoral dissertations who either chronicled the experiences of themselves and those around them or made sense of events long past. The sources I used can be found in the endnotes to this book, but a few more accessible works for readers wishing to take a deeper dive into the story of U.S. nationhood follow. The best single-volume biographies of Bancroft and Simms are Lilian Handlin's (appropriately skeptical) *George Bancroft: The Intellectual as Democrat* (1984) and John Caldwell Guilds's (overly sympathetic) *Simms: A Literary Life* (1992). I didn't know David Blight was working on a biography of Douglass when I started this project, but was delighted to have access to his insights in *Frederick Douglass* as I was completing my book; there's no better starting point for understanding the life of this essential Founder of our liberal democratic republic; Blight's earlier book, *Race and Reunion*, guided me to Woodrow Wilson's participation in the fiftieth anniversary of the Gettysburg Address. Wilson has been shielded from proper scrutiny by a small army of hagiographic biographers, so it's difficult to recommend a general biography.

There are several specialized works I can't help but include in any *Union*-inspired reading list. If you or a friend for some reason doubt that white supremacists engaged in a reign of terror against racial equality during Reconstruction, immersion in the thirteen-volume congressional investigation entitled *Testimony Taken by the Joint Select Committee to Inquire into the Condition of Affairs in the Late Insurrectionary States* may provide enlightenment; they are government documents in the public domain and at this writing can be freely read or downloaded from Google Books and other sites. Anyone seeking to analyze D. W. Griffith's *The Birth of a Nation* in any detail will value the Rutgers Films in Print volume of the same name, edited by Robert Lang. For a synopsis of how the ethnonationalist consensus was undone in the 1940s, '50s, and '60s, start with Thomas Borstelmann's excellent *The Cold War and the Color Line: American Race Relations in the Global Arena.*

In quoting from period manuscripts, I have occasionally modified orthography and punctuation when it interfered with communicating the author's words. Specifically, I replaced certain handwriting shortcuts with the full, spelled-out words they represent, such as replacing ampersands with the word "and," and "&c" with "et cetera." In a few instances, I also deleted or moved commas when their position as written would confuse today's readers. I did not modify spelling or grammar, even though many of my subjects insisted on using British variants, a choice that would no doubt have distressed Daniel Webster.

My agent, Jill Grinberg, played an essential role in making sure this project got off on the right foot while locking down deals on my other titles on several continents. At Viking my editor, Rick Kot, gave key support and sound advice not only on this book, but on *The Lobster Coast*, *American Nations*, and *American Character* as well; we'll save the Republic yet. Thanks also to designers Colin Webber (for the jacket) and Meighan Cavanaugh (for designing the book itself), to production editor Bruce Giffords, and to copy editor Maureen Clark, who greatly improved this book with her careful attention to detail. Jacques Poitras, author and CBC–New Brunswick provincial affairs reporter, and Natacha Isabelle Bossé of Fredericton, New Brunswick, kindly helped improve my translation of Victor Hugo's never-translated poem attacking Bancroft, while Joshua D. Rothman of the University of Alabama— through the magic of Twitter—recognized Bancroft's Latin scrawls as a passage from Catullus. Thanks to all three of you for sharing your language skills with a Latin- and early-nineteenth-century-French-impaired writer. Cliff Schechtman and Steve Greenlee, editors extraordinaire at the *Portland Press Herald* and *Maine Sunday Telegram*, also helped make this book possible by letting me take the leave necessary to complete it; may state-level journalism live long and prosper.

My greatest debt is to my family. My wife, Sarah Skillin Woodard, spent more time with this manuscript than anyone else, improved it a great deal, and ran interference with the children; Henry and Sadie had to make do without me on evenings and some late winter weekends when I was hunkered down in the study, pondering ancient texts and such. Thank you, my loves; you know this would never have been finished without your contributions and sacrifices.

And thanks to you, dear readers, who make this all possible.

Freeport, Maine
January 2020

KEY TO ABBREVIATIONS
USED IN THE NOTES

Bancroft-Bliss Papers: Bancroft-Bliss Family Papers, Library of Congress, Washington, D.C.

Blassingame I: Blassingame, John W., John R. McKivigan, and Peter P. Hinks, eds. *The Frederick Douglass Papers: Series 2, Autobiographical Writings;* vol. 1, *Narrative.* New Haven: Yale University Press, 1999.

Blassingame II: Blassingame, John W., John R. McKivigan, and Peter P. Hinks, eds. *The Frederick Douglass Papers: Series 2, Autobiographical Writings;* vol. 2, *My Bondage, My Freedom.* New Haven: Yale University Press, 1999.

Letters I: Oliphant, Mary C. Simms, Alfred Taylor Odell, and T. C. Duncan Eaves, eds. *The Letters of William Gilmore Simms,* vol. 1, *1830–1844.* Columbia: University of South Carolina Press, 1952.

Letters II: Oliphant, Mary C. Simms, Alfred Taylor Odell, and T. C. Duncan Eaves, eds. *The Letters of William Gilmore Simms,* vol. 2, *1845–1849.* Columbia: University of South Carolina Press, 1953.

Letters III: Oliphant, Mary C. Simms, Alfred Taylor Odell, and T. C. Duncan Eaves, eds. *The Letters of William Gilmore Simms,* vol. 3, *1850–1857.* Columbia: University of South Carolina Press, 1954.

Letters IV: Oliphant, Mary C. Simms, Alfred Taylor Odell, and T. C. Duncan Eaves, eds. *The Letters of William Gilmore Simms,* vol. 4, *1858–1866.* Columbia: University of South Carolina Press, 1955.

Letters V: Oliphant, Mary C. Simms, Alfred Taylor Odell, and T. C. Duncan Eaves, eds. *The Letters of William Gilmore Simms,* vol. 5, *1867–1870.* Columbia: University of South Carolina Press, 1956.

Link I: Link, Arthur, ed. *The Papers of Woodrow Wilson,* vol. 1, *1856–1880.* Princeton, N.J.: Princeton University Press, 1966.

Link II: Link, Arthur, ed. *The Papers of Woodrow Wilson,* vol. 2, *1881–1884.* Princeton, N.J.: Princeton University Press, 1967.

Link IV: Link, Arthur, ed. *The Papers of Woodrow Wilson,* vol. 4, *1885.* Princeton, N.J.: Princeton University Press, 1968.

Link V: Link, Arthur, ed. *The Papers of Woodrow Wilson,* vol. 5, *1885–1888.* Princeton, N.J.: Princeton University Press, 1968.

Link VI: Link, Arthur, ed. *The Papers of Woodrow Wilson,* vol. 6, *1888–1890.* Princeton, N.J.: Princeton University Press, 1969.

Link VIII: Link, Arthur, ed. *The Papers of Woodrow Wilson,* vol. 8, *1892–1894.* Princeton, N.J.: Princeton University Press, 1970.

Link IX: Link, Arthur, ed. *The Papers of Woodrow Wilson,* vol. 9, *1894–1896.* Princeton, N.J.: Princeton University Press, 1970.

Link XIV: Link, Arthur, ed. *The Papers of Woodrow Wilson,* vol. 14, *1902–1903.* Princeton, N.J.: Princeton University Press, 1973.

Link XXIV: Link, Arthur, ed. *The Papers of Woodrow Wilson,* vol. 24, *January–August 1912.* Princeton, N.J.: Princeton University Press, 1978.

Link XXV: Link, Arthur, ed. *The Papers of Woodrow Wilson*, vol. 25, *August–November 1912*. Princeton, N.J.: Princeton University Press, 1978.

Link XXVII: Link, Arthur, ed. *The Papers of Woodrow Wilson*, vol. 27, *January–June 1913*. Princeton, N.J.: Princeton University Press, 1979.

Link XXVIII: Link, Arthur, ed. *The Papers of Woodrow Wilson*, vol. 28, *1913*. Princeton, N.J.: Princeton University Press, 1979.

Link XXXII: Link, Arthur, ed. *The Papers of Woodrow Wilson*, vol. 32, *January 1–April 16, 1915*. Princeton, N.J.: Princeton University Press, 1980.

Link XXXIII: Link, Arthur, ed. *The Papers of Woodrow Wilson*, vol. 33, *April 17–July 21, 1915*. Princeton, N.J.: Princeton University Press, 1980.

Link XLVII: Link, Arthur, ed. *The Papers of Woodrow Wilson*, vol. 47, *March 13–May 12, 1918*. Princeton, N.J.: Princeton University Press, 1984.

Link XLVIII: Link, Arthur, ed. *The Papers of Woodrow Wilson*, vol. 48, *May–July 1918*. Princeton, N.J.: Princeton University Press, 1985.

Link LV: Link, Arthur, ed. *The Papers of Woodrow Wilson*, vol. 55, *February 8–March 16, 1919*. Princeton, N.J.: Princeton University Press, 1986.

Link LXIII: Link, Arthur, and J. E. Little, eds. *The Papers of Woodrow Wilson*, vol. 63, *September–November 5, 1919*. Princeton, N.J.: Princeton University Press, 1990.

McKivigan I, Book 1: McKivigan, John R., ed. *The Frederick Douglass Papers*: Series 2, *Autobiographical Writings*; vol. 3, *Life and Times of Frederick Douglass*; book 1: *The Text and Editorial Apparatus*. New Haven: Yale University Press, 2012.

MHS Bancroft Letters: George Bancroft Papers, Massachusetts Historical Society, Boston, Massachusetts.

NOTES

CHAPTER ONE

1. Edward M. Riley, ed., "St. George Tucker's Journal of the Siege of Yorktown," *William and Mary Quarterly*, n.s., 5 (July 1948): 375–95.

2. Riley, "St. George Tucker's Journal"; Ebenezer Denny, *Military Journal of Major Ebenezer Denny, an Officer in the Revolutionary and Indian Wars* (Philadelphia: J. P. Lippincott, 1859), 43–45; Edward Lengel, *George Washington: A Military Life* (New York: Random House, 2005), 340–44.

3. Liah Greenfeld, *Nationalism: Five Roads to Modernity* (Cambridge, Mass.: Harvard University Press, 1992), 423–24; Joseph M. Torsella, "American National Identity, 1750–1790: Samples from the Popular Press," *Pennsylvania Magazine of History and Biography* 112, no. 2 (April 1988): 174.

4. For a detailed discussion, see Colin Woodard, *American Nations: A History of the Eleven Rival Regional Cultures of North America* (New York: Viking, 2011).

5. *New York Mercury*, August 27, 1764, quoted in Jack P. Greene, "The Background of the Articles of Confederation," *Publius* 12, no. 4 (Autumn 1982): 35.

6. Jonathan Boucher, *Reminiscences of an American Loyalist, 1738–1789* (Port Washington, N.Y.: Kennikat Press, 1967), 133.

7. John Dickinson to William Pitt, December 21, 1765, Chatham Papers, PRO 30/8/97, National Archives (Kew, U.K.), quoted in Greene, "Background of the Articles of Confederation," 35.

8. Paul Wentworth, "Minutes Respecting Political Parties in America and Sketches of the Leading Persons in Each Province [1778]," in *Facsimiles of Manuscripts in European Archives*, comp. B. F. Stevens (London: Malby & Sons, 1889); "London, January 6," *South-Carolina Weekly Gazette*, April 10, 1784, 2; Edward Bancroft to William Frazer, Philadelphia, November 8, 1783, in George Bancroft, *History of the Formation of the Constitution of the United States*, vol. 1 (New York: D. Appleton, 1882), 331–33.

9. George Washington to Benjamin Harrison, Mount Vernon, Va., January 18, 1784, and George Washington to John Jay, Mount Vernon, Va., August 15, 1786, in Washington Papers, National Archives, Washington, D.C.

10. Thomas Jefferson, "Explanation of the Three Volumes Bound in Marbled Paper," February 4, 1818, in *The Complete Anas of Thomas Jefferson*, ed. Franklin B. Sawvel (New York: Round Table Press, 1903), 26.

11. Greenfeld, *Nationalism*, 425–27; John M. Murrin, "A Roof without Walls: The Dilemma of American National Identity," in *Beyond Confederation: Origins of the Constitution and American National Identity*, ed. Richard R. Beeman et al. (Chapel Hill: University of North Carolina Press, 1987), 341–43.

12. Daniel Boorstin, *The Americans: The National Experience* (New York: Vintage, 1965), 339–56; Sydney G. Fisher, "The Legendary and Myth-Making Process in Histories of the American Revolution," *Proceedings of the American Philosophical Society* 51, no. 204 (April–June 1912): 64–67.

13. Jaap Verheul, "'A Peculiar National Character': Transatlantic Realignment and the Birth of American Cultural Nationalism after 1815," *European Journal of American Studies* 7, no. 2 (2012): 9.

14. Noah Webster, *Dissertations on the English Language* (Boston: 1789), 179. Webster was at work on his comprehensive dictionary from 1808 to 1825.

15. Michael Kamen, *Mystic Chords of Memory: The Transformation of Tradition in American Culture* (New York: Alfred A. Knopf, 1993), 65; Etsuko Taketani, "The North American Review, 1815–1835: The Invention of the American Past," *American Periodicals* 5 (1995): 111, 119; Nathaniel Parker Willis, "Letter XVI," in *The Prose Works of N. P. Willis* (Philadelphia: Henry C. Baird, 1852), 243–44.

CHAPTER TWO

1. Paul Revere Forthingham, *Edward Everett: Orator and Statesman* (Boston: Houghton Mifflin, 1925), 10–11; Benjamin Thomas Hill, *Life at Harvard a Century Ago, as Illustrated by the Letters and Papers of Stephen Salisbury, Class of 1817* (Worcester, Mass.: Davis Press, 1910), 3–6, 11–14; Bailyn, "Why Kirkland Failed," in *Glimpses of the Harvard Past*, ed. Bernard Bailyn et al. (Cambridge, Mass.: Harvard University Press, 1986), 25.

2. Lucretia Bancroft to Jane Gheraldi, Worcester, Mass., February 28, 1828, in Mark Antony De-Wolfe Howe, *The Life and Letters of George Bancroft*, vol. 1 (New York: Charles Scribner's Sons, 1908), 13–16; Benjamin Rumford, "Essay III. Of Food; and Particularly of Feeding the Poor," in *Count Rumford's Experimental Essays, Political, Economical, and Philosophical* (London: T. Cadell & W. Davies, 1796), 183–297.

3. Howe, *Life and Letters of George Bancroft*, 1:2–10; Aaron Bancroft, *A Sermon Delivered at Worcester* (Worcester, Mass.: Clarendon Harris, 1836), 18–19, 38–40.

4. Woodard, *American Nations*, 57–64.

5. Lilian Handlin, *George Bancroft: The Intellectual as Democrat* (New York: Harper & Row, 1984), 7–10.

6. Samuel Eliot Morrison, *Three Centuries of Harvard, 1636–1936* (Cambridge, Mass.: Harvard University Press, 1937), 208; Dale H. Freeman, "A Changing Bridge for Changing Times: The History of the West Boston Bridge, 1793–1907" (master's thesis, University of Massachusetts Boston, 2000), 33–34, 45, 47; Forthingham, *Edward Everett*, 10–11; Hill, *Life at Harvard*, 9–10 (quoting from the *Laws of Harvard College*, 1807); Bailyn, "Why Kirkland Failed," 21–24.

7. Bailyn, "Why Kirkland Failed," 25–26; Oscar Handlin, "Making Men of the Boys," in *Glimpses of the Harvard Past*, 54–55.

8. Daniel Walker Howe, *The Unitarian Conscience: Harvard Moral Philosophy, 1805–1861* (Cambridge, Mass.: Harvard University Press, 1970), 1–17; Lilian Handlin, *George Bancroft*, 33–34.

9. Nuriya Saifulina, "Harvard's Habeas Corpus: Grave Robbing at Harvard Medical School," *Harvard Crimson* 28 (September 2017); Frothingham, *Edward Everett*, 19–30, 34; Lilian Handlin, *George Bancroft*, 46–47; George Bancroft to President Kirkland, Göttingen, Germany, January 17, 1819, in Howe, *Life and Letters of George Bancroft*, 1:53–55.

10. Oscar Handlin, "Making Men of the Boys," 55; *Life, Letters and Journals of George Ticknor* (Boston: James R. Osgood & Co, 1876), 1: 73n.

11. George Bancroft, "An Incident in the Life of John Adams," in *The Century Illustrated Monthly Magazine, May 1887 to October 1887* (New York: Century Company, 1887), 434–36.

12. George Bancroft to Henry Cabot Lodge, Washington, June 12, 1877, in Howe, *Life and Letters of George Bancroft*, 1:31.

CHAPTER THREE

1. "A Historical Sketch of the College of Charleston, South Carolina," in *The American Quarterly Register*, vol. 11, ed. B. B. Edwards and W. Cogswell (Boston: American Education Society, 1839), 164–68.

2. "A Historical Sketch of the College of Charleston," 169; Minutes of the Trustees of the College of South Carolina, October 27, 1817, College of Charleston archives, Charleston, S.C.

3. Edward McGrady, *History of South Carolina under the Proprietary Government, 1670–1719* (New York: Macmillan, 1897), 511–12; Forrest Andrews Nabors, "The Problem of Reconstruction: The Political Regime of the Antebellum Slave South" (doctoral dissertation, University of Oregon, June 2011), 429–31.

4. John Caldwell Guilds, *Simms: A Literary Life* (Fayetteville: University of Arkansas Press, 1992), 4–6; The death dates of these family members are recorded on the same headstone in Charleston's St. Michael's Cemetery; Simms mentions his father's hair going white in "Personal Memorabilia," Charles Carroll Simms Collection, South Caroliniana Library, University of South Carolina, Columbia, S.C.

5. W. Gilmore Simms to James Lawson, Woodlands, S.C., December 29, 1839, *Letters I*, 160–61; *City Gazette & Daily Advertiser* (Charleston), October 23, 1798, quoted in *The South Carolina Historical and Genealogical Magazine*, vol. 7, ed. A. S. Salley (Charleston: South Carolina Historical Society, 1906), 101–2; Kinloch Rivers, "Simms, the Man," *Simms Review* 2, no. 2 (Winter 1994): 30; Guilds, *Simms*, 7 (citing his in-person 1978 interviews with Simms's granddaughter, Mary C. Simms Oliphant.)

6. W. Gilmore Simms to John Esten Cook, Woodlands, S.C., April 14, 1860, in *Letters IV*, 216; Simms to Lawson, December 29, 1839, *Letters I*, 161–64; *Letters I*, lxii–lxiii.

7. Will of Thomas Singleton, Charleston, June 19, 1783, Probate Court, Charleston County, S.C., bk. 1793–1800, 561–563; Simms to Lawson, December 29, 1839, *Letters I*, 161; W. Gilmore Simms to Rufus W. Griswold, Charleston, June 20, 1841, in *Passages from the Correspondence and Other Papers of Rufus W. Griswold* (Cambridge, Mass.: W. M. Griswold, 1898), 77.

8. Guilds, *Simms*, 8–9; Simms to Griswold, June 20, 1841, *Passages*, 78; Simms to Lawson, December 29, 1839, *Letters I*, 161.

9. United States Census for 1820, Marion County, Mississippi ledger, 87; Miriam J. Shillingsburg, "The Senior Simmses—Mississippi Unshrouded," *Simms Review* 6, no. 1 (1998): 24–26.

10. Guilds, *Simms*, 9–11; Simms to Lawson, December 29, 1839, *Letters I*, 161.

11. *Letters I*, lxi; Eric H. Walther, *William Lowndes Yancey and the Coming of the Civil War* (Chapel Hill: University of North Carolina Press, 2006), 5; John Belton O'Neall, *Biographical Sketches of the Bench and Bar of South Carolina*, vol. 2 (Charleston, S.C.: Courtenay & Co., 1859), 11–12, 14, 411; O'Neall, vol. 1, 53–57.

12. Simms to Lawson, December 29, 1839, *Letters I*, 161.

13. Simms to Lawson, December 29, 1839, *Letters I*, 161; Simms to Griswold, June 20, 1841, *Passages*, 78.

CHAPTER FOUR

1. Blassingame I, 116–17.

2. Blassingame I, 117–18; Frederick Douglass, "My Bondage, My Freedom (1855)," in Blassingame II, 23–27.

3. Blassingame II, 24–25.

CHAPTER FIVE

1. George Bancroft to John Kirkland, Göttingen, August 15, 1818, MHS Bancroft Letters; Bryan F. Le Beau, *Frederic Henry Hedge: Nineteenth Century American Transcendentalist* (Eugene, Ore.: Pickwick, 1985), 6.

2. Le Beau, *Frederic Henry Hedge*, 396–98; "Göttingen during the Summer of 1818, (Concluded)," *Edinburgh Magazine and Literary Miscellany*, June 1819, 514–22; Thomas Hodgskin, *Travels in the North of Germany, Describing the Present State of the Social and Political Institutions, the Agriculture, Manufactures, Commerce, Education, Arts and Manners in That Country, Particularly in the Kingdom of Hannover*, vol. 2 (Edinburgh: Archibald Constable, 1820), 308–18.

3. Hans Kohn, *The Idea of Nationalism: A Study in Its Origins and Background* (New York: Macmillan, 1944), 350–52; Hans Kohn, *Prelude to Nation-States: The French and German Experience, 1789–1815* (Princeton, N.J.: D. Van Nostrand, 1967), 178–83, 210–11.

4. George Bancroft to John Kirkland, Göttingen, August 13, 1818, MHS Bancroft Letters; Fred L. Burwick, "The Göttingen Influence on George Bancroft's Idea of Humanity," *Jahrbuch für Amerikastudien* 11 (1966): 194; George Bancroft to Lucretia Bancroft, Göttingen, November 25, 1818, in Howe, *Life and Letters of George Bancroft*, 1:51.

5. George Ticknor to Elisha Ticknor, Göttingen, August 10, 1815, in *The Letters and Journals of George Ticknor*, vol. I (Boston: James R. Osgood., 1877), 74–75; Thomas Hodgskin, *Travels in the North of Germany, Describing the Present State of the Social and Political Institutions, the Agriculture, Manufactures, Commerce, Education, Arts and Manners in That Country, Particularly in the Kingdom of Hannover*, vol. 1 (Edinburgh: Archibald Constable, 1820), 340–43; Bancroft to Lucretia Bancroft, November 25, 1818, *Life and Letters of George Bancroft*, 1:51; Edward Everett's diary quoted in Stuart Horn, "Edward Everett and American Nationalism" (doctoral dissertation, City University of New York, 1972), 59–60; George Bancroft to [Andrews Norton?], Göttingen, June 21, 1819, MHS Bancroft Letters; Gaius Valerius Catullus, Poem 37 (circa 30 BC).

6. Bancroft to Andrews Norton, September 5, 1818, MHS Bancroft Letters; George Bancroft to Aaron Bancroft, October 3, 1818, in Howe, *Life and Letters of George Bancroft*, 1:46; Hodgskin, *Travels in the North of Germany*, 2:274; Konrad H. Jarausch, "American Students in Germany, 1815–1914," in *German Influences on Education in the United States to 1917*, ed. Henry Geitz et al. (New York: Cambridge University Press, 1995), 196–97.

7. George Ticknor to E. Ticknor, Göttingen, November 18, 1815, in *Letters and Journals*, 1:81–82; George Bancroft to John Kirkland, Göttingen, January 9, 1819, MHS Bancroft Letters.

8. George Bancroft to John Kirkland, Göttingen, April 2, 1820, MHS Bancroft Letters; George Bancroft to John Kirkland, Göttingen, September 17, 1820, in Howe, *Life and Letters of George Bancroft*, 1:84; Bancroft to Lucretia Bancroft, Göttingen, November 25, 1818, in *Life and Letters of George Bancroft*, 1:51–53.

9. George Bancroft to Andrews Norton, Göttingen, December 31, 1818, MHS Bancroft Letters.

10. [Edward Everett], review of Bancroft's translation of *Reflections on the Politics of Ancient Greece*, *North American Review*, April 1824, 390–95; George Bancroft (translator) and Arnold Heeren, *Reflections on the Politics of Ancient Greece* (Boston: Cummings, Hilliard, 1824).

11. Howe, *Life and Letters of George Bancroft*, 1:38, 66–70; Bancroft to Kirkland, January 9, 1819, MHS Bancroft Letters.

12. Eric Scott Saulnier, "'They Could There Write the Fates of Nations': The Ideology of George Bancroft's *History of the United States* during the Age of Jackson" (doctoral dissertation, University of California Los Angeles, 2016), 53–54.

13. George Bancroft, "Toasts for the 4th of July 1820, Göttingen" (and attached speech), MHS Bancroft Letters.

14. Howe, *Life and Letters of George Bancroft*, 1:87–96; Kohn, *Prelude to Nation-States*, 248–51.

15. Howe, *Life and Letters of George Bancroft*, 1:101–10; Russell Nye, *George Bancroft: Brahmin Rebel* (New York: Alfred A. Knopf, 1944), 50–52.

16. George Bancroft to Andrews Norton, Geneva, October 12, 1821, in Howe, *Life and Letters of George Bancroft*, 1:124–28.

17. George Bancroft to John Kirkland, Rome, February 10, 1822, in Howe, *Life and Letters of George Bancroft*, 1:141–43.

18. Nye, *George Bancroft*, 55–57; Howe, *Life and Letters of George Bancroft*, 1:147–51; C. Herbert Gilliland, "Byron Visits the American Navy: Two Unpublished Diary Entries," *Byron Journal* 45, no. 1 (2017): 67.

19. Howe, *Life and Letters of George Bancroft*, 1:152–53.

CHAPTER SIX

1. Henry Deleon Southerland and Jerry Elijah Brown, *The Federal Road through Georgia, the Creek Nation, and Alabama, 1806–1836* (Tuscaloosa: University of Alabama Press, 1989), 61–63; A. Levasseur, *Lafayette in America in 1824–1825* (New York: White, Gallaher & White, 1829), 77.

2. Levasseur, *Lafayette in America*, 91–93; William Gilmore Simms, *The Social Principle: The True Source of National Permanence* (Tuscaloosa, Ala.: Erosophic Society, 1843), 7.

3. "Biographical Sketches of Living American Poets and Novelists, No. IV: William Gilmore Simms, Esq.," *Southern Literary Messenger* 4, no. 8 (August 1838): 535; William Gilmore Simms, "Reminiscences of South Carolina," *XIX Century* 2 (May 1870): 920–23.

4. Shillingsburg, "The Senior Simmses," 23–25.

5. William Gilmore Simms to the *City Gazette* (Charleston), "Notes of a Small Tourist, No. 5," Mobile, Alabama, March 19, 1831, in *Letters I*, 24; Southerland and Brown, *Federal Road through Georgia*, 72–89; Levasseur, *Lafayette in America*, 77.

6. Mell Frazer, *Early History of Steamboats in Alabama* (Auburn: Alabama Polytechnic Institute, 1907), 26–27; William Gilmore Simms to the *City Gazette* (Charleston), "Notes of a Small Tourist, No. 9," April 10, 1831, in *Letters I*, 32.

7. Simms, *Social Principle*, 6; Simms to *City Gazette*, April 10, 1831, *Letters I*, 33; William Gilmore Simms, "The Grave in the Forest," *Southern Literary Messenger* 4, no. 11 (November 1838): 690–91.

8. Miriam Jones Shillingsburg, "Literary Grist: Simms's Trips to Mississippi," *Southern Quarterly* 41, no. 2 (Winter 2003): 124, 133n; Guilds, *Simms*, 10.

9. Guilds, *Simms*, 10–12.

10. Shillingsburg, "The Senior Simmses," 23–25; United States Census, 1830, White County and Wilson County, Tennessee; Guilds, *Simms*, 4, 11.

11. William Gilmore Simms, *Wigwam and the Cabin* (New York: Redfield, 1859), 74, 176–78.

12. John Caldwell Guilds and Charles Hudson, eds., *An Early and Strong Sympathy: The Indian Writings of William Gilmore Simms* (Columbia: University of South Carolina Press, 2003), 9, 16; Simms, *Social Principle*, 37–38.

13. Simms quoted in Guilds, *Simms*, 12.

14. Guilds, *Simms*, 18–21.

15. Simms to Lawson, December 29, 1839, *Letters I*, 164.

16. James Everett Kibler Jr., "The Album (1826): The Significance of the Recently Discovered Second Volume," *Studies in Biography* 39 (1986): 66–68; Shillingsburg, "Literary Grist," 119–22; William Gilmore Simms, "North American Indians (1828)," in Guilds and Hudson, *An Early and Strong Sympathy*, 15–16.

CHAPTER SEVEN

1. Blassingame II, 28.

2. Blassingame II, 28.

3. Woodard, *American Nations*, 47–56.

4. Blassingame II, 37–40, 330; Beth Pruitt, "Reordering the Landscape: Science, Nature and Spirituality at Wye House" (doctoral dissertation, University of Maryland, College Park, 2015), 15–47, 128–166.

5. Blassingame II, 330.

6. Blassingame II, 29–30.
7. Blassingame II, 43–46; Blassingame I, 27.
8. Blassingame II, 73–74, 340; Blassingame I, 23, 26.
9. Blassingame I, 15–16; Blassingame II, 48–53, 322.
10. Blassingame I, 15–16; Blassingame II, 50–52, 58–61, 322, 334.
11. Blassingame I, 28; Blassingame II, 77–78, 341.
12. Blassingame II, 76–79.

CHAPTER EIGHT

1. George Bancroft to S. A. Eliot, Cambridge, Mass., September 24, 1822, MHS Bancroft Letters.
2. Bancroft to Eliot, September 24, 1822, MHS Bancroft Letters; Saulnier, "'They Could There Write the Fates of Nations,'" 76.
3. George Bancroft to Andrews Norton, Worcester, Mass., September 18, 1822, MHS Bancroft Letters; Bancroft to Eliot, September 24, 1822, MHS Bancroft Letters; Bancroft to Eliot, Cambridge, Mass., April 2, 1823, and May 10, 1823, MHS Bancroft Letters; Thomas Wentworth Higginson, "Göttingen and Harvard Eighty Years Ago," *Harvard Graduates' Magazine* 6, no. 21 (September 1897), 17n.
4. Nye, *George Bancroft*, 64; Lilian Handlin, *George Bancroft*, 85–88; Reverend Andrew Peabody quoted in *Proceedings of the American Antiquarian Society* (April 1891), 153.
5. Nye, *George Bancroft*, 64–65; "Poems by George Bancroft" (book review), *Philobiblion*, January 1863, 8–10.
6. Howe, *Life and Letters of George Bancroft*, 1:167–77; George Bancroft to Samuel Eliot, Cambridge, Mass., December 3, 1822, in Howe, *Life and Letters of George Bancroft*, 1:161–63.
7. George E. Ellis, "Recollections of Round Hill School," *Educational Review* 1, no. 4 (April 1891): 341–42.
8. Nye, *George Bancroft*, 76–81; Howe, *Life and Letters of George Bancroft*, 1:180–83.
9. George Bancroft, *An Oration Delivered on the Fourth of July, 1826, at Northampton, Mass.* (Northampton, Mass.: T. Watson Shepard, 1826), 19–24.
10. Lilian Handlin, *George Bancroft*, 97–98; Nye, *George Bancroft*, 75–76.

CHAPTER NINE

1. Jeffery J. Rogers, *A Southern Writer and the Civil War: The Confederate Imagination of William Gilmore Simms* (New York: Lexington Books, 2015), 28; for more on Simms's views, see Colin D. Pearce, "The Metaphysical Federalism of William Gilmore Simms," *Studies in the Literary Imagination* 42, no. 1 (Spring 2009), 125–26.
2. Rogers, *A Southern Writer and the Civil War*, 27–29.
3. William P. Trent, *William Gilmore Simms* (Boston: Houghton Mifflin, 1892), 63–64; Rogers, *A Southern Writer and the Civil War*, 31; Simms to James Lawson, Summerville, S.C., November 25, 1832, in *Letters I*, 47–48.
4. Simms to Lawson, November 25, 1832, *Letters I*, 47–48; *Letters I*, lxvii–lxviii; Trent, *William Gilmore Simms*, 65.
5. Simms to Lawson, December 28, 1839, *Letters I*, 163.
6. Simms to Lawson, December 29, 1841, in *Letters I*, 162–65.

CHAPTER TEN

1. Woodard, *American Nations*, 92–100; David W. Blight, *Frederick Douglass: Prophet of Freedom* (New York: Simon & Schuster, 2018), 36–37.
2. Blassingame I, 30; Blassingame II, 79–80, 343.

3. Blassingame I, 31; Blassingame II, 81–83.
4. Blassingame I, 31–32; Blassingame II, 83–84.
5. Blassingame I, 32–34; Blassingame II, 97–98; Caleb Bingham, *The Columbian Orator* (Baltimore: Phillip Nicklin, 1811), v–vi, 7–33, 50–53, 102–18, 240–42.
6. Blassingame II, 89–90.
7. Blassingame II, 87–88, 105.
8. Blassingame II, 99–101, 334.
9. Blassingame II, 105.

CHAPTER ELEVEN

1. Harry N. Scheiber, "A Jacksonian as Banker and Lobbyist: New Light on George Bancroft," *New England Quarterly* 37, no. 3 (September 1964): 363–65; Harry N. Scheiber, "The Commercial Bank of Lake Erie, 1831–1843," *Business History Review* 40, no. 1 (Spring 1966): 48–50, 52.
2. Scheiber, "A Jacksonian as Banker and Lobbyist," 365–66; Scheiber, "The Commercial Bank of Lake Erie," 51–53.
3. Scheiber, "A Jacksonian as Banker and Lobbyist," 366–68; Howe, *Life and Letters of George Bancroft,* 1:190–91.
4. Bancroft to Sarah Dwight Bancroft, Washington, December 25 and 27, 1831, and January 11, 17, 18, and 23, 1832, in Howe, *Life and Letters of George Bancroft,* 1:191–204.
5. Bancroft to Sarah Dwight Bancroft, January 18, 1832, in Howe, *Life and Letters of George Bancroft,* 1:201–2.
6. Nye, *George Bancroft,* 98.
7. See Richard C. Vitzthum, "Theme and Method in Bancroft's *History of the United States,*" *New England Quarterly* 41, no. 3 (September 1968): 362–80.
8. Nye, *George Bancroft,* 94–95.
9. George Bancroft, *A History of the United States: From the Discovery of the American Continent to the Present Time,* vol. 1 (Boston: Charles Bowen, 1834), 3–4.
10. His home on the slope of Round Hill is described by a visitor in Howe, *Life and Letters of George Bancroft,* 1:220.
11. Bancroft (1834), *A History of the United States,* viii.
12. Bancroft, *A History of the United States,* 2–4.
13. Bancroft, *A History of the United States,* vii.
14. Bancroft, *A History of the United States,* 50, 505–8.
15. Bancroft, *A History of the United States,* 248–49, 261–62.
16. Edward Everett to George Bancroft, Charlestown, Mass., October 5, 1834, in Howe, *Life and Letters of George Bancroft,* 1:205–7; Arnold Heeren to George Bancroft, Göttingen, September 1, 1835, in Howe, *Life and Letters of George Bancroft,* 1:209–10. Prescott and Everett quoted in Nye, 182.
17. Alan Nevis, *The Diary of John Quincy Adams, 1794–1845* (New York: Longman, Greens, 1928), 513; [N. Beverley Tucker], review of George Bancroft's *A History of the United States, Southern Literary Messenger* 1, no. 10 (June 1835): 587–91; Tucker's authorship is noted in a reprint of this review in William & Mary Law School's *Faculty Publications,* no. 1294.
18. Boorstin, *The Americans,* 372; Sacvan Bercovitch, *The Office of the Scarlet Letter* (Baltimore: Johns Hopkins University Press, 1991), 36–38; Saulnier, "'They Could There Write the Fates of Nations,'" 165; Anna O. Marley, "Painting History in the Capitol Rotunda," *Capitol Dome* 55, no. 1 (2018): 33.

CHAPTER TWELVE

1. Woodard, *American Nations,* 65–72; Charles Hemstreet, *Literary New York, Its Landmarks and Associations* (New York: G. P. Putnam's Sons, 1903), 167–82; Edwin G. Burrows and Mike Wallace, *Gotham: A History of New York City to 1898* (New York: Oxford University Press, 1998),

588–93; Lawson lived at 32 Wall Street as per Thomas Longworth, *New York City Directory, 1832–33* (New York: Thomas Longworth, 1832), 424.

2. *Letters I*, lxviii, lxx; Guilds, *Simms*, 36–37; James L. West III, *American Authors and the Literary Marketplace since 1900* (Philadelphia: University of Pennsylvania Press, 1991), 81.

3. *Letters I*, xviv, cviii, ci, cix–cxi; Guilds, *Simms*, 36–38.

4. Simms to Lawson, November 25, 1832, and Simms to Lawson, Charleston, January 19, 1833, in *Letters I*, 47–50.

5. *Letters I*, lxvii–lxxi; review of *Guy Rivers* in H. W. Herbert (ed.), *The American Monthly Magazine*, vol. 3 (New York: Monson Bancroft, 1834), 302.

6. William Gilmore Simms, *The Yemassee: A Romance of Carolina* (Richmond: Johnson Publishing, 1911), 88.

7. Simms, *The Yemassee*, 141.

8. Bancroft, *A History of the United States*, 2; Simms, *The Yemassee*, 423.

9. *The Knickerbocker*, April 1835, 341–43; Guilds, *Simms*, 59–60; John Bassett, *Defining Southern Literature: Perspectives and Assessments, 1831–1952* (Cranbury, N.J.: Fairleigh Dickinson Press, 1997), 23.

10. Simms to James Lawson, [Oak Grove, S.C.], April 15, 1836, in *Letters I*, 83–84.

CHAPTER THIRTEEN

1. Blassingame II, 115.
2. Blassingame II, 110, 114–16.
3. Blight, *Frederick Douglass*, 60; Blassingame II, 118–24.
4. Blassingame I, 49.
5. Blassingame I, 51–52.
6. Blassingame II, 138–41; Blassingame I, 53-55.
7. Blassingame II, 151–53.
8. Blassingame II, 170–72.
9. Blassingame II, 173.

CHAPTER FOURTEEN

1. Howe, *Life and Letters of George Bancroft*, 1:212–13, 218; "George Bancroft," *Newburyport Herald*, November 7, 1834.
2. Lilian Handlin, *George Bancroft*, 140–41; Howe, *Life and Letters of George Bancroft*, 1:215–16; Lucretia Bancroft to George Bancroft, Clinton, La., December 21, 1836, in Howe, *Life and Letters of George Bancroft*, 1:219.
3. Saulnier, "'They Could There Write the Fates of Nations,'" 120–23.

CHAPTER FIFTEEN

1. Simms to Lawson, January 27, 1836, Midway, S.C., in *Letters I*, 90; *Letters I*, lxxvii, 90n.
2. Guilds, *Simms*, 74; William Cullen Bryant, "Simms," in *Little Journeys to the Homes of American Authors* (New York: G. P. Putnam's Sons, 1853), 157–66.
3. Guilds, *Simms*, 77; Simms to Lawson, January 27, 1836, *Letters I*, 78.
4. Guilds, *Simms*, 82–93; Simms to Philip C. Pendleton, Charleston, August 12, 1841, in *Letters I*, 265.
5. Simms to Lawson, Woodlands, March 3, 1841, in *Letters I*, 235; Lilian Handlin, *George Bancroft*, 132–43.
6. Simms to Carey and Hart, Charleston, May 7, 1842, in *Letters I*, 308; *Letters I*, 311n; Guilds, *Simms*, 133, 140.

7. Simms to the *New York Mirror,* [Woodlands], S.C., May 25, 1839, in *Letters I,* 142–43; Guilds, *Simms,* 86, 94; William Cullen Bryant to Simms, New York, November 1840, in *Letters of William Cullen Bryant,* vol. 2, *1836–1849,* ed. William Cullen Bryant II and Thomas G. Voss (New York: Fordham University Press, 1977), 139–140n; Bryant to the *New York Evening Post,* Barnwell District, S.C., March 29, 1843, in *Letters of William Cullen Bryant,* 2:204–8.
8. Guilds, *Simms,* 112–14.

CHAPTER SIXTEEN

1. McKivigan I, Book 1, 140–46; Dickson J. Preston, *Young Frederick Douglass: The Maryland Years* (Baltimore: Johns Hopkins University Press, 1980), 146–47.
2. McKivigan I, Book 1, 146–47; Frederick Douglass, "The Editor's Visit to the Old Shipyard in Baltimore," *New National Era* (Washington, D.C.), July 6, 1871, 2.
3. Leigh Fought, *Women in the World of Frederick Douglass* (New York: Oxford University Press, 2017), 46–51.
4. McKivigan I, Book 1, 150–52; Blassingame II, 72–73.
5. McKivigan I, Book 1, 150–52.
6. McKivigan I, Book 1, 154–55.
7. McKivigan I, Book 1, 155.
8. McKivigan I, Book 1, 156.
9. McKivigan I, Book 1, 156; Blight, *Frederick Douglass,* 82–83.
10. McKivigan I, Book 1, 157; Blassingame II, 75.
11. Stephen Jaffe, "David Ruggles' Committee of Vigilance," *Lapham's Quarterly* (online), May 21, 2018.
12. Blassingame II, 366; "More Slave Trouble," *New York Herald,* April 12, 1837; [Witness testimony], *New York Herald,* April 19, 1837; Blassingame II, 158.
13. McKivigan I, Book 1, 159; Blassingame II, 196, 367; Jaffe, "David Ruggles' Committee of Vigilance."
14. Jaffe, "David Ruggles' Committee of Vigilance"; McKivigan I, Book 1, 159; Blassingame II, 76.
15. McKivigan I, Book 1, 159.

CHAPTER SEVENTEEN

1. William Cullen Bryant to George Bancroft, New York, August 18, 1843, in *Letters of William Cullen Bryant,* 2:244.
2. William T. Davis, *Plymouth Memories of an Octogenarian* (Plymouth, Mass.: Memorial Press, 1906), 133, 440; Henry Cabot Lodge, *Early Memories* (New York: Charles Scribner's Sons, 1913), 18.
3. Simms to Israel Keech Tefft, Charleston, October 27, 1843, in *Letters I,* 379–80; Nye, *George Bancroft,* 130–32.

CHAPTER EIGHTEEN

1. Blight, *Frederick Douglass,* 87; McKivigan I, Book 1, 160.
2. McKivigan I, Book 1, 160.
3. Blight, *Frederick Douglass,* 89; McKivigan I, Book 1, 161–62; Herman Melville, *Moby-Dick* (Boston: St. Botolph Society, 1892), 36–37.
4. McKivigan I, Book 1, 162; Blight, *Frederick Douglass,* 92–93.
5. Blight, *Frederick Douglass,* 91–93; McKivigan I, Book 1, 162–65.
6. Blight, *Frederick Douglass,* 94–95; McKivigan I, Book 1, 165.
7. James Oakes, *The Radical and the Revolutionary* (New York: Norton, 2007), 8–9.
8. Blight, *Frederick Douglass,* 98; McKivigan I, Book 1, 167.

9. Blight, *Frederick Douglass*, 99; McKivigan I, Book 1, 167–68.

10. "Southern Slavery and Northern Religion: Two Addresses Delivered in Concord, New Hampshire on 11 February 1844," *Herald of Freedom* (Concord, N.H.), February 16, 1844, in *The Frederick Douglass Papers*: Series 1, vol. 1, *Speeches, Debates and Interviews, 1841–46*, ed. John W. Blassingame (New Haven: Yale University Press, 1979), 23–26; "Partial Speaking Itinerary, 1939–46," in *Frederick Douglass Papers*: Series 1, vol. 1, *Speeches, Debates and Interviews*, lxxxvii-lxxxviii.

11. Letter from William A. White, Newcastle, Ind., September 22, 1843, *Liberator*, October 13, 1843, 3; Blight (2018), 112–36; McKivigan I, Book 1, 179.

12. Preston, *Young Frederick Douglass*, 171; Benjamin Quarles, "Introduction," in *Narrative of the Life of Frederick Douglass, an American Slave*, by Frederick Douglass (Cambridge, Mass: Harvard University Press, 1960), i–xii; Blight, *Frederick Douglass*, 139.

13. McKivigan I, Book 1, 180–81.

CHAPTER NINETEEN

1. "Mr. Bancroft's Letter of Acceptance, Boston, August 15," *Niles' National Register*, September 7 1844, 4–5.

2. Robert E. Bonner, *Mastering America: Southern Slaveholders and the Crisis of American Nationhood* (New York: Cambridge University Press, 2009), 25–33; Mirabeau Lamar, *Letter on the Subject of Annexation Addressed to Several Citizens of Macon, Georgia* (Savannah, Ga.: Thomas Purse, 1844), 43.

3. J. L. O'Sullivan, "Democracy in Literature," *United States Magazine and Democratic Review* 9 (August 1842): 199; J. L. O'Sullivan, "Annexation," *United States Magazine and Democratic Review* 17 (July 1845): 7, 9; see also John D. Wilsey, "'Our Country Is Destined to Be the Great Nation of Futurity': John L. O'Sullivan's Manifest Destiny and Christian Nationalism, 1837–1846," *Religions* 8, no. 68 (2017): 1–17.

4. Theodore Parker to George Bancroft, West Roxbury, Mass., November 18, 1845, in Octavius Brooks Frothingham, *Theodore Parker: A Biography* (New York: G. P. Putnam's Sons, 1880), 382–85.

5. "Eulogy of George Bancroft, Secretary of the Navy," in *Andrew Jackson and Early Tennessee History*, vol. 2, by S. G. Heiskell (Nashville: Ambrose Printing Co., 1920), 626, 633.

6. Lilian Handlin, *George Bancroft*, 213–14.

7. Simms to John C. Calhoun, Woodlands, S.C., February 10, 1847, in *Letters II*, 267; Simms to James Henry Hammond, Woodlands, S.C., March 29, 1847, in *Letters II*, 289; Simms to James Lawson, Charleston, S.C., July 6, 1847, in *Letters II*, 332–33; Frederick Merck, "Dissent in the Mexican War," in *Dissent in Three American Wars*, ed. Samuel Eliot Morison et al. (Cambridge, Mass.: Harvard University Press, 1970), 35–44, 49.

8. Lilian Handlin, *George Bancroft*, 207–8; Howe, *Life and Letters of George Bancroft*, 1:292–93.

9. Elizabeth Davis Bancroft, *Letters from England, 1846–1849* (New York: Charles Scribner's Sons, 1904), 3–7.

CHAPTER TWENTY

1. James Henry Hammond, *Gov. Hammond's Letters on Southern Slavery* (Charleston, S.C.: Walker & Burke, 1845), 4–6; *Congressional Globe* 27 (February 1, 1836): 614; Drew Gilpin Faust, *James Henry Hammond and the Old South: A Design for Mastery* (Baton Rouge: Louisiana State University Press, 1982), 72–79.

2. Martin Bauml Duberman, "'Writhing Bedfellows': 1826; Two Young Men from Antebellum South Carolina's Ruling Elite Share 'Extravagant Delight,'" *Journal of Homosexuality* 6, no. 1 (Fall/Winter 1980): 86–89; Carol Bleser, ed., *Secret and Sacred: The Diaries of James Henry Hammond,*

a Southern Slaveholder (New York: Oxford University Press, 1988), 19, 170–76, 180, 231; Faust, *James Henry Hammond and the Old South*, 70–71.

3. Faust, *James Henry Hammond and the Old South*, 235–38.

4. Simms to Armistead Burt, Woodlands, January 26, 1845, in *Letters II*, 22–24; Simms to James Lawson, Woodlands, February 11, 1845, in *Letters II*, 25; Simms to James Henry Hammond, Woodlands, March 26, 1845, in *Letters II*, 45; Simms to James Lawson, Woodlands, April 7, 1845, in *Letters II*, 47–48.

5. Guilds, *Simms*, 114–17; Bleser, *Secret and Sacred*, 170–71; Faust, *James Henry Hammond and the Old South*, 242–45, 253–54.

6. Guilds, *Simms*, 122–23.

7. Guilds, *Simms*, 245–47.

8. Simms to Lawson, July 6, 1847, in *Letters II*, 332–33.

CHAPTER TWENTY-ONE

1. Blight, *Frederick Douglass*, 140–41; Dale Cockrell, ed., *Excelsior: Journals of the Hutchinson Family Singers, 1842–1846* (Stuyvesant, N.Y.: Pendragon Press, 1989), 315n.

2. Cockrell, *Excelsior*, 317, 319, 321.

3. Blassingame I, 190; Blight, *Frederick Douglass*, 143–47; Frederick Douglass, "Thoughts and Recollections of a Tour in Ireland," 1886, manuscript, Frederick Douglass Papers, Library of Congress, Washington, D.C., 6.

4. Patricia Ferreira, "'All but a Black Skin and Wooly Hair': Frederick Douglass's Witness of the Irish Famine," *American Studies International* 37 (June 1999): 77–79; Douglass, "Thoughts and Recollections," 18.

5. Blight, *Frederick Douglass*, 145–48, 169–70.

6. Blight, *Frederick Douglass*, 163, 169.

7. Blight, *Frederick Douglass*, 170–72; Douglass to John Veitch, Coventry, U.K., January 22, 1847, in *The Frederick Douglass Papers: Series 3, vol. 1, Correspondence, 1842–1852*, ed. John McKivigan (New Haven: Yale University Press, 2009), 199.

8. Blassingame, Series 1, vol. 1, lvii–lxi.

CHAPTER TWENTY-TWO

1. William L. Welch, "Lorenzo Sabine in Maine," *New England Quarterly* 70, no. 4 (December 1997): 642–43; Colin Woodard, "The War That Made Maine a State," *Maine Sunday Telegram*, June 24, 2012, E1; George F. W. Young, *The British Capture and Occupation of Downeast Maine, 1814–1815/1818* (Stonington, Maine: Penobscot Books, 2014).

2. Lorenzo Sabine, *The American Loyalists, or Biographical Sketches of Adherents to the British Crown in the War of the Revolution* (Boston: Charles C. Little and James Brown, 1847), 29–32.

3. William Gilmore Simms, "South Carolina in the Revolution," *Southern Quarterly Review*, July 1848, 37; Simms to John Pendleton Kennedy, Woodlands, S.C., April 5, 1853, in *Letters III*, 174–75.

4. Simms to Nathaniel Beverley Tucker, Woodlands, January 30, 1850, November 27, 1850, and March 12, 1851, in *Letters III*, 8–9, 76, 98–99.

5. Simms to John Henry Hammond, April 2, 1850, in *Letters III*, 23–24, 24n; John Henry Hammond to Simms, Silver Bluff, S.C., December 23, 1850, in *Letters III*, 87n.

6. Charles S. Watson, "Simms's Review of *Uncle Tom's Cabin*," *American Literature* 48, no. 3 (November 1976): 365–68.

7. William Gilmore Simms, *Woodcraft* (New York: A. A. Armstrong, 1882), 113, 509.

8. William Gilmore Simms, "The Morals of Slavery," in *The Pro-Slavery Argument* (Philadelphia: Lippincott, Grambo, 1853), 264–72.

9. William Gilmore Simms, *Southward Ho!* (New York: A. A. Armstrong, 1882), 389, 394, 440–41.

CHAPTER TWENTY-THREE

1. Blight, *Frederick Douglass*, 179–80.
2. Blight, *Frederick Douglass*, 186–89.
3. Ida Husted Harper, *The Life and Works of Susan B. Anthony*, vol. 1 (Indianapolis: Bowen-Merrill, 1899), 56–61; Nancy Hewitt, *Women's Activist and Social Change: Rochester, 1822–1872* (Lanham, Md.: Lexington Books, 2001), 35–42.
4. Blight, *Frederick Douglass*, 190–91, 200–201.
5. Blight, *Frederick Douglass*, 194–95, 204–9, 211–12, 221, 243.
6. James Hughes, "Those Who Passed Through: Unusual Visits to Unlikely Places," *New York History* 86, no. 3 (Summer 2005): 290–94; Kate Clifford Larson, *Bound for the Promised Land: Harriet Tubman, Portrait of an American Hero* (New York: Ballantine, 2004), 93–95.
7. S. Jay Walker, "Frederick Douglass and Woman Suffrage," *Black Scholar* 4, no. 6/7 (March–April 1973): 26–27; Frederick Douglass, "A Day and Night in 'Uncle Tom's Cabin,'" *Frederick Douglass' Paper*, March 4, 1853; Frederick Douglass, "To Captain Thomas Auld, Formerly My Master," *North Star*, September 7, 1848; Blight, *Frederick Douglass*, 196, 253, 281–82; "Silence of Booth and Rycraft," *Frederick Douglass' Paper*, February 9, 1855, 3.
8. Frederick Douglass, *Oration, Delivered in Corinthian Hall, Rochester* (Rochester, N.Y.: Lee, Mann, 1852), 9, 35.

CHAPTER TWENTY-FOUR

1. Lilian Handlin, *George Bancroft*, 231–32; Bancroft to James Buchanan, London, February 3, 1847, in Howe, *Life and Letters of George Bancroft*, 2:10; Bancroft to James Polk, London, May 14, 1847, in Howe, *Life and Letters of George Bancroft*, 2:17–18.
2. Lilian Handlin, *George Bancroft*, 236–42; Bancroft to William H. Prescott, London, March 3, 1847, in Howe, *Life and Letters of George Bancroft*, 2:15.
3. Lilian Handlin, *George Bancroft*, 247–49; Sandra Matuschka, "American Beauty Returns to Rosecliff in 'Timeless Style,'" *Newport Daily News*, June 18, 2015.
4. Lilian Handlin, *George Bancroft*, 256–57; George Bancroft, *A History of the United States*, vol. 4 (Boston: Little, Brown & Co., 1852), 13, 55, 302, 459–62.
5. Lilian Handlin, *George Bancroft*, 259–60; George Bancroft, *A History of the United States*, vol. 7 (Boston: Little Brown, 1858), 295–96; George Bancroft, *The necessity, the reality, and the promise of the progress of the human race: An Oration given before the New York Historical Society, November 20, 1854* (New York: New York Historical Society, 1854), 14–15.
6. George Bancroft to Elizabeth Bancroft, Savannah, Ga., March 8, 1855, in Bancroft-Bliss Papers; George Bancroft to Elizabeth Bancroft, St. Augustine, Fla., March 20, 1855, in Bancroft-Bliss Papers; George Bancroft to Elizabeth Bancroft, Columbia, S.C., April 4, 1855, and April 8, 1855, in Bancroft-Bliss Papers; "Death of Hon. William C. Preston," *Columbia* (SC) *Carolinian*, May 23, 1860.
7. George Bancroft to Elizabeth Bancroft, near Dubuque, Iowa, June 9, 1854, in Bancroft-Bliss Papers; George Bancroft to Elizabeth Bancroft, near St. Louis, June 12, 1854, in Bancroft-Bliss Papers; William J. Petersen, "The Grand Excursion of 1854," *Palimpsest* 14, no. 8 (August 1933): 301–14.
8. *Illinois State Register* (Springfield), June 15, 1854, 2.

CHAPTER TWENTY-FIVE

1. Oakes, *The Radical and the Revolutionary*, 52–53, 61–69.
2. Carl F. Wieck, *Lincoln's Quest for Equality: The Road to Gettysburg* (Dekalb: Northern Illinois University Press, 2002), 18–40.

3. Henry C. Whitney to William Herndon, Chicago, August 27, 1887, in *Herndon's Informants: Letters, Interviews, and Statements about Abraham Lincoln*, ed. Douglas L. Wilson and Rodney O. Davis (Urbana: University of Illinois Press, 1998), 633; George Bancroft, *An Oration Delivered before the New York Historical Society, November 20, 1854* (New York: New York Historical Society, 1854), 9, 28; Roy P. Basler, ed., *The Collected Works of Abraham Lincoln*, vol. 3 (New Brunswick, N.J.: Rutgers University Press, 1953), 250, 255, 266. For more on the influence of Bancroft and Parker on Lincoln's thought and speeches, see Garry Wills, *Lincoln at Gettysburg: The Words That Remade America* (New York: Simon & Schuster, 1992), 102–12; Stewart Winger, "'To the Latest Generations': Lincoln's Use of Time, History, and the End Time, in Historical Context," *Journal of the Abraham Lincoln Association* 23, no. 2 (Summer 2002): 19–36.

4. Roy P. Basler, ed., *The Collected Works of Abraham Lincoln*, vol. 2 (New Brunswick, N.J.: Rutgers University Press, 1953), 266.

5. Basler, *Collected Works of Abraham Lincoln*, 2:255–56.

6. Basler, *Collected Works of Abraham Lincoln*, 2:276.

CHAPTER TWENTY-SIX

1. *The Congressional Globe*, vol. 28, pt. 2 (Washington, D.C.: John C. Rives, 1854), 1515–17.

2. *Congressional Globe*, vol. 28, pt. 2, 1518–19.

3. Charles Sumner, *Defense of Massachusetts: Speeches of Hon. Charles Sumner on the Boston Memorial for the Repeal of the Fugitive Slave Bill* (Washington, D.C.: Buell & Blanchard, 1854), 11–14.

4. *Appendix to the Congressional Globe Containing Speeches and Important State Papers, Etc., of the First Session, Thirty-Fourth Congress* (Washington, D.C.: John C. Rives, 1856), 530–31, 535.

5. *Appendix to Congressional Globe*, 540–44.

6. *Appendix to Congressional Globe*, 545.

7. "Speech of Hon. L. M. Keitt," July 16, 1856, in *Appendix to Congressional Globe*, 838; William W. Freehling, *The Road to Disunion*, vol. 2: *Secessionists Triumphant, 1854–1861* (New York: Oxford University Press, 2008), 82.

8. Freehling, *The Road to Disunion*, vol. 2, 82.

9. *Appendix to Congressional Globe*, 831–39.

10. *The Complete Works of Ralph Waldo Emerson: Miscellanies*, vol. 11 (Boston: Houghton Mifflin, 2014), 247.

11. William Gilmore Simms to Lorenzo Sabine, Charleston, September 8, 1856, and October 12, 1856, Lorenzo Sabine Papers, New Hampshire Historical Society, Concord, N.H.; Lorenzo Sabine, "The 'American Loyalists' Edition of 1847 and South Carolina in the Revolution, References to the Work in Congress," memo, Lorenzo Sabine Papers; Lorenzo Sabine, *Biographical Sketches of Loyalists of the American Revolution, with an Historical Essay*, vol. 1 (Boston: Little, Brown, 1864), pp. 37–44. Sabine explains his reaction to the 1856 events in these statements in his revised edition, which appeared during the Civil War.

12. Simms to James Henry Hammond, Charleston, September 7, 1856, in *Letters III*, 446.

CHAPTER TWENTY-SEVEN

1. Simms to Benson John Lossing, Woodlands, S.C.: May 22, 1856, in *Letters III*, 434–36.

2. Simms to George Bancroft, William Cullen Bryant and Others, New York, November 3, 1856, in *Letters III*, 456.

3. Simms to James Lawson, Buffalo, November 12, 1856, in *Letters III*, 456–58.

4. William Gilmore Simms, "South Carolina in the Revolution; A Lecture," in *Letters III*, 521–23, 548.

5. *Buffalo Commercial Advertiser*, November 12, 1856, in *Letters III*, 456n; *Evening Post*, November 12, 1856, in *Letters III*, 457n.

6. "Quattlebum in Rochester," *Rochester Democrat and Chronicle*, November 14, 1856, in *Letters III*, 458n; Miriam J. Shillingsburg, "Simms's Failed Lecture Tour of 1856," in *"Long Years of Neglect": The Work and Reputation of William Gilmore Simms*, ed. John Guilds (Fayetteville: University of Arkansas Press, 1988), 191–92.

7. *New-York Tribune*, November 19, 1856, in *Letters III*, 462n, 463n.

8. Simms to James Chestnut, Jr., Woodlands, S.C.: December 16, 1856, in *Letters III*, 472; *New York Herald*, November 22, 1856, in *Letters III*, 459n; Trent, *William Gilmore Simms*, 224.

9. James Henry Hammond to Simms, November 27, 1856, in *Letters III*, 465n.

CHAPTER TWENTY-EIGHT

1. Franklin Benjamin Sanborn, *Memoirs of John Brown* (Albany, N.Y.: printed by J. Munsell, 1878), 96.

2. Frederick Douglass to John Brown, Rochester, N.Y., December 7, 1856, in *The Frederick Douglass Papers*: Series 3, vol. 2, *Correspondence, 1853–1865*, ed. James McKivigan (New Haven: Yale University Press, 2018), 200.

3. *Report of the Special Committee Appointed to Investigate the Troubles in Kansas; with the Views of the Minority of Said Committee*, House Report No. 200, 34th Congress, 1st sess. (Washington, D.C.: Cornelius Wendell, 1856), 1193–99; McKivigan I, Book 1, 229–30, 236–37.

4. McKivigan I, Book 1, 229–31; E. N. Vallandigham, "John Brown—Modern Hebrew Prophet," *Putnam's Magazine*, December 1909, 288–96.

5. Blight, *Frederick Douglass*, 295, 298–300; McKivigan I, Book 1, 236; Dann J. Broyld, "Harriet Tubman: Transnationalism and the Land of a Queen in the Late Antebellum," *Meridians* 12, no. 2 (2014): 85.

6. Blight, *Frederick Douglass*, 296–98; McKivigan I, Book 1, 245–47; Hughes, "Those Who Passed Through," 294; Broyld, "Harriet Tubman," 87–88.

7. McKivigan I, Book 1, 247.

8. McKivigan I, Book 1, 248–50.

9. McKivigan I, Book 1, 239–40.

10. McKivigan I, Book 1, 240–42, 251–53; Blight, *Frederick Douglass*, 309–17.

11. McKivigan I, Book 1, 253–54; Blight, *Frederick Douglass*, 315–17.

12. Frederick Douglass, "The Chicago Nominations," *Douglass' Monthly*, June 1860.

CHAPTER TWENTY-NINE

1. "Hon. George Bancroft's Oration," in *Inauguration of the Perry Statue, at Cleveland, on the Tenth of September 1860* (Cleveland: Fairbanks, Benedict, 1860), 45.

2. Howe, *Life and Letters of George Bancroft*, 2:122–26.

3. Bancroft to Dean Milman, Newport, R.I., August 15, 1861, in Howe, *Life and Letters of George Bancroft*, 2:134.

4. "Our Influence Abroad," *Frederick Douglass' Paper* (Rochester, N.Y.), December 22, 1854, 2.

5. Howe, *Life and Letters of George Bancroft*, 2:125–33.

6. Bancroft to Elizabeth Bancroft, Charleston, S.C., May 26, 1858, in Bancroft-Bliss Papers; James Redpath, *The Roving Editor, or Talks with Slaves in the Southern States* (New York: A. P. Burdick, 1859), 54, 58–62; William P. Leeman, "George Bancroft's Civil War: Slavery, Abraham Lincoln, and the Course of History," *New England Quarterly* 81, no. 3 (September 2008): 469.

7. Bancroft to Elizabeth Bancroft, May 26, 1858, in Bancroft-Bliss Papers.

CHAPTER THIRTY

1. "The Democracy on Lecturing," *Boston Daily Atlas*, December 15, 1856; *Charleston Mercury*, May 27, 1857, in *Letters III*, 490n; Simms to Mary Lawson, Woodlands, S.C., March 15, 1857, in *Letters III*, 493–94.
2. Guilds, *Simms*, 262–63.
3. Guilds, *Simms*, 262–63, 267, 351–52; Simms to William Porcher Miles, Woodlands, November 26, 1859, in *Letters IV*, 180; Simms to James Henry Hammond, Charleston, September 24, 1858, in *Letters IV*, 93–94.
4. Simms to James Henry Hammond, Charleston, August 2, 1858, in *Letters IV*, 88–89; Simms to William Porcher Miles, Pocotaligo, S.C., July 15, 1860, in *Letters IV*, 249.
5. Simms to James Lawson, Woodlands, November 13, 1860, in *Letters IV*, 266; Simms to John Jacob Bockee, Woodlands, December 12, 1860 (as printed in *Charleston Mercury*, January 17, 1861) in *Letters IV*, 301–4.
6. Simms to William Porcher Miles, Charleston, March 21, 1858, in *Letters IV*, 39.
7. Faust, *James Henry Hammond and the Old South*, 338–40; Bleser, *Secret and Sacred*, 270–71; Simms to James Henry Hammond, Woodlands, January 28, 1858, in *Letters IV*, 16.
8. "Speech of Hon. J. H. Hammond," in *Appendix to the Congressional Globe, First Session, 35th Congress* (Washington, D.C.: John C. Rives, 1858), 71.
9. Faust, *James Henry Hammond and the Old South*, 347; Simms to Harry Hammond, Charleston, March 27, 1858, in *Letters IV*, 41.
10. George Fitzhugh, "The Revolutions of 1776 and 1861 Contrasted," *Southern Literary Messenger* 37, no. 12 (November–December 1863), 772–73.
11. [William Falconer], "The Difference of Race between the Northern and Southern People," *Southern Literary Messenger* 30, no. 26 (June 1860): 401–9; John Quitman Moore, "The Past and Present," *De Bow's Review* 30, no. 2 (February 1861): 197–98.
12. Simms to James Henry Hammond, Woodlands, January 28, 1858, in *Letters IV*, 16; Simms to James Lawson, Woodlands, November 13, 1860, and November 20, 1860, in *Letters IV*, 266, 268.

CHAPTER THIRTY-ONE

1. Woodrow Wilson, "Abraham Lincoln: A Man of the People," in *Abraham Lincoln: The Tribute of a Century, 1809–1909*, ed. Nathan William MacChesney (Chicago: A. C. McClurg, 1910), 14.

CHAPTER THIRTY-TWO

1. Simms to James Lawson, Woodlands, S.C., December 19, 1860, in *Letters IV*, 311–12.
2. Simms to James Lawson, Woodlands, S.C., December 31, 1860, in *Letters IV*, 313.
3. Jeffery J. Rogers, "'Art Ready for Battle': William Gilmore Simms and the Civil War" (doctoral dissertation, University of South Carolina, 2004), 52–81; Simms to James Henry Hammond, Woodlands, S.C., November 18, 1861, in *Letters IV*, 382–85.
4. Simms to Hammond, November 18, 1861, *Letters IV*, 382–85; Simms to James Henry Hammond, Woodlands, S.C., December 2, 1861, in *Letters IV*, 389.
5. Simms to William Porcher Miles, Woodlands in Ruins, April 10, 1862, in *Letters IV*, 399–401; David Flavel Johnson to Richard Yeadon, Burwood, S.C., March 29, 1862, in *Letters IV*, 399n; Simms to James Henry Hammond, Woodlands in Ruins, April 10, 1862, in *Letters IV*, 401–4.
6. Simms to William Porcher Miles, April 10, 1862; Rogers, "'Art Ready for Battle,'" 95, 98–99; Simms to Hammond, April 10, 1862, *Letters IV*, 401–4.

CHAPTER THIRTY-THREE

1. For the weather conditions in Washington: "Diary of Horatio Nelson Taft, 1861–1865, Volume 1, January 1, 1861—April 11, 1862," Library of Congress, Washington, D.C.
2. William Howard Russell, *My Diary North and South* (Boston: T.O.H.P. Burnham, 1863), 32, 375–77; Doris Kearns Goodwin, *Team of Rivals* (New York: Simon & Schuster, 2005), 355–57.
3. Bancroft to Elizabeth Bancroft, New York, September 12, 1861, MHS Bancroft Letters; Bancroft to Dean Milman, August 15, 1861, in Howe, *Life and Letters of George Bancroft,* 2:136; George Bancroft, "The Place of Abraham Lincoln in History," *Atlantic Monthly,* June 1865, 762–65.
4. Bancroft, "The Place of Abraham Lincoln"; Bancroft to Milman, August 15, 1861, in Howe, *Life and Letters of George Bancroft,* 2:136.
5. George Bancroft to Abraham Lincoln, New York, November 15, 1861, and Abraham Lincoln to George Bancroft, Washington, November 18, 1861, in Abraham Lincoln Papers, Library of Congress, Washington, D.C.
6. Lilian Handlin, *George Bancroft,* 275; Russell, *My Diary North and South,* 393–96, 403–4; P. G. Bruff, "Army Map of the Seat of the War in Virginia," Washington, D.C.: Hudson Taylor, 1862, archived in Civil War Maps, Library of Congress, Washington, D.C.
7. George Bancroft to Elizabeth Bancroft, Washington, December 16, 1861, in Howe, *Life and Letters of George Bancroft,* 2:145–47; Russell, *My Diary North and South,* 37–38; Bancroft, "The Place of Abraham Lincoln."
8. George Bancroft to Elizabeth Bancroft, Washington, December 16, 1861, and February 24, 1864, in Howe, *Life and Letters of George Bancroft,* 2:145–47, 155–56; William P. Leeman, "George Bancroft's Civil War: Slavery, Abraham Lincoln, and the Course of History," *The New England Quarterly* 81, no. 3 (September 2008).
9. Bancroft to Elizabeth Bancroft, Washington, December 16, 1861.

CHAPTER THIRTY-FOUR

1. Frederick Douglass, "Our Work Is Not Done," speech delivered at the annual meeting of the American Anti-Slavery Society held in Philadelphia, December 3–4, 1863, in *Proceedings of the American Anti-Slavery Society at Its Third Decade* (New York: American Anti-Slavery Society, 1864), 116; Blight, *Frederick Douglass,* 406.
2. McKivigan I, Book 1, 274–78.
3. Goodwin, *Team of Rivals,* 548–50.
4. John Stauffer, *Giants: The Parallel Lives of Frederick Douglass and Abraham Lincoln* (New York: Twelve, 2008), 3–6; Goodwin, *Team of Rivals,* 456–57.
5. Frederick Douglass to George L. Stearns, Philadelphia, August 12, 1863, in *The Civil War: The Third Year by Those Who Lived It,* ed. Brooks D. Simpson (New York: Library of America, 2003), 457–60; Stauffer, *Giants,* 9–12.
6. Douglass to Stearns, August 12, 1863, *Civil War,* 457–60; Douglass, "Our Work Is Not Done," 116.
7. Douglass to Stearns, August 12, 1863, *Civil War,* 457–60; Douglass, "Our Work Is Not Done," 116–17.
8. Douglass to Stearns, August 12, 1863, *Civil War,* 457–60; Douglass, "Our Work Is Not Done," 116–17.
9. Douglass to Stearns, August 12, 1863, *Civil War,* 457–60; Douglass, "Our Work Is Not Done," 116–17.
10. Douglass to Stearns, August 12, 1863, *Civil War,* 457–60; Douglass, "Our Work Is Not Done," 117–18.

CHAPTER THIRTY-FIVE

1. "Report of Samuel Weaver," Gettysburg, Pa., March 19, 1864, in *Revised Report of the Select Committee Relative to the Soldiers' National Cemetery, Together with the Accompanying Documents, as Reported to the House of Representatives of the Commonwealth of Pennsylvania* (Harrisburg, Pa.: Singerly & Myers, 1865), 149–51; Wills, *Lincoln at Gettysburg,* 20–21.

2. Goodwin, *Team of Rivals*, 583–87; Wills, *Lincoln at Gettysburg*, 30–31; Abraham Lincoln, "Remarks to Citizens of Gettysburg, Pennsylvania," November 18, 1863, in *Collected Works of Abraham Lincoln*, vol. 7, ed. Roy P. Basler (New Brunswick, N.J.: Rutgers University Press, 1953), 16–17.

3. "Address of Hon. Edward Everett," Gettysburg, Pa., November 19, 1863, in *Revised Report of the Select Committee*, 182–209; Wills, *Lincoln at Gettysburg*, 213.

4. Abraham Lincoln, "Address Delivered at the Dedication of the Cemetery at Gettysburg," November 19, 1863, in *Collected Works of Abraham Lincoln*, 7:23.

5. Jared Elliot Peatman, "Virginians' Responses to the Gettysburg Address, 1863–1963" (master's thesis, Virginia Polytechnic Institute and State University, 2006), 26; Harold Holzer, "'Thrilling Words' or 'Silly Remarks': What the Press Said About the Gettysburg Address," *Lincoln Herald* 90 (Winter 1988): 144–45.

6. Leeman, "George Bancroft's Civil War," 481–82.

7. Oakes, *The Radical and the Revolutionary*, 219, 223; "Our Martyred President," *Rochester Democrat and American*, April 17, 1865, in *The Portable Frederick Douglass* (New York: Penguin Press, 2016), 361.

8. "The President at Gettysburg," *Chicago Times*, November 23, 1863.

9. Peatman, "Virginians' Responses to the Gettysburg Address," 28–46.

CHAPTER THIRTY-SIX

1. Robert Bober, "Young Woodrow Wilson: The Search for Immortality" (doctoral dissertation, Case Western Reserve University, 1980), 136; Luke Joel Swabb, "The Rhetorical Theory of Rev. Joseph Ruggles Wilson" (doctoral dissertation, Ohio State University, 1971), 56–61; Joseph R. Wilson, *Mutual Relations of Masters and Slaves as Taught in the Bible* (Augusta, Ga.: Steam Press of Chronicle & Sentinel, 1861), 10, 18, 21.

2. Bober, "Young Woodrow Wilson," 154; John Milton Cooper Jr., *Woodrow Wilson: A Biography* (New York: Alfred A. Knopf, 2009), 24.

3. Bober, "Young Woodrow Wilson," 173–74.

CHAPTER THIRTY-SEVEN

1. Simms to William Gilmore Simms Jr., Woodlands, S.C., December 27, 1864, and January 13, 1865, in *Letters IV*, 473–74, 478–84; Simms to Harry Hammond, Woodlands, S.C., January 24, 1865, in *Letters IV*, 482–84.

2. Simms to Andrew Gordon Magrath, Woodlands, S.C., January 9, 1865, in *Letters IV*, 475–76, 476n.

3. Simms to Evert Augustus Duyckinck, Charleston, May 1, 1867, in *Letters V*, 45; William Gilmore Simms, "Woodlands," *Columbia Phoenix*, April 12, 1865, in *Letters IV*, 484–85n.

4. William Gilmore Simms, "The Sack and Destruction of Columbia, South Carolina," in *Memorabilia and Anecdotal Reminiscences of Columbia, S.C., and Incidents Connected Therewith* by Julian A. Selby (Columbia, S.C.: R. L. Bryan, 1905), 157–58.

5. William Gilmore Simms, "The Sack and Destruction of Columbia," 166–67.

6. William Gilmore Simms, "The Sack and Destruction of Columbia," 177; Thom Bassett, "Was the Burning of Columbia, S.C., a War Crime?," *The Opinionator* (blog), *New York Times* (online), March 10, 2015.

7. Simms to James Lawson, Columbia, S.C., June 13, 1865, in *Letters IV*, 498–99.

8. Rogers, "'Art Ready for Battle,'" 181–82.

9. Rogers, "'Art Ready for Battle,'" 183.

CHAPTER THIRTY-EIGHT

1. Goodwin, *Team of Rivals*, 697–99; Abraham Lincoln, "Second Inaugural Address," March 4, 1865, in Abraham Lincoln Papers, Series 3, Library of Congress, Washington, D.C.

2. McKivigan I, Book 1, 286-87.

3. Goodwin, *Team of Rivals*, 718–21.

4. Goodwin., *Team of Rivals*, 738–39; derringer John Wilkes Booth used to assassinate Abraham Lincoln, artifact, National Park Service, Ford's Theatre National Historic Site, Washington, D.C.

5. Lilian Handlin, *George Bancroft*, 282–83; Bancroft to Samuel Cox, New York, January 28, 1865, in Howe, *Life and Letters of George Bancroft*, 2:157–58; Andrew Johnson, "First Annual Message," Washington, D.C., December 4, 1865, in *A Compilation of the Messages and Papers of the Presidents, 1789–1897*, ed. James D. Richardson (Washington, D.C.: Government Printing Office, 1897), 6:353–71.

6. Lilian Handlin, *George Bancroft*, 291–92.

7. George Bancroft, *Memorial Address on the Life and Character of Abraham Lincoln, Delivered, at the Request of Both Houses of the Congress of America, Before Them, in the House of Representatives at Washington, on the 12th of February, 1866* (Washington, D.C.: Government Printing Office, 1866), 17, 19, 35, 41.

8. Bancroft, *Memorial Address on the Life and Character of Abraham Lincoln*, 7–9, 49–50.

CHAPTER THIRTY-NINE

1. Joseph A. Goddard, "Jefferson Davis, a Prisoner in Macon, Georgia, After His Capture," in *Proceedings of the Second Annual State History Conference* (Indianapolis: Indiana Historical Commission, 1921), 14–17; James L. Swanson, "Was Jefferson Davis Captured in a Dress?," *American Heritage*, Fall 2010.

2. Cooper, *Woodrow Wilson*, 18.

3. Ella Gertrude Clanton Thomas, *The Secret Eye: The Journal of Ella Gertrude Clanton Thomas, 1848–1889* (Chapel Hill: University of North Carolina Press, 1990), 268–69.

CHAPTER FORTY

1. Simms to Evert Augustus Duyckinck, Columbia, S.C., June 15, 1865, in *Letters IV*, 501–4; Col. James C. Beecher to Maj. Stewart M. Taylor, Summerville, S.C., October 6, 1865, and September 23, 1865, in Robert R. Singleton, "William Gilmore Simms, Woodlands, and the Freedmen's Bureau," *Mississippi Quarterly* 50, no. 1 (Winter 1996–1997): 18–37.

2. James C. Beecher, court-endorsed ruling, Branchville Sub District, Bamberg, S.C., June 23, 1865, in Singleton, "William Gilmore Simms."

3. Simms to Lawson, June 13, 1865, *Letters IV*, 499–500; Simms to Duyckinck, June 15, 1865, *Letters IV*, 502.

4. Simms to Lawson, June 13, 1865, *Letters IV*, 499–500; Simms to Duyckinck, June 15, 1865, *Letters IV*, 502.

5. Rogers, "'Art Ready for Battle,'" 183–84; Julian A. Selby, "Anecdotes About Good People," in *Memorabilia*, 24–25.

6. Simms to Edward Roach, Columbia, S.C., June 25, 1865, in *Letters IV*, 504–7.

7. Beecher to Maj. Taylor, September 23, 1865; Beecher to Maj. Taylor, October 6, 1865; and Simms to Evert Augustus Duyckinck, Columbia, S.C., August 12, 1865, in *Letters IV*, 514–16.

8. Simms to Duyckinck, June 15, 1865, and August 12, 1865, *Letters IV*, 504, 515.

9. Beecher to Maj. O. D. Kinsman, Summerville, S.C., October 7, 1865, and October 15, 1865, in Singleton, "William Gilmore Simms"; Beecher to Maj. Taylor, October 6, 1865, in Singleton, "William Gilmore Simms."

10. Beecher to Maj. Kinsman, October 15, 1865, in Singleton, "William Gilmore Simms."

11. Simms to Evert Augustus Duyckinck, Columbia, S.C., October 1, 1865, in *Letters IV*, 523.

CHAPTER FORTY-ONE

1. David Blight, *Race and Reunion: The Civil War in American Memory* (Cambridge, Mass.: Harvard University Press, 2001), 44–46.
2. Eric Foner, *Reconstruction: America's Unfinished Revolution, 1863–1877* (New York: Harper Perennial, 2014), 198–202.
3. Foner, *Reconstruction*, 235–36.
4. Captain W. A. Poillon to Carl Schurz, Mobile, September 9, 1865; W. A. Poillon to Brig. Gen. Swayne, Mobile, July 29, 1865; Col. Charles H. Gilchrist to Maj. W. A. Gordon, Jackson, Miss., September 17, 1865, in Carl Schurz, *Report on the Condition of the South*, December 1865, U.S. Senate Executive Document No. 2, 39th Congress, 1st sess. (Washington, D.C.: Rivers, 1865).
5. Foner, *Reconstruction*, 276–78, 447–48; S. Jay Walker, "Frederick Douglass and Woman Suffrage," *Black Scholar* 4, no. 6 (March–April 1973), 27–29; Brenda Wineapple, "Ladies Last," *American Scholar*, Summer 2013; Ellen Carol DuBois and Richard Cándida Smith, eds., *Elizabeth Cady Stanton, Feminist as Thinker: A Reader in Documents and Essays* (New York: New York University Press, 2007), 137–38; Laura Free, *Suffrage Reconstructed: Gender, Race, and Voting Rights in the Civil War Era* (Ithaca, N.Y.: Cornell University Press), 151.
6. Walker, "Frederick Douglass and Woman Suffrage," 30.

CHAPTER FORTY-TWO

1. Walter J. Fraser Jr., *Charleston! Charleston!: The History of a Southern City* (Columbia: University of South Carolina Press, 1989), 264–69, 275; Simms to Evert Augustus Duyckinck, Charleston, December 19, 1865, in *Letters IV*, 529.
2. John Townsend Trowbridge, *My Own Story with Recollections of Noted Persons* (Boston: Houghton Mifflin, 1903), 301–2.
3. Simms to Evert Augustus Duyckinck, Charleston, February 10, 1866, and March 5, 1866, in *Letters IV*, 537, 541; Simms to James Lawson, Charleston, May 25, 1866, in *Letters IV*, 559; Simms to William Gilmore Simms Jr., Columbia, S.C., September 20, 1865, in *Letters IV*, 522.
4. Simms to Evert Augustus Duyckinck, Columbia, S.C., October 1, 1865, in *Letters IV*, 523; Simms to Duyckinck, December 19, 1865, *Letters IV*, 528.
5. Simms to Lawson, May 25, 1866, *Letters IV*, 559–60; Simms to William Hawkins Ferris, Charleston, May 25, 1866, in *Letters IV*, 561.
6. Simms to Clara Victoria Dargan, Charleston, February 20, 1867, in *Letters V*, 18.
7. Simms to Evert Augustus Duyckinck, Charleston, December 13, 1866, in *Letters IV*, 624; Simms to Evert Augustus Duyckinck, Charleston, May 1, 1867, in *Letters V*, 44–46; Philip M. Hamer, *The Papers of Henry Laurens*, vol. 1 (Columbia: University of South Carolina Press, 1968), xxvi–xxvii.
8. Simms to Robert Barnwell Rhett Jr.[?], Midway, S.C., c. May 6, 1867, in *Letters V*, 50–51; Simms to *Charleston Courier*, May 8, 1867, and December 25, 1867, in *Letters V*, 50n, 104n; "Guide to the Southern Famine Relief Commission Records, 1867–1868," finding aid, New-York Historical Society Museum & Library, created August 12, 2014; "The Distribution of Food Among the Destitute of the South," *New York Times*, March 27, 1867; Simms to William John Gayer, Charleston, May 8, 1868, in *Letters V*, 128–29; Simms to John Reuben Thompson, Charleston, March 20, 1867, in *Letters V*, 30.
9. Simms to William Hawkins Ferris, Charleston, March 7, 1867, in *Letters V*, 22.
10. Simms to John Esten Cooke, Charleston, May 9, 1868, in *Letters V*, 131.
11. Robert K. Scott, gubernatorial proclamation, c. December 1868, in *Reports of Committees of the House of Representatives, Second Session of the Forty-Second Congress, 1871–1872* (Washington, D.C.: Government Printing Office, 1872), 1255–56.
12. Simms to James Lawson, Woodlands, S.C., December 18, 1869, and May 10, 1870, in *Letters V*, 280, 315–16; Simms to William Hawkins Ferris, Charleston, March 20, 1867, and Brooklyn,

September 11, 1869, in *Letters V*, 29, 248; Simms to Justus Starr Redfield, Charleston, February 16, 1870, in *Letters V*, 296.

13. Guilds, *Simms*, 413n.

CHAPTER FORTY-THREE

1. Cooper, *Woodrow Wilson*, 19–20.
2. John M. Mulder, *Woodrow Wilson: The Years of Preparation; Wilson Supplemental Volumes* (Princeton, N.J.: Princeton University Press, 1978), 12–13.
3. A. K. McClure, "Jefferson's Prophecy Fulfilled—South Carolina Legislature," *Daily Cleveland Herald*, February 2, 1870; H.H.J., "Editorial Correspondence No. 3," *Georgia Weekly Telegraph and Georgia Journal & Messenger* (Macon), March 23, 1875; Ray Stannard Baker, *Woodrow Wilson: Life and Letters*, vol. I: *Youth, 1856–1890* (New York: Doubleday, 1927), 58–59, 64–65; Cooper, *Woodrow Wilson*, 20.
4. Baker, *Life and Letters*, 1:72.
5. John S. Reynolds, *Reconstruction in South Carolina, 1865–1877* (Columbia, S.C.: The State Co., 1905), 74–91.
6. Reynolds, *Reconstruction in South Carolina*, 107–8, 118–20.
7. "The Legislature," *Charleston Courier*, August 18, 1868; Monroe N. Work et al., "Some Negro Members of Reconstruction Conventions and Legislatures and of Congress," *Journal of Negro History* 5, no. 1 (January 1920): 94, 101.
8. Horace V. Redfield, "South Carolina Scenes," *Georgia Weekly Telegraph and Georgia Journal & Messenger* (Macon), January 7, 1875; James Shepherd Pike, *The Prostrate State: South Carolina Under Negro Government* (New York: D. Appleton, 1874), 14–16.
9. Blight, *Race and Reunion*, 108–20; Francis B. Simkins, "The Ku Klux Klan in South Carolina, 1868–1871," *Journal of Negro History* 12, no. 4 (October 1927): 621; "Testimony of William M. Champion," in *Testimony Taken by the Joint Select Committee to Inquire into the Condition of Affairs in the Late Insurrectionary States*, vol. 1, *South Carolina* (Washington, D.C.: Government Printing Office, 1872), 365–66.
10. Baker, *Life and Letters*, 1:59; Link I, 20–25, 28, 43–46, 54–56; Bober, "Young Woodrow Wilson," 216–17.
11. Janet Woodrow Wilson to Woodrow Wilson, Columbia, S.C., May 20, 1874, in Link I, 40; Bober, "Young Woodrow Wilson," 218, 233–35.

CHAPTER FORTY-FOUR

1. Blight, *Frederick Douglass*, 477, 481, 527–32.
2. Blight, *Frederick Douglass*, 490–92.
3. Frederick Douglass, "Our Composite Nationality: An Address Delivered in Boston, Massachusetts, on 7 December 1869," in *The Frederick Douglass Papers: Series 1, Speeches, Debates and Interviews*, vol. 4, *1864–1880*, ed. John W. Blassingame (New Haven: Yale University Press, 1991), 242–59.
4. "The Claims of Our Race: An Interview with President Andrew Johnson in Washington, D.C., on 7 February 1866," in *Frederick Douglass Papers: Series 1*, 4:96–106.
5. "Bombast," *New National Era*, November 10, 1870, 2; Frederick Douglass, "The Unknown Dead: An Address Delivered in Arlington, Virginia, on 30 May 1871," in *Frederick Douglass Papers: Series 1*, 4:289–91.
6. Blight, *Frederick Douglass*, 523, 532–33, 554–55.
7. Blight, *Frederick Douglass*, 575–76; Congressional Research Service, *African American Members of the United States Congress: 1870–2018*, RL 30378 (Washington, D.C.: CRS, December 28, 2018), 5–8.

8. Foner, *Reconstruction*, 512–13, 523, 525–27; Jerome Mushkat, *The Reconstruction of the New York Democracy, 1861–1879* (Rutherford, N.J.: Fairleigh Dickinson University Press, 1981), 244.

9. Blight, *Frederick Douglass*, 556–57.

CHAPTER FORTY-FIVE

1. George Bancroft, manuscript account, August 17, 1867, in Howe, *Life and Letters of George Bancroft*, 2:169–71; Henry Blumenthal, "George Bancroft in Berlin: 1867–1874," *New England Quarterly* 37, no. 2 (June 1964): 226; Lilian Handlin, *George Bancroft*, 301.

2. Lilian Handlin, *George Bancroft*, 301–3; Bancroft to Hamilton Fish, Berlin, October 18, 1870, in Howe, *Life and Letters of George Bancroft*, 2:245–47; Blumenthal, "George Bancroft in Berlin," 233.

3. Alan W. Palmer, *Bismarck* (New York: Charles Scribner, 1976), 144; George Bancroft to Count Bismarck, Berlin, September 30, 1870, in Howe, *Life and Letters of George Bancroft*, 2:254–55; Victor Hugo, "Bancroft," in *L'Année terrible* (Paris: Michel Lévy frères, 1872), 62–63.

4. George Bancroft to Reverdy Johnson, Berlin, January 2, 1868, in Howe, *Life and Letters of George Bancroft*, 2:184–87; Reverdy Johnson, *A Further Consideration of the Dangerous Condition of the Country* (Baltimore: Sun Job Printing Establishment, 1867), 5–21.

5. Lilian Handlin, *George Bancroft*, 318–19.

CHAPTER FORTY-SIX

1. "Plan of the Campaign of 1876," in *South Carolina During Reconstruction*, by Francis Butler Simkins (Chapel Hill: University of North Carolina Press, 1932), 515, 515n, 564–69.

2. "The Political Condition of South Carolina," *Atlantic Monthly*, February 1877; Foner, *Reconstruction*, 570–75.

3. Foner, *Reconstruction*, 530–31, 576–89; Blight, *Race and Reunion*, 138; Blight, *Frederick Douglass*, 578–79.

4. Woodrow Wilson, "Draft of a Speech: The Union," November 15, 1876, in Link I, 228.

5. Frederick Douglass, "There Was a Right Side in the Late War: An Address Delivered in New York, New York, on 30 May 1878," in *Frederick Douglass Papers*: Series 1, 4:492.

CHAPTER FORTY-SEVEN

1. Ray Allen Billington, *Frederick Jackson Turner: Historian, Scholar, Teacher* (New York: Oxford University Press, 1973), 10–11, 17–18, 31–32.

2. "Account of Hugh M'Farlane," in *History of Columbia County, Wisconsin* (Chicago: Western Historical Company, 1880), 430–31; John Muir, *The Story of My Boyhood and Youth* (Boston: Houghton Mifflin, 1913), 52–53; Billington, *Frederick Jackson Turner*, 15–17; Richard D. Durbin, *The Wisconsin River: An Odyssey Through Time and Space* (Madison: University of Wisconsin Press, 1997), 35–38.

3. Donald J. Berthong, "Andrew Jackson Turner: 'Workhorse' of the Republican Party," *Wisconsin Magazine of History* 38, no. 2 (Winter 1954–55): 77–79; "The Colored Man of the South to Be Eliminated from Politics," *Wisconsin State Register* (Portage), May 5, 1877; "Fred Douglass' lecture at Pettibone Hall To-Nite," *Wisconsin State Register* (Portage), December 11, 1875; Frederick Douglass, "A Lecture on Our National Capital," in *Frederick Douglass Papers*: Series 1, 4:443–74.

4. James Robert Hester, *A Yankee Scholar in Coastal South Carolina: William Francis Allen's Civil War Journals* (Columbia: University of South Carolina Press, 2015), 1–13; William Francis Allen, *History Topics for the Use of High Schools and Colleges* (Boston: D. C. Heath, 1886), 104; Billington, *Frederick Jackson Turner*, 26–30.

5. Billington, *Frederick Jackson Turner*, 17–25.

6. Billington, *Frederick Jackson Turner*, 33–35; James D. Bennett, *Frederick Jackson Turner* (Boston: Twayne, 1975), 23–25.
7. Billington, *Frederick Jackson Turner*, 36–57.

CHAPTER FORTY-EIGHT

1. Baker, *Life and Letters*, 77–80.
2. Henry Wilkinson Bragdon, *Woodrow Wilson: The Academic Years* (Cambridge, Mass.: Harvard University Press, 1967), 15–19, 42–43, 47; Jennifer Schuessler, "Princeton Digs into Its Fraught Racial History," *New York Times*, November 6, 2017, C1.
3. Bragdon, *Woodrow Wilson*, 21–22, 44–45; Woodrow Wilson shorthand diary, entries for June 19, 1876; July 4, 1876; November 8, 1876, in Link I, 143–49, 222; Woodrow Wilson marginal notes, in Link I, 388; Janet Woodrow Wilson to Woodrow Wilson, Wilmington, N.C., December 1, 1876, and May 13, 1879, in Link I, 233, 479–80.
4. Bragdon, *Woodrow Wilson*, 65–68, 87; Woodrow Wilson to Richard Heath Dabney, Wilmington, N.C., February 1, 1881, in Link II, 17–18; Woodrow Wilson, "Stray Thoughts from the South," c. February 22, 1881, in Link II, 27–28.
5. Woodrow Wilson to Robert Bridges, Atlanta, April 29, 1883, in Link II, 343–44; James Woodrow to Joseph Ruggles Wilson, Columbia, S.C., March 14 and April 11, 1883, in Link II, 317–18, 335–36; Bragdon, *Woodrow Wilson*, 92–93.
6. Lawrence A. Spalla, "Herbert Baxter Adams: A Pioneer in History Education" (doctoral dissertation, University of Pittsburgh, 1992), 24–29; Niels Aage Thorsen, "The Political and Economic Thought of Woodrow Wilson, 1875–1902" (doctoral dissertation, Princeton University, 1981), 94–96.
7. Woodrow Wilson to Ellen Louise Axson, Baltimore, October 16, 1883, in Link II, 479–80.
8. M. Karen Crowe, "Southern Horizons: The Autobiography of Thomas Dixon, a Critical Edition" (doctoral dissertation, New York University, 1982), 230–31; Anthony Slide, *American Racist: The Life and Films of Thomas Dixon* (Lexington: University Press of Kentucky, 2004), 19; "Dixon's Lecture," *Emporia* (Kansas) *Weekly Gazette*, October 16, 1902, 8.
9. Thomas Dixon Jr. to Woodrow Wilson, Raleigh, N.C., February 15, 1885, in Link IV, 258–59; Thomas Dixon Jr. to Woodrow Wilson, Wake Forest College, N.C., June 7, 1887, in Link V, 515–16.
10. Bragdon, *Woodrow Wilson*, 113, 145–46; "From Wilson's Confidential Journal," Bryn Mawr, Pa., October 20, 1887, in Link V, 619.
11. Bragdon, *Woodrow Wilson*, 188–89; Woodrow Wilson to Herbert Baxter Adams, Bryn Mawr, Pa., April 2 1886, and April 8, 1886, in Link V, 150–52, 155; Herbert Baxter Adams to Woodrow Wilson, Baltimore, April 7, 1886, in Link V, 154; "Editorial Note: Wilson's Teaching at Bryn Mawr and The Johns Hopkins, 1887–88," in Link V, 600–602.

CHAPTER FORTY-NINE

1. Baker, *Life and Letters*, 1:176–77.
2. Frederick Jackson Turner to Caroline Mae Sherwood, Baltimore, February 13, 1889, in Link VI, 88.
3. Ray Allen Billington, *The Genesis of the Frontier Thesis: A Study in Historical Creativity* (San Marino, Calif.: The Huntington Library, 1971), 88–91, 106–9; Richard Hofstadter, *Social Darwinism in American Thought* (Boston: Beacon Press, 1955), 40–41, 56–60. See also James Woodrow, *Evolution: An Address Delivered May 4th 1884 Before the Alumni Association of Columbia Theological Seminary* (Columbia, S.C.: Presbyterian Publishing House, 1884).
4. Frederick Jackson Turner to William E. Dodd, Cambridge, Mass., October 7, 1919, in Wendell H. Stephenson, "The Influence of Woodrow Wilson on Frederick Jackson Turner," *Agricultural*

History 19, no. 4 (October 1945): 249–53; Woodrow Wilson to Frederick Jackson Turner, Middletown, Conn., August 23, 1889, in Link VI, 369.

5. Turner to Dodd, October 7, 1919, "The Influence of Woodrow Wilson on Frederick Jackson Turner," 252–53.

CHAPTER FIFTY

1. "Dinner to the President," *Washington Post*, February 22, 1883, 4; "Society," *Washington Post*, May 6, 1887, 3; "Bancroft's Banquet," *Washington Post*, January 11, 1878, 4; Howe, *Life and Letters of George Bancroft*, 2:278, 280–81.

2. Howe, *Life and Letters of George Bancroft*, 2:218; "George Bancroft—Mrs. J.J. Astor Gives a Banquet in His Honor," *Boston Daily Globe*, October 4, 1886, 8; "Grant Dined by Arthur," *Washington Post*, March 23, 1882, 4.

3. "Bancroft's Daily Life," *New York Times*, July 31, 1883; "Bancroft's New Work," *Washington Post*, January 16, 1887, 7; Howe, *Life and Letters of George Bancroft*, 2:282–83; M. E. Powell, "Some of Our Founders," *Bulletin of the Newport Historical Society*, April 1915, 15–16.

4. "Bancroft in Nashville," *Washington Post*, April 17, 1887, 1; Howe, *Life and Letters of George Bancroft*, 2:312–13; Lilian Handlin, *George Bancroft*, 340.

5. George Bancroft, *History of the United States of America: The Author's Last Revision*, vol. 1 (New York: D. Appleton, 1883), 3; David W. Noble, *Historians Against History: The Frontier Thesis and National Covenant in American Historical Writing Since 1830* (Minneapolis: University of Minnesota Press, 1965), 37–38.

6. George Bancroft, "Annual Address of the President of the American Historical Association, Delivered in New York, April 27, 1886," in *Papers of the American Historical Association* 2, no. 1 (1887): 7–13; Lilian Handlin, *George Bancroft*, 341–42.

7. Lilian Handlin, *George Bancroft*, 335–38.

8. "Bancroft's Last Days," *Washington Post*, February 15, 1891, 4; "Notes," *The Critic* 16, no. 10 (May 1890): 241.

9. Howe, *Life and Letters of George Bancroft*, 2:315–16; Lilian Handlin, *George Bancroft*, 343.

10. "Funeral of Bancroft," *Washington Post*, January 21, 1891, 6.

CHAPTER FIFTY-ONE

1. Blight, *Frederick Douglass*, 581-84; McKivigan I, Book 1, 334.

2. Blight, *Frederick Douglass*, 587–88, 604, 628.

3. McKivigan I, Book 1, 344–52; Blight, *Frederick Douglass*, 597.

4. McKivigan I, Book 1, 353; Blight, *Frederick Douglass*, 619.

5. Blight, *Frederick Douglass*, 630–31, 634, 643.

6. McKivigan I, Book 1, 395–401.

7. Blight, *Frederick Douglass*, 649–50.

8. Blight, *Frederick Douglass*, 661.

9. Blight, *Frederick Douglass*, 666–75.

CHAPTER FIFTY-TWO

1. Billington, *Frederick Jackson Turner*, 82–89; Bennett, *Frederick Jackson Turner*, 28–29.

2. Woodrow Wilson to Reuben Gold Thwaites, Middletown, Conn., December 26, 1889, in Link VI, 457–58.

3. Frederick Jackson Turner, "The Significance of History (1891)," in *Frontier and Section: Selected Essays of Frederick Jackson Turner*, ed. Ray Allen Billington (Englewood Cliffs, N.J.: Prentice-Hall, 1961), 11–27.

4. Turner, "Significance of History (1891)," 6–27; Billington, *Frederick Jackson Turner*, 97–99.
5. Frederick Jackson Turner, "Problems in American History (1892)," in Billington, *Frontier and Section*, 28–36.
6. Billington, *Frederick Jackson Turner*, 106.
7. Woodrow Wilson to Charles Kendall Adams, Princeton, N.J., December 23, 1892, in Link VIII, 61, 61n; Wilson to Dodd, October 7, 1919, in Stephenson, "The Influence of Woodrow Wilson on Frederick Jackson Turner," 253; "Editorial Note: The Madison Conference on History Civil Government and Political Economy," in Link VIII, 61–63.
8. Billington, *Frederick Jackson Turner*, 106–7.

CHAPTER FIFTY-THREE

1. Bragdon, *Woodrow Wilson*, 232–34.
2. Bragdon, *Woodrow Wilson*, 161; Stockton Axson, *Brother Woodrow: A Memoir of Woodrow Wilson* (Princeton, N.J.: Princeton University Press, 1993), 202; Richard H. Titherington, "The Baptist Church in New York," *Munsey's Magazine*, April 1892, 11.
3. William Peterfield Trent to Woodrow Wilson, Richmond, Va., June 5, 1887, in Link V, 514–15; Woodrow Wilson, *Division and Reunion, 1829–1889* (New York: Longmans, Green & Co., 1893), x–xii, 117, 194.
4. Wilson, *Division and Reunion*, viii; Bragdon, *Woodrow Wilson*, 233–35.
5. Wilson, *Division and Reunion*, 11.
6. Wilson, *Division and Reunion*, 123, 125–27.
7. Wilson, *Division and Reunion*, 121, 203, 212.
8. Wilson, *Division and Reunion*, 268, 274–75.
9. Wilson, *Division and Reunion*, 127–28, 298–99.
10. Wilson, *Division and Reunion*, 299.
11. Frederick Jackson Turner to Woodrow Wilson, Chicago, July 16, 1893, in Link VIII, 278–79; *The Nation*, April 13, 1893, in Link VIII, 185–90; Hermann Eduard von Holst, review of *Division and Reunion*, *Educational Review* 6 (June 1893), in Link VIII, 222–24; *New Orleans Picayune*, May 28, 1893, in Link VIII, 218–19.
12. Kent Plummer Brattle, review of *Division and Reunion, North Carolina University Magazine*, n.s., 12 (May 1893), in Link VIII, 203–5; New York *Church Union*, April 15, 1893, in Link VIII, 191.
13. Turner to Wilson, July 16, 1893, Link VIII, 278–79; "Editorial Note: Wilson's 'Short History of the United States,'" in Link VIII, 279–81; John Ireneaus McCain to Woodrow Wilson, Due West, S.C., April 29, 1893, in Link VIII, 202–3; Bragdon, *Woodrow Wilson*, 240–41.

CHAPTER FIFTY-FOUR

1. "The Late President Hyppolite of Hayti," *Chautauquan*, May 1896, 238; Jacques Nicolas Léger, *Haiti: Her History and Her Detractors* (New York: Neale Publishing Company 1907), 243–45; Louis Martin Sears, "Frederick Douglass and the Mission to Haiti, 1889–1891," *Hispanic American Historical Review* 21, no. 2 (May 1941): 226.
2. McKivigan I, Book 1, 456.
3. Blight, *Frederick Douglass*, 704–5; McKivigan I, Book 1, 441.
4. Sears, "Frederick Douglass and the Mission to Haiti," 235; McKivigan I, Book 1, 452; Léger, *Haiti*, 246–47.
5. Blight, *Frederick Douglass*, 706–8.
6. Blight, *Frederick Douglass*, 709.

7. Haitian Secretary of State's Office to Frederick Douglass, Port-au-Prince, February 11, 1892, in Frederick Douglass Papers, Library of Congress, Washington, D.C.

CHAPTER FIFTY-FIVE

1. David Burg, *Chicago's White City* (Louisville: University Press of Kentucky, 1976), 3–6, 42–43.
2. Trumbull White and W. M. Igleheart, *The World's Columbian Exposition, Chicago 1893* (Boston: John K. Hastings, 1893), 495–590; Erik Larson, *The Devil in the White City* (New York: Vintage, 2003), 175, 193, 222–25, 252–54.
3. Francis Bellamy, "The Story of the Pledge of Allegiance to the Flag," *University of Rochester Library Bulletin* 8, no. 2 (Winter 1953).
4. Elliott M. Rudwick and August Meier, "Black Man in the 'White City': Negroes and the Columbian Exposition, 1893," *Phylon* 26, no. 4 (October 1965): 354–55; Anna R. Paddon and Sally Turner, "African Americans and the World's Columbian Exposition," *Illinois Historical Journal* 88 (Spring 1995): 22–23.
5. Frederick Douglass, "Inauguration of the World's Columbian Exposition," *Campbell's Illustrated Weekly*, March 1893, 300.
6. Blight, *Frederick Douglass*, 727–28; Frederick Douglass, "Haiti and the Haitian People," address in Chicago, January 2, 1893, in *The Frederick Douglass Papers: Series 1*, vol. 5, *Speeches, Debates and Interviews, 1881–85*, eds. John W. Blassingame and John R. McKivigan (New Haven: Yale University Press, 1992), 509–11
7. Larson, *Devil in the White City*, 235–38.
8. Burg, *Chicago's White City*, 235–38.
9. Billington, *Frederick Jackson Turner*, 124–25.
10. Richard White, "Frederick Jackson Turner and Buffalo Bill," in *The Frontier in American Culture*, ed. James R. Grossman (Berkeley: University of California Press, 1994), 9–10, 27; Joy S. Kasson, *Buffalo Bill's Wild West: Celebrity, Memory and Popular History* (New York: Hill and Wang, 2001), 113–17.
11. Turner, "Significance of the Frontier," 37–38.
12. Turner, "Significance of the Frontier," 39, 46, 48, 51–58.
13. Turner, "Significance of the Frontier," 55–58, 61.
14. Billington, *Frederick Jackson Turner*, 129.
15. Woodrow Wilson to Ellen Axson Wilson, Chicago, July 25, 1893, in Link VIII, 283.
16. Woodrow Wilson, "An Address at the World's Columbian Exposition," July 26, 1863, in Link VIII, 285–92; "Knowledge for All: General Education Congresses in Full Swing," *Daily Inter Ocean* (Chicago), July 26, 1893, 8.
17. Rudwick and Meier, "Black Man in the 'White City,'" 359–60.
18. Blight, *Frederick Douglass*, 734–35.
19. Blight, *Frederick Douglass*, 736–37.
20. Blight, *Frederick Douglass*, 737; Rudwick and Meier, "Black Man in the 'White City,'" 360–61.
21. Rudwick and Meier, "Black Man in the 'White City,'" 361n.

CHAPTER FIFTY-SIX

1. Blight, *Frederick Douglass*, 740.
2. Frederick Douglass, *Why Is the Negro Lynched?* (Bridgewater, U.K.: John Whitby & Sons, 1895), 2–3, 24–25.
3. Douglass, *Why Is the Negro Lynched?*, 2–3, 24–25.
4. Douglass, *Why Is the Negro Lynched?*, 38.
5. Blight, *Frederick Douglass*, 752.
6. Blight, *Frederick Douglass*, 753.

CHAPTER FIFTY-SEVEN

1. Billington, *Frederick Jackson Turner*, 188–93; Frederick Jackson Turner, "The Problem of the West," in Billington, *Frontier and Section*, 74–76; Bennett, *Frederick Jackson Turner*, 50.

2. Bennett, *Frederick Jackson Turner*, 52–53; Noble, *Historians Against History*, 40–44; Billington, *Frederick Jackson Turner*, 186.

3. Bennett, *Frederick Jackson Turner*, 51–53; Billington, *Frederick Jackson Turner*, 185–86, 190; "The Educational Convention," *Los Angeles Times*, July 13, 1899; "To Study Education," *Daily Messenger* (St. Alban's, Vt.), July 7, 1899 (describing a Chicago convention).

4. Billington, *Frederick Jackson Turner*, 130, 209–12; Frederick Jackson Turner to Constance Lindsay Skinner, Cambridge, Mass., March 15, 1922, in *Wisconsin Witness to Frederick Jackson Turner*, by O. Lawrence Burnette Jr. (Madison: State Historical Society of Wisconsin, 1961), 66–67.

5. Billington, *Frederick Jackson Turner*, 215–16, 219; Turner to Skinner, March 15, 1922, Burnette, *Wisconsin Witness*, 66–67.

6. Frederick Jackson Turner, "Problems in American History," in *Congress of Arts and Science: Universal Exposition, St. Louis, 1904*, vol. 2, ed. Howard J. Rogers (New York: Houghton, Mifflin, 1906), 186–87, 190.

7. Billington, *Frederick Jackson Turner*, 133–34.

8. Billington, *Frederick Jackson Turner*, 153–57.

CHAPTER FIFTY-EIGHT

1. Woodrow Wilson, *The State: Elements of Historical and Practical Politics* (Boston: D. C. Heath, 1889), 1–3, 24–25; "Ethnographic Map," *Meyers Konversations-Lexikon*, 4th ed. (Leipzig, Germany, 1885–90).

2. Woodrow Wilson, "The Ideals of America," *Atlantic Monthly*, December 1902.

3. Woodrow Wilson, "The Reconstruction of the Southern States," *Atlantic Monthly*, January 1901.

4. "Remarks by Prof. Woodrow Wilson," *Annual Report of the American Historical Association for the Year 1896*, vol. 1 (Washington, D.C.: Government Printing Office, 1897), 292–96.

5. "Southern History Society," Charleston *Weekly News and Courier*, April 29, 1896, 2; Bethany Leigh Johnson, "Regionalism, Race, and the Meaning of the Southern Past: Professional History in the American South, 1896–1961" (doctoral dissertation, Rice University, May 2001), 31, 50–53, 79n.

6. Patricia O'Toole, *The Moralist: Woodrow Wilson and the World He Made* (New York: Simon & Schuster, 2018), 18–19.

7. Edwin A. Weinstein, *Woodrow Wilson: A Medical and Psychological Biography; Supplementary Volume to the Papers of Woodrow Wilson* (Princeton, N.J.: Princeton University Press, 1981), 106–7; Woodrow Wilson to Ellen Axson Wilson, S.S. *Ethiopia*, June 9, 1896, in Link IX, 512; Woodrow Wilson to Ellen Axson Wilson, Carlisle, Pa., June 28, 1896, in Link IX, 528; Woodrow Wilson to Ellen Axson Wilson, Oxford, England, July 9, 1896, in Link IX, 537–38; Woodrow Wilson to Ellen Axson Wilson, Winchester, England, July 13, 1896, in Link IX, 538.

8. Bragdon, *Woodrow Wilson*, 247–51.

9. Link IX, 398–462.

10. "Cleveland Host of Roosevelt," *Trenton Evening Times*, October 17, 1902, 7; Theodore Roosevelt to Woodrow Wilson, Washington, D.C., October 18, 1902, in Link XIV, 147–48.

11. Link XIV, 248–52, 282–83, 345–46.

12. Link XIV, 286–87, 309–13; Bragdon, *Woodrow Wilson*, 251.

13. Woodrow Wilson, *A History of the American People*, vol. 5 (New York: Harper & Brothers, 1902), 20–21, 46, 59–63.

14. Wilson, *History of the American People*, 5:185, 212–13.

15. Wilson, *History of the American People*, 5:294–300.

CHAPTER FIFTY-NINE

1. Billington, *Frederick Jackson Turner*, 157–59.
2. Billington, *Frederick Jackson Turner*, 217–24.
3. Frederick Jackson Turner, *Rise of the New West, 1819–1829* (New York: Harper & Brothers, 1906), 8–9.
4. Frederick Jackson Turner, "Is Sectionalism in America Dying Away?," in *Papers and Proceedings, First Annual Meeting, American Sociological Society*, vol. 1 (Chicago: University of Chicago Press, 1907), 45–59; "Discussion: Professor Frank W. Blackmar, University of Kansas," in *Papers and Proceedings, First Annual Meeting, American Sociological Society*, 1:60–61.
5. Frank Freidel, *Franklin D. Roosevelt: The Apprenticeship* (Boston: Little, Brown, 1952), 61; Henry Miller Littlefield, "Textbooks, Determinism and Turner: The Westward Movement in Secondary School History" (doctoral dissertation, Columbia University, 1967), 246–47; Francis FitzGerald, *America Revised: History Schoolbooks in the Twentieth Century* (Boston: Little, Brown, 1979), 59; Billington, *Frederick Jackson Turner*, 285.
6. Paul M. Maginnis, "The Social Philosophy of Frederick Jackson Turner" (doctoral dissertation, University of Arizona, 1969), 64–67.

CHAPTER SIXTY

1. *The Mirrors of Washington* (New York: G. P. Putnam's Sons, 1921), 50–55.
2. Bragdon, *Woodrow Wilson*, 344–45, 387.
3. Bragdon, *Woodrow Wilson*, 388–91, 394–95.
4. Bragdon, *Woodrow Wilson*, 401; O'Toole, *The Moralist*, 32, 36.
5. O'Toole, *The Moralist*, 43–44.
6. O'Toole, *The Moralist*, 41–50.
7. O'Toole, *The Moralist*, 58–59.

CHAPTER SIXTY-ONE

1. "Tumultuous Scenes of Popular Greeting Mark Inauguration," *Atlanta Constitution*, March 5, 1913, 3; "Wilson Assumes Reins of Government; 250,000 Watch Inauguration," UPI, March 4, 1913.
2. "Wilson and Marshall Become Heads of Nation," *Washington Post*, March 4, 1913, IE1.
3. "Hungarians Assail Wilson as Unfair," *New York Times*, February 12, 1912, 2; "Lincoln Central Figure: 'The Southerner' by Thomas Dixon Jr.," *Boston Daily Globe*, June 12, 1913, 4; *Atlanta Journal*, April 17, 1912, and *Nashville Banner*, March 3, 1913, both quoted in Samuel Lonsdale Shaffer, "New South Nation: Woodrow Wilson's Generation and the Rise of the South, 1884–1920" (doctoral dissertation, Yale University, December 2010), 239–40.
4. Woodrow Wilson, "An Address to the New York Southern Society," December 17, 1912, in Link XXV, 593–96; Woodrow Wilson, "An Address at Mary Baldwin Sanctuary, Staunton, Virginia," December 28, 1912, in Link XXV, 627; "South Welded to Nation by Election of Wilson, Taft Tells Dixie Women," *Atlanta Constitution*, November 13, 1912, 1.
5. *Atlanta Constitution*, March 5, 1913; National Park Service, "Joseph Lamar Boyhood Home," www.nps.gov/nr/travel/augusta/lamarhouse.html (viewed May 14, 2019); "How Wilson Was Sworn In," *New York Times*, March 5, 1913.
6. "Southern Men Return to Dominate U.S. Government After 52 Years," *St. Louis Post-Dispatch*, March 9, 1913, 1; *Evans v. Newton*, 382 U.S. 296 (1966); "How Wilson Was Sworn In," *New York Times*, March 5, 1913.
7. "Southerners Hold Reins in Capitol and White House," *Washington Post*, March 9, 1913, 4; *Atlanta Constitution*, November 13, 1912; *St. Louis Post-Dispatch*, March 9, 1913; W. Joseph Campbell, "'One of the Fine Figures of American Journalism': A Closer Look at Josephus Daniels of the Raleigh *News and Observer*," *American Journalism* 16, no. 4 (Fall 1999): 37–55.

8. "How Wilson Was Sworn In," *New York Times*, March 5, 1913.

9. "When Wilson Took the Oath," *New York Times*, March 5, 1913.

CHAPTER SIXTY-TWO

1. E. David Cronon, ed., *The Cabinet Diaries of Josephus Daniels, 1913–1921* (Lincoln: University of Nebraska Press, 1963), 32–33.

2. Cronon, *Cabinet Diaries of Josephus Daniels*, 32–33; Eric S. Yellin, *Racism in the Nation's Service: Government Workers and the Color Line in Woodrow Wilson's America* (Chapel Hill: University of North Carolina Press, 2013), 117–18.

3. Cronon, *Cabinet Diaries of Josephus Daniels*, 33.

4. May Childs Nerney to Oswald Garrison Villard, New York, September 30, 1913, in Link XXVIII, 404; Cleveland Green, "Prejudices and Empty Promises: Woodrow Wilson's Betrayal of the Negro, 1910–1919," *The Crisis*, November 1980, 383.

5. Morton Sosna, "The South in the Saddle: Racial Politics in the Wilson Years," *Wisconsin Magazine of History* 54, no. 1 (Autumn 1970): 33; Nerney to Villard, September 30, 1913, Link XXVIII, 404.

6. Nerney to Villard, September 30, 1913, Link XXVIII, 403–7; Nicholas Patler, *Jim Crow and the Wilson Administration: Protesting Federal Segregation in the Early Twentieth Century* (Boulder: University Press of Colorado, 2004), 18–20; Yellin, *Racism in the Nation's Service*, 119; "For Colored Only," *Washington Bee*, July 19, 1913; "What the Democratic Presidential 'Victory' Means to Our People in Washington, DC and the Entire Country," *Cleveland Gazette*, July 26, 1913; William Gibbs McAdoo to Woodrow Wilson, Washington, D.C., April 10, 1913, in Link XXVII, 283–84, 284n.

7. Patler, *Jim Crow and the Wilson Administration*, 19; "What the Democratic 'Victory' Means," *Cleveland Gazette*, July 26, 1913.

8. Yellin, *Racism in the Nation's Service*, 11–38; Patler, *Jim Crow and the Wilson Administration*, 14.

9. Patler, *Jim Crow and the Wilson Administration*, 20–21, 32–33.

10. Booker T. Washington to Oswald Garrison Villard, Tuskegee, Ala., August 10, 1913, in Link XXVIII, 187.

11. Oswald Garrison Villard to Woodrow Wilson, New York, July 21, 1913, in Link XXVIII, 60–61.

12. Woodrow Wilson to Oswald Garrison Villard, Washington, D.C., July 23, 1913, in Link XXVIII, 65.

13. Casey Cep, "Legacy of a Radical Black Newspaperman," *New Yorker*, November 25, 2019.

14. Patler, *Jim Crow and the Wilson Administration*, 175–85.

CHAPTER SIXTY-THREE

1. "Old Soldiers to Hear Talk by President," *Detroit Free Press*, June 29, 1913, 2.

2. "North and South Flock to Field of Gettysburg," *Atlanta Constitution*, June 29, 1913, 1; Blight, *Race and Reunion*, 8–9, 384.

3. "Gettysburg Again Hears the Rebel Yell," *Hartford Courant*, July 2, 1913, 1.

4. Blight, *Race and Reunion*, 8, 385–86.

5. Blight, *Race and Reunion*, 10–11.

6. Woodrow Wilson, "An Address at the Gettysburg Battlefield," July 4, 1913, in Link XXVIII, 23–26.

7. "Gettysburg Cold to Wilson's Speech," *New York Times*, July 5, 1913, 1.

CHAPTER SIXTY-FOUR

1. Frederick Jackson Turner, "Sections and Nation," in Billington, *Frontier and Section*, 136–37, 141–42; Billington, *Frederick Jackson Turner*, 368–69.

2. Turner, "Sections and Nation," 137, 151–52.

3. Turner, "Sections and Nation," 138, 152–53.

4. Bennett, *Frederick Jackson Turner*, 76–78.

5. Billington, *Frederick Jackson Turner*, 324–25, 370–73, 376, 434–35.

6. Billington, *Frederick Jackson Turner*, 370–73.

7. Freidel, *Franklin D. Roosevelt*, 61; Littlefield, "Textbooks, Determinism and Turner," 246–47; FitzGerald, *America Revised*, 59; Billington, *Frederick Jackson Turner*, 285; David Muzzey, *An American History* (Boston: Ginn and Company, 1911), 261.

8. Muzzey, *American History*, 621.

9. Muzzey, *American History*, 480–81, 486–89.

CHAPTER SIXTY-FIVE

1. Thomas Dixon Jr., *The Leopard's Spots: A Romance of the White Man's Burden* (New York: Doubleday, Page, 1902), 433–36.

2. Thomas Dixon Jr., *The Clansman: An Historical Romance of the Ku Klux Klan* (New York: Doubleday, Page, 1905), 290–91, 374.

3. Crowe, "Southern Horizons," 389–90; Thomas Dixon Jr., "Why I Wrote 'The Clansman,'" *Theatre* 6, no. 59 (January 1906): 20.

4. Raymond Allen Clark, "Thomas Dixon: His Books and His Career" (doctoral dissertation, Emory University, 1953), 133–35; Crowe, "Southern Horizons," 360.

5. Crowe, "Southern Horizons," 403; Michael R. Hurwitz, "D. W. Griffith's 1913 Film *Birth of a Nation* and Its Impact on the Cultural Landscape of America" (master's thesis, California State University Dominguez Hills, Spring 2006), 11.

6. Crowe, "Southern Horizons," 403; Melvyn Stokes, *D. W. Griffith's "The Birth of a Nation": A History of the Most Controversial Film of All Time* (New York: Oxford University Press, 2008), 53–54.

7. Stokes, *D. W. Griffith's "The Birth of a Nation,"* 23.

8. Hurwitz, "D. W. Griffith's 1913 Film *Birth of a Nation*," 12, 16–17; Cecilia Rasmussen, "Film Pioneer Griffith Rode History to Fame," *Los Angeles Times*, August 1, 1999, 37; Iris Barry, *D. W. Griffith: American Film Master* (New York: Museum of Modern Art, 1940), 20.

9. Hurwitz, "D. W. Griffith's 1913 Film *Birth of a Nation*," 21; Russell Merritt, "Dixon, Griffith, and the Southern Legend," *Cinema Journal* 12, no. 1 (Autumn 1972), 41.

10. Michael Rogin, "'The Sword Became a Flashing Vision': D. W. Griffith's *The Birth of a Nation*," *Representations* 1, no. 9 (Winter 1985): 151–52; Robert Lang, ed., *"The Birth of a Nation": D. W. Griffith, Director* (New Brunswick, N.J.: Rutgers University Press, 1994), 94.

11. Crowe, "Southern Horizons," 403; Rogin, "'The Sword Became a Flashing Vision,'" 152; Lang, *"The Birth of a Nation,"* 39, 83, 88, 110, 115.

12. Rogin, "'The Sword Became a Flashing Vision,'" 157.

13. The screenplay of the final theatrical release is reproduced in Lang, *"The Birth of a Nation,"* 43–156.

14. Lang, *"The Birth of a Nation,"* 134; Merritt, "Dixon, Griffith, and the Southern Legend," 40–43.

15. Crowe, "Southern Horizons," 404–5; Clark, "Thomas Dixon," 17.

CHAPTER SIXTY-SIX

1. Arthur Lennig, "Myth and Fact: The Reception of 'The Birth of a Nation,'" *Film History* 16, no. 2 (2004): 117–19.

2. Lennig, "Myth and Fact," 119–20.

3. Lennig, "Myth and Fact," 120–21; Crowe, "Southern Horizons," 405.

4. Crowe, "Southern Horizons," 405–6.

5. Thomas Dixon Jr. to Woodrow Wilson, New York, July 27, 1913, in Link XXVIII, 88–89; Woodrow Wilson to Thomas Dixon Jr., Washington, D.C., July 29, 1913, in Link XXVIII, 94; Adam

Edward Patterson to Woodrow Wilson, Washington, D.C., July 30, 1913, in Link XXVIII, 97–98; Yellin, *Racism in the Nation's Service*, 108–9; Crowe, "Southern Horizons," 406.

6. Crowe, "Southern Horizons," 406–7.
7. Crowe, "Southern Horizons," 407–8.
8. Thomas R. Cripps, "The Reaction of the Negro to the Motion Picture *Birth of a Nation*," *Historian*, May 1963, 347–48.
9. Thomas Dixon Jr. to Woodrow Wilson, New York, February 20, 1915, in Link XXXII, 267.
10. For a detailed discussion of this quote and its history, see Mark E. Benbow, "Birth of a Quotation: Woodrow Wilson and 'Like Writing History with Lightning,'" *Journal of the Gilded Age and Progressive Era* 9, no. 4 (October 2010): 509–33.
11. Benbow, "Birth of a Quotation," 514.
12. "President Witnesses Moving Pictures in the White House," *St. Louis Post-Dispatch*, February 19, 1915, 5; Crowe, "Southern Horizons," 408–9.
13. The conversation with White as related by Dixon in Crowe, "Southern Horizons," 409–11.
14. Lennig, "Myth and Fact," 122; John DeFerrari, *Lost Washington, D.C.* (Charleston, S.C.: The History Press, 2011), 35–39; Crowe, "Southern Horizons," 411–12; "Movies at Press Club," *Washington Post*, February 20, 1915, 5.
15. Crowe, "Southern Horizons," 413–14; Lennig, "Myth and Fact," 122; "Fighting Race Calumny," *The Crisis*, May 1915, 40.
16. Lennig, "Myth and Fact," 124–26; Merritt, "Dixon, Griffith, and the Southern Legend," 27n; "Broke All Stage Records," *Washington Post*, January 30, 1916, SM2.
17. Cripps, "Reaction of the Negro," 353–55; "Negroes Hiss Wilson's Name," *Boston Journal*, April 8, 1915.
18. Woodrow Wilson to David Wark Griffith, Washington, D.C., March 5, 1915, in Link XXXII, 325.

CHAPTER SIXTY-SEVEN

1. "'Birth of a Nation' Causes Near Riot," *Boston Globe*, April 18, 1915, 1.
2. The sources for the events of the night of April 17, 1915, are "'Birth of a Nation' Causes Near Riot"; "Trotter on the Stand," *Boston Evening Transcript*, May 3, 1915, 2; "Schoeffel a Witness," *Boston Evening Transcript*, April 30, 1915, 2; "Negroes Placed on Trial," *Boston Evening Transcript*, April 28, 1915, 2.
3. Crowe, "Southern Horizons," 417.
4. "Colored People to Storm State House," *Boston Daily Globe*, April 19, 1915, 1.
5. Lennig, "Myth and Fact," 129; "Starts Hearing Without Delay," *Boston Daily Globe*, April 21, 1915, 1.
6. "Starts Hearing Without Delay"; "Forbids Birth of a Nation," *Boston Daily Globe*, April 17, 1915, 9.
7. "Fight Is Taken to State House," *Boston Daily Globe*, April 22, 1915, 1; "Fighting Race Calumny, Part II," *The Crisis*, June 1915, 88.
8. "Branches," *The Crisis*, July 1915, 148–49; Stefanie Laufs, *Fighting a Movie with Lightning: "The Birth of a Nation" and the Black Community* (Hamburg, Germany: Anchor Academic Publishing, 2014), 26–27; "Colored Women Form a League," *Boston Daily Globe*, April 16, 1915, 9.
9. "Wilmington Bans Photo Play," *Baltimore Afro-American*, June 2, 1915, 1; "Birth of a Nation Barred by Mayor in Cedar Rapids," *Chicago Defender*, June 5, 1915, 1.
10. Joseph Patrick Tumulty to Woodrow Wilson, Washington, D.C., April 24, 1915, and Woodrow Wilson to Joseph Patrick Tumulty, Washington, D.C., April 28, 1915, in Link XXXIII, 68, 86.
11. Lennig, "Myth and Fact," 136; Merritt, "Dixon, Griffith, and the Southern Legend," 27n; *Washington Post*, January 30, 1916; Clark, "Thomas Dixon," 148.
12. Maxim Simcovitch, "The Impact of Griffith's *Birth of a Nation* on the Modern Ku Klux Klan," *Journal of Popular Film*, Winter 1972, 45–47; "Klan Is Established with Impressiveness," *Atlanta Constitution*, November 28, 1915.
13. Simcovitch, "The Impact of Griffith's *Birth of a Nation*," 48.

14. "Hundreds Brought to Atlanta by 'The Birth of a Nation,'" *Atlanta Constitution*, December 13, 1915, 5.

15. Ward Greene, review of *Birth of a Nation*, *Atlanta Journal*, December 7, 1915, in Lang, *"The Birth of a Nation,"* 179.

16. Simcovitch, "The Impact of Griffith's *Birth of a Nation*," 48; Linda Gordon, *The Second Coming of the KKK: The Ku Klux Klan of the 1920s and the American Political Tradition* (New York: Liveright, 2017), 13–15.

CHAPTER SIXTY-EIGHT

1. On the Zimmermann cable and the code breakers, see Paul Gannon, *Inside Room 40: The Codebreakers of World War I* (Hersham, U.K.: Ian Allen, 2010), and Erik Larson, *Dead Wake: The Last Crossing of the* Lusitania (New York: Broadway Books, 2016), 77–88.

2. Colin Woodard, *American Character: A History of the Epic Struggle Between Individual Liberty and the Common Good* (New York: Viking, 2016), 139; United States Congress, *United States Statutes at Large*, vol. 40, *Public Acts of the 65th Congress, 2nd sess.*, chap. 75, 553.

3. Woodrow Wilson, "Address at Pueblo, Colo., September 25, 1919," in *Congressional Serial Set: Senate Documents, 66th Congress, 1st sess.*, vol. 2 (Washington, D.C.: Government Printing Office, 1919), 359.

4. Daniel A. Gross, "The U.S. Confiscated Half a Billion Dollars in Private Property During WWI," Smithsonian.com, July 28, 2014.

5. "During World War I, U.S. Government Propaganda Erased German Culture," *All Things Considered*, National Public Radio, April 7, 2017.

6. Allison Keyes, "The East St. Louis Race Riot Left Dozens Dead, Devastating a Community on the Rise," Smithsonian.com, June 30, 2017; Cameron McWhirter, *Red Summer: The Summer of 1919 and the Awakening of Black America* (New York: Henry Holt, 2011), 13, 216–20, 225.

7. "Negroes Appeal to Wilson," *New York Times*, August 1, 1919; McWhirter, *Red Summer*, 106–8, 157.

8. Woodrow Wilson, "An Address in New York on Behalf of the American Red Cross," May 18, 1918, in Link XLVIII, 54.

CHAPTER SIXTY-NINE

1. John Graham Royde-Smith and Dennis E. Showalter, "World War I," *Encyclopedia Britannica* (online), accessed April 25, 2019.

2. Anthony Gaughan, "Woodrow Wilson and the Legacy of the Civil War," *Civil War History* 43, no. 3 (1997): 240–41; Woodrow Wilson, "An Address in Billings, Montana," September 11, 1919, in Link LXIII, 172.

3. Lloyd E. Ambrosius, "Woodrow Wilson and *The Birth of a Nation*: American Democracy and International Relations," *Diplomacy and Statecraft* 18 (2007): 689–718; Lloyd E. Ambrosius, *Woodrow Wilson and American Internationalism* (New York: Cambridge University Press, 2017), 108–10.

4. Jesse Richardson Hildebrand to Joseph Patrick Tumulty, Washington, D.C., April 20, 1918, in Link XLVII, 388, 388n. Generations of historians have tried to pass off his comment that it was an "unfortunate" production as belated criticism of the film, when it was made in response to his press secretary's raising concerns about "the forthcoming production here at popular prices" of the film and its effect on Liberty Loan and Red Cross subscriptions.

5. Shaffer, "New South Nation," 404–5.

6. Reginald Kearney, "Japan: Ally in the Struggle Against Racism, 1919–1927," *Contributions in Black Studies* 12 (1994): 117–18; Nguyen Ai Quoc to U.S. Secretary of State, Paris, June 18, 1919, Record Group 256: Records of the American Commission to Negotiate Peace, 1914–1931, National Archives, College Park, Md.; Christopher Woolf, "The Little-Known Story of Vietnamese

Communist Leader Ho Chi Minh's Admiration for the US," *The World*, Public Radio International, September 18, 2017; Cep, "Legacy of a Radical Black Newspaperman."

7. Woodrow Wilson to James Phelan, May 3, 1913, in Link XXIV, 382–83; Kearney, "Japan," 118–19.
8. Shizuka Imamoto, "Racial Equality Bill: Japanese Proposal at Paris Peace Conference—Diplomatic Manoeuvers and Reasons for Rejection" (master's thesis, Macquarie University, 2006), 80–99.
9. Weinstein, *A Medical and Psychological Biography*, 296, 336–39.
10. Weinstein, *A Medical and Psychological Biography*, 345–46.
11. Weinstein, *A Medical and Psychological Biography*, 340–47.
12. Weinstein, *A Medical and Psychological Biography*, 348–49; Ambrosius, *Woodrow Wilson*, 142–45.
13. Weinstein, *A Medical and Psychological Biography*, 355.
14. Weinstein, *A Medical and Psychological Biography*, 355–57.
15. Weinstein, *A Medical and Psychological Biography*, 357–59.
16. Weinstein, *A Medical and Psychological Biography*, 361–62.
17. Gordon, *Second Coming of the KKK*, 2–3; Simcovitch, "The Impact of Griffith's *Birth of a Nation*," 48–51.
18. "Speech by Robert H. Clancy, April 8, 1924," in *Congressional Record, 68th Congress, 1st sess.*, vol. 65 (Washington, D.C.: Government Printing Office, 1924), 5929–32; Tom Gjelten, *A Nation of Nations: A Great American Immigration Story* (New York: Simon & Schuster, 2016), 89–90.
19. "Silenced by Thunder," *Los Angeles Times*, June 5, 1914, 11.

CHAPTER SEVENTY

1. Billington, *Frederick Jackson Turner*, 393–95.
2. Billington, *Frederick Jackson Turner*, 375–77.
3. Frederick Jackson Turner, "Middle Western Pioneer Democracy," *Minnesota History Bulletin* 3, no. 7 (August 1920): 405; Billington, *Frederick Jackson Turner*, 371–72.
4. Billington, *Frederick Jackson Turner*, 371–72.
5. Billington, *Frederick Jackson Turner*, 409–15.

EPILOGUE

1. "From the Diary of Dr. Grayson," March 10, 1919, in Link LV, 471; Thomas Borstelmann, *The Cold War and the Color Line: American Race Relations in the Global Arena* (Cambridge, Mass.: Harvard University Press, 2001), 23, 30, 33–34.
2. Adolf Hitler, *Mein Kampf* (London: Hurst and Blackett, 1939), 240; John Peter, Horst Grill, and Robert L. Jenkins, "The Nazis and the American South in the 1930s: A Mirror Image?," *Journal of Southern History* 58, no. 4 (November 1922): 667–94; Borstelmann, *The Cold War and the Color Line*, 36–40.
3. Borstelmann, *The Cold War and the Color Line*, 76–77, 105, 109, 164–66; Mary L. Dudziak, *The Cold War and Civil Rights: Race and the Image of American Democracy* (Princeton, N.J.: Princeton University Press, 2011), 40.
4. Borstelmann, *The Cold War and the Color Line*, 58–60; "Remarks of President Kennedy on Nationwide Television and Radio," June 11, 1963, in *Congressional Record: Proceedings and Debates of the 88th Congress, 1st sess.*, vol. 109, pt. 8 (Washington, D.C.: Government Printing Office), 10965–66.
5. "Special Message to Congress: The American Promise, March 15, 1963," in *Public Papers of the Presidents of the United States: Lyndon B. Johnson, 1965*, bk. 1 (Washington, D.C.: Government Printing Office, 1966), 284.
6. Martin Luther King Jr., "I Have a Dream" (speech), August 28, 1963, https://kinginstitute.stanford.edu /king-papers/documents/i-have-dream-address-delivered-march-washington-jobs-and-freedom.

INDEX

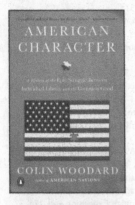
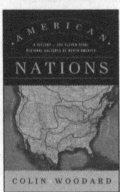